SYLVIA PLATH
— DAY BY DAY —
Volume 1

SYLVIA

PLATH

DAY BY DAY

Volume 1: 1932–1955

CARL ROLLYSON

UNIVERSITY PRESS OF MISSISSIPPI / JACKSON

The University Press of Mississippi is the scholarly publishing agency of
the Mississippi Institutions of Higher Learning: Alcorn State University,
Delta State University, Jackson State University, Mississippi State University,
Mississippi University for Women, Mississippi Valley State University,
University of Mississippi, and University of Southern Mississippi.

Designed by Peter D. Halverson

www.upress.state.ms.us

The University Press of Mississippi is a member
of the Association of University Presses.

First printing 2023

∞

Library of Congress Cataloging-in-Publication Data

Names: Rollyson, Carl E. (Carl Edmund), author.
Title: Sylvia Plath day by day, volume 1 : 1932–1955 / Carl Rollyson.
Description: Jackson : University Press of Mississippi, 2023. | Includes
bibliographical references and index.
Identifiers: LCCN 2023009941 (print) | LCCN 2023009942 (ebook) | ISBN
9781496835000 (hardback) | ISBN 9781496845191 (epub) | ISBN
9781496845207 (epub) | ISBN 9781496845214 (pdf) | ISBN 9781496845221 (pdf)
Subjects: LCSH: Plath, Sylvia. | Poets, American—20th century—Biography.
| LCGFT: Biographies.
Classification: LCC PS3566.L27 Z8495 2023 (print) | LCC PS3566.L27
(ebook) | DDC 811/.54—dc23/eng/20230329
LC record available at https://lccn.loc.gov/2023009941
LC ebook record available at https://lccn.loc.gov/2023009942

British Library Cataloging-in-Publication Data available

Nature doesn't disdain what lives only for a day.
It pours the whole of itself into each moment.
—TOM STOPPARD, *SHIPWRECK*

CONTENTS

SYLVIA PLATH
—— DAY BY DAY ——
Volume 1

INTRODUCTION

SINCE SYLVIA PLATH'S DEATH IN 1963, SHE HAS BECOME THE SUBJECT of an unceasing succession of books, biographies, and articles. She has been hailed as a groundbreaking poet for her starkly beautiful poems in *Ariel* (1965) and as a brilliant forerunner of the feminist coming-of-age novel in her semi-autobiographical *The Bell Jar* (1963). The literature about her has expressed a wide range of opinions about the causes of her suicide—often tied to the breakup of her marriage to Ted Hughes. Each new biography has offered new insight and new sources with which to measure Plath's life and influence. At this point, what is needed is a work that can offer a distillation of this data without the inherent bias of a narrative.

Biographical narratives, because they are designed as stories, inevitably discard many precious details and the feel of what it is like to live day by day. This is especially true in Plath's case because she began writing diaries at the age of twelve, and for many of her days, months, and years, she kept calendars and journals full of details that no narrative biography can possibly include. Volume 1 commences with Plath's birth in Boston in 1932, records her response to her elementary and high school years, her entry into Smith College, and her breakdown and suicide attempt, and ends on February 14, 1955—the day Plath wrote to Ruth Cohen, principal of Newnham College at the University of Cambridge, to accept her admission as an "affiliated student at Newnham College to read for the English Tripos."[1] That decision marked a turning point in her life that leads directly to the second volume of *Sylvia Plath Day by Day*.

Every effort has been made to do justice to her assiduous recording of her life so as to recover the diurnal Sylvia Plath, to write in the present tense about past events as if they are happening now. Entries for individual days include specific times when Plath recorded them. Many entries end without a period, with her activities marked off by commas, in order to suggests fragments of a life in progress. I have also retained, in most instances, Plath's misspellings (e.g., "juicey" and "apatchies") and her inconsistent capitalization. In effect, you are presented with the raw data, without commentary, so that *you* become the biographer. There are still gaps where I cannot account for certain days, identify the full names of her teachers and others, or explain the context of certain cryptic entries. Perhaps other researchers will come along to fill some of those voids, prodded by what I have included or overlooked. If I provide no narrative, I do provide brief signposts that signal the important events and turning points in Plath's life.

My approach is inspired by Jay Leyda's *Melville Log* (1951), that bedrock of Herman Melville biography. Leyda wanted to establish a groundwork for the biographies yet to come. Although Plath has many biographers, there is no reason to suppose that others will not appear in this and the next millennium so long as this world and its literature survives. Even with the most recent one-thousand-page biography, the biographer has acknowledged that, because of the exigencies of a one-volume work, she had to cut more than three hundred pages. Her biography may have been the better for such deletions, but that is not to say that within those discarded pages there are not the kinds of vital details that this book attempts to recover.

Sylvia Plath Day by Day is for readers of all kinds with a wide variety of interests in the woman and her work. The entries are suitable for dipping into and can be read in a minute or an hour, by the bedside or propped against another book or other suitable support during a meal. It is difficult to read several Plath biographies side by side, but this book, by ranging over several sources, stimulates several points of comparison between biographies and other sources, including Plath's own diaries, journals, letters, stories, and other prose and poetry. The entries in this book are shorter than the sources they are taken from. My principle of selection has been to record the most striking events and comments that reveal Plath but also to minimize repetition, except when the repetition of certain sentiments and events seem important in characterizing Plath's daily activities.

The details in her calendars, diaries, journals, and letters sometimes read like the minutes of her life, giving us a granular Plath. More importantly, by accounting for her activities, she also particularizes the culture of her time, what it was like for a young girl growing up in the 1940s, a young woman making her way in the 1950s, and a mature woman entering the 1960s. Whenever possible, I have provided brief descriptions of the games Plath played and the books she read, especially during her teenage years, and of her favorite radio programs, with links (if available) to the episodes she listened to, provided in the endnotes. In some cases, as with *The Great Gildersleeve*, links to certain programs do not seem available.

What holds true for another book of this kind, *Marilyn Monroe Day by Day* (2014), also holds true for this one: it is for anyone who delights in savoring all aspects of becoming and being a self. Reading Sylvia Plath day by day yields many different Plaths and perhaps suggests new angles and perspectives.

SOURCES AND ABBREVIATIONS

I HAVE CONSULTED ALL THE BIOGRAPHIES OF SYLVIA PLATH, THE TWO volumes of her published letters, and her journals, as well as her calendars, diaries, and archives, in addition to Peter K. Steinberg's online blog and website. Entries for 1944–1949 and 1951–1956 rely on diaries and calendars in the Sylvia Plath papers in the Special Collections, Lilly Library, Indiana University in Bloomington. Entries derived from Sylvia Plath's letters are from Steinberg and Karen V. Kukil, eds., *The Letters of Sylvia Plath: Volume I. 1940–1956* (New York: Harper, 2017); and *The Letters of Sylvia Plath: Volume 2. 1956–1963* (New York: Harper, 2018). Entries derived from Plath's journals for the period of 1950–1962 have been collected in Karen V. Kukil, ed., *The Unabridged Journals of Sylvia Plath: 1950–1962* (New York: Anchor Books, 2000). Other entries for 1962 are from the Letts Royal Office Tablet diary in the Sylvia Plath collection, Mortimer Rare Book Library, Smith College in Northampton, Massachusetts. Curly brackets (i.e., {}) identify other sources for entries, outlined below by their abbreviations.

AW: Andrew Wilson, *Mad Girl's Love Song: Sylvia Plath and Life Before Ted* (New York: Scribner, 2013)

Bells: Notation in Plath's Smith College calendar referring to sitting at a desk "on watch," recording entrants into Haven House and Lawrence House

BW: Plath's abbreviation in her calendars for waiting on tables, usually at breakfast, as part of her Smith College scholarship obligations

EB: Edward Butscher, *Sylvia Plath: Method and Madness* (New York: Seabury Press, 1976)

HC: Heather Clark, *Red Comet: The Short Life and Blazing Art of Sylvia Plath* (New York: Knopf, 2020)

HR: Harriet Rosenstein research files on Sylvia Plath, 1910–2018, Stuart A. Rose Manuscript, Archives, and Rare Book Library, Emory University, Atlanta, Georgia

LP1: Peter K. Steinberg and Karen V. Kukil, eds., *The Letters of Sylvia Plath: Volume I. 1940–1956* (New York: Harper, 2017)

LWM: Linda Wagner-Martin, *Sylvia Plath: A Literary Life* (London: Palgrave Macmillan, 1999)

MLLE: Plath's abbreviation for *Mademoiselle*

PA: Paul Alexander, *Rough Magic: A Biography of Sylvia Plath* (New York: Da Capo Press, 1991)

PJ: Karen V. Kukil, ed., *The Unabridged Journals of Sylvia Plath: 1950–1962* (New York: Anchor Books, 2000).

PKS: Peter K. Steinberg, *Sylvia Plath* (New York: Chelsea House, 2004)

PM: Plath manuscripts, Special Collections, Lilly Library, Indiana University, Bloomington, Indiana, last updated 2022, http://webapp1.dlib.indiana .edu/findingaids/view?doc.view=entire_text&docId=InU-Li-VAC4841

RB: Ruth Beuscher's McLean Hospital notes in HR

SPL: LibraryThing, "Sylvia Plath Library," n.d., https://www.librarything .com/profile/SylviaPlathLibrary

PRINCIPAL PERSONAGES

Aaron, Daniel: Smith college professor Plath consulted about her senior thesis and other academic matters

Abels, Cyrilly: *Mademoiselle* editor and Plath's mentor during her month at the magazine

Akutowicz, Edwin: a Harvard PhD who taught at Massachusetts Institute of Technology and became sexually involved with Plath and her roommate Nancy Hunter

Aldrich, Henry and Elizabeth (aka "Uncle Henry" and "Aunt Elizabeth"): Wellesley, Massachusetts, neighbors, with nine children: Duane, Peter, Stephen, John, Mark, Elizabeth, Ann, Amy, and Sarah

Anderson, Jane: a patient at McLean Hospital who befriended Plath and dated Dick Norton

Auden, W. H.: important twentieth-century poet and visiting professor Plath consulted at Smith College

Aunt Dot: *see* Schober, Dorothy "Dot"

Aunt Elizabeth: *see* Aldrich, Henry and Elizabeth

Aunt Frieda: *see* Heinrichs, Frieda Plath

Aunt Hazel: actually Hazel M. Purmot, a friend of Aurelia's who taught at Boston University

Aunt Louise: *see* Schober, Louise

Aunt Mildred: *see* Norton, Mildred

Barnhouse, Ruth Tiffany: *see* Beuscher, Ruth

Benny, Jack: popular comedian and radio personality and one of Plath's favorites

Benotti, Joseph: Plath's uncle, married to Dorothy Schober

Bets: *see* Powley, Betsy "Bets"

Beuscher, Ruth (aka Ruth Tiffany Barnhouse): Plath's therapist who began treating her after her suicide attempt

Bev: *see* Newell, Beverly "Bev"

Bragg, Frances: Wellesley neighbor

Brawner, Philip: Wellesley friend and Princeton undergraduate

Buckley, Maureen: Plath's Smith College classmate

Buckley, William F., Jr.: prominent conservative author; Plath reported on his lecture at Smith College

Cantor, Billy: *see* Cantor, Margaret

Cantor, Joan: *see* Cantor, Margaret

Cantor, Margaret: employed Plath as a mother's helper in Chatham, Massachusetts, to look after the children Billy, Joan, and Susan and also to write to the Cantors' oldest daughter Kathy; Mrs. Cantor became a friend of Plath and of her mother

Cantor, Susan: *see* Cantor, Margaret

Cochran, Bob: Plath dated Cochran during her summer working for Mrs. Margaret Cantor

Cohen, Eddie: one of Sylvia Plath's most important correspondents during her college years, with an ability to astutely analyze her feelings and motivations

Crockett, Wilbury: Plath's high school teacher and mentor

Davidow, Ann: Plath's first year roommate and lifelong friend

Davis, Robert Gorham: Smith College professor and one of Plath's mentors

Davison, Peter: A magazine and later trade book editor Plath befriends.

Drew, Elizabeth (aka "Miss Drew"): Smith College professor, important literary critic, and Plath mentor

Dunne, Patricia "Patty" Ann: childhood playmate in Wellesley

Egan, Marcia: childhood playmate in Wellesley

Epstein, Enid: Smith College classmate and good friend

Fisher, Albert: Smith College professor Plath consulted about her poetry

Fraser, Marilyn: childhood playmate in Wellesley

Freddie: *see* Mayo, Mrs. Frederick

Freeman, David: childhood playmate in Winthrop, Massachusetts, brother of Ruth Freeman

Freeman, Ruth "Ruthie": David Freeman's sister and a childhood playmate in Winthrop but also a frequent visitor to the Plath home in Wellesley

Friedman, Elinor: a Smith classmate and good friend

Gaebler, Max: son of Otto's old friend Hans Gaebler

Gebauer, George: Amherst College student who dated Plath and impressed her with his erudition

Geisel, Ruth "Ruthie": childhood playmate in Wellesley

Gendron, Val: a pulp magazine writer that encouraged Plath's writing projects

Goodie: *see* Goodkind, Anne "Goodie"

Goodkind, Anne "Goodie": Smith College classmate

Grammy: *see* Schober, Aurelia

Grampy: *see* Schober, Frank

Halliburton, Richard: a travel writer whose adventures Plath enjoyed reading about

Heinrichs, Frieda Plath: Otto Plath's sister

Hodges, John: Wellesley boyfriend

Humphrey, Bob: dated Plath while she was at Smith College

Hunter, Nancy: Smith College classmate who attended Harvard University summer school with Plath and dated Edwin Akutowicz

Irish, Frank: coeditor with Plath of their high school newspaper

Joey: *see* Mayo, Mrs. Frederick

Kamirloff, Gregory "Gary": UN translator who dated Plath during her month at *Mademoiselle* in New York City

Kassay, Attila: Hungarian boyfriend

Kazin, Alfred: important literary critic and visiting professor at Smith College who encouraged Plath's writing

Kramer, Art: a Yale University student Plath dated and whom she found intellectually stimulating

LaMeyer, Gordon: An Amherst College student who dated and traveled with Plath, inspired by her romantic and intellectual sensibility

Lincoln, Eleanor Terry: Smith College professor for Plath's class on John Milton

Longsworth, Maury: Wellesley friend and Amherst College undergraduate

Lotz, Myron: Yale University undergraduate who first dated Plath in her sophomore year

Loungway, John: childhood playmate during visits to Maine

Loungway, Margot: childhood playmate during visits to Maine

Mark, Enid: One of Plath's Smith College classmates who Plath corresponded with

Mayo, Mrs. Frederick: Plath's employer in Swampscott, Massachusetts, the mother of three children, Joanne ("Joey"), Esther ("Pinny"), and Frederic ("Freddie")

McCurdy, Philip: Wellesley neighbor who dated Plath and corresponded with her

McKay, Barbara: childhood playmate in Wellesley

McNealy, Jim: Yale student who dated Plath

Miss Drew: *see* Drew, Elizabeth

Moore, Clement: Warren Joseph Plath's friend, married Susan Allison, poet and anthropologist, who found her way to Ted Hughes's bed the night Plath died

Moore, William "Willy": schoolmate

Mowgli: family cat

Neupert, Hans-Joachim: German pen pal

Newell, Beverly "Bev": wife of Richard Newell

Newell, Richard "Rit": Perry Norton's roommate who befriended Plath at a summer job at Cape Cod, Massachusetts, in 1951, and husband of Beverly Newell

Norton, Mildred (aka "Aunt Mildred"): mother of Dick and Perry Norton and a Plath family friend

Norton, Perry: Richard Norton's younger brother and Plath's close friend

Norton, Richard "Dick": dated Plath while she attended Smith College

Norton, William (aka "Uncle Bill"): father of Dick and Perry Norton and a Plath family friend

O'Reilly, Maureen Buckley: *see* Buckley, Maureen

Patty: *see* Dunne, Patricia "Patty" Ann

Phillips, Claiborne: one of Plath's friends and a Smith College classmate

Pill, Ilo: an Estonian working with Sylvia at the farm where she earned money for her first year at Smith College; although he shocked her with his sexual aggressiveness, he became a friend she later visited in New York City

Pinny: *see* Mayo, Mrs. Frederick

Plath, Aurelia Schober (1906–1994): Plath's mother, whom Plath simultaneously adored and hated as she felt burdened by her mother's self-sacrifice and overprotectiveness and yet desirous of Aurelia's approval and happiness

Plath, Otto (1885–1940): Plath's father, a renowned entomologist who died when Plath was eight, leaving behind a powerful impact that Plath spent her life trying to absorb and surmount

Plath, Warren Joseph (1935–2021): Plath's stalwart and high-achieving brother, a graduate of Phillips Exeter Academy, and a Harvard University PhD

Powley, Betsy "Bets": a Wellesley friend; she and Plath played together nearly every day and went to the same summer camp

Prentice Smith, Alison: friend and Smith College classmate

Prouty, Olive Higgins: popular novelist and one of Plath's benefactors

Rit: *see* Newell, Richard "Rit"

Rosenthal, Jon K.: Amherst College student who dated and corresponded with Plath

Russel, Donnie: schoolmate

Ruthie: *see* Freeman, Ruth "Ruthie" or Geisel, Ruth "Ruthie"

Sassoon, Richard: a sophisticated Yale undergraduate Plath fell in love with

Schober, Aurelia (1887–1956): Plath's maternal grandmother with whom Plath stayed during her father's illness

Schober, Dorothy "Dot" (1911–1981): Plath's aunt married to Joseph Benotti

Schober, Francis "Frank" (1880–1963): Plath's maternal grandfather

Schober, Louise (1920–2002): Frank Richard Schober's wife and Plath's aunt

Schober, Frank Richard (1919–2009): Plath's uncle

Scott, Ira: Harvard instructor Plath met during Harvard summer school in 1954

Sherk, Kenneth: professor of chemistry, Smith College

Sidamon-Eristoff, Constantine: Plath met him at a party, and they dated; Plath later visited him at Princeton University

Skouras, Plato: son of movie mogul Spyros Skouros, met Plath at a party and dated her

Smith, Joan: Smith College classmate who roomed with Plath and Nancy Hunter during Harvard summer school session of 1954

Steele, Prissy: childhood playmate in Wellesley

Sterling, Wayne: Plath's boyfriend in Winthrop, Massachusetts

Stout, Tony: friend from Wellesley and a Harvard University student

Tapley, Arden: childhood playmate in Wellesley

Totten, Laurie: *Mademoiselle* guest editor from Wellesley

Uncle Bill: *see* Norton, William

Uncle Frank: *see* Schober, Frank Richard

Uncle Henry: *see* Aldrich, Henry and Elizabeth

Uncle Joe: *see* Benotti, Joseph

Webber, Sydney: classmate in history class at Smith with an interest in drama

Weller, Sue: Lawrence House friend and classmate

Whittemore Betsy: A Plath classmate whose wedding Plath attended

Wilbor, Guy: Amherst College student who dated Plath during her first year at Smith

Willy: *see* Moore, William "Willy"

Wilson, Eric Lane: Yale student Plath dated

Woods, Jeanne: Wellesley friend

Woody, Melvin: Yale undergraduate, roommate of Richard Sassoon, and one of Plath's correspondents

Wunderlich, Raymond: Columbia University medical student who dated Plath 1952–1953

TIMELINE

NOTE: IN CERTAIN ENTRIES, IT IS NOT CLEAR WHAT PLATH HAD IN mind, and I have speculated—usually in the endnotes, which perhaps will find answers from readers of this book. It is not always possible to tell the order in which Plath accomplished her daily tasks, although her recording of specific times provides some guidance about her agenda. I have not been able to supply the month or day for all entries. Entries feature highlights and revealing passages but are not complete transcriptions or reports of all that Plath wrote or experienced. Entries with quotation marks, underlining, misspelling, strikethroughs, all caps, and lowercase usage are verbatim transcriptions of Plath's diaries, journals, and letters, and italics indicate formative moments in Plath's life.

1929

Aurelia Schober, daughter of Austrian parents, goes to college and aspires to be a writer.

Aurelia enrolls in Professor Otto Plath's course in Middle High German. {HC}

1932

January 4: Aurelia (twenty-five) marries Otto Plath (forty-seven) in Carson City, Nevada, after he obtains a divorce in Reno, Nevada, from his estranged wife. {HC}

October 27: Sylvia Plath is born in Boston, Massachusetts, and lives with her mother, Aurelia, and father, Otto in their house on 24 Prince Street in Jamaica Plain, a Boston neighborhood.

Aurelia preserves a lock of Sylvia's hair in a baby book with details about Sylvia's infancy. {PM}

Aurelia relinquishes her dream to be a writer, collaborates with her husband on his scholarly work, and dotes on her new baby.

1933

May: At eight months, Sylvia utters her first words: "mama," "dad," "bye-bye," and "tick-tick." {HC}

Mid-May: For an hour each morning and afternoon, Aurelia gives Sylvia a sunbath. {HC}

June: Aurelia, concerned that Sylvia is a small eater, begins recording her weight. {HC}

October 20: "Birdie!" {HC}

November 1: "I tee" for "I see" and "haw" for "hot" and "ba" for "bath" and "bad" for "ball." {HC}

December 19: "Daddy!" {HC}

1934

Otto Plath publishes Bumblebees and Their Ways, *a landmark study that his wife and former student, Aurelia, collaborated on.*[1]

February: Aurelia reports, Sylvia "gets excited about plants and flowers and wants to smell them immediately." {HC}

September 14: Sylvia takes her first steps. {HC}

1935

January: To get attention, says "ga-ga." {HC}

October: Sees a stop sign and says "pots." {HC}

April 27: Warren Joseph Plath is born and lives with the family in Jamaica Plain. {HC}

1936

The family sells their Jamaica Plain house and moves to 92 Johnson Avenue in Winthrop, Massachusetts, close to Aurelia's parents.

Summer: Sylvia and Warren spend much of a hot summer with their grandparents. {HC}

1937

Sylvia walks a short distance from her home to half-day sessions at Winthrop's Sunshine School, a private elementary school. She adjusts well to this new experience and returns home at noon to tell her mother and brother all about her activities. {HC}

December: Learns to read and writes first poem, "Thoughts": "When Christmas comes smiles creep into my heart. / I'm always happiest when I'm singing a song or skipping along." {HC}

1938

Aurelia preserves a lock of her daughter's hair. {PM}

Sylvia walks a longer distance to attend second grade at the Annie F. Warren Grammar School in Winthrop and performs well in her studies and enjoys her classes. {HC}

September 21: A Category 3 hurricane strikes southern Massachusetts, killing 564 people, injuring 1,700, and damaging and destroying thousands of trees, power lines, homes, boats, and other structures. Winthrop sustains significant damage. From her father's downstairs study, Sylvia can hear the frightening holocaust overhead.[2] {HC}

December 7: Wayne Sterling's seventh birthday party. She begins to cry, and as he tries to comfort her, Aurelia (helping out with the party) hovers, "watching over" him. {HR}

1939

April 8: Aurelia writes note of congratulations to her daughter for her all-A report card. {HC}

Otto Plath's health declines and his daughter spends more time with her grandparents at 892 Shirley Street, on the edge of the sea.[3] {HC}

1940

Sylvia enrolls in E. B. Newton School, draws and writes, and receives the highest grades. {HC}

With friends, sneaks in a funeral home and sees a dead body for the first time, a terrifying experience. {HR}

Typescripts: Poems—"Motherly Love" and "Pearls of Dew." {PM}

Undated: Drawing of a girl's head. {PM}

February 20: Staying with grandparents at Point Shirley in Winthrop, writes to her mother about the high waves and encloses a self-portrait of her holding a wand next to her Aunt Dorothy ("Dot" Schober, Aurelia's sister). {LP1}

October 12: Otto Plath's leg is amputated.

November 5: Otto Plath, suffering from diabetes, dies. Aurelia decides not to have her children attend the funeral.

Aurelia Plath, a single mother, struggles to support her family but has the support of her parents.

1941

January: Aurelia finds temporary work teaching German and Spanish in a Jamaica Plain high school. {HC}

April 19: Sylvia is the flower girl at the wedding of her Aunt Dot, who marries Joseph Benotti. {LP1}

July 30: Aurelia preserves a lock of Sylvia's hair. {PM}

August 10: "8-Year-Old Poet," *Boston (MA) Herald*, B-8, Sylvia's first published poem.

1942

August: Aurelia preserves a tress of Sylvia's hair. {PM}

August 2: "Funny Faces," *Boston (MA) Herald*, B-10: Sylvia wins children's art contest with drawing of an older, overweight society woman.

Autumn: *After the Winthrop homes are sold, Aurelia, her children, and her parents move to 26 Elmwood Road in Wellesley, Massachusetts. The white clapboard house in a suburban-looking neighborhood deprives Sylvia of the sea, which is such an important part of her poetry and prose. She shares a room with her mother. Aurelia secures a teaching post at Boston University. Sylvia repeats the fifth grade at Marshall Livingston Perrin Grammar School, and her family begins attending the Unitarian Church.*

October 27: Sylvia celebrates her tenth birthday.

1943

Undated: Typescript—"April Blossoms." {PM}

January: Letter to Mother: "Warren and I have been very good," which means she is not teasing Warren, she is doing her music lessons, and there are no "mishaps."[4]

March 20: Reports to her mother in letters about staying with "Grammy," Aurelia Schober, having a good breakfast and bath, and encloses poems—one of them about two kittens and a mouse and a fairy who all live together in a "tiny little house" and another about a fairy that can "pass a conversation with / a friendly butterfly." Summarizes the plot of a book, *A Fairy to Stay* (1928), by Margaret Beatrice Lodge. Pamela, a little girl, is rescued by a fairy who promises to discipline the aunts who have punished her.

Plath prepares for her first camp stay away from home, beginning a lifelong pattern of departures in which she returns, nearly every day, to home in the form of letters to her mother detailing the days and hours while away.

June: Aurelia suffers a gastric hemorrhage, Sylvia sent to her Camp Weetamoe in Ossipee, New Hampshire. Postcards to Mother from Ossipee Lake.

June 28: Sylvia sends a note to her mother with a drawing of a chicken with four eggs, captioned "A proud mother." She finds a quarter and nickel and spends twenty cents on Rita Hayworth and Hedy Lamarr doll books,[5] saving the remaining five cents for a defense stamp.

June 29: Letter to Mother: encloses a drawing of daffodils and asks her how she likes it, draws a pitchfork and mentions she has been haying.

July 2: Misses her mother "alot." Counts her hearty meals—all three of them—and what various items, like a bathing cap, cost her and asks her mother for one-cent stamps.

July 5: Sends Mother a postcard about a train trip from camp to Mountainview, New Hampshire, explaining the trip began and ended with a jerk. In the pouring rain, they sang around a fireplace and ate cocoa, baloney sandwiches, and Toll House cookies, then organized their tents and ate some more.

July 6: Reports to Mother about lots of eating and swimming, asks for one-cent stamps, mentions in another postcard receiving a letter from Mowgli (the family cat). "I can't describe what a wonderful time I'm having." A good view of the lake from her tent and more swimming, asks for a pillow and pillowcase.

July 9: Wants to know how her mother is doing and is happy with letters from home, including Warren's drawing. She has written two more poems.[6]

July 10: To Mother: mentions writing every day. "I miss you an awful lot."

July 12: Tells her mother that one girl has gone home crying, tries to comfort her, and the girl tells Sylvia she is "nice." A "bath every week and a shampoo every 2 weeks."

July 16: Hayride, picnic, campfire, mountain climbing. "Write soon," she urges her mother. "I received your check for rest of month."

July 17: Misses home, draws a heart, and sends "loads of love."

July 18: No letter from Mother yesterday: "I hope you are all right." Worries that her mother is not receiving all the letters because of missing answers to her "dead" letters, "xxx Sylvia."

July 20: Complains about two new girls who are not "well brought up." "They don't speak well saying ain't and youse and such . . . just hurts my ears. I long for my family's soft, sweet talk." Letters from home help. "xxxxxxx Sylvia."

July 21: Misses home and yet feels "lucky to be staying for a month." Boating several times and wonderful muffins and melons. "I have received all your letters, Mowgli's card, and, do thank Grammy for my sneakers. . . . xxxxxxx xxxxxxx xxxxxxxx ******** ********."

July 24: Hayrides and blueberry picking and only two weeks before returning home. "I am very glad Mowgli got that chicken leg he deserves it." Working in arts and crafts, having spent two cents on camp paper. "The view across the lake is beautiful. The sun and clouds cast shadows on it from time to time."

July 28: A "red letter day" with three letters from Mother and one from Mrs. Marion Freeman.

July 29: Receives the suitcase she requested from her mother, then "devoured the funnies eagerly," sends her train itinerary for trip home

July 31: Home soon with two things she has made in arts and crafts for her mother and a "change purse for Grammy with flowers here and there." Includes drawing of the purse. Camp is already seeming like a "happy dream." Notifies her mother that "you will see a great difference in my caracter."

Christmas Eve: Max Gaebler and his brother Ralph come for dinner with a gift, *The Yearling*.[7]

Christmas morning: "Warren and I examined our stockings and opened our presents": a half pound box of chocolate creams, two velvet hair ribbons, a jar of paste, overshoes, mittens, skates, an apron, two books on Spanish for beginners, a puzzle, two bars of chocolate, one dollar and fifty cents, "a silver dollar from out West," a necklace, nail polish, and a pocket diary.

"Memoranda Christmas 1943"—"the most joyous one I had because my Uncle Frank [Frank Richard Schober] and my Aunt Louise [Schober] came home from Spokane, Washington to stay until New Years Day."

December 27: Uncle Frank introduces a friend, Gibby Wyer, he met in the Africa Medical Corps in Egypt and in the "campaign to chase Rommel out of Africa. He was with Montgomery's 8th army. They went from El Alamein to Tunis." Wyer shows off a German bayonet, a German pistol, a German camera, a German belt, a German helmet, and German binoculars.

December 28: Betsy Powley gives Sylvia two paper dollars, and Marcia Egan gives her a notebook.

1944

Sylvia attends the Alice L. Phillips Junior High School, publishes poetry in the school newspaper, and keeps a diary. In class, she is praised for her recitals of Edwin Markham's "Rules for the Road," Henry Wadsworth Longfellow's "The Courtship of Miles Standish," and Emily Dickinson's "Sunset and Sunrise."

Undated: Poems—"In the Corner of My Garden," "A Wish upon a Star," and "The Snowflake Star." {PM}

January 1: Resolves to be "nice to everyone and make people think I am not stuck-up." Ice sliding.

January 2: At Sunday school, enjoys Mr. Hales sermon "very much," writes a jingle about the New Year "bringing in cheer," listens to *Jack Benny*[8] and *The Great Gildersleeve*.[9]

January 3: Likes school more than vacation, "sometimes . . . fun in Scouts."

January 4: Notes her mother's twelfth wedding anniversary, both Sylvia and Marcia Egan are "ahead of the class in book reports."[10]

January 5: Notices a "blonde and very handsome" boy.

January 6: Draws and shares pictures with Marcia Egan.

January 7: Plays in the wet blanket of snow, with the boys showering the girls with snowballs, Willy Moore stuffs snow down her back, does not like Willy anymore.

January 8: Reads *A Forest World* (1942) by Felix Salten in bed until 9:15 a.m., Saturday sledding.

January 9: So much ice she does not go to Sunday school, listens to *Jack Benny*[11] and *The Great Gildersleeve*.[12]

January 10: Willy pushes her around: "Willy laughed and talked with me which is an honor to any girl."

January 11, 4:00 p.m.: Wears a black velvet suit skirt with embroidered red and white flowers and suspenders Aurelia sews on for eleven-year-old Barbara McKay's birthday party.

January 12: Teacher leaves the room "noisy as a waterfall" while Sylvia cuts out airplanes from blotters.

January 13: Ice skating interrupted by giving chase to boys who have stolen Betsy Powley's skating sock and Sylvia's doll.

January 14: Delivers to Joanne Rodgers thirty-seven "funny books" for her collection, collects forty-three more and has "lots of fun reading them with Warren."

January 15: Saturday reading of the funnies with Warren, after lunch, a snowball fight with Warren after failing to make a "crazy statue of Hitler in the snow."

January 16: At Sunday school, listens to speaker urging the class to put "feelings into what we say." Builds miniature igloo for her doll.

January 17: Puts together a Scout log about South America, "got sort of tiresome after awhile and most of us were glad when 5:00 came and we went home."

January 18: Enjoys teacher's reading from *The Odyssey*, thinks William Moore is "<u>so</u> handsome." Igloo melts.

Minstrel shows at school and camp were a staple of Plath's early upbringing and reflected the vestigial racism that children absorbed as simply entertainment.

January 19: A cold, plays with her dolls, no "minstrel."[13]

January 20: Misses school because of a cold. A dull day, reads *The Ring of the Nibelungen* (1939) by Richard Wagner and plays with paper dolls.

January 21: Feels better but her mother won't let her attend school, Sylvia cuts out the rest of her Jane Arden paper dolls,[14] listens to the radio, and does Sunday school work.

January 22: "Yippee!" Out of bed and "feeling fine." Listens to *Carmen* and works on music lesson on a "gorgeous" day, wishes she had gone out.

January 23: Assigned to memorize ten Bible verses in Sunday school, finishes pasting movie-star pictures in scrapbook, listens to *Jack Benny* with Alexis Smith as guest star,[15] and listens to *The Great Gildersleeve.*[16]

January 24: Works on "Roman People Places, and Things" problem paper, two boys steal her cookies when she goes to get a straw for her milk, finishes work for Scout's World Knowledge badge.

January 25: Celebrates high grades in history and music with some ice sliding.

January 26: Buys nineteen valentines.

January 27: Works on penmanship, asks her teachers how she ranks compared with other students and is pleased to know that she is even better than Donald Cheney, who got 100 percent once while she scored 100 percent three times.

January 28: Mentions a Scout Patrol meeting.[17]

January 29, 8:00 a.m.: Awakes and practices piano.

Does housework, works on Scout Reader badge.

January 30: With a cold, works on Scribe badge,[18] listens to *The Great Gildersleeve.*[19]

January 31: Despises William Moore and vows never to mention him in her diary again "unless it is important," during a trip to the fire station, Sylvia and Marcia Egan shine the fire pole "a little way."

February 1: During a snowstorm, Aurelia makes a surprise visit to school with Sylvia's lunch.

February 2: Sylvia is instructed in class to choose one of three Raphael Madonnas and selects Sistine Madonna to do a report on.

February 3: Receives 100 percent on a "Problem Paper," with grades so far of 100, 90, 100, and 100 percent, works on somersaults and headstands in gym, no cartwheels: "I do not know how."

February 4: Collects stamps of Abraham Lincoln and other famous Americans at a total cost of thirty cents.

February 5: Aurelia reads aloud *The Yearling.*

February 6: Watches choir rehearsal at church, practices piano, listens to *The Great Gildersleeve*.[20]

February 7: At school, reads her topic (Raphael) and is told that it sounds "as though it came right from the book," twenty-one blank order forms for Girl Scout cookies to sell.

February 8: Three more orders for cookies. Reads in bed until 9:15 p.m., "Unknown to mummy."

February 9: Twenty-five orders for cookies, *Calling All Girls*[21] magazine arrives. "I was very good today so mummy helped me to bed."

February 10: "I gave those boys a good lecture and now they won't take my hat any more. They said Marcia [Egan] & I were good sports."

February 11: A nasty cold: "It probably is because one of those horrid boys taking off my hat." Practices piano, Toll House cookies for dessert at dinner, Aurelia reads from *The Yearling*.

February 12, 8:15 a.m.: Wakes up and practices piano.

4:00 p.m.: Joan Wilson's Valentine's party, plays five games.

6:00 p.m.: Returns home, cuts out one of her dolls from her paper-doll books.

February 13: Out with Grammy, Warren, and Mother for a walk, finishes reading *Maida's Little House* by Inez Haynes Irwin,[22] makes a snow house for her doll in the dazzling white snow.

February 14: Passes out valentines: "I got 1 from every girl in my room . . . 1 from [Aunt] Dot and [Uncle] Joe and 1 from Ruth F[reeman] (28 in all)." Goes to Mrs. Robinson's for Child Care badge.[23]

February 15: "I made a picture of a girl on a windy hill in art."

February 16: "Today all the slush froze and it was wonderful for sliding." In the afternoon, practices piano, listens to *Superman*,[24] *Terry and the Pirates*,[25] and *The Lone Ranger*.[26]

February 17: Turns in her Scout cookie list and learns several girls have done better and win prizes.

February 18: Does poorly on her arithmetic paper, a 64 percent.

February 19, 9:15 a.m.: Wakes up and practices piano.

Spends part of the day at Hathaway Bookshop, "the oldest house in Wellesley."[27]

February 20: Sunday school, piano practice, plays in the woods, collects pretty pieces of ice. "Marcia [Egan] hit me over the head with an ice cake and gave me a big sore bump there . . . I did not get to sleep 'till 11:00 because of that bump."

February 21: Visits the Hathaway Bookshop and gets *The White Isle*.[28]

February 22: Finishes reading *The White Isle*, five games of "Turock"[29] with Warren, Mother, and Grammy.

February 23: Piano practice in the morning, sees *Lassie Come Home*.[30]

February 24: Reads Bobbsey Twins[31] and plays with her Rita Hayworth paper-doll book.

February 25, 8:00 a.m.: Wakes up.

Practices piano after breakfast, walks, and plays cards with Warren and Grammy.

February 26: Cleans her room, practices piano, visits Hathaway Bookshop.

February 27: In Sunday school, rehearses eleven Bible verses, finishes reading *A Girl of Limberlost* by Elnora Comstock,[32] "a wonderful book," listens to *Silver Theater*,[33] *The Great Gildersleeve, Jack Benny*,[34] the *Quiz Kids*,[35] and *Charlie McCarthy*.[36]

February 28: In Scouts: "when Mrs. Clifford told us to we held out our hands and got marked on our cards my hands got 2 (for the neatest) we got a red feather."

February 29: Sylvia works on maps of Europe: "I love to do that."

March 1: Sees movies *Scarlet Pimpernel*[37] and *Love Crazy*.[38] "We brought our dollies."

March 2: Reads *The Glorious Adventure* (1927) by Richard Halliburton. "I have 'Old Ironsides' for my poem for March."[39] Piano practice at home.

March 3: Miss Norris reads *The Trumpeter of Krakow* by Eric P. Kelly[40] to class, Sylvia plays dolls with Betsy Powley and Prissy Steele in Sylvia's room, dividing it into screens, Prissy spanks her doll because it "called her names."

March 4: Sylvia plays hide-and-go-seek with Warren and another friend and later musical chairs at a party, borrows *The Secret of the Barred Window*[41] (1943) by Margaret Sutton from Prissy Steele.

March 5: Piano practice, a double bill, *Riding High*[42] and *Flesh and Fantasy*, the first she likes, the second one is awful.

March 6: Over to Betsy Powley's[43] to learn how to chop wood, plays on the stumps for about five minutes, then listens to *Terry and the Pirates*.[44]

March 7: Finishes reading *The Secret of the Barred Window* and an issue of *Calling All Girls*, Miss Norris finishes reading about the opera *Aida* by Giuseppe Verdi.

March 8: Piano practice, makes a first-aid kit ("I love it all ready"), cleans out garage with Grammy, tired after jumping rope, listens to *The Lone Ranger*.

March 9: Does her first cartwheel: "(If it could be called that) and everybody laughed."

March 10: Marcia Egan and Sylvia have their stories published in *The Townsman*. "I am very proud of my name in the papers." For Sylvia's, see "Troop 5 Valentine Party," *The Townsman*, 4.

March 11: Housecleaning: "I feel I am being quite a help lately." The Nortons come for lunch. "Dick [Norton], Perry [Norton], Warren, and I Played 'Sky Ryders.'[45] Perry won."

March 12: A long walk with Grammy and Warren.

March 13: "Hercules [William Moore] is a surprisingly good dancer." Listens to *The Lone Ranger*: "He congratulated the Girl Scouts on their 32 anniversary. (I think he's wonderful)."

March 14: Miss Norris talks about illuminated letters that the class will be working on in art on Friday, finishes floor maps in art.

March 15: Piano practice, trades playing cards with Diana Lou and Dori Lou: "The old craze is probably coming back." Plays dolls with Prissy Steele, "loads of fun" taking their dolls to a party.

March 16: "Our 2 girl army attacked the boys. As a result we were soaked when we came in . . . I got my face washed in snow."

March 17: Works on illuminated letters.

    4:00–5:00 p.m.: Piano practice.

March 18: Jumps rope 109 times, builds a "lovely sand castle" with Betsy Powley, "a sweet sweet girl."

March 19: Sunday school test: Sylvia's score of 58 is second best. Piano practice, listens to *Silver Theater*, *The Great Gildersleeve*,[46] *Jack Benny*,[47] and "two others."

March 20: Snow up to the knees, snowball fights, listens to *The Lone Ranger*.

March 21: With Warren, presents a cardboard house to Mowgli for his birthday.

March 22: Watches *Madame Curie*,[48] "sad but beautiful."

March 23: Practices penmanship and makes snow statues.

March 24: Warm weather melts snow fort.

March 25, 9:00 a.m.: Wakes up.

    Small breakfast, piano practice, stomach trouble, plays with Mowgli, wrapping him in a blanket.

March 26: Sunday school, piano practice, misses her programs because radio is not working.

March 27: Sings "Happy Birthday" to Mowgli.

March 28: Miss Townsend reads *Robin Hood* to the class, learns she has to pay ten cents for every badge: "I don't think it's quite fair."

March 29, 6:45 a.m.: Wakes up.

    7:00–7:30 a.m.: Piano practice.

    In the afternoon, with Marcia Egan, watches *Riding High*[49] and *What a Woman!*[50]

March 30: In gym, an obstacle race, her team has to "jump over a rope (knee high) on one foot": "I made a running leap and tripped and fell down flat. Boy! did every one laugh. It wasn't very funny to me because I got several scratches and was very dirty."

March 31, 9:45 a.m.: Fun in art, working on designs for illuminated letters.

April 1: Trip to the Jamaica Plain arboretum.

April 2: Has a cold, does not attend Sunday school. "I can't wait 'til our Court of Awards[51] in Scouts."

April 3: Picked as leader of kickball team.[52]

April 4: Presents a report on the *Trumpeter of Krakow* (1928) by Eric P. Kelly, draws faces in art class.

April 5: Practices penmanship and piano.

    2:00 p.m.: Bus to the dentist in Boston: "Not one filling did I have!" *Jane Eyre* (1943) is "such a wonderful picture," she watches it twice.

April 6: Plays jump rope,[53] and after orchestra class, on the school trapeze.

April 7: Plays on the slide with Betsy Powley: "We did our regular farewell and we always will."

April 8: Reads *Jane Eyre* (1847) by Charlotte Brontë and a second Bobbsey Twins book.

April 9: Works in Grammy's garden on a "beautiful Easter day" with singing robins.

April 10: Plays kickball and dodgeball,[54] obtains a Bette Davis autograph in Scouts, puts it in movie-star scrapbook under pictures of Davis.

April 11: Essay about Marie Curie.

April 12: Miss Norris gives class a "talking to" about boys who have broken windows resulting in $200 in damage.

    Sylvia practices piano, cuts out a skirt for a paper doll.

April 13, 6:45 a.m.: Piano practice at home.

    Plays piano in orchestra on stage.

    Reads in bed until 9:15 p.m. "unknown to mummy."

April 14, 6:45 a.m.: Thirty minutes of piano practice.

    A- on Marie Curie composition.

April 15: At the Nortons', allowed to hold and feed baby David William Norton: "He was so cuddly and was 1 month & a half old. . . . He had the cutest little smile!"

April 16: Choral rehearsal at Sunday school, piano practice, finishes *Jane Eyre*, reads *Gone with the Wind* (1936) by Margaret Mitchell, listens to the radio.

April 17: Reads comic strips, then gets "down to business" cleaning out cellar and playroom—a "mess with toy railroad tracks, trains, blocks and other things thrown around," rests at lunch, reads an issue of *Calling All Girls*, tired out after cleaning the cellar: "I am so proud to have done such a job." Too tired for piano practice.

April 18: Reads *When a Cobbler Ruled the King* by Augusta Huiell Seaman,[55] plays by a pond, Dori Lou starts talking about "people going insane. (She must be herself) when a man moved slowly toward us thru the bushes. We didn't stop to look but fled home." Mother nearly finishes reading *Johnny Tremain* by Esther Forbes.[56]

April 19: Gets up late after reading in bed, practices piano, plays baseball with Dori Lou, Tommy Duggin, Billy, and Warren: "The boys didn't play fair so we stopped playing until they admitted their babyish cheating." Mentions she has a collection of one hundred books: "I am in a reverie of happiness for I love books." Mother finishes reading *Johnny Tremain*.

April 20: Gets up early, practices piano, mentions measles epidemic, sews and gathers two hundred pine cones with Warren, uses chicken feathers for her dolls' hats.

April 21, 8:00 a.m.: Piano practice, housework.

11:00 a.m.: Betsy Powley calls, they go over to her house, play with dolls, gargle milk "to see who could hold their milk in the longest!" Dishwashing, plays Monopoly, Betsy loses part of her Sugar Daddy,[57] but Sylvia finds it later "sticking to the seat of my pants."

6:00 p.m.: Returns home: "We had a wonderful afternoon & full of fun."

April 22: Reads *The Lucky Sixpence* by Emile Benson Knipe and Alden Arthur Knipe,[58] "wonderful," plays in the garden.

April 23: In Sunday school, rehearses a choral reading, learns that "Bruce Bullard had died 10 minutes after he was in the ambulance. I am so sorry and he was such a lovely boy!" Finishes birthday present for Mother.

April 24: Receives a 100 percent in her "last Social Studies Test!!! I am even with Donald Cheney!!!" Miss Norris and some students attend Bullard's funeral. "I can't believe Bruce is dead."

April 25: Works on composition about Marie Curie, colors stained glass windows in art class.

April 26: Reports on *Treasure of Carcassonne* by Albert Robida.[59]

April 27: Gives Warren twelve shells from the Museum of Natural History for his birthday, makes a new friend with "Nancy B. something," who has "brown hair and blue eyes. She seems to be very nice."

April 28: "Miss Norris said that Donald [Cheney] was the only boy going to Jr. High with straight a average and I was the only girl!" Buys a ticket to a junior high school performance of *The Pirates of Penzance*.

April 29, 9:00 a.m.: Gets ready for Warren's party.

3:00–5:00 p.m.: Warren's party.

Tired after party, so no piano practice.

April 30: A "slight congestion of the throat," so no Sunday school, reads *Happy House* by Jane D. Abbott,[60] all right "but unless by miracle it could not have happened," listens to *Those We Love*, *Silver Theater*, and *The Great Gildersleeve*[61] "which is as funny as ever."

May 3: "We started to do our third paragraph on our Madame Curie composition."

Plays baseball: "I made two homers!"

May 2: Reads *Eight Cousins* by Louisa May Alcott,[62] *A Boy of the Lost Crusades* by Agnes Danforth Hewes,[63] paints stained glass windows purple, blue, and yellow.

May 3: Walks to the junior high to see *The Pirates of Penzance*: "It was wonderful and had two sets one on a beach and one in a castle. The lights, costumes and pictures were lovely."

May 4: Plays baseball in eighty-eight-degree weather, reads *Kilmeny of the Orchard* by Lucy Maud Montgomery,[64] and packs a bag for an overnight hike.

May 5: Reports on her reading of *Eight Cousins*.

4:00 p.m.: Off to hike, sleeps only "1 1/2 hrs. Our loft counted Jane W.'s coughs 169 times."

May 6, 6:00 a.m.: Up for breakfast before a walk in the woods with "loads of daffodils."

Ice cream on the way home, takes a bath "as I was filthy and went to bed."

May 7: Decides to name the kinds of flowers in Sunday school. Today: white carnations and ferns. Piano practice, listens to *Those We Love*: "nothing special happened as usual." Flowers in bloom in the home garden: a tulip, violets, forget-me-nots, forsythia, plum blossoms. Soon to bloom: carnations, lilacs, narcissus, lilies of the valley, honeysuckle, roses, and "many others." Listens to *The Great Gildersleeve*[65] and *Charlie McCarthy*.

May 8: Reports on *The Wind in the Willows* by Kenneth Grahame.[66]

May 9: Recites "In Flanders Fields," by John McCrae[67] asks Miss Norris to assign a book report who says she will do so tomorrow: "She is a lovely teacher."

May 10: Demands the book report assignment on *Freckles* by Gene Stratton-Porter,[68] draws a picture of Alice in Wonderland for Betsy Powley: "We had loads of fun." Piano practice.

9:00 p.m.: Reads in bed, "unknown to mummy."

May 11: Reports on *Nadita* by Grace Moon.[69]

Noon: Riding with Prissy Steele on her bicycle, runs into a little boy, who suffers a cut. She feels "awful," goes to minstrel.[70]

May 12: "Our apple tree is in the glory between buds and full bloom," fixes her doll house.

May 13: Eats ten of her mother's homemade molasses cookies, listens to a "very funny" Corliss Archer program,[71] plays Russia[72] all morning after piano practice.

May 14: On *Those We Love*: "we got wind that something was going to happen next Sunday. I think Anne is going to get killed." Plays Russia for practice, reads the funnies, reads in the apple tree, eating cookies and drinking milk, listens to *The Great Gildersleeve*[73] and *One Man's Family*.[74]

May 15: A test identifying countries of the "Old World on a map without names! I am no good at that," plays Russia with Betsy Powley, who wins, learns in Scouts that she will get ten badges and an attendance star.

May 16: In language class, receives a D, an "awful mark," plays Russia with Marcia Egan.

Noon: Walks home with Betsy Powley to see her "beautiful tulips," plays Russia with Marcia again.

May 17: "Minstrel" in the afternoon.[75]

May 18: Plays baseball, kickball, and Russia, reads *The Story Girl* by Lucy Maud Montgomery,[76] a "solid hour" of piano practice, at supper, Aurelia asks Sylvia and Warren "some funny riddles."

May 19: A bird walk: "We saw lots of redwinged blackbirds and an oriole and its nest."

In the evening, plays Russia with Diana Lou "till 8:45."

May 20, 9:00 a.m.: Waters the flower garden, reads two Bobbsey Twins books.

May 21: Makes the honor roll with only two absences, makes dresses for dolls with Prissy Steele that they will take to camp, plays Russia with Prissy Steele until 6:00 p.m.

May 22: Reports on *Heidi* by Johanna Spyri.[77]

6:30 p.m.: At school with Grammy and Mother for Court of Awards and joins the minstrel singing.

May 23: A "too wonderful" awards night yesterday with ten badges: Bird Finder, World Knowledge, Group Music, Childcare, Reader's, Scribe, Campcraft, Foot Traveler, Boating, and Weaving. Finishes *The Little Colonel's Holiday* by Ann Fellows Johnston.[78]

May 24: Reads *The Diary of Selma Lagerlof*[79] and *An Old Fashioned Girl*.[80]

May 25: Starts working on maps of Australia.

7:30 p.m.: Trades hat pins with Betsy Powley.

8:30–9:00 p.m.: Listens to *Henry Aldrich*.[81]

May 26: After school, plays with Prissy Steele and Ruth Geisel: "Ruthie rode me on her bike to my home where we played statues and had molasses cookies. We invented a <u>new</u> way of riding a bike with two people."

May 27, 9:00–10:15 a.m.: Wakes up and practices piano.

10:15 a.m.: Reads *Calling All Girls*.

11:00 a.m.: Plays ball and rides bikes with Ruth Geisel.

3:00–5:00 p.m.: Plays with Ruth Geisel.

May 28: Sleeps late, piano practice after breakfast, goes to country club for a swim with Mother, Warren, and Prissy Steele, swims out over her head: "I put on mother's beach robe and Pris and I climbed on top of the life guard chairs and had him jumping off."

May 29: At recess, plays Russia and baseball.

May 30, 7:40 a.m.: Wakes up, gets into Scout uniform for Memorial Day parade: a three-hour march, five miles long.

3:30 p.m.: Returns home and rests, plays Russia: "For once I was one game ahead of somebody."

May 31: Music lesson, plays Russia. "Grammy was so hot that we thought she was going to faint."

8:00 p.m.: Returns home since Grammy feels faint.

June 1: At the Wellesley Hills library, checks out *Susie Sugarbeet* by Margaret Asmum[82] and *The Blue Aunt* by Elizabeth Orne White.[83]

June 2: Works on two penmanship papers, plays Russia, walks home with Betsy Powley. "I showed her two new games I made up to play a ball with."

June 3: Off with Betsy Powley to Fairy Rock[84] for a picnic with watermelon, sandwiches, milk, and cookies: "We ate with gusto and we spit out all the melon seeds at once. We both wore our braids up on our heads with a carnation." Shops at Filene's, returns home to find that Grammy has bought her a blue bathing suit and two pairs of pajamas.

June 4: After breakfast, piano practice, reads *Uncharted Ways* (1935) by Caroline Dale Snedeker,[85] plays Russia with herself, Mowgli accompanies her to catch dragonflies, listens to *Those We Love*, reads the funnies.

8:00–9:00 p.m.: Listens to *Silver Theater*, *The Great Gildersleeve*,[86] and *The Army Hour*,[87] "with some of our greatest comedians."

June 5: Plays baseball and Russia with Betsy Powley and Patty (Patricia Ann Dunne), goes into the woods to get double buttercups and other flowers to press.

June 6: Works on pressed flowers and social studies report and on a flower girl painting in art class, accepted for first two weeks at Camp Weetamoe: "Yippee!!" Enters a contest to "enlarge the picture of a Wac."

June 7: Reports on *Uncharted Ways*, home late and her mother slaps her, Grammy drives Sylvia and Warren to Aunt Elizabeth's (Aldrich) for a big dinner with strawberry pie: "Uncle Henry [Aldrich] gave Warren and I each a dollar. Aunt Liz gave us each a funny book and Warren a soldier cut out doll and me a girl. We sat on the porch and cut them out."

6:30 p.m.: Thirty minutes of piano practice.

June 8: Reports on *Blue Aunt*, checks out *Otto of the Silver Hand* by Howard Pyle[88] and *Edward MacDowell and His Cabin in the Pines* by Opal Wheeler[89] from the library.

June 9: Sunday school report card: "one Fair, 2 Good's, and 3 Excellents." Reads *Mozart the Wonder Boy* by Opal Wheeler,[90] makes paper houses in art, goes over to Betsy Powley's in the afternoon, then to Sylvia's home where they "'smelled' some iris and pansies."

June 10, 9:00–11:00 a.m.: Piano practice, a picnic at Morses Pond,[91] catches a baby fish, and swims with David Freeman and Ruth Geisel, goes home and upstairs with Ruth, reads and plays doctor, David plays popular tunes by ear on the piano, Sylvia plays "La Chatelaine."

7:45 p.m.: A "happy day."

June 11: Sylvia reads in bed, listens to *Those We Love*, goes to the country club to get Grammy, reads *Gone with the Wind*, listens to *The Great Gildersleeve*,[92] *Quiz Kids*, and Gracie Fields, substituting on *Charlie McCarthy*.

June 12: Reports on *Mozart the Wonder Boy*, plays kickball and Russia, reads up to page 700 of *Gone with the Wind*, reads *Edward MacDowell and His Cabin in the Pines* for a report.

June 13: Reports on *Edward MacDowell and His Cabin in the Pines*, in art class, almost finishes with white paper house (blue shutters), goes swimming at Morses Pond.

7:00 p.m.: Returns home.

9:30 p.m.: Goes to bed.

June 14: Sees *Up in Arms*[93] and *Passport to Destiny*,[94] over to Mrs. Becker's house to eat "2 hotdogs, 2 rolls, 2 cups of cocoa, 23 animal crackers, 1 piece of cake, 1 helping ice cream," reads funny books and plays on the swing. Grammy picks her up, and Grace Dickinson stays overnight.

June 15: Miss Norris reads *Blacksmith of Vilno: A Tale of Poland in 1832* (1930) by Eric P. Kelly to the class.

June 16: End of school, plans to attend a carnival at night with Patty Dunne and Betsy Powley, Scout Day Camp registration, rains during the carnival sending them to a drugstore, "soaked after running a few yards."

June 17: Sylvia has a rare treat for breakfast: cinnamon toast. Piano practice for a half hour, reads *Gone with the Wind* for an hour, plays ball by herself and does some drawing, another trip to the carnival, rides on the "chair-plane"[95] and Ferris wheel.

June 18: Housecleaning: "The house was neat as a pin."

5:00 p.m.: Large supper with Aunt Dot, Uncle Joe (Joseph Benotti), Paul Aldrich, Esther Aldrich, Uncle Henry, and Aunt Elizabeth: "2 helpings of chicken salad, ham, a dish of ice cream, a brownie, and a glass of milk." Grownups have fun playing cards. Uncle Henry gives Sylvia one dollar.

Sylvia goes to sleep after they leave.

June 19: Sylvia is in the advanced swimmer's group at day camp, canoes, builds a hut, sings songs before everyone goes home.

June 20: Miserable day at camp with no sun, reads comic books, canoes, plans for an Indian skit: "I am going to be an Indian Princess." At home, a hot bath and bed, "for I was frozen."

June 21: No day camp because of rain. Mother does not want her to play outdoors.

11:00 a.m.: Betsy Powley comes over to play with paper dolls.

Sylvia reads *Mademoiselle*, washes dishes after supper, practices piano.

June 22: Makes totem poles and "Scalp Sticks" for the following day's play. "I am not to be the princess because I was not there yesterday but I am to be her brother." Eats a lot and rehearses for the play, more singing and cutting out paper dolls, reads "funny book that Warren got."

June 23: Grammy takes Sylvia to day camp. She passes fifty-yard swimming test.

11:00 a.m.: Start of an all-day canoe trip over to Sandy Bottom[96] for a picnic, paddles under scenic bridges: "I never had such a wonderful time in my life. . . . I was chief in our indian play tonight because Pat didn't come. I like the nursery school play best. It was 'Snow White.' The costumes were charming."

5:45 p.m.: Home for supper, forty-five minutes of piano practice.

June 24, 8:00 a.m.: Makes breakfast for herself and Warren.

Cuts out paper dolls of seven movie stars, helps with housework.

June 25, 9:00 a.m.: Helps mother and Grammy prepare for lunch with Aunt Helen.[97]

12:30 p.m.: Lunch with Aunt Helen, who gives Sylvia and Warren fifty cents each and announces she has lost twenty-five pounds on a diet.

4:30 p.m.: Sees *Lost Angel*[98] and *Rationing*[99] at the theater: "It was wonderful and we saw lots of others that we knew there."

8:45 p.m.: Returns home for a late supper.

June 26: Day camp: archery, a skit, cleanup, reads funny books in her hut, off to the beach. "I was victim for demonstration of artificial respiration." Grammy takes her home.

June 27: Day camp: practices skit, hikes to get some wild roses. "I have never been as hot." Home for shower and right to bed.

June 28: Day camp: fixes up the hut with cushions, hikes around the lake, reads funny books. At home, plays outside with Warren, comes in, dries dishes, and brushes her hair.

June 29: Day camp: play practice, plays pencil games,[100] canoes. "I was stern paddler with Mrs. Hayden. She said I made an excellent landing." Presentation of plays in the afternoon, Dr. Berton gives Sylvia a "camp examination."

June 30: Last day of day camp.

11:45 a.m.–12:15 p.m.: Sylvia swims fifty yards to the float and back. "I felt wonderful afterwards." Plays hangman[101] with Betsy Wiley during rest hour, a half hour of swimming, at home, rests on porch. "Mrs. Freeman sent me a beret like Ruthie [Freeman] has."

July 1, 8:30 a.m.: Grammy and Grampy (Francis "Frank" Schober) leave for a two-week vacation. Dries the dishes and makes the beds, writes a thank-you letter to Mrs. Freeman for sending a "plastic band."

Ca. noon: Swims at Morses Pond, a picnic lunch packed by Mother.

1:30–2:30 p.m.: Rests.

2:30–3:00 p.m.: Swimming.

3:00–3:15 p.m.: Rests.

3:15–3:35 p.m.: Swimming.

5:00 p.m.: Home with a sunburn, rests, works on a crossword puzzle.

July 2: After breakfast, makes beds, washes dishes, and reads.

10:30–11:15 a.m.: Arrives at Morses Pond for a swim.

12:00–1:00 p.m.: Mother arrives with lunch.

2:00–2:45 p.m.: Sylvia swims.

3:30–4:00 p.m.: Uncle Joe picks Sylvia up.

Sylvia sleeps overnight at Aunt Dot's, reads funnies before bedtime.

July 3, 6:00 a.m.: Gets up, prepares for train trip to camp.

8:00 a.m.: "Mother saw me off." On train to Mountainview with Audrey Young.

Arrives at camp in time for lunch and receives ration stamps, railroad tickets, and money, assigned to tent four, makes her bed and unpacks before supper, singing in the lodge.

9:00 p.m.: Bedtime.

July 4: Wakes up before "taps," writes two letters to Mother[102] and one to Betsy Powley, keeps accounts of what she eats and spends, swims, arts and crafts (makes a tile for Mother's Christmas present), after supper, plays steal the bacon.[103] Miss Jane reads *The House at Pooh Corner* (1928) by A. A. Milne[104] at bedtime.

July 5: Before reveille, Sylvia writes a third letter to her mother and one to Grammy and Grampy, swims before breakfast, tent inspection, rest hour, a treasure hunt for candy kisses, games before bed, and a thunderstorm that has everyone doubling up in beds.

July 6: Arts and crafts, boating, swimming after rest hour, and first letters arrive from home along with an issue of *Calling All Girls*. Sylvia plays "Sink the Ship"[105] after dinner: "loads of fun." The moon rises, "first red, orange, and then light yellow."

July 7: Sylvia writes a fourth letter to mother, swims, in arts and crafts, works on a coaster with a raven painted on it, learns how to dive.

July 8: Finishes reading *Calling All Girls*, shellacs her coaster, swims, dives "so straight that I fell right to the bottom and at first thought I broke my neck," finishes *Mystery at the Moss-Covered Mansion*,[106] more swimming.

July 9: "The same somebody as last night blew Reville at 5:30 and woke me and many others up. 'Bev' has an awful wart on the bottom of her foot and makes too much of it." Very hot, Sylvia swims some more.

July 10: Arts and crafts, swimming, tent inspection.

July 11: Makes potholder in arts and crafts, has a picnic in the rain that ends up in a tent, which floods.

July 12: Makes a second potholder, doesn't feel like swimming, reads Bobbsey Twins, more thunderstorms, sleeps with Gloria in her bed.

July 13: Reads letters that arrived yesterday. She has received seventeen letters at camp. Swims and has a scavenger hunt.

July 14: Doesn't feel like swimming, writes letters,[107] and draws. At supper: "A toy frog was put in the salad and we spilled milk and were very bad. We played games and popped corn on the beach before supper."

Writes a postcard to Mother and includes drawings of potholders and coasters made in arts and crafts and an itemization of expenses at camp. "I am going to try to look neat coming home." Reports she swam one-hundred-yard sidestroke: "I never thought I could do it!"

July 15: A boat trip with a "nosebag supper[108] on the lake because we won inspection with 4.0." Eats supper in the middle of the lake, sends a postcard home reporting on patriotic day at camp with a drawing of her red, white, and blue clothing.

July 16: Packs up to return home, singing after lunch, at weigh-in: a two-pound loss. At Scouts, a minstrel show, sad to think she has to leave tomorrow.

July 17: Finishes packing, puts on her pinafore and bow, writes to Mother that she is packed, itemizes expenses, draws a heart.

3:05 p.m.: Departs on train from Mountainview.

6:31 p.m.: Train arrives.

At home, greets Uncle Frank, Aunt Louise, Aunt Dot, Uncle Joe, Grammy, Grampy, and Warren.

10:00 p.m.: Mother gives her a bath before bed.

July 18, 11:00 a.m.: Feels rested after a "wonderful sleep."

Helps Warren pick beans in the garden, finishes a "wonderful book," *Fog Magic* by Julia L. Sauer,[109] wins at croquet with Uncle Frank, Aunt Louise, and Warren, plays Liverpool,[110] comes in second, apple picking: "one hit me right in the eye when it fell! They feel hard." A "hearty supper," Uncle Frank teaches Warren and Sylvia card tricks before they drive to Grammy and Grampy's house.

July 19: Sylvia does housework, reads *An Ear for Uncle Emil* by Eva Roe Gaggin,[111] copies the beautiful illustrations and one of the etchings of a "little Swiss girl sitting in the midst of some flowers playing an accordion." Off to Morses Pond for a swim, finishes the picture at home, the "best I have ever drawn," dries supper dishes, reads, and goes to bed.

July 20: Shops at Filene's for a pink wool sweater, a blue checkered dress, and a yellow long-sleeved jersey, a supper cookout: "loads of fun." More card tricks with Uncle Frank, sleeps on the porch.

July 21, 7:30 a.m.: Draws in bed, reads, plays Monopoly with Warren.

4:00–4:30 p.m.: Swims at Morses Pond.

5:15–5:30 p.m.: Returns home, small supper since she is not feeling well.

July 22, 7:15 a.m.: Wakes up "feeling miserable," one eye "closed with pus" and a "sore throat." Washes, gargles, feels better. Betsy Powley comes over to play with paper dolls.

4:45 p.m.: Betsy bikes home. Sylvia has supper on the porch couch "as I was tired." Before going to bed, shines her "luminous figures."

July 23, 6:00 a.m.: Wakes up with a closed eye, cleans it, and goes back to sleep.

9:30 a.m.: On porch, has a terrible earache that disappears at lunch.

Cuts out paper dolls, reads, a "delicious supper" on porch couch, after supper, plays turock with Grammy, Mother, and Warren: "I won 1 game with Grammy. I won 1 by myself when Mother & Warren played against me."

July 24, 5:15 a.m.: Wakes up, cleans out her eyes, a hearty breakfast on the porch couch.

Reads and cuts out paper dolls, goes shopping with Grammy and Mother, lunch at home.

3:15 p.m.: Grammy arrives with a country-club fruit basket.

Because of her eye, Sylvia stays home while everyone else goes to Morses Pond for swimming. Puts roast in the oven, plays cards after supper before going to bed.

July 25: Reads *Cornelli* by Johanna Spyri.[112]

9:00 a.m.: Listens to radio while making her own paper doll and drawing clothes for it.

1:30 p.m.: Lunch alone while Warren is at Grammy's and Mother is at a Boston University teachers' meeting.

2:30 p.m.: Mother returns, they play cards.

After supper, Sylvia walks to the library, but it is closed, returns home for dessert, listens to *A Date with Judy*[113] and *Mystery Theatre*.[114]

9:45 p.m.: "We [Sylvia and her mother] went to bed together."

July 26, 7:15 a.m.: Wakes, breakfast with Mother.

9:00 a.m.: Mother attends another teachers' meeting. Sylvia works on the paper doll she made and plays cards by herself.

Eats the lunch Mother prepared for her. Listens to radio all day.

3:30 p.m.: Mother returns home with a paper-doll book.

After supper, they play cards and listen to *The Lone Ranger* and *Mr. and Mrs. North.*[115] "They are both so exciting."

July 27: While Mother goes to another teachers' meeting, Sylvia accompanies Uncle Frank and Aunt Louise to Morses Pond. At home, plays turock when Mother returns, reads, tries on dresses and sweaters that Louise has outgrown.

July 28: Helps Mother make the beds, reads, plays cards with Aunt Louise, goes to country club to get Grampy for a swim at Morses Pond. Uncle Frank and Aunt Louise leave, and Sylvia notes: "This is the last I will see of them on their furlough. I feel sadly."[116] Washes dishes and listens to *The Lone Ranger* before bed.

July 29: Still has some problems with an eye infection made worse by swimming. Does housework, dishwashing, reads *Ladies Home Journal*, paints dresses for paper dolls. "Mother gave me some ideas." Mother sews the hems of Sylvia's dresses.

9:00 p.m.: Sylvia makes a point of reporting she said "good night" to Warren.

July 30: Weighs eighty-eight pounds in the morning and ninety pounds at night, makes more dresses for her paper dolls, plays turock.

July 31: Finishes reading a book in the Little Maid series. Makes paper-doll dresses and listens to the radio. Reads another Little Maid book: "always good no matter how many times I read them."[117] Listens to radio until supper.

7:30–8:00 p.m.: Listens to *The Lone Ranger.*

8:00–8:30 p.m.: Listens to *Cavalcade of America.*[118]

August 1: Plays Monopoly with Warren and later plays with Ruth Geisel, who teaches her a new way to play checkers, plays outside until 5:00 p.m., showers, and listens to *A Date with Judy.*

August 2: Plays with Warren and Ruth Geisel, washes dishes, gets ready for bed, Mother brushes Sylvia's hair while they listen to *Mr. and Mrs. North.*

August 3: Sylvia cleans the house to prepare for visitors, off to Morses Pond, plays turock with Warren, Mother, and Grammy after supper.

August 4: Gets up just before 10:00 a.m., practices piano after breakfast, does a little housework, finishes reading *The Little Prince* (1943) by Antoine de Saint-Exupéry and *You Wouldn't Know Me from Adam* (1944) by Frederick Chase Taylor, off to swim: "Warren and I were bad and pushed each other underwater. Then we made friends and caked ourself with wet sand so we had to wash off." Plays turock after supper.

August 5: Piano practice in the morning, goes to see *Destination Tokyo*[119]: "wonderful (and tense!)."

August 6: Weeds the gravel sidewalk, Mother braids Sylvia's hair, Sylvia has a cookout with Grammy and Grampy: "The flies were awful! I lay on the hammock and only ate cake, ice cream, and a fruit drink as I felt ill! I felt much better when they left."

August 7: Sylvia has a sore throat, listens to radio all day, plays cards, reads *Schoolgirl Allies* by Rebecca Middleton Samson,[120] and then listens to *I Love a Mystery*[121] and *The Lone Ranger*.

August 8, 8:00 a.m.: Wakes up and reads *Pollyanna* (1913) by Eleanor H. Porter again.[122]

Draws in a camp notebook, plays cards until lunch, listens to radio, does more drawing.

4:00–6:00 p.m.: Naps.

Listens to radio after supper: *Ginny Simms*[123] and *A Date with Judy*.

August 9: "My throat was better after mother blowing Sulphuric down it last night." Mother goes to the Wellesley Square library for books. Sylvia goes to bed "sore and weary," listens to *The Lone Ranger* and *Mr. and Mrs. North*, "which cheered me somewhat."

August 10: Finishes *A Little Maid of New York* (1921) by Alice Turner Curtis: "It was one of the best I have read."[124] Finishes reading *The Open Gate*.[125] Taken to see Dr. Berger, a homeopath: "He is fat and sloppy like his office." Sylvia starts reading *The Middle Moffat*,[126] plays turock.

August 11: Does housework and puzzles with Warren, "almost finished 'Peace and Plenty.'"[127] He finished 1 and started a 2nd. As it was too hot to sleep in my room mother and I went out and stargazed for a few mins."

August 12: Reads the September issue of *Calling All Girls*, Grammy takes her to the library, and Sylvia checks out two mysteries, listens to music on the radio.

August 13: Dressed by 9:00 a.m., good breakfast, makes the beds, off to Morses Pond with Mother, Warren, and Grammy.

August 14: Sets up a tent with mosquito netting, finishes a puzzle of Crater Lake,[128] sits in her tent until supper, does "embroidering on the bureau scarf for mother's Christmas present."

August 15: Swims, has a picnic, collects shells with Warren, sits in the shade of an umbrella with Warren, sits on the shore and lets the waves splash on her and Warren, after supper, sits in the apple tree with Ruth Geisel, and then listens to *A Date with Judy*.

August 16, 8:00 a.m.: Awakes.

10:00 a.m.: Drives to "wonderful" Children's Morning Esplanade Concert, swims out to the "second raft" with Mother and Ruth Geisel.

Ca. 9:30 p.m.: Asleep.

August 17: Plays "death and war" with Ruth Geisel, swims out to the "second raft."

August 18: Another game of war with Ruthie, after the rain, sits in the apple tree, swims with a flutter board[129]: "The waves were large and did we have fun." On the school playground, swings and slides, stargazing on the way home.

August 19, 5:45 a.m.: Mother departs for "a day in Lynn," Massachusetts. Sylvia plays cards with Ruth Geisel (war and solitaire), lunch with Grammy, who takes a nap while Sylvia cleans the kitchen to surprise her: "We scoured the walls and sink, stove and table. I polished the toaster till it look like a mirror. She was surprised." Over to Aunt Dot's to pick apples.

August 20: Uses wax paper to make the playground slide slippery, to Morses Pond with Betsy Powley for a swim, Grammy picks them up, plays cards until supper with Ruth Geisel and Betsy (156 pickup).[130]

August 21: Plays with paper dolls with Nancy Brewer, Maureen, and Paula (Brown?).

August 22: Plays with paper dolls with Nancy Brewer at her house, home for lunch, Mother calls to say Sylvia has received a letter from Hedy Lamarr and that she will send it. Sylvia goes swimming with Ruth, plays hoist the green sail.[131]

August 23: Sleeps in the same bed with Ruth at the Freeman home, sorts out paper dolls and listens to records, talks with Mother on the phone, reads a Mary Poppins book.[132]

August 24: Shops with Mrs. Freeman, buys a Greer Garson paper-doll book for ten cents, sees *Home in Indiana*[133] and *The Scarlet Claw*.[134]

August 25: Tries to fly kites on the beach, Ruth rips hers, and Sylvia's won't fly, but David Freeman's "Fu Man Chu" "sailed fine." Sylvia is on to Boston to meet Mother.

August 26: Helps with housework and cleaning, cuts out Greer Garson dolls, an artist, Elizabeth Kent, brings her "an art pad, 3 special pencils, and a scratch pad. We two talked about art after supper."

August 27: Sylvia works on an illustration of a poem for the *Boston Sunday Herald* "Good Sport" page contest, plays "relivo"[135] with Prissy Steele and Betsy Powley.

August 28: Washes dishes, makes her bed, plays on the playground ropes, and makes huts in the woods with Prissy Steele, Ruth Geisel, and Betsy Powley: "Ours was a stick frame work wound in and out with ferns and wild plans. We have a camouflaged cubby hole and a big door."

August 29: Practices piano before breakfast at 8:00 a.m.

Works with Betsy Powley on enlarging their hut, which can now hold around eight people.

6:10 p.m.: Home and listens to *A Date with Judy* with Mother.

August 30, 8:00 a.m.: Wakes up, breakfasts, practices piano.

Over to the hut, avoiding the poison oak, plays on the ropes, and buys a fifteen-dollar bike at a girls bike sale. "It's mine! I rode home and was there by 4:00." Washes dishes after supper and listens to *The Lone Ranger* and *Mr. and Mrs. North*.

August 31: Bike riding before breakfast, finishes reading *Come Soon, Tomorrow*,[136] starts *Cousins' Luck in the Louisiana Bayou Country*.[137] Rides bike to Morses Pond, sunbathes with Mother, more bike riding after supper.

September 1: Cleans house with Mother, practices piano, rides bike, listens to *The Lone Ranger, Blondie*,[138] and *Kenny Aldrich*.[139]

September 2: Bikes, sees Hedy Lamarr and William Powell in *The Heavenly Body*[140]—"wonderful"—and Lynn Bari in *Tampico*[141]—"poor."

September 3: "I didn't get the prize on the [*Boston Sunday Herald*] Good Sport Page." Gives Warren a ride on her bike "around up hills and down dales," returns home "exhausted. He actually pedaled the pedals. He is learning to ride." Reads *The Golden Skylark, and Other Stories* by Elizabeth Goudge.[142] "There were only 2 stories I didn't care for. I got some of my planning for Christmas done." More bike riding. "I am not going to try for another contest for quite awhile." Makes a necklace out of cantaloupe seeds and puts it on her cat who promptly loses it.

September 4: Arranges her paper dolls in another book, practices piano, rides bike, birthday card for Uncle Frank. "Grammy is going to make a cake for him and send it." Plays turock with Warren and her grandparents: "As usual I lost while all the rest won from my big loss!!"

September 5: Piano practice, bike riding, into Boston with Mother to shop and to have tea at the "Wilding Whites": "I met a very interesting Italian girl going to Radcliffe. We had a good time only I found the older talk rather boring but do not show it."

September 6: Practices piano, plays nurse in her hut, builds a tent, reads "funny books," rides her bike, gets ready for junior high school tomorrow. *Enters junior high school.*

September 7: Takes bus to school, listens to the home room teacher talk about junior high.

September 8: On the 7:40 bus with schedule cards for math, physical education (PE), chorus, English, and orchestra, draws after supper.

September 9: Bikes to the library after helping Betsy Powley with housework, cuts her elbow when her bike tips over in the garage, listens to Mother read *The Yearling*.

September 10: Sleeps in on Sunday, bikes to get the newspaper, cleans out her drawers, using one for her drawings, listens to *The Great Gildersleeve*[143] while eating supper, biking, and homework.

September 11: "Miss Raguse (the old dear) complimented me on the good book report I wrote on my card." Homework, turock.

September 12: Elected secretary of the math club, lunch: "Boy! Do I get hungry." Does her homework in Grammy's room, rides her bike, reads *Calling All Girls* "cover to cover."

September 13: Plays one piece in orchestra: "It gives me a wonderful thrill."

6:00 p.m.: Mother and Grammy are home after attending a performance of *Othello*.

September 14: "A hurricane going over 140 mi. an hour is expected tonight & tomorrow morning." Homework during a "tense and humid" evening: "There is now a small wind and thunder and rain! I will tell about everything tomorrow if I live through it! (I hope)."

September 15: Sleeps through the hurricane "what there was of it," which hits Cape Cod and then goes out to sea: "we just got the tail end of it." Earns a credit for seeing that all the tables are in "perfect order" for lunch, tries out the piano in orchestra, rides bike to Nancy Brek's in the Wellesley Hills neighborhood. Nancy shows her drawings, and they play rummy[144] and Go Fish,[145] Sylvia rides home on her bike.

September 16: Hair braiding, homework, biking while her hair dries, plays turock with Warren and Mother: "Won."

September 17: Eats breakfast "in the warm sun on the porch." Bikes, reads in the apple tree with the warm sun on her, bikes over to Betsy Powley's, builds a miniature fern hut with plans for a snow hut, listens to *Charlie McCarthy* before going to bed at 9:00 p.m.

September 18: PE games in the gym and a question test in social studies. "I got one wrong which gave me B."

September 19: Assigned to write a composition or poem about "first impressions of Jr. High," reads from *The Rise of Our Free Nation*[146] in social studies, assigned to report a current event by memory tomorrow. Plays with Betsy Powley, returns home to do homework.

September 20: At orchestra, Mr. Leach sends her to Guidance (the school counselor), saying "he was going to try me on something else. I wonder what."

September 21: Her choice of clubs: "1. Art, 2. Jr Dramatics, 3. Dancing."

September 22: Mr. Leach assigns her to play the bass viola. Betsy Powley calls to ask whether Sylvia can stay overnight: "The answer was yes!" Bikes over to Betsy's, they read and play checkers, tell ghost stories: "Was it fun! I didn't get to sleep until around eleven o'clock."

September 23: Sylvia stays in bed with Betsy until 10:30 a.m., they make their beds and have breakfast, Sylvia rides home for lunch to be ready for Mr. Leach, who is bringing the "big violin." He doesn't come. Betsy comes over for tea in a house they make out of blankets, pillows, poles, and three trees. After supper, Sylvia reads *Pollyanna's Door to Happiness*.[147]

September 24: Warren leaves the garage door open, and the car freezes. Sylvia makes a hut with Warren "like I did yesterday," goes to the country club with Grammy. The chef gives them a bag of pears, peaches, and bananas. Sylvia reads the paper, bikes home, packs her school bag.

September 25: Mails off entry to the *Boston Sunday Herald* "Good Sport" puzzle page.

September 26: Reads *The Rise of Our Free Nation*, creates a cartoon out of a news article in social studies.

September 27: Her cartoon is praised in social studies. Makes a rug with Betsy Powley in the backyard.

September 28: "In study I have Miss Siok. She's rather pretty but her nose is like a sea-hawk." Plays cards and wishes "something would happen nothing has for a long time."

September 29: Chestnut collection now totals eighty-four. "We sang lovely songs in chorus. I love it. . . . It has happened!!!!!!! Tomorrow I am going to meet Mrs. Haynes (our new Scout leader) at the end of El. [Elmwood] Rd." In her car with Betsy Powley and two others. "We are going to visit a radio broadcast given by the Wellesley Boy Scouts. (Youth on parade)."

September 30: Attends the broadcast. "The stars that sang were swell! There was a little freckle-face fellow who was 'Popcorn.' It was hilarious the way he acted! There were three pairs of twins! It was over too soon." After supper, plays dress-up with Ruth Geisel as a "Senorita" and Sylvia as an "old fashioned girl." Experiments with shadows in front of a streetlight. "I wore the high heeled shoes. I got right ready for bed for this has been one of the biggest days of this year for me."

October 1: A wonderful preacher at Sunday school, Grampy quizzes her on social studies test.

October 2: "In English our new teacher talked & talked. She is very interesting." Plays dodgeball,[148] goes to a Scout meeting.

October 3: Gets four questions wrong in social studies for a "77.5/9%! Sort of bad!" Bikes to the library, checks out *The Riddle of River Acres*[149] and *Shark Hole: A Story of Modern Hawaii* (1943) by Nora Burglon.

October 4: "Our 7th Grade Assembly was wonderful! 11 people took part and 7 were from our room," playing trumpet, piano, drums, and violin.

October 5: "In S. S. Study I did page 32 and made up a grand thing about Columbus."

October 6: Relay races in PE, sings beautiful songs in chorus, makes defense stamps. "In orchestra Mr. Leach made me play almost all the time for last week I guess."

October 7: Worn out after doing the beds, dishwashing, and dusting. "I had settled down for a quiet rest when the telephone rang—Bets

[Powley]—I was over her house in a jiff. We sat in her back yard and used my printing set to print a circus folder." Breathtaking fall scenery, Caroline stays for supper, "a beautiful sweet girl. She wore the prettiest dress."

October 8: An ordeal at Sunday school: the girls were "so rude but mother took care of them and put them in their place." Sylvia bangs her knee while biking, does math homework after supper, listens to the radio, reads before bed. "I have had a hard day."

October 9: Wears Scout uniform to school, paints fall leaves and flowers in art class, works on Wellesley Award papers in social studies, hopes she is one of the ten best.

October 10: Pastes movie-star pictures in scrapbook.

October 11: Attends an assembly talk about posture, elected president in social studies.

October 12: After lunch, rakes leaves and feels "woozy," walks with Ann Geisel across the baseball field as a shot whizzes past them: "Did we jump!"

October 13: Cuts knee in beat ball,[150] but a "nice Fri 13" anyway in orchestra, gets some colored candle stubs, and plays turock.

October 14: Warren at the dentist with Mother, Sylvia cleans his room, dries dishes, and makes beds, at Nancy's house draws pictures, reads, plays piano. "Warren had left the house in a mess and when mother & Grammy came home from the movies they scolded him something awful."

October 15: A "wonderful time" in Sunday school. "The girls were so responsive." Grammy drives Sylvia to the Wellesley College campus, they walk around the lake, enjoying the "beautiful foliage." Sylvia has a hearty lunch, bikes, works on a "portfolio for my drawings" and an oral presentation for English. Listens to *The Great Gildersleeve*, *Jack Benny*,[151] *Quiz Kids*, and *Charlie McCarthy*.

October 16: Learns more about percentages in math, in Scouts, plays red rover.[152] "I fell against Mrs. Haynes' basement screen and for a minute I thought I had gone thru it. I am now black & blue."

October 17: Drilled and drilled and drilled in music class, the topic is French and Spanish colonies in social studies, burns her colored candle, and reads from *Swiss Family Robinson*,[153] "which is a very [virtuous] book."

October 18: A movie in assembly about South America. "It was fun." Oral presentations in English, works on Halloween poem, candle burning.

October 19: Paints an ocean scene in art, "Marcia [Egan] said mean things to me but I don't care," asked to write an article for *The Phillipian* about "seventh grade girls after school sports!" In social studies, writes a fictional diary of a "Spanish child in days of Columbus," tries a charcoal drawing for the first time: "terribly messy and fades out right away." Works on birthday invitations.

October 20: Sees *Double Indemnity* (1944), listens to a "hilarious" episode of *The Great Gildersleeve*, "Gildersleeve's Ghost."

October 21: Homework, biking, Monopoly, paper dolls, "I had fun opening the packages for my party (baskets, candy, napkins, etc.)."

October 22: "In Sunday School we learned more about Paul." Takes a drive along Cliff Road, a new route, sees the "deep blue reservoir and bright colored oaks . . . islands in the reservoir covered with pine trees."

October 23: Makes charts of the human body and posture in health class, relay races and dodgeball in PE, writes the "first draft on my biography."

October 24: In English, reads book report on her biography, and Miss Raguse approves it "highly."

October 25: Finishes reading the latest issue of *Calling All Girls*, "interesting and novel," rides her bike to the drug store for Grammy.

October 26: Some of her pictures exhibited at school, Sylvia pastes pictures on cardboard for one of the games for her birthday party the next day.

October 27: Lists birthday presents: a kerchief, bicycle carrier, a two-year subscription to *American Girl*, money from Aunt Dot. Dancing class before the party and learns to "keep time."

6:00 p.m.: Party starts with opening presents, then supper and games, "Who Am I"[154] and "Things our Grandmother's missed," makes clay models.

Guests leave, and Sylvia joins Ruthie in telling stories before they go to sleep.

October 28: With Ruth Geisel, gathers birch tree seeds in back yard, a party at Betsy Powley's: "we each had a number and were blindfolded and went down the cellar 1 by 1. First we shook hands with Frankenstein (a glove filled with wet sand) felt his brains (cold gooey macaroni) & felt his innards (raw liver)," bobbing for apples, everyone a prize winner.

October 29: Sunday school with Ruth Geisel, reading and candle burning, writes thank-you letters,[155] reads *Pollyanna Grows Up* (1915) by Eleanor H. Porter.

8:00 p.m.: Tired after all the late parties.

October 30: "In Health I was elected <u>President</u>!"

October 31: Works on the colonies in social studies, rides home, does homework, "I am too old to go out now as I am twelve. I have just as much fun watching Warren go out as I would if I had gone myself. Some boys, bent on ruining property took our outside light bulbs and did damage."

November: Sylvia publishes an article about seventh-grade girls after school sports in *The Phillipian*.

November 1: In Guidance, Miss Borgatti talks about the importance of manners. "Why am I so happy! I am in love! He smiled at me today and He's wonderful."

November 2: In art, drawing faces "according to real proportion," Sylvia takes a wild bicycle ride before supper in the "drear" November evening air, riding "no hands all up the road."

November 3: Begins reading *Rebecca of Sunnybrook Farm*.[156] "I did not fall off the balance beam!" Walks home and hears someone following her. She speeds up and then sees John Loungway grinning at her "like a Cheshire Cat. . . . I about died!" Learns to waltz "pretty well" and does the Virginia Reel.

November 4: Says "something to Mama and she got unreasonable and made me clean Warren's bookcase and room." Milk and cookies at Aunt Dot's, cuts out paper dolls, makes a house on top of a rock under pine trees.

November 5: More about Paul in Sunday school, a half hour of "'Paderewski' practicing,"[157] reads the papers, washes dishes with Grammy, fun playing turock with Aunt Dot and Uncle Joe, who says she made no mistakes.

November 6: Snowing, drawing faces in art.

November 7: Elected vice president in math, burns another candle.

November 8: "Roosevelt's president!" A sore throat, reads and draws in bed.

November 9: Self-portraits in art, Miss Siok compliments her on her penmanship, gym girls do "fantastic stunts on the desks to get rid of any nervousness" before PTA meeting, Sylvia gets stage fright just before the curtain is pulled but does not fall off the balance beam, "everything was fun."

November 10: Rains hard, Grammy drives her to school on Armistice Day, second-period talk by an American Legion member, a soldier, and a sailor, Grammy drives her to dancing class: "Bruce A. came too. We teased him sort of. He is so silly." They learn how to do the Lindy.

November 11: Has a cold and listens to radio all day, cutting out paper dolls, all her meals in bed. "My eyes were all watery so I couldn't read so I wrote down the words to some old sweet songs that I heard on radio. My nose is so stiff and red that it feels like a washing board."

November 12: Sleeps late and misses Sunday school, listens to radio and cuts out paper dolls, plays piano and does homework, listens to *The Great Gildersleeve*, looks over her answers on the English colonies assigned for social studies class before bed.

November 13: Reads her sentences about Armistice Day to the class, Miss Raguse points out sentence fragments but says "they expressed my poetic nature." Sylvia reads *Calling All Girls* and *American Girl*.

November 14: Miss Raguse comments on her English report: "You go too fast and do not give us enough time to follow your points. You have a gift in that and should build it up." Sylvia sees *Greenwich Village*[158] in technicolor.

November 15: New officers elected in Guidance. "I am only supervision hostess. Miss Borgatti said, 'You are doing so well that I will let you keep the job during the whole year. You can pile up 4 credits!'" Sylvia finishes reading a book in the Bibi series[159] in English class.

November 16: Window shopping and homework, reads *Road to Down Under* by Maribelle Cormack[160] before and after supper.

November 17: In chorus, Miss Hough plays *The Nutcracker Suite*. "It <u>was</u> <u>wonderful</u>." Miss Raguse mentions expecting ten book reports. An "aghast" Sylvia finishes her homework and turns to the "task of ten book reports."

November 18: Rereads three books and writes reports, hopes to get the other six done the next day. "I am enjoying writing them although it is quite a task to do ten in three days."

November 19: Spends time in the woods and starts to make a "small garden . . . up against a moss covered tree." Two more book reports completed and more reading of *Road to Down Under*: "I am at peace in the world."

November 20: A bike accident: "I thought the end had surely come! I flew somewhere, and landed up on the street on my carrier which broke. I let out one shriek. I was helped by a lady to Mrs. Haynes who made a fuss over me. She bathed my dripping knees and bandaged them."

November 21: Rides home on her battered bike with stiff knees, gets three books from the library.

November 22: "Ah! Bliss! In Guidance Miss Borgatti chose <u>me</u> to read two stories (on A. G. Bell & T. A. Edison)," publishes an article in the new issue of *The Phillipian*.

November 23: Housework, sketching at the playground, a walk in the woods before Thanksgiving lunch: a twenty-four-pound turkey with all the fixings, two kinds of pie for dessert, and "frosted cookies and tiny cakes" [a drawing], talks and plays a duet with Warren, goes to bed, has "fun thinking thoughts in the gray of night."

November 24: Snowing: "Large Lacey white flakes are slowly drifting down and the evergreen trees reach their fingertips to catch it." Piano practice, Monopoly with Betsy Powley after lunch, perfects the Lindy, the waltz, the polka, and the Virginia reel, reads about Donn Fendler,[161] plays turock with Grammy, Mother, and Warren, Mother plays Christmas songs before bed while it continues to snow.

November 25: Sees *Snow White*, "awfully sweet," plays pickup sticks[162] at the playground, goes to the library with Mother, reads and draws before supper, makes up a list of her credits after supper, a sleepless night.

November 26: Thanksgiving turkey for lunch, completes ninth and tenth book reports after lunch, gets to sleep very late.

November 27: Very sleepy, weighs ninety-one pounds in health class, works on bracelets at Scouts: "My but they are hard to begin!" Wraps Christmas presents.

November 28: Sings Christmas songs in music class, reads *All Aboard the Whale!*[163] Has a glass of Ovaltine and then happily goes to bed.

November 29: Works on Christmas projects, including "beautiful Christmas cards" that Miss Chadwick shows the class how to do.

November 30: Stays after school to make a Christmas border for Miss Lowe's blackboard.

December 1: Eager to start her viola lessons, has dancing lessons.

December 2: Warren sick with pneumonia, Sylvia bikes over to the Perrin School to see two plays: *Gingerbread House* and *High School Days*. Sunday school and Scouts homework.

December 3: Sunday school lesson about Saul, a "wonderful dinner," does her book report and a drawing for her Christmas booklet while listening to the radio, wraps up Grampy's Christmas present.

December 4: In health, everyone walks around the room to show their posture, works on bracelets in Scouts.

December 5: Drawing and homework.

December 6: Very tired on walk to bus stop, copies an outline of Braddock's Campaign[164] in social studies.

December 7: Makes three stencils in art. In English, the class composes a draft of a letter to Miss Raguse, who is out west to visit her very sick sister, test on the Albany Plan of Union.[165]

December 8: Plays basketball: "I made a basket!" Begins viola lessons, then dancing school.

December 9: Fun wrapping Christmas presents.

December 10: Reads *The Magical Walking-Stick*,[166] works on her Christmas booklet, listens to *The Great Gildersleeve* and *Jack Benny*.[167]

December 11: Works hard on her Christmas booklets, plays basketball, rehearses play in Scouts.

December 12: "What a rush!" Works on Christmas booklet, finishes a drawing in social studies, rehearses carols in music, another outline in social studies, music and other homework. "I got to be on time for once (!!!!!!!!)."

December 13: A beautiful Christmas assembly.

December 14: "What a day." Stays home with a cold, reads in Grammy's room, makes a tiny doll out of Kleenex, eats a large lunch. "What an awfully boring day." Calls up Nancy to find out about schoolwork, goes to bed after a "useless day."

December 15: In English, Christmas booklets are passed around. "In room 15 I met my dream boy, (Robert Fisk)."

December 16: Dancing and skating the day away, plays pickup sticks with Arlene: "What fun!" Copies one of her Christmas cards.

December 17: "In church two birds got in by some strange chance and evidently beat themselves to death against the walls." Skating on ice that looks like glass, colors a Christmas card at home, and listens to the radio "a long while. I do so love everyone. I saw my Jon. He's nice (not to me)."

December 18: Viola practice, works on Christmas cards, rehearses play at Scouts.

December 19: Works with Warren on Christmas wreath, sees *Holiday Inn*[168] and *A Night of Adventure*,[169] both "good," reads after supper.

December 20: A "snowy, sunny day" with "clear fresh blue air," sledding and sliding, finishes reading *Bright Morning*.[170] So far, she has received one Christmas card and made five for Warren to send to his friends. Listens to *The Lone Ranger* and *Mr. and Mrs. North*.

December 21: Cleaning and dusting, Mrs. Bates, Sylvia's viola teacher, arrives. "Boy! Was I tired after she taught me how to hold and play my viola. (I know how to play a song of two different notes!)." Scout rehearsal, starts reading *The Silver Pencil* by Alice Dalgleish.[171]

December 22: "Today is my big day." Reads and draws before lunch, a shampoo, dresses for dancing party, ties with Prissy Steele for first prize for costumes, discovers her "dream-man—Frank [Irish]," cuts in on him during a waltz, but feels hopeless when he does not ask her to dance a polka. He asks her to dance a Virginia reel. "I'd love to," she says. He is "sweet" to her in games, followed by a picnic supper, a candlelight investiture, and a play.

December 23: Puts up Christmas tree, lights, and ornaments: "It looks divine." Cleans house before noon, sings Christmas carols, wraps two Christmas presents for Mother, puts other presents under the tree.

December 24: "I was so excited this morning!" To church and Christmas service, models a "lovely lady" out of snow, skates, sings carols with Warren, and "tucked in by mother" after an exciting day.

December 25: Announces a full account of Christmas in a new "yearbook" received today as a present, over to Aunt Dot's for a "wonderful turkey dinner," Uncle Joe takes the kids down to the cellar to blow glass, the family returns home after a "wonderful afternoon."

December 26: Sylvia sleeps late and has breakfast in bed "royally," finishes reading *New Worlds for Josie*,[172] Marcia Egan comes over with an autographed copy of *Donn Fendler*, Sylvia has viola and piano practice, writes to Aunt Frieda (Frieda Plath Heinrichs), thanking her for a lovely leather diary, more beautiful than the one she wrote in last year, enjoys writing every day as an exercise in completing sentences, reads over last year's diary and finds it is full of spelling mistakes, hopes that her aunt can come from California for a visit in the fall when the New England color is so brilliant.

December 27: Sleeps late, calls Ruthie for a long talk, Warren and his friend experiment with gun powder, which explodes in a lighted fireplace, Sylvia and Warren open bank accounts accompanied by Grammy and Mother, Sylvia types one of her poems after lunch.

December 28: "I got right down to business as soon as I got up."

10:30 a.m.: Viola lesson with Mrs. Bates, arms ache after holding the instrument for fifteen minutes.

Sketches after lunch, flies down a steep slope on her sled, with the wind whistling through her until she is "brought to earth by sunset."

December 29: A "wonderful nights sleep," viola practice, spaghetti and strawberry shortcake dinner, plays piano, sledding in backyard: "Such fun!" Dancing lesson and then rest: "What a lovely home I have."

December 30: Cleans house, viola practice, sledding with Arden Tapley.

December 31: Sleeps late and has breakfast in bed, skates with Warren and then coasts downhill. "I stood up most of the time and fell off once" [drawing], walks home dragging her sled as Ray and Will pass by. Ray says "'Hi!' so nicely."

1945

Undated: Poems—"Dreams," "Camp Helen Storrow," "The Fairy Scarf," "March." {PM}

Proposes a rule for her diary: "not to be written in after 8 p.m."

January 1: Asleep when the year changed, "Warren waked from peaceful slumbers (the little vixen) and I was alone, asleep, the only one in the family who did not welcome 1945!" Balances her budget and arranges Warren's "bridge-table laboratory," practices viola and piano, works on a school assignment on Henry Ford and a Sunday school lesson, listens to *The Lone Ranger* before going to bed.

January 2: At school, is called to the office by Miss Bahnor who says, "'You didn't dust the counter or the principal's desk this morning Please do it now!' I could have cried and I did apologize about five times."

January 3: Watches a movie in assembly: *How Raytheon Makes Radio Tubes*, hemming an apron in household arts, in social studies, "where my love lies," gets started on "our wonderful 'Story's of the American Revolution.' I'm glad I am tall because I was one of the lucky 10 who had theirs pinned up on the bulletin board." Does an outline map of the northern colonies: "I do so love Miss Chadwick, she makes everything so wonderfully interesting." Homework and viola practice, Mother stays over on a visit to the Freemans in Winthrop.

January 4: Talk in art about *Saturday Evening Post* artists, "I am in a terrible forgetful mood today—on the bus I remembered that I forgot to take home my legging and mittens and when I got home I remembered I left my math book in school!" No longer gets tired holding her viola, the children call Mother. "Oh! How I miss my mother."

January 5: Sylvia draws a colonial flag, reads *Peddler's Pack* by Mary Owen Lewis,[173] calls her mother: "I can't wait till she comes home soon." Listens to *Henry Aldrich*, "What a laugh! I went to bed in the best of spirits."

January 6: A music lesson and painting flowers, tells funny "tongue twisters" with Tommy Duggin and Warren, Mother returns, Sylvia goes shoe shopping, comes home "ice cold and tired and warmed up in bed with mother," after supper practices viola and has fun.

January 7: "It's snowing, hooray!" Stays home instead of going to Sunday school, goes out in the snowstorm, reads *A Separate Star* by Loula Grace Erdman,[174] begins scrapbook with her poems, drawings, and stories.

January 8: Finishes Valentine border for Miss Lowe's blackboard, talks about house types and plans in art, "Miss Raguse is back! I love her!" Finishes a drawing on twelve causes of the American Revolution, a beautiful day for "coasting," viola practice and card play with Uncle Joe and Aunt Dot.

January 9: After an oral presentation, Miss Raguse says: "You talk too fast but have style." Writes a poem, "Faces and Spirit" or "Lines to Ruth," with a series of questions, including "Is there a face where wisdom and beauty dwell?" Concludes with "A face like this could never be!" The rest is "pretty weak. The poem is meant for Miss Chadwick, but it doesn't do her lovely face and spirit justice."

January 10: Two-minute campaign speeches in assembly, "full of fun," slogans: "Think twice and think Whirty." "The treasury grows with the grower." Works on an assignment to write a poem, story, or letter about a star, with a "right good will," she produces "King of the Ice" and "another even better 'The Snowflake Star.'"

January 11: Goes to Barbara McKay's "rowdy party," gets sick but wins a prize: "chocolate which I'm allergic to)." At home, rereads *The Little Prince*.

January 12: Dancing class: "It isn't as much fun as it used to be because a certain person isn't there any more." At home, listens to *The Lone Ranger*, collects her poems, stories, and pictures for "Sylvia's Scrapbook," on pastel green and peach paper.

January 13: Viola lesson, "now I can play two notes with my fingers!" Later plays new songs on her viola for Mother, Grammy, and Warren, likes viola better than piano.

January 14: Works on "Sylvia's Scrapbook," listens to *The Great Gildersleeve*, "still about the marriage suit) and went right to bed (<u>early</u> for once!)."

January 15: In art, a movie about doing pottery, does homework, enjoys herself "thoroughly."

January 16: Awful blizzard, one of only three students to pass a quiz on the two Continental Congresses.

January 17: Studies grammar in English, Donald "Donnie" Russel asks her out to a band concert and dance, not her "dream man," but he's all right. "Those are the breaks kid."

January 18: "Odds and ends": dusts, goes over notebooks, draws, works on Continental Congress drawing and maps, viola practice, works on a "living room plan."

January 19: "Today is a big day for me. I am all excitement for the dance and concert tonight." Studies English grammar, "As I was eating supper Donald Russel called up (I knew the set up was too perfect) saying his mother had decided, <u>Decided</u> mind you—to go to a movie and would I please take myself." Grammy, "the dear," takes her to the dance, wears a flowered dress [drawing]. A lovely concert. "The dance was wonderful (I stayed till 11:00)."

January 20: "Today is the biggest day of my life. I have a dreamless sleep and woke as fresh as dew on spring buttercups. All day I was in another world, far better than this." Takes the bus to Boston with Mother and Warren to see William Shakespeare's *The Tempest* (ca. 1610–1611) at the Colonial Theatre: "too perfect for words." Keeps the program as a souvenir, on the train home, sits next to a "young sensitive boy from the navy," with wavy blond hair and blue eyes: "In all my life I will never love anyone as I did him." They talk about travel and Shakespeare.

January 21: Pastes into her diary an image of Andrew Jackson, one of the "Heroic Americans," with the headline "The Federal Union—it must and shall be preserved." Off to Scouts and, after supper, gets ready for bed while listening to *The Great Gildersleeve* and *Charlie McCarthy*.

January 22: Writes "don't die of nervous shock! <u>We</u> (Room 18) got 100% in stamp sales!" Learns folk dances in PE, works on Hostess and Dancing badges in Scouts, piano practice.

January 23: Works with Betsy Powley on a large snow house with secret passages. "As we were walking up the hill . . . My foot caught in my shovel and down the hill I went! An idea was born—The rest of the afternoon we spent in sliding down the hill" [includes drawings].

January 24: "In Guidance some talked on their close (family) relatives in the service." Asked to write down likes and dislikes in sewing, "so to flatter Miss Lowe I put first under like 'teacher.' I had to sweep the whole room and pick the dirt off the mop as Superman's advertiser says 'with bare hands etc.)," practices viola and reads *Calling All Girls*.

January 25: Works on a picture in art, a pastel of an oak or maple in fall foliage overlooking cornstalks and pumpkins. "I called it 'Harvest Bountiful' or 'Wigwammed Cornstalks.' (The titles outdo the pictures)." Her side wins in basketball. She makes "5 baskets or 10 points or half the score."

January 26: Visits a radio station, WNAC, a part of the Mutual Broadcasting Network, returns home to a "wonderful supper," rereads *Jane Eyre*, sleeps soundly after an "ecstatically happy and joyful day."

January 27: Reads *Girl of the Limberlost* (1909) by Gene Stratton-Porter in bed, viola practice, "playing with my third finger" [drawing], coasts down hills and bumps with Betsy Powley, gets "soaking wet," rips the seat of her ski pants, over to Betsy's for refreshing cake and milk, wears Betsy's dry clothes and plays at "Romance."

January 28: At Sunday school, the boiler steams up and, fearing an explosion, Sylvia is ready to "jump out the window with mother and her belongings." Skates and coasts all afternoon, comes home "after a strenuous day."

January 29: "What an awful day!" Snow, slush, ice, gymnastics at school [drawings].

January 30: Works on prepositional phrases in English, Miss Frank shows "slides on the Revolution" and gives explanations in a "delightful story form, asking questions about each one in such a way I didn't realize they were questions."

January 31: Elected vice president in Guidance and also senator but has to choose one (chooses vice president), the life of Robert Louis Stevenson is read to students in assembly.

February 1: Finishes house-plan scheme in art: "dark green, walnut woodwork and furniture, pale yellow wallpaper, a deep dull violet-purple, gold; and a flowered pattern with the latter color predominating, and a flowered pattern with green, gold, and white, as the main colors." In study period, puts up her map, "The Story of the American Revolution," after school, goes to Marylin's "semi-private art class while she drew my face in crayon."

February 2: Walks on the balance beam in gym, touching her toes without falling off, jumps "horse n' buck" [drawing]: "I did it with a straight legged sitting position. Then we had the ropes. What fun! My hands got red and sore from slipping so often and my face turned color as I came down hard on the floor [drawing]. Boy! Was I banged around!" Dancing class, homework, Mother comes home from her tea "dead tired."

February 3: Sleeps late, fixes herself a "delicious breakfast. (You see—I can do it.)" Viola lesson, coasting: "Then I got to business." Works on math, English, a letter to Frank Irish, Sunday school work.

February 4: Studies Christian symbolism in Sunday school, coasts and skates for an hour, after a wonderful lunch, works on English notebook, draws, shows Mother pictures drawn at school, listens to *Charlie McCarthy, The Great Gildersleeve, Jack Benny*,[175] and *Quiz Kids*.

February 5: Ice covered with "muddy slush. I am waiting with expectation for signs of recognition from Frank [Irish]. (I sent him the invitation for our Scout Dance on Friday the 16th)." Weighs ninety-three and one quarter pounds in health. Learns about "compound Subjects and Predicates" in English, draws a picture of a girl in armor, marching drill in gym, makes wipes in Scouts "folded gauze piece to wipe away blood and such. I am also the 'Juliet Low' girl."[176]

February 6: "In math I was all excitement for I was sure in my first study period that my Frank [Irish] would scorn going to the Scout dance with me and shake his head the wrong way but he gave me an engaging grin and nodded assent!"

February 7: Assembly talks about "different characters of different people, and of foreign lands," spelling bee: "I went down on odor! (What a stup!) I spelled it Oder!" In social studies, Mr. Thistle examines Sylvia's map: "He crooked up the corner of his mouth in a heart warming smile and said, 'That is a wonderful map and the drawings are beautiful.'"

February 8: A blizzard. "In Art I started a heart-shaped pickaninni for a valentine face," wins a five-cent prize for a heart-shaped drawing of Madame Chiang Kai-shek's face, after school, helps a women driver who cannot get into her driveway: "I shoveled out her whole driveway and she got her car in thru. She went in the house and immediately pressed a dollar upon me but I ran home before she could give it to me." Grammy, Warren, and Mother get stuck and leave the car in the driveway all night.

February 9: Sylvia wakes to snow up to her waist, shovels the walk, holiday from school "(Hurray!!!!!!!!!!!!)."

February 10: A viola lesson, shovels out the car: "My back almost broke but, I did it!"

February 11: Pastes image of Thomas Edison as a "Heroic American": "Genius is about two per cent inspiration and ninety-eight per cent perspiration." Studies Christian symbolism in Sunday school, works for Scout Dancing badge and on valentines.

February 12: No-school whistle blows, Sylvia runs home to spread the "glad tidings!" Lunch with Uncle Frank and Aunt Louise, who talk about their travels across the country and Frank's time in the army, pastes an image of Abraham Lincoln in her diary.

February 13: Tells Frank Irish the Scout party and dance has been postponed. "I don't like him any more. (Strictly on the Q. T.—I would if he was rich or handsome (not stuck up) but since he's not rich or handsome but self conscious of his so called self.) Do I despise him? Yes!" Copies part of the Declaration of Independence for her map, practices piano and viola at home.

February 14: A fun time in art making fruit baskets.

February 15: Reads poems about Lincoln, in art, "using different techniques in powder paint with the new brushes." Out to the store for milk.

"I waited <u>and</u> waited for the milk but one (whom I thought was a Black Market customer) was arguing about roast beef."

February 16: No school: "Those busses are certainly scared of a few lacey flakes of snow!!" Happily runs home to help Grammy with the house cleaning, finishes *The Forgotten Daughter* by Caroline Snedeker,[177] "loved it for the excitement it was packed with. Never has the life of slaves been more interesting. (I guess part of the attraction was the love it was full of.)" Dancing lesson, a Monopoly game with Prissy Steele and cake and cocoa, Uncle Frank comes to dinner and talks about his army training. Sylvia draws and listens to *Henry Aldrich* with Warren while the grownups talk.

February 17: "My Viola lesson was <u>not</u> good (I played flat)." Digs a tunnel in the snow, working toward Warren's cave, but is not able to finish it.

February 18: With Warren's help, finishes a magnificent cave in the snow, with three outlets, one "secret," and "steps on the top and sides and a pillar in the middle."

February 19: "I'm all in a dither!" Music lesson, baking cookies, at Scouts working on valentines, tells Tommy Duggin she cannot go to a dance with him, beginning to like Bob Stockbridge but wonders if he is "just fooling," plays truth or consequences at the dance and has to write her name with her toes in order to kiss Bob, but she refuses to do it after learning he had asked the judges to ask her to do so.

February 20: Works on a cardboard house for Scouts.

February 21: Sleeps late as usual, until 10:30 a.m., last night in bed a "flash," and finishes her poem, "Snowflake Star," works on drawings with Ruthie after supper.

February 22: Twenty inches of snow, Monopoly with Prissy Steele and Betsy Powley: "We played a good (nice I mean) game and mother called us in to the dining room and in candle light we had tea." Finishes making four dolls.

February 23: Works on a rag doll [drawings and exact measurements given]. Sees *Kismet* (1945), starring Ronald Colman and Marlene Dietrich [drawing], "(alias 'Legs'), all she "expected (swell!) in technicolor—the exotic romantic city of old Baghdad with its mirrored halls and glamorous native-dancing girls and fairy-tale romance. . . . We came home our spirits still in the dreadful beauty of fairytale Bagdad."

February 24: Coasting with Ruthie: "We made the most of our hour together." Plays turock with Mother and Warren after supper, loses eight cents in spite of having "played well."

February 25: Car is stuck in driveway ice, rush is on to get to Sunday school by bus, afterwards, Sylvia chops ice and makes up a poem about March "which is weak but pretty." Listens to *Those We Love* at lunch, viola practice, "which is tough," reads comic strips, goes to a church meeting: "Prissy [Steele] and I were the only girls there. We sang two hymns and Mrs. Grimes gave us a long talk on 'Depending on other nations.' We said a prayer and had a collection and were dismissed."

February 26: Sylvia makes a color wheel in art and discusses medical terms in health, drilled on marching in gym, makes molasses cookies: "jolly good fun." Scout meeting about setting up a miniature day-camp exhibition at the library.

February 27: Arden Tapley lends her a book, *The Adventure of Princess Sylvia*,[178] which is why Sylvia reads about a "beautiful young princess" who is supposed to marry an emperor she has always loved but who has never seen her. But she does not want an arranged marriage and decides to disguise herself, seeking to win his love as a "middle class girl and not a princess." After school, reads *Calling All Girls*, practices viola: "I have the 5th finger now."

February 28: In health, stews white sugar all over prunes and puts raisins in the core holes of baked apples: "Yum!!!" Listens to *Mr. and Mrs. North* "(alone in my room)."

March 1: In art, begins a "central balance design[179] in two opposite colors (or intermediates)."[180] Works on a "Treaty of Peace" map in social studies: "That is something I will keep to show my children!" Over to the playground, races to the "top rung of the bench backs to see who could get to the center first. We both fell and hurt ourselves and as we were nursing our wounds, who should come riding across the icy pond on his bike but Edor Nelson. We three had a long talk and then went our ways."

March 2: Fun in math "playing a game in geographical planes and solids," in gym, ring toss, darts, beanbags, bowling. Miss Raguse reads from *The Pickwick Papers* (1936) by Charles Dickens and "we almost died laughing for it (the book) was so comical." Dismissed from dancing class "because of some of them fooling (not me)."

March 3: Does "pretty well" in viola lesson with her little finger, dusts, works on homework, plays with Warren, draws a picture of the "water from the road [which] has dug deep trenches as it runs down the hill to the brook."

March 4: Misses Sunday school because of laryngitis, plays with Warren by the brook, near the road that is half washed away.

March 5: Another central balance design in art, 100 percent on a geometry test, draws herself measured to be "5 ft 3½2 in!" Plays guard in basketball, "certainly helping us win (if I say so myself). I flew here and there catching the ball."

March 6: Goes to see *Thirty Seconds over Tokyo*,[181] "very sad in the 'almost' end."

March 7: Writes the Pledge of Allegiance in Guidance "from memory," listens to Miss Chadwick's heirloom music box, "a lost art."

March 8: Long bicycle ride, piano and viola practice, reads *The Middle Button* by Kathryn Worth.[182]

March 9: Full day playing on the apparatus in gym, basketball, rehearsal for a "Flag program," works on a social studies map, dancing class, visit to an art exhibit at the library, arrives at home to work on a poster for Scouts.

March 10: Joins Betsy Powley and Prissy Steele in game night at Cushing House. They explore the "dark, cold nooks and crannies of one of the oldest Wellesley (most spooky) houses."

March 11: Sunday school "dictation on Christian Symbolism," biking, on to the brook—"it hummed to me," a walk with Mother after lunch, draws at home and listens to *The Great Gildersleeve.*

March 12: Against a team of ruffians in PE, loses a basketball game and is scratched on her leg and elbow and gets a swollen eye, four-mile-plus bike ride through Wellesley with Ruth Geisel, they ride their "tired carcasses home" in the rain and snow.

March 13: In social studies, Sylvia reads *The Rise of Our Free Nation*, Miss Chadwick instructs the class on good behavior since "important guests" arrive tomorrow and will visit "all the rooms!" Sylvia practices an oral presentation for English: "If I don't have it perfect tomorrow I will do something drastic (probably cry all day)."

March 14: One comment after her oral report in English: "a lovely speech," she had "a beautiful clear tone of voice and made not one mistake. (I feel sort of proud of myself)."

March 15: In art, finishes a central balance color design, draws cartoon for *The Phillipian*, at home, dresses in her Scout uniform for a Scout exhibit.

March 16: In dancing class, reviews the rhumba, foxtrot, and waltz, comes home to garden, plants tulip bulbs now that "Spring is really here! . . . but not yet have 'daffodils their gold unfurled.'"[183]

March 17: Enjoying her viola lessons "more and more." Bikes in the fresh spring air before lunch, reads the *Arabian Nights* (first English edition from ca. 1706–1721) while "minding our Scout exhibit," rereads *Fog Magic.*[184]

March 18: Working on slide of Christian symbols in Sunday school, talks with Mother and Warren on the Babson Institute[185] grounds, collecting "many, many pussywillows," a walk with Mother after lunch, and has her hair "washed to a glinting, sparkling, electric mass of golden, red-brown (mostly brown) waves."

March 19: "Wonderful News! After school Mr. Leach called me to him and said, 'Perhaps if you'll work hard enough you may be one of the lucky 7 to play for the senior graduation!' I was knocked over with a bombshell [drawing] but said calmly, 'Yes, Mr. Leach.'" Works on a third color wheel—"darn it, in my sleep I'll see them doing a hula-hula dance" [drawing], almost finished with Hostess and Dancing badges, expects to complete one more badge before the Court of Awards, describes the "pussywillows creeping out," the "robins hop about," the unfurling golden daffodils, "the shyest violets," all marching in "Nature's Spring Parade!"

March 20: "Beautiful snow!" Watches movies on colonial buildings and customs, bikes to Morses Pond in a "cold breeze (from the water still covered with a thin coating of ice)," walks out on a long pier, takes off shoes and socks, breaks through the ice and christens the pond with bare feet [drawing with caption: "BRR"], bikes home, cools off with "tall, sparkling glasses of ice water" [drawing].

March 21: In Guidance, lesson in how to be popular, assembly play "centered on the post war world," viola practice, "duets with a boy" [drawing], listens to *Mr. and Mrs. North.*

March 22: Draws a profile in art of Arden Tapley that does not do her justice, to bed with the rain playing a lullaby on the roof, singing her to sleep.

March 23: In gym, shimmies up "only a small way" on the ropes, puts three poems in *The Phillipian* box, copies more poems in to "Life Poem Book": one about strolling in March "Under the arch / Of flowering boughs," another about the advent of spring with a tulip "nodding her head to the breeze."

March 24: Has "putrid" viola lesson, plays in tulip garden at home, discovers three very tiny buds just emerging from the ground, bikes to piano lesson, plays "quite well" for Mrs. Bates, rushes over to Ruth Geisel's to get her to watch "The Centerville Ghost"[186] and *Show Business.*[187]

March 25: Daffodils in Sunday school prompts a quotation from William Wordsworth: "Brighter than the stars that shine and glitter on the Milky Way. They stretched in never ending line along the margin of a bay."

March 26: Works on two topic paragraphs in English: "Last night on my way home I had a terrible fright" and "My favorite shop window." On bus with Scouts to Boston with windows open, whistling at soldiers, sailors, and marines [drawing], visits the *Christian Science Monitor* building and its Mapparium: "We learned that it was made of over 600 pieces of ¼ inch thick stained glass," visits the printing room, the room where the paper is cut, and the library, and sees two great, lighted globes, goes home on bus "after a magic afternoon."

March 27: The faculty play the ninth graders: "The teachers wore blouses and sneakers. They look so human after school. Miss Lachett's blouse ripped when she made a basket so she was out." The faculty wins the game by five points.

March 28: Works on memorizing the preamble to the Constitution, viola practice.

March 29: Works on poems for a "Spring Booklet," to bed "happy and was sung to sleep by the birds."

March 30: "I got up before anybody else and went out in the dewy, early morning and transplanted violets and lilies-of-the valley into my garden." Helps Grammy with housework and practices piano, bikes, writes a summary of George Washington's life and draws his silhouette on the cover, works in the garden: "looks lovely as it is full of sprouting green leaves and sweet smelling, fresh overturned earth. I saw the most beautiful bird today. It was a little smaller than a robin and had the most beautiful blue plumage and red breast. I found out later that it was a bluebird and the first I have seen this spring."

March 31: The first forsythia buds are swelling, Sylvia bikes over to Betsy Powley's. They read poems "overexpressively and overgegesturingly," a terrible night vomiting and retching.

April: Publishes "The Spring Parade" and "March" in *The Phillipian*.

April 1: Still sick, listens to the radio.

April 2: Recovered, in school, paints a forsythia bush, Grampy brings a Japanese place card from the country club.

April 3: Studies the Constitution in social studies, not ready to give talk about the "development and modern use of the automobile." As her name is called, she hears "Ring! 'Whew!' I thought, 'saved by the bell.' Miss Raguse said that I would be the first to have my oral talk tomorrow."

April 4: Her talk takes "2 min. 10 sec. I made no pauses and <u>said</u> it alright but I don't know about the content of it."

April 5: Puts together George Washington booklet, draws picture of her bouquet of pink phlox and golden dandelions in a blue vase, vaults about five feet on her bamboo pole: "It is fun fun to fly though the air. Almost as much fun as that, is the swinging on the apple tree bough! I am getting more and more bird-like in play as the years go by. So I may grow wings (<u>not</u> angels)."

April 6: Volleyball in gym: "I made no good serves but once I had a tapping up with a girl over the net and the ball went back and forth about eleven times . . . Our side won—31–13!"

April 7: A successful viola lesson, bikes to a "bad forest fire," Mr. Goble calls her mother to ask Sylvia to give a "responsive reading" in Sunday school "tomorrow! I finally gave in and said I would. Gee! Am I scared!"

April 8, 9:00 a.m.: Goes to church with misgivings, Mr. Goble gives her pointers. She is robed and at the pulpit: "I began in a clear distinct voice and was told afterward by many how they enjoyed it! I felt at home once

I stood in the pulpit but mother told me later that I looked awfully pale. There was a terrible pause after I had finished as the organist was trying to get the choir to sing. Finally they began and I went happily back to my seat. The rest of the service was a pleasure."

April 9: Gets quite professional in volleyball, clothing drive in Scouts, joins a group writing a report about visiting the *Christian Science Monitor* building.

April 10: Submits poem for *The Phillipian* describing the March "wind-wolves prowling about" and "majestic skies" that "loom vast and gray" as "The powerful Master of March holds sway." Starts on a "spree of flower pressing."

April 11: New officers elected in Guidance, with Sylvia assigned to take care of defense stamps, receives an A for a cooking lesson, scrambles eggs that come out "savory and just delicately browned," Miss Raguse plays a "lovely game," reciting a few lines of a poem, letting them guess the author.

April 12, 4:00 p.m.: "ROOSEVELT DIES!" Sylvia mentions he was having his portrait painted and then fainted away at 3:35 p.m. "of a brain hemorage! . . . He died, like Lincoln, soon—very soon before the peace treaty and end of a long, cruel war!"

April 13: "This is really a day of mourning. We were to school just for a short 2 hours of worship and prayer." Sylvia gets two poems and a cartoon published in *The Phillipian* plus an editor's comment: "The excellence and abundance of Sylvia Plath's poems!" Later sunbathes for two hours, goes to a party in the evening: a "thrilling ride" in a beach wagon at night under "starry skies" to Needham, Massachusetts, and sees *The Fighting Lady*.[188]

April 14: Sleeps late and wakes up "as stiff as a log from walking so far yesterday." In the afternoon, a "weenie roast" at Arlene's: "I don't want to ever see another weenie. We had such fun though! Before eating we all had to entertain—so—I played the Moonlight Sonata."

April 15: In Sunday school, learns about Albert Schweitzer,[189] comes home, presses apple blossoms, marigolds, and other flowers, which is becoming an obsession, bikes, watches Warren collect fish eggs at the pond, Grampy brings woodland violets to plant in her garden.

April 16: In the flower garden after breakfast, Sylvia is pleased with the new planted violets, has piano practice, goes back to the garden: "Billy and Jo believe that a fairy lives there so I dressed Cynthia my beautiful blonde doll, in a white dress, blue veil and pink ribbon and scattered white flowers over her and set her in my bed of violets. I called the children over and they believed it was a real fairy! Billy said in a soft, shy voice, 'Can I hug her?' It was such fun to see the sweet little children get flowers to give to this 'fairy.'" Sleeps overnight at Aunt Dot's in a room that looks like a "walnut shell lined with pink. The wallpaper and dressing table were pink and white with pink roses and blue forgetmenots the pink and white spread covered a walnut bed and the one chair and the dressing table chair were painted silver gray!"

April 17: Notes the trillium on her dresser, pancake-and-rhubarb breakfast, dries the dishes, and out to the greenhouse to transplant lettuce, finds a wake robin trillium, a "lovely wine color," has a scrumptious lunch of "egg fried on toast (a hole in the toast) in butter with peach-icebox cake," washes dishes, walks in the woods, "Blue violets grew everywhere!" Cool in the pines on a hot day: "We saw a big ant hill about 3 ft. high and 10 feet around." A cool shower after four hot miles of walking.

April 18: Draws a flower chain of violets while in bed, breakfast of rhubarb, two doughnuts and two cups of cocoa, helps Aunt Dot hang up the wash and weed the lettuce, makes a dandelion chain, visits Mother at Aunt Dot and Uncle Joe's to bring home two chickens, "dead and cleaned of course," for supper, chicken livers, bread, and rhubarb pie for lunch, afternoon sunbathing and sunburn, cool bath and cool clothes, writes letters with illustrations to Uncle Frank and Aunt Louise,[190] cooks chickens in fireplace charcoal stove. "Boy! They sure were superb. I never tasted anything like them! (They were broiled!)."

April 19: Packs her trunk and gives her aunt and uncle an anniversary card she made the previous night, drives home, a viola lesson, bikes to Wellesley Square to see marathon racers: "I really think it is silly because some of the men were perspiring and some looked so tired!" Works on making clothing for her doll.

April 20: With Warren, cleans up the house, gives Warren a ride on her bike to his cub meeting, helps Mrs. Chapman house clean after a gallbladder attack: "I could not refuse." Scrubs floors of dining room, living room, sunporch, and kitchen "(backboards too!)," waxes the floors on her knees and brings in rugs. "I received a dollar for my work which I felt . . . was not too much for all the work!"

April 21: Cleans upstairs today to show "I could do some work at home." At Gardner Museum for a tour, mentions John Singer Sargent's *The Dancer* in "special wing built just for it." Listens to Gordon String Quartet: "Magnificent!" Admires the museum flower court "colors from orange red—gold blue—to red violet and white, calla lilies—tulips—rarities of flowers," a "beautiful sight!"

April 22: In church: white snapdragons, tulips "with touches of gold or pink arrayed in lush green leaves." Plays in her garden, works on her dark blue "Union Booklet" with a "flame of the colonies flying behind the words 'Plans of Union,'" finishes "Spring Booklet," wishes for more time: "I could have gotten twenty five more poems at least!"

April 23: Lecture in English about "Character," Miss Raguse on Sylvia's spring booklet: "an exquisite piece of work." Sylvia reads a Japanese poem, "Spring," to the class. Everyone raises their hands when Miss Raguse asks whether they enjoyed it. "She gave me an understanding sort of wink as if to say, 'It's beautiful, Japanese or not!'" Plays a "Pirate game" in Scouts.

April 24: Looking at spring booklets: "Elizabeth Burdoin had the funniest poem (original)" in "Italian dialect," titled "The Jailbirds Conversation." On a flower-pressing mission after school: "it really is fun for the people are almost always <u>very</u> willing to give us flowers (only two of a kind)." Listens to *A Date with Judy*, "which made me go to sleep with a smile."

April 25: Makes scrumptious muffins in household arts, she has received an A on all her lessons.

April 27: Pastes an image of Ulysses S. Grant into diary under heading "Heroic Americans," with the phrase "Let us have peace." Two birthday presents for Warren: an X-Acto jackknife and a model-boat kit. "He was greatly pleased." Aunt Dot and Uncle Joe arrive with blue jeans. "In every pocket there was some money. Warren ended up by finding $1.31! I went to bed brimful of birthday."

April 28: Reads *American Girl* and *Reader's Digest*: "my entry was <u>not</u> included in the Picturesque Speech and Pattern." Into the "marshy wood" in search of flowers, finding "one beautiful magenta 'fringed milkwort'!" Checks out Kate Seredy's *The Open Gate*[191] from the library.

April 29: Plants lettuce for Grammy, reads comic books: "They are awful! I don't want to see another one of them for they ruin my eyes!" [drawing]. Listens to the radio.

April 30: "I feel sort of squelched as I asked Miss Raguse if it would be alright to have one page and three fourths instead of one page but she smiled in a queer way and said, 'I'm sorry—it counts <u>points</u> against you and you <u>should</u> learn how to condense!'"

May 1: After school, sees *Meet Me in St. Louis* (1944) with Judy Garland and Margaret O'Brien: "It was magnificent!"'

May 2: In social studies, copies the Dumbarton Oaks plan for international peace, to the woods to gather wildflowers for her pressed flowers book.

May 3: Enjoys watching a movie about glass blowing, pleased with her grade of an A for her "Plans of Union Notebook."

May 4: A busy day with Scouts out in the woods, then a hearty supper of hot vegetable soup, bread and jam, cheese and crackers, and milk, plus toasting marshmallows while telling stories: "Bets [Powley] and I slept with our heads together and watched the shadows flicker."

May 5: A walk in the woods, roasting hot dogs, acrobatic games.

May 6: A miserable cold, reads *The Little Colonel's Holidays*[192] "just to pass the time away," listens to the radio, a refreshing alcohol rub, a "delicious supper of soup, milk, & 5 crackers & cheese and two peeled & sliced apples."

May 7: Germany surrenders: "WAR WITH EUROPE OVER!" Sylvia plays baseball: "I made one run and no outs!" Reads *Children of the Nineties* (1936) by Anna Rose Wright, "which is a book that tells of a family of motherless children living in the 1890s. It's endsheets are some of the advertisements of the older days over fifty years ago."

May 8: Listens to President Harry S. Truman proclaiming V-E Day. Quotes him: "To show the appreciation of our victory in Europe we must do work, work, work and more work and still remember that there is a war to be won in the East." Elected secretary in English, discusses the presidency of John Adams in social studies, practices viola and listens to Arturo Toscanini direct Ludwig van Beethoven's Fifth Symphony.

May 9: In assembly, girls play piano, Donnie Russel leads three other boys in a "hot jitterbug," Sylvia learns how to set a table perfectly in household arts, pleased that her secretary's reports have all been "approved as read. I hope to keep it up." In social studies, Miss Chadwick takes the whole period to read the "Man without a Country" about Philip Nolan.[193]

May 10: A drawing about the Monroe Doctrine, starts an "interesting drawing" in art club: "First, you put one of the lighter color crayons (pink, yellow, green etc.) on a paper and then a dark color over it heavily. With a compass we scratched off the outer dark color and formed any picture we wish so the lighter color would show through."

May 11: "In Chorus we came in so noisily (I was among the few who did not talk or make noise [drawing]) that we have to stay for an 8th period." Rushes to see *Thunderhead, Son of Flicka* (1945): "It was a technicolor brilliancy!" The other movie *Brazil*[194] stars Virginia Bruce and "romantic Tito Guizar." On the way home, Sylvia spots a blue jay "pecking a hole in a baby sparrow that was knocked down from its nest" and carries the sparrow home.

The entry below about the baby sparrow prefigures a similar event when Plath and Ted Hughes later try to save the life of an injured baby bird.

May 12: Bikes with Betsy Powley into the woods, finds "a bed of pink lady slippers hidden from the dull eye" in a grotto, an awful viola lesson: "quite disappointed in myself." Names her baby sparrow Dickie, "cuddling cozily in a box filled with flannel rags. . . . Thirstily drinking milk form an eye dropper and eating wheat germ around a tooth-pick."

May 13: In Sunday school: "white snapdragons and green ferns in a gold vase." Feeds Dickie "bits of worms (freshly killed and still squirming) on a tooth-pick that we stuff down his gullet and pull out empty." He sleeps in warm flannel in a large, screened box.

May 14: Designs a book jacket for *Children of the Nineties* "coming along finely." In English, Donnie Russel recites "Rules for the Road": "Stand Straight, step firmly . . . / The good gray road is faithful to your tread." Sylvia works on a hut in the woods: "We are going to weave it in with pine boughs and water proof it."

May 15: In social studies, learns about the War of 1812, later listens to *A Date with Judy*.

May 16: In assembly, Robert Chase, a "wonderful soldier," speaks about his sixty-four missions in such an "easy way of talking." Sylvia has a Riverside Park[195] picnic with the Nortons: Dick Norton times who "hangs from a bar in one position for the longest time." She wins at two and a half minutes. Loring Brace, an older boy, beats her in the thirty-yard run by a quarter of a second. They race privately neck and neck. "I love him."

May 17: Wins first prize in social studies for drawing of the Monroe Doctrine. Writes a nineteen-line poem, "How I'll Spend My Vacation": "I found a sparrow scarce alive. / I said to myself I'll bring him up / Can't you see how I'll spend the summer time?"

May 18: Shoe shopping: "They look like this [drawing] Brown and white."

May 19: Sleeps twelve and a half hours and wakes up at 9:15 a.m. for a breakfast of delicious, crystallized honey "because butter is almost unobtainable nowadays." Dickie has recovered and won't let himself be fed. "He gives me quite a lively chase about the porch and Mowgli is so tantalized by the sight of that fat, fuzzy, (juicy to him), young sparrow fluttering about the porch that he cries sorrowfully about the window."

May 20: After Sunday school, Sylvia walks along Lake Waban at Wellesley College, then hangs from a tree branch over "clear cool water," comes home with a bouquet of wildflowers, draws a striped tulip.

May 21: "100% in stamp sales today!" Weighs "only 95," writes an eleven-line poem, which begins "Awake! Awake! Behold the lake— / A diamond rare beneath the sky" and ends with "A new spring day is born!"

May 22: Makes a list of expressive words and phrases for "The Courtship of Miles Standish."[196]

May 23: Before school, sets Dickie free, watching him circling "ever upward, to the tip of the top branches of a tree—probably I'll never see my darling Dickie again!" Donnie Russel reads the play he has made out of "The Courtship of Miles Standish." She enjoys his hand gestures. "It was riotous the way he spoke in a deep, gruff voice to imitate Miles Standish, a natural voice of John Adler and a high voice that dropped to low note to imitate Priscilla! We almost split our sides." She plays a part of the *Peer Gynt* suite for piano. A poll in Guidance has Lux Radio Theatre as the favorite program, Sylvia reads *Reader's Digest* since there is no assembly.

May 24: In social studies, writes "How I Would Travel and by What Route I would travel to get to Northern Illinois if I lived in Boston in 1830." Bruce Mansfield pushes his seat next to hers so they can consult his atlas. Another assignment is to write a letter from Thomas Jefferson to Congress explaining the Louisiana Purchase.

May 25: "In Chorus we had two friendly dogs come in and they would <u>not</u> be pulled out. Finally one of the big boys (with few brains) got up and took one dog under each arm and carried them out bodily!" Sylvia plays Russia with Betsy Powley after school.

May 26: Reads all of *Treasure Island* (1883) by Robert Louis Stevenson up in the apple tree: "I did somersaults on the branches of the tree. While cutting Scotch tape with a knife I cut off my skin on my third finger on my left hand. It bled until it filled a bandage, hankie, and sink. MY BLOOD."[197]

May 27: A "lovely program in church. Warren looked so sweet as Samuel praying."

May 28: At Scouts, awarded a Hostess badge, Dancing badge, an attendance pin, and a service pin.

May 29: In social studies, traces a map of North America and reads about Russia in current events period.

May 30: Plays scrub[198] with Warren and Bradford.

May 31: Goes to Aunt Louise's party with a cake decorated with rosebuds and the words "Happy Birthday Louise" in pink and white icing and Sylvia's present: a box of candy and a pack of Johnny-jump-up[199] seeds and a card.

June 1: Only fifteen more days of school: "I love to be just on the brink of a long vacation and to feel that I can always look forward to the golden rays of holidays ahead without feeling that one precious minute is eaten out of the promising vacation days." Later reads in her apple tree in the afternoon and "just as the suns rays were slowly fading in the west I jumped into bed (at 8:30)."

June 2: A good viola lesson even though she has had a sore finger for a week. A baby robin dies of fright run over by a car. "I picked the poor baby bird up and laid him by the wayside to rest forever." Finishes the "thrilling" novel *She*[200] by H. Rider Haggard: "It kept me in suspense until it ended." Copies a Norman Rockwell drawing.

June 3: Sees *National Velvet* (1944): "the story of an ex-jockey, a girl, and a horse, and a faith that moved mountains. It was in technicolor. Velvet was Elizabeth Taylor, the jockey—Mickey Rooney . . . exceptional!"

June 4: In art, starts another etching—not "too promising," in English, volunteers are asked to recite Markham's "Rules for the Road." Inadvertently, she raises her hand, even though she doubts she can say the whole poem. But from "sheer fright" she recites the poem perfectly.

June 5: Donnie Russel signs her "autograph book": "To the girl I sit next to in my home room. What a pleasure." Does a drawing "by Norman Rockwell of characters of well known books."

June 6: In assembly, watches a play about the four freedoms.[201] In social studies, there is a panel discussion of great inventions and inventors. Sylvia reads "The Mummy's Foot,"[202] "The Necklace,"[203] and "Lulu's Triumph."[204]

June 7: In English, recites Dickinson's "Sunset and Sunrise," in social studies, completes a map of the United States and all of its possessions, outdoor sketching, memorizes John Masefield's poem, "Roadways," which begins "One road leads to London, / One road leads to Wales, / My road leads me seaward / To the white dipping sails."

June 8: Mother, Warren, and Sylvia work on the laborious process of making molasses candy, "developed from brown, so dark that it was almost black, to a deep brown, to (very slowly) a middle brown, and still more slowly, to an ochre. At last my candy turns a light, golden brown," delicious and superior to "any cheap store candy."

June 9: A good viola lesson, biking, Warren brings home a catch of "five little kivvers"[205] for supper: "They were tasty but had too many tiny bones."

June 10: "I am devouring my molasses candy so fast that by the afternoon I had only five pieces left." Sylvia trapezes in the apple tree before it begins to rain.

June 11: A new poem, "Enchantment," which ends "A book may lead each girl and boy / From darkest night to brilliant day."

June 12: "Enchantment" is mounted on yellow paper with a green trim in the classroom. "My! Isn't that lovely," Miss Raguse says. Baseball in the "broiling sun": "we played very well (if I say so myself)."

June 13: Cleaning up in household arts for next year: "It was some job. For recompense Miss Lowe made us some fudge which was slightly burned but was nevertheless, good." Last piano lesson of the year.

June 14: "After school I had an interview with Miss Lawson. She accepted me for a critic on the literary staff on the Phillipian next year! I am so happy!" Sylvia tells Miss Raguse, who hugs her and says, "Be sure to tell your mother."

June 15: "Today is really a broiler . . . cooler in the gym! In English every time I raised my hand the paper that I was working on came up with it and stuck to my hand." Dismissed early from school. "Boy!" A large thunder shower: "It was very close!" Cooler, off to the carnival with Marilyn Fraser to ride on the "Ferris wheel once, chairplane 4 times," spends forty-four cents: "Lost supper after getting home."

June 16: Wonderful viola lesson, "feel quite proud of myself." A swim in Morses Pond is a "great relief after such a muggy day," a "long, relaxing sunbath on the sand fell asleep for a while."

June 17: Hunting for Warren at Morses Pond, wears her white shoes, "unsuspecting of all the booby traps down there. First I tripped and my leg went knee deep into a mucky hole and then I tripped and fell in the brook before I found him fishing."

June 18: Writes a poem, "My Garden," "a haven of wild flowers / The Kingdom of birds and bees."

June 19: Number games in math. In music, tells the story of the *Peer Gynt* suite composed by Edvard Grieg. In a storm, arrives home sopping wet after tripping in a puddle and falling with a "great splash." Plays flinch,[206] arranges a notebook for camp.

June 20: Wins the Wellesley Award for the seventh grade and is presented with Charles Lamb and Mary Lamb's *Tales from Shakespeare* (1807): "In English Miss Raguse gave me congratulations that really mean more than anyone else's."

June 21: Wins two creative writing awards and one for her supervision of the war stamp sales, Marilyn Fraser does her portrait in chalk and crayon. {PM}

June 22: "Yahoo! School is out!" Swamped with "requests for autographs and it was fun." *The Phillipian* publishes her poem "Rain."

June 23: Works with Betsy Powley on a camp diary, draws up an index "with quite a bit of difficulty."[207]

June 24: Plays blindman's bluff[208] with Warren and Betsy Powley, then "Fish"[209] and "Social Solitaire."[210]

June 25: Draws Betsy Powley after her waist-length, thick braids are cut: "Her hair looked lovely. It is cut shoulder length and curled under (not permanented!)." Sunbathing, "but my skin stayed the same old dirty brown." Copies a picture from Kate Seredy's book, *Singing Tree.*[211]

June 26: Goes to Nancy Wiggins's house: the "most gigantic and beautiful house that I have ever seen. A mirror about ten feet by 25 feet! We played out on her glassed in porch which was cool as the rain lightning and thunder were wreaking havoc outside." They act in a play Marilyn Fraser makes up and then Sylvia illustrates a story. They are served a "delicious luncheon by a 'Ritzy' maid." Mrs. Wiggins takes them to a drug store for a "vanilla frappe."

June 27: Sylvia reads in bed, washes and dries breakfast dishes and makes all the beds "by myself," bikes to Betsy Powley's, works on their camp notebook, begins a poem, "Transparent depths so still / Bright as dew of Sapphire hue." Copies poems from *Sung under the Silver Umbrella.*[212]

June 28: Has the sniffles, over to Betsy Powley's: "We have so many happy plans for going to camp!" They make up poems together.

June 29: "My cold is at its height today but I am up and have been baking in the sun for about 3 and one-half hours. I feel as if I am all dried up." Runny nose, nose spray, feeling "loads better and full of vigor," packs her duffel bag for two weeks at camp.

June 30: Her cold vanished, she quotes Ogden Nash: "A mighty creature is the germ, though smaller than the pachyderm." Makes a bank deposit with the grand total of savings to date: twenty-seven dollars and seventy-six cents. "I have sent into <u>so</u> many contests that I wish I would win <u>something</u>!"

July 1: Trouble sleeping, excited about camp, packed and ready to go, a beautiful drive to Cape Cod with Betsy Powley and her family, arrives at Camp Helen Storrow at 3:30 p.m., looking forward to "2 joyous weeks."

July 2: Awake at 5:00 a.m. with birds "singing sweetly. . . . One would trill up and down the scale again and again." Reveille and a rush to the latrines, crafts, swimming tests: "I cannot be in any of the high ones [groups] as I cannot swim under water." Writes letters, sings "Jenny Cracked Corn"[213] around the campfire.

Postcard to Mother: "My bed is so cozy and I am all unpacked and every thing is neatly put away." Describes camp activities and supper: "fresh spinach, sliced turkey, 2 baked potatoes, brick (vanilla, strawberry chocolate) ice cream, and four cups of milk! I am well and overwhelmingly happy."

Postcard to Warren: "I love camp. You would love to be here. There are trees every where; and at night the fireflies are countless, and they light up the earth and sky."

July 3: Items purchased at trading post: Kleenex, tie, and bathing cap for a total of seventy-five cents. Swimming and boating.

Postcard to "Dearest Mother": "The food is wonderful. . . . I'm fine! Xxx Love, Sylvia."

July 3–4: Postcard to "Dear Mummy": Going for a swim after rest hour. "Our cabin is so nice and cozy."

July 4: A ceremony on the beach, folk dancing, and refreshments.

July 5: Cleans out her cabin, boating, writes a "big fat letter" to Mother and Warren, a "lovely card" from Grammy and Grampy, "Dash" (a camp counselor) tells a "story about everyone! How we love her."

To Mother and Warren: Describes last night after the flag lowering on the beach watching the "perfect tawny-red ball of sun sink slowly out of sight in the West," reads her part of the ceremony and is "complimented on it by 'Dash.'" Boating and basking in the sun, mentions her full stomach after a huge meal of coffee cake, chocolate cake with marshmallow sauce, three cups of milk, haddock, nineteen carrots, lettuce and tomatoes, cucumber, punch, two potatoes, and four slices of watermelon. "Boy!"

July 6: "For capers we had to clean the John's. . . . It was a smelly job . . . fun in a queer sort of way." Boating on the lake with the setting sun flooding the lake "a pale pink color."

Postcard to Mother: Promoted from lowest (red cap) to next highest class (white) in swimming: "I am quite happy." Dash compliments her on braiding her hair "so neatly and so often! I love camp, and it is near enough to you so that I never feel homesick Yahoo!" Mentions getting a big fat letter from her mother with drawings, which she shows to the whole unit. "If any one says I can draw I'll know I inherited it from you. P.S. I have a reputation with my unit leader for eating more than any one!"

Postcard to "Dearest Mummy": More heroic eating. "Give my love to Warren," draws a heart.

July 7: Sylvia and Betsy Powley are on the winning softball team, an 8–2 score.

Postcard to Mother: Mentions writing to Grammy and Grampy.[214] Begins a poem about watching the stars and listening to the grass "whispering to the moon / Which shines above the hill."

July 8: Boating and a refreshing swim, gargantuan eating: "I feel like a stuffed turkey." Crafts and singing by the campfire before taps. "Dash let me lie against her."

Postcard to Mother: "If you're hard up on ration points when I come home you can have Joe slaughter me and you can eat me for pork."

July 9: Drawing and games, "Loose Caboose,"[215] "Musical Chairs," and potato-sack races.

Postcard to Mother: Mentions sleeping on the beach "tonight!!" Completes a second verse of her poem about the flitting fireflies "gleaming in the frosty air."

July 10: "Our minstrel show was a great success! I dressed like a little pickanninny girl and when one of the darkies danced I had to say 'I love dat man!'" [drawing].

July 11: A firefly in the cabin: "He blinked his greenish light a few times before he flew away."

Postcard to Mother: Describes the minstrel show. "I got your big fat letter with the map. Everybody envies me—receiving such meaty letters! . . . I received dear Warrens letter and thought it one of the loveliest I've received."

July 12: A five-mile hike: "At least, after we thought we could bear it no longer, we reached the ocean and saw the white sandy dunes, and cliffs which housed the belted kingfisher, and smelled the salty, tangy air!" Sketches the cove. "I got quite a sunburn by the time I was ready to go home. I was practically caked with salt!"

July 13: Dresses for a masquerade as a black widow.

Postcard to Grammy and Grampy: Describes excursion to the ocean. "I had to laugh at some of the girls because I was the only one who dared to go in first for the waves were strong and cold until you ducked."

Postcard to Mother: draws the cove and cliff and her having fun riding the waves.

July 14: "Dash (that mean hypocrite) has gone to Boston to stay overnight to pick up the new campers coming in tomorrow."

July 15: Returning home from camp. "Everyone is sorry to see us go! . . . I'm glad to be home."

July 16: "I slept around the clock and made up for every moment of sleep that I lost while at camp." Reports on progress in the garden, the back of the house "ablaze with fall colors of orange, gold, deep Indian reds and browns." Plays turock with Mother and Warren. "I lost as usual but had a grand time anyway."

July 17: Housework, dish washing, dusting, making beds, piano practice beginning with Beethoven's "Moonlight Sonata" and Ignacy Jan Paderewski's Minuet in G Major, begins an original sketch of a "mermaid reclining on a rock in the River Rhine and waving to someone in the towers of an old German castle on the bank of a river."[216] Answers a letter from Marcia Egan, bikes to the library to check out *White Stag* by Kate Seredy[217] and *Stand Fast and Reply* by Lavinia R. Davis.[218]

July 18: Grammy makes a deposit in Sylvia's bank account. Since December 27, Sylvia has accumulated thirty dollars, "all earned myself too." Off with Betsy Powley to Morses Pond for swimming, diving, and sunbathing.

6:30 p.m.: An angry Mrs. Powley picks them up because it is "way past supper time. Mother didn't scold me though!"

July 19: After chores, gets "down to business," writes letters to friends,[219] finishes reading library books, arranges for a new, bigger bookcase.

July 20: Visits Harvard's Peabody Museum in the company of Max and Carolyn Gaebler and mentions the "famous glass flowers, minerals and precious stones, ancient sculls of Java men and such, animals (preserved)." On to the Fogg Museum, where Max explains "in detail, all of the old Chinese art, which he is so familiar with." A perfect day.

July 21: Stocks new bookcase, completes this enjoyable job, shampoos hair, and, while it is drying, mows part of the lawn since the grass is "terribly thick and it was a terrific task."

July 22: Mows the front lawn after chores, rakes the lawn after lunch, reads *Schoolgirl Allies* (1917) again, packs suitcase for a trip to Portland, Maine, tomorrow with Mother and Warren to visit the Loungways.[220]

July 23: Travel by train and bus to Portland. On the crowded bus, Sylvia stands behind the bus driver who tells her about the scenery.

July 24: A "dreadful night's sleep" because of Warren's coughing, draws Christmas cards, Margot and Johnny Loungway, Warren, and Sylvia play "keep away" with a football,[221] the girls are bruised and vow never to play that "dreadful and rough game again!" Sylvia works with Margot on making a paper doll and designing a few dresses for it. With Warren in the house and Sylvia and Aurelia in a cabin, they get a good night's sleep.

July 25: Makes candle bottles with Margot, plays croquet, a short swim, sleeps with Margot: "We had such fun."

July 26: Reads in bed with Margot, plays badminton and with paper dolls, designs more dresses. "After lunch Margot and I escaped doing dishwashing and went down in the back field in a cozy little shack to read" [drawing]. At supper, reports on two planets, Saturn and Mercury, Margot on Mars and Jupiter, after supper, dishwashing with Margot.

July 27: After household tasks, croquet with Margot, they make a picnic lunch, off to a hilltop overlooking Lake Thompson: "a glittering sapphire in the warm July sunshine." Sylvia draws flowers and scenery.

July 28: Plays baseball with the boys, draws, and plays piano, pretending with Margot to be mutes: "We really spoke not <u>one</u> word during the meal." They play checkers after supper.

July 29: A baby squirrel in the cabin, blueberry pie for dessert made of the blueberries Sylvia picked with Margot in the morning.

July 30: Bible school with Margot and twenty-five other children learning about the Roman persecution of the Christians, "childish games such as 'drop the handkerchief,'[222] 'the Flying Dutchman,'"[223] rows across the lake, lunches, swims, fishes.

July 31: Drawing of shooting stars, a lesson in Bible school on the "symbol of a fish," learns to turn somersaults under water at Thompson Pond, swims and eats, eats and swims: "Never in my life have I seen such a clear, star spangled sky. We saw some brilliant shooting stars (The 1st that I've ever seen and the Milky Way was like a gossamer scarf flung across the sky.)" Writes a poem, "The Fairy Scarf," comparing the spread of stars to a fairy scarf, which falls to the ground but in the "faintest rays of the sun" the scarf vanishes like "fairy things—it did not last."

August 1: Shooting stars: "I saw four of them, two large, bright ones. Margot and I rolled up in blankets, 'Indian style,' and lay on the lawn on our backs. This way we received a much better view."

August 2: A drive into Lewiston, Maine, purchases a scrapbook for her pressed flower collection, plans "murder plays" with Margot and the boys to present to their parents the next day.

August 3: Puts up with Mr. Dunstan's "drivel about the bad side of Christianity through a mass of loudly-chewed gum!" Writes a seventeen-line poem, "The Wind."

August 4: Sunbathes, makes spatter prints[224] on stationery, "Mr. Beatty came over and 'Beatted' us up. He evidently was suffering the after effects of too much alcoholic drink! He tried to choke me with my braids (not in fun, either) but Margot came to my rescue in time."

August 5: Sylvia goes off with Margot to a secret place in the woods to write. "We lay on soft pine needles in a large clearing enclosed by pine trees. The needles covered a rocky ledge which was very smooth. We had a lovely time." A long letter to Arden Tapley, sorts out stamps, and plays hide-and-go-seek with the boys.

August 6: Picks "nice, juicey blackberries" for her cereal, works with Margot on their stamp collections, plays "Kick the Can"[225] and "Hide and Go Seek" with the boys. "After supper we 4 darkened the living room so it was pitch black and played murder which was terrible exciting."

August 7: Mails an entry to the "Draw Me" contest, plays hide-and-seek in the barn with Warren, Margot, and Johnny Loungway, works with Margot on their stamp collections, plays murder with Margot and two boys: "I had fun all the time and everyone came out of the dark with bruises—John[ny] with a black eye, Warren with a bruised face, Margot with a strained back, and I with a sprained neck." An upset stomach after dinner, rests and draws.

August 8: "Atom bomb!" On the way home from Maine, reads the first reports about the bombing of Hiroshima and is shocked to learn that 60 percent of the city is destroyed. President Truman says the bomb can be used for "constructive as well as destructive purposes."

August 9: Goes through collection of Swedish stamps that John Stenberg, "my first love," has given her, soaks the stamps off of postcards, trades some US stamps with Warren, embroiders flowers on a guest towel purchased in Lewiston for her mother's Christmas present.

Thanks Margot "ever so much for the perfect time I had at Innisfree in the past seventeen days. I have never felt better and I have gained two pounds. (Must be due to those five potatoes I consumed one night for supper)." Wakes that morning in horror but then "sighed with relief as I saw the moose head at the foot of my bed rapidly dwindle into a bedpost! You see, your imaginative influence still clings to my mind" [moose head drawing]. Reports a dream about a "rainstorm soaking all the valuable stamps in the world from albums and washing them up to my doorstep sorted out and in perfect condition." Encloses three Swedish stamps, looks forward to a Boston trip to get a new stamp album.

August 10: [Drawing] "JAPS OFFER TO QUIT." Mows the lawn since Warren has had an asthma attack, embroiders, listening to *Quiz of Two Cities*[226] and *Henry Aldrich*, "Tokyo radio says Japan ready to accept Potsdam terms if Hirohito can seek throne! Moscow gets offer through ambassador—Japs say Swiss bringing terms—Fighting continues. . . . No official word from Japan yet."

August 11: Irons embroidered guest towel for Mother's Christmas present, arranges stamps according to continents, writes to Jamestown Stamp Company asking to buy stamps on approval, writes to Uncle Frank and Aunt Louise,[227] bikes to the library.

August 12: A sultry, humid day, writes a letter to Dash,[228] listens to the radio, walks to the mailbox.

August 13: Takes a bus to Boston to buy a stamp album, "navy blue and gilt lettering," at the Harris Stamp Company, buys a "frap"[229] at the drugstore, goes to a Loews Theatre to watch *The Valley of Decision* (1945), starring Greer Garson, Gregory Peck, and Lionel Barrymore: "The story and acting were superbly done." Takes bus home, supper, and before bed, pastes stamps in the new album.

August 14: [Drawing] "PEACE." Puts US stamps in her album. "All through the day we hear news broadcasts (very contradictory) about the news that was expected from Japan about the acceptance of unconditional national surrender." Checks out *A Separate Star*[230] and Robert Louis Stevenson's *Strange Case of Dr. Jekyll and Mr. Hyde* (1886) from the library.

7:00 p.m.: Hears "official word . . . that Pres. Truman has received the note from Japan saying 'We surrender unconditionally.' The end of World War II!!!!!! My How the people shouted! How the whistles blue. At night we set off firecrackers and rockets. We all thank God for answering our prayers."

August 15: Firecrackers and cannons roaring, still celebrating peace, Sylvia works on stamps with Warren, takes a walk with Mother, Warren, and Grammy: "The sky put on its rainbow colors for peace. Pale pink cloud streamers hung across the azure sky. The west was a golden red-yellow glow and hazy white clouds floated here and there, but best of all, there was a bright <u>blue</u> crescent moon in the heavens."

August 16: Housework, off to Morses Pond, sunbathing, swimming, two friction burns on her bottom from the water slide (hot in the middle), copies poems in her notebook while "reclining in the apple tree," viola practice after supper.

August 17: Piano practice and biking, makes a notebook of all the poems written since she was five, at Aunt Dot's: chocolate cake, cookies, and milk. Listens to *Quiz of Two Cities* before going to bed.

August 18: Receives long letter from Margot Loungway containing "a few very nice stamps for me," checks out three books from the library, writes to Margot saying she is happy to have found "someone that writes really worthwhile letters," thanks her for the stamps and describes her stamp-collecting trip to Boston and her new album, asks about friends at Bible school, draws pictures of them. Everyone is joyful about the end of the war. Mowgli has disappeared. Asks about the sex of Margot's cats: "Some morning you may wake up and find a dozen little apatchies or gray and white kittens climbing all over your bed and still more peeping down from the bats roost [arrow pointing at drawing of bedroom] in your room."

August 19: Goes to church with Mother for a thanksgiving service for the end of the war, has a picnic at Lake Waban.[231]

August 20: Paints her bicycle geranium red, reads a "nice letter" from Dash, Betsy Powley talks about her summer in New York, Sylvia builds a tree house with Betsy made of ferns and with leaves covering it: "Light still comes through but tomorrow we hope to perfect it."

August 21: Going to have her braids cut, taken into a little booth where the hairdresser tries to persuade her not to cut her hair, which makes her "feel all the worse," draws her new haircut but misses her braids, goes to Betsy's after mother takes her picture, "dismayed to find our woodsy house full of gapping space where the ferns had dried. However after one hours work we had the house looking lovely as ever."

August 22: Paints outdoor beach chairs white, weaves ferns for a hut at Betsy's: "Someone at the top of the hill started out throwing stones down so we quickly built a secret fern room in the back of our spacious retreat."

August 23: Quite tired after a sleepless night "spent on hard pin [drawing] curls." Sees *Son of Lassie*,[232] "all war (ugh)," and *Gentle Annie*,[233] starring James Craig and Donna Reed. "An improvement on the first picture."

August 24: Has three teeth filled at a Boston dentist, goes to Harris Stamp Company to purchase one hundred Danish stamps.

August 25: Bikes over to Betsy Powley's, supper at home with Uncle Frank, Aunt Louise, Aunt Dot, and Uncle Joe, stays up until 11:30 p.m. to listen to Frank and Louise tell stories about their life in New York.

August 26: "When I got up this morning I had a laughing spell for about ½ hr. and only saw the comic side of everything." Reads *Anne of Green Gables* (1908), designs a few dresses for her handmade paper dolls after lunch.

August 27: Housework and paper-doll dress designing: a "pale blue evening gown, a Mexican costume [drawing] and a suit-blue skirt red jerkin and white long sleeved sweater," Mother then begins the "gruesome task of washing and setting my hair." Sylvia is in curlers when Betsy Powley arrives, starts a letter to Margot Loungway, listens to *Bulldog Drummond*[234] before bedtime.

August 28: Receives five hundred stamps on approval from the Jamestown Stamp Company, divides them up with Warren, spends the afternoon sorting and hinging stamps, bikes to the library and checks out *Invincible Louisa* by Cornelia Meigs,[235] a biography of Louisa May Alcott.

August 29: Sorts out duplicate stamps, goes to Morses Pond "for a few happy hours on the beach and in the water," sunbathing for an hour, feels "healthy the rest of the day."

August 30: A tour of Wayside Inn, "about which Longfellow made up his famous poem. We saw old fashioned rooms with nameplates of various famous people on the doors. I had a lovely time."

Letter to Margot Loungway: "I heartily agree with you concerning Mr. (I won't disgrace churches or minister by associating him (or his Name) with 'Reverend) Morbid Religious Drible' Dunstan" [a caricature drawing of him]. Thinks her new haircut is "quite presentable!!" [drawing of back and front views].

August 31: Has the sniffles.

September 1: Remains in bed with a cold, lunches, and plays solitaire on the porch, "I have called all the girls (four) that I'm inviting to lunch on Tuesday and all have accepted."

September 2: Plays cards with Betsy Powley and gets her notebooks ready for school.

September 3: Helps mother with housework, goes to the "fern hideaway" with Betsy, they name the main room "Fern Forest Inn" and the larger of two secret rooms, "Restabit Hideaway." Betsy's parents visit the fern house but have trouble finding the hidden door. "Finally we showed them." Returns home after a "perfect day."

September 4: A discussion of camp experiences at the lunch Sylvia hosts. She made place cards for her guests. After lunch, under the shade of a birch tree, they play "Spit,"[236] "I Doubt It,"[237] and other card games. "We all (save quiet sensible Marilyn [Fraser]) dressed up in funny costumes and old rags and went to one house to pretend we were refugees, but, fortunately, (for us, probably), no one was home." Mother reads a chapter of Willa Cather's novel *Death Comes for the Archbishop* (1927) by Willa Cather to Sylvia.

September 5: Sylvia prepares reluctantly for school the next day, dries her hair in the sun after a shampoo: "I looked somewhat like Medusa [drawing] when my curlers were taken out."

September 6: Enters the eighth grade, meets her teachers but no classes, Grammy takes her swimming on a "very, very, hot, humid and uncomfortable" day.

September 7: Sylvia has an enjoyable day at school, Mrs. Warren, an English teacher, has a "mainia for oral topics. She usually stops in the middle of a sentence to tell us a long story about something it reminds her of." Sylvia has her first meeting with *The Phillipian* staff: "We really are aiming to put out a super magazine." Off to Morses Pond: "I swam over my head and stood on my hands under water."

September 8: An hour of swimming with Warren, picks apples with Mrs. Eaton after supper.

September 9: Stays over night at Arden Tapley's, plays cards and games, "I got almost no sleep at all."

September 10: In social studies, the issue of *Junior Review* is "all about the atomic bomb." Mrs. Warren gives a lesson about facial expressions.

September 11: Reads aloud in class from *Gulliver the Great* by Walter A. Dryer[238] and is told to "Slow Down!"

September 12: Elected president of her class, draws a picture of her jump "off the high dive" at Morses Pond.

September 13: Makes a fruit cup (bananas, apples, grapes, oranges, cherries, grapefruit) for Miss Lowe.

September 14: Tries to make gingerbread men: "I opened the oven door and, to my profound dismay I found the mess of hot dough all over the oven and dripping from the tray. I called in Warren to get the cookie mold and he broke a gallon jug of molasses all over the floor in the attempt! Everyone came home in the midst of this. The grownups comforted us and I found out my mistake was putting 2–3 cups of molasses and such instead of 2/3 (It was written 2–3)."

September 15: Reads Edgar Allan Poe's "The Gold Bug," plays turock with Uncle Joe, Mother, and Warren.

September 16: After lunch, Mrs. Bates arrives to discuss giving up the viola.

September 17: Elected secretary in English, on bus during a "genuine laughing fit" with Betsy Powley: the "people around us joined in. As we left the bus they all were looking at us and laughing hard."

September 18: Mrs. Warren compliments Sylvia on reading aloud "very nicely."

Letter to Margot Loungway: Says she enjoyed her "dignified letter," discusses how to manage her allowance and buy stamps, encloses British stamps, describes how she dropped her bus ticket and was on her knees hunting for it when "Betsy [Powley] sat on my head. Everybody around us was laughing fit to kill." Expresses interest in Margot's suggestion to write to someone in a foreign country, includes several drawings.

September 19: Plays soccer, colors a lantern slide in "General Science," has a multiplication drill in math, piano lesson, counts her stamp collection at home: "I have exactly 471."

September 20: Chooses her clubs: art, stamp collecting, recreational reading. Goes home with a cold.

September 21: [Drawing] "ACHOOOOOOOOOOOOOOOOOOOO-OOOOO." A 100 percent on three quizzes in social studies. Goes to bed early, still sneezing.

September 22: Has a breakfast pancake that fills up the whole pan. Her cold is "drying up."

September 23: Finishes *A Sea Between*[239] by Lavinia R. Davis, walks with Mother in the woods in the afternoon: "The leaves were beautifully colored and all the asters were a purple mist on the hills."

September 24: Has a deep cough, paints a swan and her "little babies," a "nice letter from Margot," which she begins to answer.[240]

September 25: Plays field hockey, gives a talk on the constellation Cassiopeia in general science, her team wins 8–5 in softball.

September 26: Sylvia is so hoarse in Guidance she can hardly call the meeting to order. Yawns through a "boring lecture on cafeteria table manners and quotas and prices of the next Peace Bond Drive," at home, begins a painting of "a little girl gazing at a fairy in a petunia bed," practices piano and viola after supper.

September 27: Makes cream of corn soup, "tasty although watery," checks out *Daddy-Long-Legs*[241] from the library: "too mushy and impossible."

September 28: Reads a "trashy" Nancy Drew mystery and regrets wasting her time, has a physical exam: "We girls stood shivery (stripped to the waste) in a room with open windows and cold drafts. I felt very ill but the doctor (an old codger, shaking all over) pronounced me as perfect in every way!" Sylvia plays cards and sorts stamps that Mother had brought home from the stamp collection of a fellow teacher: "There are many beauties from Jamaica, US, Italy and such!"

September 29: Mother comes home with a "lovely new dress," Sylvia helps Warren hinge his stamps.

September 30: A Sunday school family reception, a country walk with Grammy, Mother, and Warren, writes a thank-you letter to Miss Mower for the stamp-album gift.[242]

October 1: Drizzling and freezing rain, viola and piano practice, puts about twenty stamps in Warren's album.

October 2: Miss Baldwin teaches "perfect posture" that will command authority, Sylvia is doing well in science and math, does stamp arranging with Warren.

October 3: Has an "icy game" of field hockey.

October 4: Gets first choice: art club. At home, reads *American Girl*, homework and viola lesson, Debby Bates gives her a "nice pumpkin."

October 5: Sylvia goes to a reunion Scout meeting with seventh- and eighth-grade girls, with singing, refreshments, and "technicolor movies of Scout camps."

October 6: Sunday school cookout with games and "frankfurts, tomatoes, potato chips, olives and other yummy things."

October 7: A good ninety-minute piano practice.

October 8: "In stamps today we reached the mark and sold ten dollars worth."

October 9: Volleyball: learns to serve with "average skill," gives a report about Percival Lowell,[243] listens to *Tello-Test*,[244] "the question is up to $75."

October 10: A "brisk game of hockey and I got tangled up on the sticks and came out of the jumble with a temporarily crushed finger and a likewise strained foot! (What a martyr I am!)." Returns home to paint a sea nymph.

October 11: A test on the planets in general science, mounts two watercolors in art class. "(Honestly—nothing new) I began a picture of a cobweb fairy. . . . Dear Diary—you're one of the 'musts' for peace of mind."

October 12: A "nice" country walk with Mother, with the sun "hanging low in the west and shining through the graceful milkweed in crisp, 'Octoberish' air" that turns frosty when they return home.

October 13, 8:00 a.m.: Church.

Hiking to the "glorious summit of Mount Monadonock," eating lunch in a howling, icy wind, below is a "tiny pool of water" beside the "autumn red-gold countryside," the fresh air and sun make for a "wonderful time."

October 14: Mrs. Harrington is an "Awful!!!" substitute in Sunday school, Sylvia has a "nice long telephone talk with Betsy [Powley] before bed."

October 15: Dusts and washes mirrors for Miss Lowe. "She said that I will make a good wife! (Ha! Ha!)." Reads about Marie Curie: "I do enjoy that book so much."[245]

October 16: In English, "Oh! Joy!," the whole period is devoted to poetry and prose. After school, works with Betsy Powley and Prissy Steele on the Star-Find badge for Scouts.

October 17: Comes in first in mathematics for the third time.

October 18: In Foods class, makes some "delicious 'supperish' surprise muffins."

October 19: In English, works on book reports, in science, work on season maps is interrupted by an "unseasonable fire drill," Sylvia submits three poems to *The Phillipian*, elected secretary in Girl Scouts.

October 20: Bikes around Wellesley College grounds in beautiful weather.

October 21: A nice walk with Mother and Grammy on a country road in Weston, rides her bike as well and comes home with it covered in "colored leaves and sumac."

October 22: In music appreciation, listens to "lovely recordings of a harpsichord." Starts on a crayon picture of birch trees for an art exhibit and a chart in general science showing the phases of the moon, a "dreadful time" in math with mortgages, everyone confused.

October 23: Sylvia browses Hathaway House bookshelves.

October 24: Weighed in health, "99 lbs!!!!" Finishes reading about Madame Curie.

October 25: A spelling test with "usual <u>100%</u>," makes baking-powder biscuits—burned but "tasted very good just the same." In math, Miss Chadwick says, "'One excellent example of neatness is Sylvia's work and she seldom gets below ninety!' Boy! What an unexpected compliment."

October 26: Sylvia plays in an orchestra concert: "pleased with myself because I was able to play everything (even the Knightsbridge-March) and kept in good time."

Sylvia Plath becomes a teenager, and her mother marks the moment with a poem.

October 27: Pastes a picture of Theodore Roosevelt into her diary with the motto "Speak softly and carry a big stick." Everyone sings happy birthday to her. Gifts: two kerchiefs, fourteen dollars and sixty-six cents, a book, *Green Peace* (1945) by Marjorie Hayes, and some "lovely stamps," bubble bath, and socks. Makes frosting and decorates her birthday cake with pink roses and green leaves. Sylvia's mother writes a poem, "To My Sylvia," her darling, her "<u>teen</u>-age girl!" Life is opening "so many doors," but she has to "keep on growing" in "mind and soul" and keep this as her goal as she enters "the teens / With laughter and song."

October 28: Sylvia takes a nice walk on a beautiful day.

October 29: "In math I beg to get into my thick skull the kinds and uses of life insurance."

October 30: "Steps in English Grammar"—"a gruesome task. . . . In Monitor meeting we were shown some things with which we could fill a Red Cross kit. It was interesting to see how many nice things could fit into such a small box." After school, an "old tiresome rehearsal for parent Teachers Night."

October 31: Gives an oral report on *Madame Curie* (author and publication date uncertain).

November: Publishes "My Garden," *The Phillipian*, 7.

November 1: In Foods, makes melted cheese and butterscotch biscuits, a "yummy lesson."

November 2: Reads *The Perilous Seat* by Caroline Dale Snedeker[246] "once more." Watches Danny Kaye in *Wonder Man* (1945) and Tom Conway in *The Falcon in San Francisco* (1945): "(nutsy). Danny Kaye played the part of twin brothers. One was a dancer in burlesque and the other was a bookworm. The picture is hilarious and the dancing is super."

November 3: Gets to see a movie for free for Girl Scouts: *National Velvet* (1944), reads *The Story Girl*[247] and *The Golden Road*, both books by Lucy Maud Montgomery,[248] before going to bed.

November 4: "In church [drawing] we had rusty aster for flowers. . . . The world around our house was touched with a filmy band of cold white lace." Makes a "big snowman" with Warren.

November 5: Goes shopping with Grammy for dancing shoes but "to no avail." To the Nortons' for supper, Mrs. Marion Norton drives her and Perry Norton to their first dancing lesson with Mr. Batitste: "It was really fun."

Letter to Margot Loungway: Sends a thank-you for "your nice birthday card." Mentions receiving a "whole pile of lovely stamps," including some from Cape Juby[249]—"three of which are alone worth $2.50," sent by the Harris Company as a "special birthday gift. . . . I have 51 Austrian Stamps and would like more on approval." Mentions playing the viola at a teachers' convention in Boston:[250] "it was my first public appearance and it was fun!" Mentions enjoying field hockey: "I really think that it is relaxing."

November 6: The snowman is now just a "big lump of snow," which she makes into a snow house decorated with stones and a "little man standing in front of it" [drawing].

November 7: In Guidance, discusses "boxes for the armed forces overseas." Armistice Day in assembly: a "multitude of speakers on war and such." Works on the cover of her English work to be presented at a PTA meeting: "an open book covered with green and edged with gold. On each page I'm having a verse of my original poem, 'Enchantment.' I'm bordering each page with vines of purple grapes."

November 8: In Foods, makes "delicious big cookies which were full of delicious dates and were flavored with lemon extract. I did enjoy mine!" In art, completes a drawing of "some poor people."

November 9: Mother brings home gold for the edge of a book cover for a school project, an assignment on William Jennings Bryan.

November 10: Sylvia hikes and has a cookout with Scouts that completes her work on her "Outdoor Cook Badge."

November 11: Plays a new card game, GI Joe,[251] with Uncle Frank and Aunt Dot.

November 12: Has a sore throat, rereads *The Wind in the Willows*,[252] listens to the radio, lunch in bed, draws pictures of fairies and pretty girls, dresses for dinner and then dancing class: "I had a super time and never knew before that dancing could be so much fun."

November 13: Sore throat is improving. Volleyball, excused from PTA rehearsal with Mother's note.

November 14: A boring PTA rehearsal. "I tried to make a slide of Abraham Lincoln but did not succeed very well." A piano lesson, "I condescended to talk to little Bruce, whereupon his mother was very joyous and was nice to me. I went to bed early!!!!!!!!!!!!!!!!!!"

November 15: Home after school for a rest in bed, "mother served me my supper," to the PTA: "It went off beautifully." Sees a shooting star on the way home.

November 16: Stays home in bed all day with a miserable cold, listens to the radio all day long and draws, reads the paper, rests, plans Christmas presents for Warren: stamps and a model boat.

November 17: Shoe shopping: "finally got some ill-fitting patent leathers."

Writes to Margot Loungway: "How are you old top?" Encloses a photograph of herself: "my favorite picture of me with my little brown jug."[253] Mentions her performance in a tableau at PTA with an exhibition of student work, wants to know what stamps and from which countries Margot wants, mentions starting a book of poems—"5 real ones, and have about 5 medium and about 15 jingles," asks to see Margot's stories, mentions visiting the mummy at the Museum of Fine Arts and meeting a "queer old man" who wants to show the girls his treasures. "Off he went into a dark corridor. I immediately wanted to go home for my feet hurt and the two others were interested and I had, evidently, been reading too many 'Nancy Drew' stories. I, of course, stayed with them." The man returns wearing a new suit and a "queer shaped sort of magnifying glass" and begins to show them Egyptian jewelry. "One little box contained an agate eye! It looked (to shivering me) like the real thing. The man cackled when he saw my terror and held out the glass—He held the glass over the eye and, as though it were jelly, the eye wriggled and the pupil contracted as the man tipped the glass!" He laughs and asks them to "come down the dark corridor to see some more relics," but Sylvia, feeling ill, grabs the girls and rushes out, reminding them it is lunch time. Later Prissy Steele says, "The eye was terrible." Sylvia tells her "condescendingly, 'Oh! That's only natural for someone who hasn't had as much experience as I have.'" Mentions dreams in which eyes come toward her "at a terrific rate and whizzing past just in time. When I work with stamps too much this happens too. Take my advice—never take eyes too lightly. They really are supernatural sometimes."

November 18: "I wanted very much to go to church (Thanksgiving Sunday) but Mother thought I was not well so I didn't. I surprised her by doing the dishes & beds in her absence," sorts out Warren's stamps.

November 19: Happy to return to school, plays with baby David William Norton at the Nortons, and is praised for learning a new step in dancing class.

November 20: Reads *Absolute Pitch* (1939) by Florence Choate, an interesting book about opera singers. With a few other girls, packs cookies for the "poor and shut-in people of Wellesley": "We really had quite a good time."

November 21: Dismissed early from school for Thanksgiving, works on stamps with Warren: "We're in desperate need of hinges."

November 22: Thanksgiving: "a real day to be thankful for," reads while having a "delicious breakfast served luxuriously in bed," a shampoo and hair up with curlers, listens to radio while cleaning out a trunk of paper supplies.

November 23: Plays Monopoly with Warren, visits Grampy at the country club, and consumes two pieces of apple and pie and ice cream.

November 24: A "beautiful frosty day," sunny and no wind, a walk with Grammy in the woods: "The air was crisp and clean and sweet. We had a beautiful time."

November 25: In Sunday school, a Jewish girl gives a "very interesting" talk about Jewish customs and beliefs. She promises a visit to a synagogue. "I had a beautiful time listening to her."

November 26: One of her poems, "'My Garden' (which is no good) is published in the *Phillipian*." Returns home and tells a happy Grampy about her good grades. He gives her some money and hugs her, "which means more than any money to me although money is handy around Christmas time."

November 27: In general science, watches an "interesting movie on the ways and techniques of glass blowing."

November 28: An interesting debate (two on each side) in assembly about compulsory military training, which she opposes, reads *Calling All Girls*.

November 29: Eats a "whole lot" of delicious oatmeal cookies made in Foods class.

November 30: Snowing hard, no school, shovels the front walk with Warren, finishes embroidering two pairs of socks.

December 1: Visits Ruthie Freeman in Winthrop with Mother, snowball fight with David Freeman before supper, hide-and-seek with Ruthie after supper: "We had a wonderful time."

December 2: Works on making a newspaper with Ruthie, including sections on society, sports, advertisements, comics, lost and found, poetry, and a serialized story, "The Pine Tree Special," returns home after a "wonderful time."

December 3: Sings Christmas carols in music, dancing class with Perry Norton.

December 4: Basketball is now her favorite game. In a science experiment, nearly scalds one hand and freezes the other, a "nice letter" from Margot Loungway.

December 5: In Guidance, students grade themselves on "various traits." Joe Mitchel Chappel, a "wonderful speaker," gives an amusing talk about his meetings with former President Warren G. Harding, Bette Davis, Amelia Earhart, and Thomas Edison. He imitates their mannerisms, including Mae West's "Come up and see me sometime." Returns home, "Mother went to bed with me for once. I was really surprised."

December 6: In Foods, Sylvia makes "pop corn balls" (boiled molasses, karo, vinegar, and salt poured over "wheat sparkies").[254] Pouring rain, arrives home "like a drowned rabbit."

December 7: Sees *The Prisoner of Zenda* (1937), "thrilling," and *Top Hat* (1935), "<u>very</u> old fashioned and makeuppy."

December 8: Helps Mother with breakfast dishwashing and cleaning up the kitchen, walks with Warren to the library, taking out nine books, before bed, finishes reading *Mary Poppins Opens the Door*: "fascinating."

December 9: Mr. William Norton teaches Sunday school, writes a thank-you note to Mrs. Freeman for "my happy weekend."

December 10: Listens to some records with Perry Norton at the Norton house, dancing class.

December 11: "I have a few mysterious white bumps on my face but figure that they are only pimples."

December 12: A Jamestown Stamp Company offer arrives: "Warren and I gloated over the stamps." He has the first choice and chooses the biggest stamp she has ever seen. Altogether, they have "$7.00's worth."

December 13: A terrible, itching rash on her face that the school nurse swabs with alcohol that "almost asphyxiated me."

December 14: Itchy red welts (poison sumac) all over her face and arms, a sore throat, and head cold, no school, listens to the radio all day and draws pictures, can't read because of her stinging, watering eyes, wraps Christmas presents for the Loungways. Margot Loungway is to receive *Downright Dency* (1927) by Caroline Snedeker.

December 15: More itching and more listening to the radio.

December 16: Stays home from Sunday school, writes Christmas cards, writes to Margot Loungway in bed, mentions rash and cold and that she is in a "dither" about two book reports for tomorrow. "I often remember the perfect time we had at your house this summer." Sends her love and promises to write a longer letter when she is better.

December 17: Plays the first movement of the "Moonlight Sonata" for the school musical program, "I got Ruthie's Xmas and birthday present some flowered notepaper and exquisite book plates."

December 18: [Drawing] "Eclipse of Moon from 7:37 to 12:02," makes half the baskets in basketball, for a paper on air pressure she gets "(horror of horrors, and, thank goodness, rarities) a C!!!!!!!!" The eclipse: "only a pale ball of faint light hung in the sky."

December 19: Heavy snow, describes a show as having wonderful choir and costumes but a drab stage with a squeaking and ragged curtain—"the back hanging was cheap cheesecloth and was a dirty beige."

December 20: "Hooray": no school because of the piles of snow, shovels the walk with Warren, rash is better, wraps presents, feels better after a shampoo.

December 21: Finishes *The Forgotten Daughter*[255] once more.

December 22: Sleeps lates and rejoices over a week without school, puts up Christmas tree with lights [drawings].

December 23: Morning Christmas service, finishes trimming the tree with Warren.

December 24: Puts presents under the tree, watches Grampy "have his Christmas as he won't be here tomorrow. Grampy was touchingly happy with all of his gifts as we made him the center of attention for, I believe, the first time in his life."

December 25: Enumerates her gifts from mother, grandparents, Uncle Frank and Aunt Louise, and Uncle Joe and Aunt Dot, including a pencil case, "much needed stamp hinges," mittens, a nighty, slippers, a red sweater, an address book, a diary, a pocketbook, a "handmade aluminum hammered bracelet," and from Ruthie, a sachet.

December 26: Goes to see *Our Vines Have Tender Grapes*,[256] starring Margaret O'Brien, James Craig, Frances Gifford, Jackie Jenkins, Agnes Moorehead, and Edward G. Robinson.

December 27: Reads in bed, helps Mother with housework, climbs the apple tree, listens to the radio, and colors napkins for Aunt Dot's New Year's party, now has twenty-one napkins out of thirty-eight done.

December 28: A "gorgeous day," listens to the radio and works on napkins, writes some thank-you letters,[257] gets sick, throws up, and faints.

December 29: Sick and stays in bed, Mother brings "gruel and junket,"[258] can't do much except cut out pictures from old Christmas cards.

December 30: Pastes Christmas card pictures into scrapbook, listens to "twelve good programs before going to bed."

December 31: Listens to a few "corny programs. . . . I am sort of optimistic of the new year for me. I hope you enjoy the New Year too. I have a nice new diary but you have been the record of one of the most beautiful years I've ever had in my life."

1946

Undated: Poems in scrapbook—"The Scarlet Beacon," "A Golden Afternoon," "Silver Thread," "Mornings of Mist," "Sea Symphony." {PM}

Typescript—"Mary Jane's Passport." {PM}

January 1: "Far away is 1945." Grammy gives her one dollar for coloring twenty-five New Year's napkins, Sylvia plays piano for Grampy.

January 2: Elmwood Road is one long slippery sheet of ice.

January 3: Sylvia does a report about Harmony Warren who went to live at "Green Peace," the home of Julia Ward Howe: "This story takes place during the Civil War." Makes a "yummy" Welsh rarebit in Foods.

January 4: With Betsy Powley, uses shovels to whiz downhill "faster than any sled would go."

January 5: Plays Russian bank[259] with Betsy.

January 6: A sermon about Job in church, sings two of her favorite hymns, "Forward Through the Ages" and "Holy, Holy, Holy," a family walk before lunch, works on her stamp list: "We had loads of fun." Grampy brings her a fountain pen with her name in gold on it. "It's beautiful."

January 7: Writes with new fountain pen in her diary: "Isn't it lovely?" No dancing class, so she works on her stamps.

January 8: She is the tallest basketball player on her team, but they still lose 18–4.

January 9: Shows Donnie Russel her old pen hoping he will buy it. "I am trying to get a little extra money by sending stamps of my own (duplicates, of course) to various members of the stamp circle."

January 10: In Foods, the meatball "lay like a bowling ball and rolled To and Fro in my stomach! I really felt quite weighed down" [drawing of a ball inside a person's stomach with the caption "cannon ball in anatomy. Warm"].

January 11: A report on Edward MacDowell,[260] a hayride organized by the Unitarian Church: "The horses trotted slowly and we had loads of fun," dancing class. [Drawing of a horse pulling a hay wagon under a yellow moon with the caption "moonlight hayride."]

January 12: Wakes up with a cold, listens to radio programs, finishes reading *A Maid of Old Manhattan* (1917) by E. B. Knipe and A. A. Knipe: "It was a touching, thrilling novel about old days in New Amsterdam."

January 13: Runny nose, skips Sunday school and listens to the radio.

Letter to Margot Loungway: describes new diary, new stamps, asks about Margot's collection, mentions her enthusiasm for Halliburton's books, *Royal Road to Romance* (1925), *Flying Carpet* (1932), *The Glorious Adventure* (1927), and *New Worlds to Conquer* (1929)—"They're full of lovely expressions and descriptions."

January 14: In art, works on advertisements for book jackets [drawing hers], works on designs "in reliefs," learns a "nice new variation" in dancing class, returns home, works on her knitting spool.[261]

January 15: Reads a "thrilling book," *The Scarlet Pimpernel* (1905) by Baroness Orczy, an "exciting story about the French Revolution" [large drawing of a guillotine surrounded by decapitated heads with the caption, "Madame la 'Guillotine'"], a "D (!!)" on science test: "I will make it up tomorrow," works on knitting spool.

January 16: "As I walked home from my [piano] lesson I was awed by the frosty splendor of the evening and so made one of my best poems":

"A Winter Sunset," with a "sky from orange to gold / And then to copen shades," a moon hanging like "a globe of iridescent light."

Letter to "Dear Grampy": encloses "A Winter Sunset."

January 17: Makes a tuna wiggle in Foods: cream sauce, tuna, and peas on toast—"very good and filling."

January 18: Reads *The Scarlet Pimpernel* in the library, dishwashing with Ruthie Freeman after dinner, listens to the radio while working on her knitting spool, Ruthie explains the game of "Kiss and Tell" with Wayne Sterling, several pillow fights before "drifting to dreamland" at midnight. [Drawing of a couple kissing with the label "kiss and tell."]

January 19: Pillow fight in the morning, skating after breakfast, plays Monopoly, several drawings of a triangular sandwich with tuna, celery, and cream cheese, cheese rolls, a slice of cake, plays "some judo trick of a sort in the living room," makes molasses candy with Ruthie, "yum yum."

January 20: To church with Ruthie, daffodils and chrysanthemums on the altar, at home, devours "twenty pieces of molasses candy apiece [with Ruthie] while playing some hot games of social solitaire," listens to radio after Ruthie leaves, a delicious supper, to bed early.

January 21: Snow is shooting "furiously . . . from the leaden sky" [drawing], icy roads, newspapers headlining "dreadful strikes all over the United States."

January 22: Trees covered with ice, folk dancing in gym class.

January 23: Walks home from school with the sun shining through the ice on the trees, making it "shimmer like diamonds."

January 24: A "horrid" cornstarch pudding in Foods class, adds some "pretty colored yarn" to her knitting spool.

January 25: To the Nortons' after school, dinner in Boston, visits the Temple of Israel, draws Star of David, pulpit made of solid white marble, in between the two slabs are the ark and the Torah, the rabbi devotes a sermon to an explanation of Judaism: "I had a beautiful Time and was impressed."

January 26: Helps Grammy with housework, sees *Her Highness and the Bellboy*,[262] starring Hedy Lamarr, June Allyson, and Robert Walker, and *Dangerous Partners*[263] with James Craig "(pant! pant!)."

January 27: Church, homework.

January 28: At the Nortons', dancing class, at the observatory: "I will never forget my first view of Saturn through the telescope! I expected a little point of light. I gasped as I saw the three rings of moonlets whirling about the silvery planet" [drawing of Saturn]. Mars, "not so spectacular," looked like a "great yellow ball."

January 29: In English, the "sugary" Mrs. Washburn substitutes for Mrs. Warren. In science, watches "a very interesting movie on synthetic rubber.

It showed how, in many ways, it is better than natural rubber." A nice letter from Margot Loungway.

January 30: Elected chaplain in Guidance, "Marvelous" assembly program: square dancing and acrobatics (cartwheels, handstands, double somersaults, rope jumps) timed to drumbeats. Writes a report about it for *The Phillipian*.

January 31: Elected narrator in a dramatization of "Horatius at the Bridge," by Thomas Babington Macaulay,[264] "Boy! Did we have fun. . . . I reveled in those bloody lines." In Foods, "Fatso Lowe" [drawing of a smiling overweight woman] checks their notebooks.

February: Publishes "A Winter Sunset," *The Phillipian*, 6; "The Snowflake Star," *The Phillipian*, 9; "Assembly Lineup: January 30" (unattributed), *The Phillipian*, 12.

February 1: Brings her star map to school: "Miss Walker was very pleased with it."

Like other children of her generation, Plath was inspired by the travels of Richard Halliburton to think of worlds elsewhere.

February 2: Shops in Wellesley with Grammy, Warren, and Mother, who buys her a "beautiful gray jacket with white trimming," at Hathaway House to pick out books to be redeemed by Christmas certificates, chooses two one-dollar books by Halliburton, *New Worlds to Conquer* and *The Glorious Adventure*, coasting with Warren on the playground: "We had a super time. The hill rose shining, white and vacant. We flew down and the stinging wind brought tears to our eyes. It was glorious!"

February 3: After church and Sunday school, coasting with Warren down a hill that curves over a bridge spanning a brook: "I felt almost nothing could beat coasting. I'll never forget the feeling of those silver runners slashing through the crusty snow!" [drawing of a coasting figure].

February 4: "Ugh! Back to school once more. How quickly the weekends flit by!" After school, coasting: "Betsy [Powley] screamed when we swooped over the bridge for the first time."

February 5: Her team wins a basketball game 20–4.

February 6: Nine As and two Bs on her report card: "pretty good considering I have gotten all a's in my major subject for almost four straight years!"

February 7: Cuts out some Valentine's decorations for the Children's Convalescent Home.

February 8: Begins reading *The Dragon's Secret*[265] by August H. Seaman.

February 9: Reads Mark Twain's *The Mysterious Stranger* (1916).

February 10: Cuts ten more valentines for a total of fifty-five.

February 11: In art, working "like mad on our big paintings."

February 12: Wellesley Award talk about her stamp collection: "I was very nervous but tried not to show it and to be very pleasant. Boy! Am I glad its over!" Mrs. Warren tells her she has a "flair" for English. "She firmly believes I have a talent for oral talks."

February 13: In Guidance, stringing up "red valentine decorations on branches coated with white."

February 14: Plays spin the bottle with Perry Norton at the Girl Scouts's Valentine's Day party.

February 15: In social studies, relieved to have given her report on a current event.

February 16: Sleeps late, "Glorious vacation has begun at last." Finishes reading *Gone with the Wind* for the third time, listens to *The Silver Theater* and *The Life of Riley.*[266]

February 17: Reads comic strips, a walk with Mother and Grammy: "We went into Weston and walked down Bogle Street (which doesn't mean much to you). We rested on the bridge of a swollen brook and I had fun gazing at the amber depths," a slow walk home "under the smell of soft pine needles. It was a lovely day."

February 18: "Ah! O how lovely it is to sleep until 8:15 in unclouded dreams. You have no idea as to how it compares with grumpily getting up at six-forty-five!" Helps Grammy with housework and practices piano, at the Nortons', takes baby David William Norton for an hour's walk around the neighborhood, dancing class at the Wellesley Country Club, returns home "footsore."

February 19: Begins "Dream Book," recording five dreams, "two of which I thought superior enough to record. Dream 1: 'Rocket Ship to Mars.' Dream 2: 'The Sled that Coasted Around the World.'" Only in dreams could she have come up with the plot with "very satisfactory" endings, visits Aunt Dot's adopted baby, Bobby: "He loves to walk holding onto my fingers."

February 20: Goes to the Unitarian dance with Mr. Norton and Perry Norton, fun trying out "dancing combinations" learned in class. Perry and Sylvia enjoy talking about comets and planets.

February 21: Shovels the glistening snow in the driveway, purchases eighteen-cents worth of stamps, trying to economize, finishes reading *Granite Harbor*[267] by D. M. Bird.

February 22: The sun glare makes her tear up as she shovels out the driveway, completes reading *A Year to Grow* by Helene Conway.[268]

Letter to Margot Loungway: Asks how many stamps Margot has of famous poets and artists, mentions her high "expenditures" on stamps for the last two months and notes "my income only covers one-fourth of it," at work on "punk" diary, which has room for only eighteen lines of writing. She no longer tries to illustrate each page. Still taking piano, viola, and dancing lessons, active in her Scout troop, looks forward to summer camp:

"The three weeks I spent in Maine last summer (believe it or not) were the most fun I've ever had. I will never forget it." Describes her streamlined sled and coasting exploits.

February 23: Wears sunglasses while shoveling the driveway.

February 24: Awful weather (sleeting), Mother shampoos her hair and, while it is drying, listens to the radio.

February 25: In art, works on "charcoal figure sketches from life."

February 26: In English, presents her book report on Raymond Ditmars,[269] sore after gymnastics routines, her basketball team wins "26–8!!!!"

February 27: A lecture on posture in Guidance, 52.5 percent on math paper: "Shh! Don't tell anyone."

February 28: "This morning was the most beautiful one I've ever seen. It rained last night and it froze. The trees were stiffly bent under the weight of branches coated with ice. The snow (as shiny as glass) was coated with a glossy crust."

March 1: In social studies, works on World War I notebooks.

March 2: A "furious sore throat," listens to the radio, and reads *New Worlds to Conquer*.

March 3: A miserable cold: "My nose is running so fast that I've already given it hundreds of blows and that hasn't even stopped it! (Laughter please!)." Draws and listens to the radio.

March 4: Angry about missing school, looks over *Gone with the Wind* while listening to *The Strange Romance of Evelyn Winters*[270] and *Bulldog Drummond*.[271]

March 5: School reports on Woodrow Wilson's Fourteen Points and the League of Nations, listens to the radio: "I went to bed with a spinning brain."

March 6: Makeup assignments at school, plays volleyball, 100 percent on her math makeup test.

March 7: Makes pie crusts, lemon filling, and meringue in Foods: "It really was quite good."

March 8: In English, notices her "eyes spinning and the black and white flashes grew worse." Feels better after a visit to the nurse's office and a three-quarters-hour rest, resumes her studies, has play rehearsal in assembly hall.

March 9: Walks to school, puts too much sugar in her eggnog ("sugared slime!"), goes through the "tortures" of hair washing, and listens to the radio while hair dries.

March 10: Reads newspaper, homework on World War I, listens to *Charlie McCarthy* while munching cheese.

March 11: "Back to the old prison once more! How those weekends do flit by!" After school, play rehearsal.

March 12: Writes paragraph about Manchuria in current events class.

March 13: In assembly, a speaker from the Boston FBI shows a movie of one case and is bombarded with questions, sees *The Mikado* (1939) at Fessenden School with Mrs. Eaton: "Super."

March 14: In Foods, makes gingerbread and whipped cream, play rehearsal after school.

March 15: Interesting movie in science about "how nature protects her animals."

March 16: Out selling tickets to the play.

March 17: Dessert at the country club: a "fifth of an apple pie with a big scoop of icecream and milk and two little bonbons," visits Aunt Dot, Bobby Schober can now walk and say "Ma-Ma, Da-Da, and Bow-Wow. He is just a precious baby."

March 18: Sells two more play tickets, does a drawing of a girl with a book looking at a clock.

March 19: Folk dancing in gym class.

March 20: In assembly, a "corny" play about the Constitution: "It would have been better if one of the characters had stayed 'in' his part seriously." Miss Siok displays Sylvia's World War I notebook much to Sylvia's embarrassment. Last piano lesson—"too much with viola and all."

March 21: In cooking class, makes a "yummy butter cake with white frosting," does a drawing of a two-layer cake, her basketball team loses 22–12.

March 22: Mrs. Warren tells Sylvia "privately" that she should attend college on a scholarship, "my assignments were all of what could be expected by some college . . . !" Walks with Aunt Dot's Bobby, "so sweet + has skin like rose petals."

March 23: With Mother, visits a "beautiful" Boston flower show, an "old Cape Cob herb garden, a garden of gold Acacia tress with green leaves, moss and a waterfall, + a rose room, a vegetable garden, a frond and rhododendron" and an "orchid room," she has a perfect silhouette made of herself.

March 24: In church, with "white Cala lilies with gold centers and shiny green leaves" [drawing], walking on Wellesley campus and spots a "new penny glimmering" and hangs over a cement platform poking at it with a stick that Warren gives her for retrieving the penny: "Happy me!"

March 25: "Ugh! I am getting very eager for vacation."

March 26: With Prissy Steele, reports on Halliburton's books *The Glorious Adventure* and *New Worlds to Conquer*, "Mum came home with a neat spring hat and perfectly lovely box coat."[272]

March 27: Bob Zock loans her *Richard Halliburton's Complete Book of Marvels* (1941) with a picture of Halliburton on the back. "I am in love with him. I feel as though I understand him. (Being on his fourth book.)"

March 28: A five-mile Girl Scout hike, stopping off at Bendslev's for a "lemon and lime," wears her hair "in a new way" [drawings of old hairdo and new, with no more bangs]. Mowgli's birthday.

March 29: Spends the night at Aunt Dot's, calls her mother before bedtime.

March 30: Sketches Bobby Schober, at home, a fire in the neighbor's garage: "Mum rang the fire alarm (thrill, thrill) and screaming engines rushed here and put it out!!!!!"

March 31: A sore throat, no Sunday school, listens to *Blondie*[273] before bed.

April: Publishes "Spring Song," *The Phillipian*, 13.

April 1: "I have just been through a serious operation (gizzards removed) and have lost my two million dollar pearl brooch set in carved jade. APRIL FOOL! (Haw!)" Reads *Barberry Gate* by Jane D. Abbott.[274]

April 2: John Stenberg tells her he has twenty-one thousand stamps. She has one thousand. "I can't wait for vacation to begin. The two or three weeks before holidays drag by so slowly!"

April 3: Rehearsal for drama club play.

April 4: "I can't wait to go to Winthrop on April 13!"

April 5: Elected vice president in English.

April 6: Checks out *Island Adventure*[275] and *Career for Jennifer*,[276] both by Adele de Leeuw, from the library. Listens to *Kitty Foyle*.[277]

April 7: Dreading her report on American art in the nineteenth and twentieth centuries. Listens to *The Great Gildersleeve* and *Jack Benny*[278] and then recites her report for her mother.

Already the life of an artist beckons.

April 8: Dreams about the "lives and works etc. of those American artists," two minutes of soap operas give her a headache.

April 9: In bed with a sore throat, her mother brings "piles of assignments" from school.

April 10: Grammy drives her to school with ten pounds of books, makes a birthday card for Mother.

April 11: Walks to the bus stop with a cute boy, John Stenberg, and has a "very interesting talk about stamps," in assembly, Bill C. acts out *The Lost Weekend* at the piano, sending Margie and Sylvia into "fits of laughter. . . . He looked the part—but def!" [Drawing of the performance.]

April 12: Dances with several boys in Donnie Russel's basement. "Dick C. asked me to sit on the couch for two beside him (is he fast!) his arm was conveniently draped over it. Dick Mills picked that moment to jump up and say 'Dancer.'" [Drawing of a heart with a couch inside it.]

April 13: Over at Ruthie's house in Winthrop, meets "my long-lost friend, Wayne Sterling. . . . Oh boy! (It's all I can say.)" They play croquet with Ruthie and David Freeman. The girls steal the boys' bikes, and later the boys climb on the roof and look in the bedroom window and start to climb in.

April 14: Wayne Sterling walks with Sylvia and Ruthie to Sunday school. "Oh! Is he cute!"

April 15: Wayne calls from Boy Scout camp. He returns, and they ride bikes together. Mrs. Freeman, David Freeman, and Wayne accompany Sylvia to the bus stop. "It's certainly nice to have two boys attentive at once—specially Wayne."

April 16: Dreams about Wayne, a "very, very sighful weekend," a "spooky and breath taking" climb up the "famous" Wellesley College tower: "OH! The view! Down below White Houses and shimmering lakes dotted a minia-ture countryside criss-crossed by ribbon-like roads—Thrilling! But I missed boys company." [Drawing of tower's spiral stairs.]

Writes to Mrs. Freeman, thanking her for the "super-wonderful time," describes the 250 steps to the Wellesley College tower after an elevator took her and Prissy Steele up four floors. They could hardly squeeze through the small and triangular "conical structure." Mentions "two ant like girls strolling chummily on the walk below. (I do hope that they don't mind the comparison.)"

April 17: "This morning mum woke me up at 7:00 by talking in her sleep."

April 18: "Last night I had the most terrible nightmares!"

April 19: A sleep over at Joan Beals's house, plays ping-pong with Joan, Dash, and Betsy Powley: "It was the first time that I had played and learned quite a bit. Betsy and I slept in a double bed in a room by ourselves. We two did not go to sleep till morning and told each other about Wayne [Sterling] and Bill et cetera."

April 20: Sees *Beloved Enemy*,[279] starring Merle Oberon and Brian Aherne—"Oh! Hubba, Hubba!"—and Dave Niven. The picture was about the struggle between France and England. "It was so beautiful that I cried during parts. The other feature was 'Come and Get It'[280]—A fair logging picture."

April 21: Easter service: draws a picture of the church, with organ, chair, and pastor. Slips on the floor while singing, and the pastor says: "Bless him who keeps ye from falling." Sylvia and Betsy Powley have to stifle "convul-sions of laughter."

April 22: "I felt so strange back in school again. Somehow I enjoy the old routine." Mentions publication of "Spring Song."

April 23: Grampy gives her a dollar for an essay in *The Philippian*.

April 24: A "grueling" play rehearsal.

April 25: In Foods, makes "delicious, juicy, elastic, flavorful rich brownies which, after all this explaining, I didn't eat. (I only took a little half.)" Works on circus drawing of a juggler "passing through a country town." Leaves her wallet on the Manor Avenue bus.

April 26: Gets up early for Mother's birthday. Presents: underpants, seven dollars from her camp fund with an "original card." The bus driver returns her wallet. "I was never so happy I came home joyous."

April 27: Presents Warren with stamps for his birthday. Studies her part in the play.

April 28: Sees Laurence Olivier's *Henry V* at Boston's Esquire Theatre: "It was beautiful and in technicolor."

April 29: "Today the most wonderful thing happened!" Sends in original "picturesque speech" to *Reader's Digest*, expects to be "overwhelmingly happy if I'd get any published: 'A milkweed parachute hitchhiked on a passing breeze.' It may sound amateurish to you later, but to me it sounded pretty good (to me that is!)."

April 30: "Today has been just about the worst in my life so far." Her ten-dollar fountain pen has been stolen. Fears she will never get it back: "I feel as bitter as gall and as awful as salt tears. My whole world has turned gray and black." Returns home and looks at the flowers.

May 1: The play, *The Patchwork Quilt*, is "quite a success," puts a notice up in the cafeteria about her lost pen, Mr. Thistle tells her she is a new "star" in dramatics and asks her to join the club. "I had a very complimentary day."

May 2: Eats some "lovely cream-puffs" she has made in Foods.

May 3: Reads *Jenny's Secret Island* by Phillis Garrard.[281]

Typescript—"A May Morning." {PM}

May 4: Dips her hands in the pond's "slime and ooze" to catch tadpoles, Warren helps her catch ten pollywogs, listens to "Oh! What It Seemed to Be!" on the *Your Hit Parade*.

May 5: Mentions "original speech and patter": "Her eyelashes brushed away the last cobwebs of slumber," "Pink scarves of phlox carelessly draped over the wall."

May 6: "Today was one great rush for me." Heavy homework, orchestra rehearsal, viola lesson, play report on J. Preston Peabody's *The Piper*.[282]

May 7: Mrs. Warren tells Sylvia she gave her report on *The Piper* "beautifully." A "mortally wounded knee" in after school sports: "To my delight it bled all over the bus and drew pitying attention and sighs."

May 8: Reads some *National Geographic*: "very interesting."

May 9: Includes a clipping from *The Townman*, listing her in the music festival as playing the viola.

May 10: Sees *The Bandit of Sherwood Forest*,[283] starring Cornel Wilde ("m-m-m") and *Masquerade in Mexico*,[284] with Dorothy Lamour and Arturo de Cordova: "Both pictures were excellent and I had a very nice time. The first movie was in technicolor."

May 11: With Prissy Steele, takes the bus to the Needham music festival: "The only bright spots were our playing and the parade." *Finlandia* was "marvelous! It sounded like waves pounding on the wet beach, tossing up mists of spray with the theme of lightning and thunder rising through the powerful melody. For two of the encores [Arthur] Fiedler conducted the 'Flight of the Bumblebee,' wonderful for strings, and 'The surrey with the Fringe on Top,' complete with sound effects. Perfect time!"

May 12: Does a report on Panama for social studies, listens to "some pleasant murder-mysteries featuring mad families and jealous heirs," tunes into *The Great Gildersleeve* and *Jack Benny*. "The murder programs told on me when, after Warren and I were alone in the house, he had to tuck <u>me</u> in bed!"

May 13: Draws figures in art, concentrates on a "bathing scene" with "some of my pretty girls."

May 14: Works on "The Pond in Spring" for *The Phillipian*.

May 15: Reads "Evangeline."[285]

May 16: In cooking class, enjoys the food, including chocolate cake and white frosting: "it was really nice, had not my complexion-conscience given me a terrible scolding."

May 17: At Margot Loungway's. "She is quite talented, (in case she hasn't already told you!) and gave me the great privilege of listening to her play the piano."

Typescript—"The Mummy's Tomb." {PM}

May 18: Writes a "frightful murder-mystery," "The Mummy's Tomb," hops in bed with Margot, and they torture each other "by reading aloud our stories."

May 19: At Margot's, Sylvia works on a "smuggler's story," "On the Penthouse Roof."

May 20: "Just think Diary, only four more weeks of school!" Has a good laugh with Betsy Powley when Miss Sanborn says to the class, "Sylvia is filling her drawing with interesting shapes." Types up "The Mummy's Tomb" and notes that "On the Penthouse Roof" "turned out terrible," starts a new, "more descriptive," story.

May 21: A miserable rainy day, "a gloomy atmosphere of foreboding pervaded the chill air. (I get those expressions from my stories.)"

May 22: Sits on the porch writing a two-page story, "A May Morning," "quite a neat job for the first time, if I do say so. I have the idea of a beautiful long fairy tale in mind."

May 23: Appears in a radio play directed by Donnie Russel, who decides to make it funny but overdoes it.

May 24: Sylvia does homework in study periods, has fun in orchestra, at the Masonic Temple for International Order of the Rainbow for Girls.[286] "It was beautiful. The love between gowned sisters was touching. There was dancing afterward, mainly girl with girl."

May 25: Before lunch, begins work on a long story: "When I went out again it had mysteriously disappeared!"

May 26: Sings three of her favorite hymns in church.

Letter to Margot Loungway: "My mother is shocked and horrified at the fact that it is over a week since I have written to you!" Sylvia mentions she has been writing stories but should have written to thank Margot for the "perfectly wonderful time that I had over your house!" Describes her stories and adds a line to one of Margot's: "The delicious smell of frying flesh reached my nostrils."

May 27: "Dear Diary—Last night I had the queerest dream about Wayne and Margot!" Home from school "soaking wet and angry with the world in general."

May 28: A lot of extra work in hopes of getting a "high A."

May 29: In assembly, a soldier speaks about "incidents of war and victory overseas, not forgetting to mention the long rows of white crosses filling the many green clearings holding the American and allied dead. It was really quite sad. Oh! But I do hope that there will be no more wars."

May 30: Finishes a notebook for social studies: "The World and the United States."

May 31: Mr. Leach drives Prissy Steele and Sylvia to the bus stop, sits in the back with Dick Knight [drawing of a heart]. "He is so handsome and in the tenth grade too. He has dark hair and eyes, and plays the sousaphone. He's so friendly to me" [drawing of three hearts].

June 1: A double bill: Maureen O'Hara and Paul Henreid in *The Spanish Main*[287] and *The Enchanted Forest*,[288] which was "a beautiful story, including many trained animals." Earns fifty cents for babysitting two boys, a five-year-old and one-year-old: "I had quite a time when the little one refused to go to bed, the big one saw that he got in."

The entry below may pinpoint the beginning of Plath's interest in attending Smith College. Mary Ellen Chase became one of Plath's mentors at Smith and arranged for Plath to teach there.

June 2: Reads *A Goodly Heritage* (1945) by Chase for a book report.

June 3: Sleeps "amid gruesome nightmares."

June 4: Volunteers to give her oral presentation first and is made chairman. "Boy! What a job!" Everyone begs her "<u>not</u> to call on them," and when she did, it was as if she had "shot them!" She gets an A+ for her social studies notebooks. After so much work, she thinks she deserves it.

June 5: Hail bounces "up and down on the grass and danced on the roof and covered the street," Sylvia rushes with Warren from window to window to watch.

June 6: "Today was my big day." She wears a pale-blue evening dress for the occasion, a "picturesque scene; the blue gowns of the seniors, and the evening dress of the orchestra and guests. The guest speaker was wonderful—Mrs. Horton, head of Wellesley college." Lovely music and a flower-decked stage: "I had a thrilling time."

June 7: "Guess What! Mother has bought me a new fountain pen to replace the one that was stolen! It is an exact duplicate, save for a slightly thicker point." After school reads all of Jules Verne's *Twenty Thousand Leagues Under the Sea* (1870).

June 8: Almost finishes Jules Verne's *Around the World in Eighty Days* (1872).

June 9: A beautiful day with an "airy sky . . . deep, intense blue, and the wind kept 'shushing' through the leafy trees."

June 10: In music, the class listens to the whole *The Nutcracker Suite*.

June 11: Sylvia goes to Filene's after school to get a white jersey and a two-piece bathing suit, a sunshade, and blue and white platform play shoes [drawing of purchases]. "I came home very pleased."

June 12: The only eighth grader to receive a "fourth letter! . . . in the shape of a pennant" [drawing of a Wellesley pennant]. At home, puts the pennant over her bookcase.

June 13: Reads *Pride and Prejudice* (1813), enjoying it "greatly. Of course the artificial speeches they made in those days are rather boring."

June 14: Autographs issues of *The Philippian*, rowing, and tanning [described in drawings].

June 15: Mows the side lawn and trims it. "It was surely some job." In the "comfortable perch" of her apple tree, begins reading *At the Back of the North Wind*[289] by George MacDonald, "one of my favorite authors."

June 16: Cleans house while Mother and Grammy are at church, goes with Warren to get the Sunday paper, digs up some ferns and lady slippers at the pond for her woodland garden.

June 17: Hangs out the wash, a viola lesson, finishes *At the Back of the North Wind*, "a lovely story."

June 18: A 103-degree fever, brings home six books from the library, including Adele de Leeuw's *Doctor Ellen*.[290]

June 19: Finishes *Doctor Ellen*, begins *Mystery in Blue*[291] by Gertrude Mallette, "rather tedious reading."

June 20: Gets a sunburn while reading Adele de Leeuw's *With a High Heart.*[292] "She ranks among my favorite authors. Most of her books are about girls beginning their life work. She must be exceptionally intelligent for she writes about many different careers in very professional language."

June 21, 7:30 a.m.: Gets up to do early marketing with Grammy.

Margot Loungway visits: "I was surprised to see how she had grown (sideways, not up.) She is the only specimen of the zombie that I have seen so rough and masculine."

June 22: Sylvia and Margot read their stories to each other. Margot's have good plots but unnatural characters. Talk about stamps with Warren, a picnic lunch, goes to Wellesley College on bikes, Sylvia and Margot begin to write their autobiographies before biking home. "Margot ganged up against me with Warren and they contented themselves with being as annoying as possible. She certainly enjoys being very odd and mean. I guess she can't help it though. Margot is my favorite friend for all her oddities."

Typescript—"Stardust." {PM}

June 23: A glorious, sunny day, the air "filled with the fragrant scent of clover and fresh grass." Diary writing, stories after breakfast, begins a second chapter of "Stardust" about "Nancy and Star's visit to the Sea Queen's Palace." "The first chapter was the one that was stolen or mysteriously spirited away. So I am going to write it over again later." Margot won't tell her the title of her story. "She is some character."

June 24: Working on "Stardust," mows half the lawn, upstairs to finish typing "Stardust."

June 25: Alone in the house with Warren, reads her story to him and is "greatly surprised at his eloquent praise of it. He described it with gestures and all that, so I was quite happy."

June 26: A "pleasant job of meeting mother in Boston and going to the dentist's." Toothaches from eating sweets: "As he was filling the third [cavity], he found the fourth. When he picked at it I practically collapsed with the pain." The dentist leaves the room and comes back with a bag of false teeth. "You can imagine how relieved I was when a woman came in and paid for them!"

June 27: Thrilled to receive a letter from a distant thirteen-year-old relative in Austria who wants to correspond: "I jumped at the chance and immediately sat down and wrote her a long four page letter."[293]

June 28: Writes to Ruth Geisel[294] and Margot Loungway, finishes packing duffel bag and suitcase, leaves for Camp Helen Storrow tomorrow.

Letter to Margot Loungway: Describes getting into a crowd of people watching a "frenzied criminal, being handcuffed by two grim police men. . . . A little shiver ran up my spine as I thought how it easily might have been you." A screaming paddy wagon arrives as Mother drags her away, "fearful it might have some influence on me." Mentions letter from Austria written by "my grandfather's half-sister's granddaughter (figure that out for me)." Wants to know about Margot's stories, hopes they can get together for some part of the summer. "Can't you just see us lying on soft pine needles and writing best-sellers in the quiet serenity of the woods?"

June 29: A farewell trip to Morses Pond: "The water was wonderful, only I couldn't swim very well because my hair always got in my face."

Postcard to "Dearest Mother": "Oh! Camp certainly is wonderful." The water is like "liquid crystal," shares a cabin with Betsy Powley that they have fixed up. "We didn't go to sleep for a while because of listening to the wind and watching fireflies. xxxx Sylvia."

June 30: Unpacking. Supper: "Boy! Was I hungry. There wasn't much to eat either." After taps, Betsy gets into her bed, and they tell jokes while the counselors "prowled outside."

July 1: Complains about the meals: toast that tastes like "scorched board." Swimming, crafts, painting, swimming, supper, and a "hilarious barn dance before flopping into our cabins to go to bed."

Postcard to "Dear Mummy": recounts activities, "Love, Remember to save the funnies."

July 2: Burnt breakfast and messy cookout lunch, one girl "upchucked at supper," rewrites first chapter of "Stardust," rainy and damp.

Postcard to "Dear Mother": Happy with sketch pad and arts and crafts, "I am having such fun."

Letter to "Dear Grammy": "Happy BIRTHDAY!" [drawing of a floral bouquet].

July 3: "Today was really something!" Betsy and Sylvia awake after Gloria sprinkles water on them, starting a water fight, a breakfast cookout, boating, swimming: "Marilyn [Fraser] had fun doing a 'Water Ballet' (if you could call it that.)" Sylvia has a hysterical laughing fit that turns into crying after the growth on her nose bleeds when the bandage is taken off. A nurse stops the bleeding. "Betsy [Powley] and Gayle were positive that I was loony and were disappointed to find that I was perfectly sane."

July 4: "Today was glorious." Boating, rowing, practicing diving: "I certainly need practice." A "wonderful" beach campfire, a gold and red sunset, ice cream.

July 3–4: Letter to "Dear Mother": Mentions her mother's lovely letter and Warren's "little bit of humor," bad fish for dinner leads to vomiting for a fourth of the camp (thirty people), lots of friends to whom she has given away some of her paintings, eats well but the food is "almost as bad as Uncle Frank's dog biscuits," explains her hysterical laughing/crying fit. She was told to go to the nurse "quick! Or you'll get cancer," but the "tumor" is actually a pimple. Plays badminton: "My stroke is really atrocious." Rehearsing for a minstrel show: she will guest star as Frank Sinatra. "I have, so they say, the perfect build. However I have the voice of a lovesick horse, and can you imagine me getting out on the floor wailing 'Prisoner of Love' off key!" She doesn't want to do it but will be a "good sport." Some good ideas for poems. "We had the most beautifully cobweb almost bigger than me, out in front of our cabin between two trees. All the cobwebs were dew spangled, and were draped about in misty beauty all over the place."

Postcard to "Dear Mother": dives from a rock that ends in a belly flop.

July 5: Sunbathing with a little burn that feels better with an application of toothpaste, a letter and postcard from Mother, rehearsal for minstrel show.

Postcard to "Dear Mother": on the beach singing songs around the campfire, enjoys rowing.

Letter to "Dear Mater": "I am in a very good mood today, which is rather odd, because my caper was to clean out the latrines." Describes enormous meals of noodle soup, potatoes and cabbage, salad, cheese, peas, eggs, three bowls of custard, a cup of milk, two of cocoa. "I'm eating so much, no matter what, or how horrible it is, that I can hardly walk after each meal."

July 6: A rainy "miserable day." Rehearses show and listens to radio in Skipper's cabin.

July 7: A sketching trip. A good meal of chicken, mashed potatoes, peas, ice cream, and cupcake.

Letter to "Dear Mother": Mentions getting letters from Grammy, Grampy, Uncle Frank and Aunt Louise. "I do not like to tell you, but I have come down with a miserable cold. I am so mad!" The minstrel/variety show was a hit: "I was dressed in white men's shirt, gray slacks, bow tie, and jacket with my hair pulled back for Frankie. I leaned against the piano for my microphone was a broom with a cup on top" [drawing]. She opened her mouth, but Betsy Powley actually did the singing. When she stopped to blow her nose, Betsy kept singing, uses her cold as an excuse so no one will sleep in her bed.

July 8: Cold is almost gone, sunbathes, a nosebag lunch after rowing a boat.

Letter to "Dear, Dear, Mother": Compares her drawings to those of other campers—"only one came up to mine." Making a nut spoon in crafts that she will give to Aunt Dot if it turns out nice, misses camping out on the beach because of her cold, has an infected, ingrown toenail.

July 9: A lovely, if cold day, works on costumes for masquerade, Betsy Powley is to be her mother and Sylvia her daughter in 1890. "Betsy made a black mosquito netting blouse. I made a long white peplum skirt.[295] I wore my hair up with a white flower in it. Betsy looked adorable all in white ruffles."

Letter to "Dear Grammy and Grampy": Thanks them for sending "nice letters." Describes her activities, including a "sketching trip," claims the food is good "only we aren't allowed to fill up on bread and potatoes, which I try to do. Draws the costumes for the masquerade, concludes by promising to write more and draws a picture of a smiling female.

Letter to Mother: Details her expenditures in camp, purchases of crafts materials, a book, postcards, and sketch pad. Describes dressing for the masquerade. "Everybody was aghast that Betsy [Powley] and I had actually made use a finished product in a few hours." Others dress up as a sultan, an Arab, a pirate, and Black people. Wins second prize for "best old-fashioned and well made costume!"

July 10: Works on a shadowgraph,[296] "rotten" lunch, softball.

Letter to "Dear Mother": During a thunderstorm Betsy Powley takes a "flying leap" into Sylvia's bed.

July 10–11: Letter to "Mother": "I felt almost like crying to hear you had not gotten a letter from me for a week!" She has written five letters and will number them from now on. Complains about tasteless meals, works on the camp newspaper, the next day a hike around the lake in cold and nasty weather, scared at night by a "most pitiful, and yet terrible cry." She has nightmares. "Almost anything can happen here. I wouldn't be surprised to hear Superman knocking at the door."

July 11: A five-mile hike that turns into eight miles with detours lasting four and a half hours

Letter to "Dear Mummie": Complains about her aching feet after the hike, mentions seeing a deer "so graceful it took my breath away." Her feet are covered with blisters.

July 12: A nature walk, listens to bird calls.

Continues letter to Mother, mentions holding a tiny garter snake while the other girls scream and back away: "It felt so nice slithering through my hands, all slippery. . . . My! I certainly like snakes, there's something about them that fascinates me." Another short sketching trip and a visit to a family graveyard: "I was so interested in the names and dates on the old stones, that I felt quite subdued and rather filled with the tragedy that pervaded the air."

July 13: "Today was my idea of a perfect day." Loves the wild and windy day, battling the waves.

Letter to "Dearest Mother": Finishes her nut spoon, now noted to be for her grandparents (instead of her aunt), mentions the two dollars her grandparents have sent, which she uses to purchase books and crafts, expects a visit from her grandparents: "I hope that they bring fruit if they can, for what we get here is mainly sour and hard." Still loves camp "for all its faults."

July 14: An exciting day, expecting the arrival of new campers, Betsy Powley is moving out, and Ruth Freeman is moving in.

July 15: "I was jumping for joy to find two cards and two big fat letters from my mother, including five good snaps of me, and some ribbons, and a stamp offer."

Letter to "Dear Grammy and Grampy": Delighted about the two dollars from them: "I never expected anything like it." She will have fun now that Ruth has arrived, complains about ingrown toenails, which have been soaked in "boiling sulfa-naphthol or something like that."

July 16: Publishes her impression of camp in the camp newspaper. She has already written a poem about the lake.

Letter to "Dearest, Most-Revered Twice Honored Mater": Thanks her for the letters and photographs—"Why you sent that glamorous one of me hunched over, and snoring under the maple tree, I will never know." Encloses her poem about the lake "a creature / Quiet, yet wild. / Rough and yet gentle— / An untamed child."

July 17: Joins a two-mile hike to a blueberry farm, paid ten cents a quart for what she picks, earning one dollar and a sunburn. Calls the blueberries the "most wonderful things I have ever seen—rows and rows of laden bushes." She is happy she can "earn some money, even though it is not much, it helps!" Tired but joyous, sleeps well.

July 18: Works on two poems.

Letter to Margot Loungway: "It was very good thinking on your part to invite Mater and Warren up while I'm away, so I won't have to come. I do hope you show this newsy letter to my Mater so I won't have to bother to write her."

July 19: Swims twelve lengths of sidestroke, sketching trip to cove beach: "I made a rather nice one of a shed."

Letter to "Dear Mother": Submits two poems to camp newspaper— "The editor, who evidently did not think too much of me, went as far as to say they were excellent!" Encloses "Morning of Mist": "Frail cobwebs of lacy filigree / Clutched by gnarled fingers / Of a tree." She is receiving her mother's daily cards "joyfully. Your latest one sounded like a lovely poem in blank verse."

Another sketching trip.

July 20: Letter to "Dear Mother": Finishing a "tremendous project" in crafts. "The end of camp is drawing to a close so speedily, that I'm afraid that I'll wake up some morning soon, and find Grammy saying, 'Better get up! Time for school.'" Praises Ruth Freeman's excellent article for the camp newspaper about blueberrying. "The sun is shining and a cool breeze is swishing through the trees and rippling up the lake." A sketching trip tomorrow. "I am now dressed in my blue shorts, white belt, socks, jersey, and saddle shoes, writing to you during rest hour while waiting for grammy and grampy to arrive." Starchy diet and poorly prepared food.

"Dear Diary": Grammy and Grampy visit bringing peaches, cherries, oranges, plums, and Ritz crackers. Gives Grampy the nut spoon. "He was very pleased."

July 21: Eats a pound of cherries and four and a half plums apiece with Ruthie, sings "Oh! God our Help in Ages Past" and "Nearer My God to Thee" in chapel.

Letter to Mother: Mentions how "goggle-eyed" she was over all the fruit Grammy and Grampy brought—"Tears fill my eyes at the thought of having such wonderfully grand grand parents! . . . It will be rather sad to get away from camp, but I will be very glad to get to my own little mummie's house."

July 22: A "red letter day": learns how to dive, tips the canoe over in the lake, jumps out, and turns it over.

Letter to "Dear Mother": Very excited about her improved diving. A counselor asks her to "draw some ideas for the cover of the paper, so I did." Misses fresh vegetables.

July 23: In crafts, finishes a plate for her mother with a "hammered 'A' in the center," works on a speech she will give at the banquet.

July 24: A hike to Fisherman's Cove, "PJ party ended in disaster."

July 25: A good meal at the banquet: roast beef, corn on the cob, apple salad, mashed potatoes, grapefruit, gravy, rolls, butter, and ice cream. "My report was evidently enjoyed the most, because they laughed in the right places, and I got plenty of applause." {PM}

Letter to "Dear Mother": "I have been overwhelmingly busy the past few days." Hiking to Fisherman's Cove—"How I love the ocean! We then hunted for sea creatures in the shallow warm pools between the rocks." At her first banquet with a "placecard and everything."

Now classified as an "intermediate swimmer."

July 26: Last day at camp, windy two-hour boat trip across the lake.

July 27: Sad to leave "all the wonderful friends I've made," but also happy to return to "dear old Wellesley." After leaving camp, exchanges visits with Ruth Freeman in Wellesley and Winthrop, topics of discussion: writing and boys. Illustrates her poems in an anthology, *Poems by Sylvia Plath*.

July 28: A "rather dull" day.

July 29: Lunch with Grammy at the country club: steak and potatoes, grilled tomatoes, "superb Italian squash cut paper thin and fried in butter," fresh peach pie à la mode, and a "tall glass of fresh, creamy milk." Staggers away with "utmost satisfactions stealing over me."

July 29–August 2: Letter to Margot Loungway: Apologizes for not writing, busy at camp with newspaper, banquet, and learning how to dive as well as rowing and hiking. "The lake water is always changing. It is more or less translucent and the white sand beneath its depths gives a rather odd color effect. Sometimes it is mirror and blue, and on other times a wild emerald green with tossing sprays of foam and rough white caps." Good to be home in her own cozy little "matchbox," starts typing lessons with Mother, works on story, "Stardust," buys oil paints in Boston and her mother gives her four canvases, asks about Margot's diary: "Sometimes mine is rather tiresome, but on the whole I really enjoy it." Annoyed with stamp companies that keep sending the same stamps for approval, loves wearing the "darling dress" Margot gave her, with "rickrack[297] on it [drawing]. . . . My mother is now dramatically plowing through the 'Tale of Two Cities'—reading aloud to my brother—who sits wide-eyed in bed, gnawing anxiously on the sheets waiting for her to go on" [drawing of wide-eyed boy and woman]. Sometimes the floor shakes as Warren bounces around in his excitement.

July 30: In Boston, purchases oil paints and a dark-brown jersey dress with "drawstring kellygreen bows [drawing of dress]. I also bought a darling black and white haltertop" [drawing]. At home, paints a scene—"what fun!"—of "three birches on a hillside, mountains in back."

July 31: Helps her mother can eight quarts of peaches, finishes the "last touches on my oil painting. (Sounds professional, doesn't it!) I certainly get a thrill out of painting in oils."

August 1: Works on a painting of a bowl of zinnias, which turns out better than she thought with just the right colors, plays cards with Warren and David Freeman.

August 2: "Today was another one of those miserable days where the wind howls like a lost child, and sheets of rain beat against the window." Enjoys her typing lessons.

August 3: Another typing lesson, Mother makes "darling applesauce cakes," takes eight of them to Betsy Powley's. They play cards until it is pitch-dark outside. Bikes home and is relieved and happy to see a "familiar figure ahead," her mother coming to meet her.

August 4: Feeling "off," bikes to get the paper and plays Monopoly with Warren, a "wonderful time" playing spit at Betsy's. The "Powley's are so nice."

August 5: A fun visit from Ruthie Freeman, after lunch, swimming at Morses Pond: "I <u>dove</u> off the low diving board for the first time in my life. It was such fun." At Betsy Powley's after supper.

August 6: Another "glorious day," plays a long game of Monopoly with Ruthie and Warren, to Morses Pond, swimming, diving.

August 7: Miserable outside, fun inside playing spit with Ruthie and Warren, eating Mother's "delicious banana bread."

August 8: Swimming, diving, Mr. Powley shows them how to play hearts,[298] "which is certainly full of suspense." After a wonderful time at the Powleys', Sylvia and Ruthie have a "hair raising time riding home in the dark."

August 9: Sad that Ruthie left after lunch but will see her Wednesday.

August 10: Gets down to work and writes letters,[299] a grand time taking speed tests for typing.

August 11: Cleans out bookcase and trunk: "It was really some job." Writes four-page letter to Anne Brown,[300] listens to *Meet Corliss Archer*,[301] "which was sorta' nutty."

August 12: Begins building a hut at Betsy Powley's.

August 13: Miserable, too many typing errors. Plays tripoli[302] at Betsy's.

August 14: Packs up for a trip to Winthrop to see the Freemans, sleeps in a big double bed with Ruthie, who is "a pain. She was mean, and made me feel sick."

August 15: Swims in the salty surf, walks to the end of a jetty, watches the "green, foamy water swirl about in strong currents."

August 16: Makes ice cream with Ruthie Freeman.

August 17: Back home, picks and helps can pole beans.

August 18: "Ah! Today is the kind of day that you can feel ambitious in." Mother praises her dives, but Sylvia feels she needs to get more spring into them. "It is such fun to cut the water like a knife."

August 19: A "tawny, miserable day," sleeps until 11:00 a.m., falls in love with a honey-colored, six-week-old cocker spaniel and draws a sketch of him sleeping.

August 20: Enjoys typing for almost two hours in the morning, rakes the lawn, diving at Morses Pond.

August 21: Typing at thirty-one words a minute with only one error, reads *Wuthering Heights* (1847).

August 22: Rereads *New Worlds for Josie*[303] in bed.

August 23: Spends the morning arranging the living room for a photo shoot using Betsy Powley's new camera: "After all this painstaking work we found that the shutter of the camera did not work right! Boy were we mad. Mum gave us some fresh gingerbread to cheer us up."

August 24: Swims at Morses Pond: "We watched eagerly when Floyd Robinson, a well built Negroe demonstrated four dives in perfect form. His summersaults were especially spectacular." Over to Betsy Powley's house: "Seemed like all we did was criticize every other girl in Wellesley."

August 25: Wakes up with a temperature over one hundred and a sore throat, finishes reading *Schoolgirl Allies*, listens to radio, writes four poems— "A Silver Thread," "October," "A Golden Afternoon," and "Simplicity." Considers "A Silver Thread," about a dream, the best: "I picked these thoughts out of the air when they came flying by on winds."

August 26: No temperature but still a sore throat. Copies her poems and listens to radio all morning, news about "trouble with Palestine, Jugoslavia, and Russia. Boy! If only there isn't another war in this world!"

August 27: A miserable day outside, listens to radio and works on stamp collection.

August 28: Listens to radio and works on letter to Margot Loungway, reads *A Tale of Two Cities* (1859).

August 29: Typing practice, reads *Wuthering Heights*.

Letter to Margot: "Can't you take a hint?" Margot has not answered her eight-page letter. Home with Grammy while mother and Warren visit in Connecticut, describes a radio program, "Disputed Passage," the "moving story of two doctors, one old—one young—only a delightful speck of romance to give it more human flavor." Listens to her favorite song, "Wanting You"—("No one else in this world will do!"), describes her sore throat as "a little man digging in my throat with a pitchfork, boy!" Asks for help in keeping track of her stamp offers, includes a postscript: "Remember! Crime doesn't pay (well enough)."

August 30: On *Wuthering Heights*—"rather dark and morbid."

August 31: Bikes to the library, finishes reading *Bright Island* by Mabel L. Robinson,[304] "a wonderful, natural story about Thankful Curtis and her life on Bright Island, owned by her family. The sea is in her background as her 'Gramp' was a sailor, and she proves her great heritage."

September 1: Mows the lawn on a beautiful day, sits in the apple tree reading, finishes *Wuthering Heights* and *Going on Sixteen* by Betty Cavanna.[305]

September 2: Apple picking (three bushels) on the Fessenden School campus (in West Newton, Massachusetts). "I enjoyed the apple orchard in the quiet solitude of the morning. It was all sweet and dewy-cool. I do love the scent of apples."

September 3: A family outing in the car to Westford, Massachusetts, to Max Gaebler's house, enjoying a country drive. "Max tortured us further by showing W + me his stamp collection (over 30,000). He had loads of valuable duplicates but would not even let us get near enough to smell them. The piker!"

September 4: Purchases a hundred African stamps: "Boy! Were they beautiful I enjoyed every moment of putting them in my album. It was really comforting to know that I had 75 more stamps in my collection. Boo to Max!" Vows to "get more stamps at less cost if it's the last thing I do."

September 5: Wakes up early, to junior high, in the ninth grade and Warren in the seventh, gets a seat in home room next to Betsy Powley, feels "good to get back in the old routine."

September 6: Second day of school and "still enjoying it," takes Latin.

September 7: "Today was truly wonderful—warm and breezily sunning." Rereads *Wuthering Heights* in the apple tree, Mother brings home *Triumph Clear* (1946) by Lorraine Beim from the library, a story about Marsh Evans, "a girl crippled by poliomyelitis, who went to Warm Springs, Georgia to be cured. The books lesson is, I guess, that we never know how much we appreciate something until we lose it."

September 8: Finishes reading *A Tale of Two Cities*: "It is the most wonderful, magnificent book I've ever read! The characters and plot are superb. Indeed, it is a book I will always want to have to refer to."

September 9: Her first "sorta steady job," babysitting Mrs. Boonisar's six-month-old baby, Philip: "She practically begged me to take care of him again after school." Takes him out for his first ride and earns twenty-five cents an hour.

September 10: Takes baby Philip out with Prissy Steele on the way to the library.

September 11: Enjoys a cartoonist's presentation at a school assembly.

September 12: Excursion with baby Philip. Reads *David Copperfield* (1849), works on poems for *The Phillipian*.

September 13: Fun with baby Philip, who tries unsuccessfully to clap his hands, "I am earning money fast."

September 14: Reads *David Copperfield*: "I get a lot of enjoyment out of [Charles] Dickens books."

September 15: Prefers to sit in the backyard and sun herself instead of going again to see *Henry V* (1944).

Plath's earliest diaries do not mention the loss of her father. The following entry is unusual.

September 16: "Ho! Hum! School once more." Sylvia has earned one dollar and eighty-seven cents so far babysitting Philip.

Returns home to be introduced to Philip McCurdy, who tells her the riveting story about how he discovered that his sister was actually his mother, that his father was actually his grandfather, and that he had never met his birth father, who remained apart from his son. Warily shares some of her own feelings about her father's death. {HC}

September 17: Wheeling baby Philip around in his carriage on a "really hot" day.

"Thought Patterns on Paper." {holograph, PM}

September 18: Checks out *Oliver Twist* (1838) from the library.

September 19: Two hours more with baby Philip on another hot day.

September 20: With Warren, bombards three boys "teasing" them with apples from their tree.

September 21: Out with baby Philip, gets a lovely letter from Claudine Dufrane.[306]

September 22: Another "dog day," stays in bed reading *Oliver Twist.*

September 23: A "horrid tawny gray day," stays up late doing homework.

September 24: Worried about algebra.

September 25: "During supper a crumb lodged in Grammys windpipe. We all were frantic, she could not breathe at all, and we all thought she was going to die." A call to Dr. Hammer who arrives in time: "We all were worn out after the strain and worry, but, thank God, grammy is alive."

September 26: Outdoor sketching on a "glorious" day, more babysitting for a total of four dollars and eighty-seven cents.

September 27: Outdoor sketching, studies ancient history.

September 28: Babysitting earnings "overbalanced any stamp expenditures."

September 29: With Warren, "family Sunday at church."

September 30: Plays soccer, after school Grampy translates a letter from Claudine Dufrane.

October 1: "Well! Now we're beginning one of my favorite months!" A clear sky, "blue, the white fluffy cirrocumulus clouds scudded across like dry leaves, blown by a biting north wind."

October 2: Entertained in assembly by a "dapper little man," Samuel Eves, who plays old songs, like "Ol' Man River" and "The Old Chisholm Trail" on a piano and accordion with a "good bass voice." They sing along to "Cuddle Up a Little Closer, Baby Mine" (perhaps "Cuddle Up a Little Closer, Lovey Mine") and other selections.

October 3: "Today was just overflowing with happiness. I got 90% in both my Algebra and Ancient History tests." Wins a book in a club writing contest: *Cape Cod Yesterdays* (1935) by Joseph C. Lincoln.

October 4: Gets an A+ in Latin and has a "swell time in orchestra."

October 5: Reads *The Count of Monte Cristo* (1844) in bed, gets a haircut: "It was really much too long and is just the right length now." [Drawing of front and back of a girl.]

October 6: Listens to a ballgame and toasts marshmallows at a picnic.

October 7: "I have to stay over the eighth period for Miss Martin, partly for talking with Betsy [Powley]." Out in the woods with Warren where they spot a "muskrat (kind of sick)."

October 8: Gets a B+ on her oral report in English. "Betsy was making faces at me, and I had all I could do to keep from having a fit of laughter."

October 9: Reports in the school newspaper about the musical assembly featuring Chopin and catchy tunes.

October 10: Babysitting, drawing figures of a woman posing.

October 11: "Today I paid a sad farewell to my good old pal Betsy Powley. I sat on her front steps and talked over all the good times we've had." Grammy drives her to Margot Loungway's house in Jamaica Plain.

October 12: "As usual I take more time filling up space with crazy drawings."

October 13: Has a miserable cold, reads *Girl without a Country* by Martha Lee Poston[307] and listens to radio in bed.

October 14: Writes up the program of a school assembly, featuring a reading, a piano solo, choral singing and reading, a harmonica solo, a skit, a vocal trio, tap dance, and an accordion solo.

October 15: A sixteen-line poem for Miss Cox, which ends "But behind the cold, white stillness / There's the promise of a spring."

October 16: Clippings about World Series games, visual-aid education, physical exams.

October 17: "World news is really discouraging—wish I could run things for a while."

October 18: Orchestra rehearsal, pleased to realize she has left her ancient history book at home, "Oh! Well! I'll get along."

October 19: Wears a yellow evening gown with black velvet bows to a dance. One boy steps on her toes, but she has fun dancing with another partner who is "very nice" [drawing of a heart].

October 20: "All the girls were talking about last night happenings and were comparing partners."

October 21: "Dear Diary, I don't know what possesses me to mess you up by such scribbling. Some old nagging things inside me prompts me to waste such nice paper. . . . From now on I won't let the weak side of my character hold sway."

October 22: No longer looking forward to her birthday with the usual excitement. She is "growing old," although it still seems strange to "take things as a matter of course."

October 23: "FAREWELL TO ALL DRAWINGS—THERE WILL BE NO MORE SUCH THINGS HEREIN! (SOB!)."

October 24: On bus to Tremont Temple in Boston, inside the temple: "very depressing—Every sound echoed and re-echoed in its huge dim interior: it was very lonely, and our rehearsal trying." Singing on the bus on the way home.

October 25: Program at Tremont Temple a "great success," Ruthie Freeman gives her a birthday present "early—a darling pink and blue flowered pinafore-apron that she made."

October 26: Plays GI Joe with Ruthie Freeman and Prissy Steele and frosts her birthday cake in green letters that spell "Sylvia."

October 27: Birthday presents: five dollars from Aunt Hazel, three dollars and ninety-three cents from Aunt Dot and Uncle Joe, stamps from Warren, a pair of nylons from Uncle Frank and Aunt Louise, a "super plaid jumper (or dress) and long sleeve blouse to go with it from Mum, an adorable gray pleated skirt from grammy, and a handsome brown belt (for my new coat) from grampy."

October 28: Big test in ancient history on all material "studied previously." Babysitting baby Philip Boonisar for thirty cents, eats an avocado, a gift from Grampy, while wheeling Philip around.

October 29: "Dear Diary: I have not written to you for so long that it is the old old story of not remembering what happens, so, I will copy one of my favorite poems in here when I am at a loss of what to say."

October 30: In assembly, a "marvelous" technicolor movie on New England fall colors.

In the fall of 1946, Plath begins to take a keen interest in Sara Teasdale (1884–1933), a lyric poet who became a touchstone figure.

October 31: Copies a Teasdale poem, "Late October."

November 1: Comments on Teasdale's "Full Moon": "What I wouldn't give to be able to write like this!"

November 2: At Ruthie Freeman's for a visit, sees *Janie Gets Married* (1946), on the porch hammock with David Freeman, Wayne Sterling, Ruthie Freeman, and Wendell: "I felt quite popular: When Wayne puts his arm around me, Dave became very annoying and tried it too."

November 3: Goes for a nice walk with Wayne, who carries her suitcase to the bus stop and runs to the next stop waving at her.

November 4: Copies a Teasdale poem, "The Fountain," with its haunting conclusion: "Nothing escapes, nothing is free."

Letter to Marion Freeman: "I still have a left-over glow from the lively time I had at your house. . . . You will always be like a second mother to me."

November 5: Copies two Teasdale poems—"Autumn Dusk" and "The Crystal Gazer," mentions a "Republican Ticket victorious! Ray! Ray!"

November 6: Copies Teasdale poem "Mountain Water" [drawing of mountains with a valley in between].

November 7: Copies Teasdale's "There Will be Stars."

November 8: Copies Teasdale's "Beautiful, Proud Sea."

November 9: Earns forty-five cents babysitting, goes to assembly in a new black dress with "gold dots all over its billowing skirt [drawing of a girl in a dress] I was very happy in it," dances with Donald White "slightly short," with Bruce Palmer, a "cute, rather short blond boy," and with Perry Norton "a good part of the time . . . the last dance with T. Duggin."

November 10: Sleepy but manages to make it to Sunday school. "I felt ambitious in a lazy way (if that is possible) and just roamed about our house, storing descriptions and thoughts in my mind to be taken out at random some day in the future. I feel a poem coming on soon, too."

November 11: Copies "The Fog" by Carl Sandburg: "Tonight I put on my raincoat and stepped out into inky blackness. The rain splattered on the street and the wind blew gusts of rain by the streetlight that made the bare slippery branches of the trees make dancing shadows on the house."

November 12: "It seemed almost good to get back to school once more!" Finishes and types, "Victory," a short story, earns thirty cents babysitting.

November 13: Admires Marylyn's "beautiful oil paintings that were like theories of masters. My dinky things looked terrible beside it, but old dope Sanburn [drawing of face] put them there."

November 14: Charcoal sketches of people in the room.

November 15: Does every "smitch" of her homework before supper.

Typescript—"Victory," with instructor's comments. {PM}

November 16: At the movies, sees *The Falcon's Alibi*[308] and *Centennial Summer*.[309] "The first picture really stank, but the technicolor picture starring Cornel (Hubba) Wilde, Jeanne Crain, and Linda Darnell (that figureful glamour girl) [drawing of a woman]. I loved the story and Cornel Wilde as a young Frenchman was simply a dream!"

November 17: High temperature and stays in bed listening to the radio.

November 18: Miserable cold with streaming nose and eyes, listens to music on the radio and draws, Warren comes home with her homework.

November 19: Mother decides another stay at home is in order, Sylvia listens to the radio, reads ancient history textbook at her desk in pajamas and a bathrobe, feels better.

November 20: Enjoys an assembly given by a deep-sea diver, in the evening, attends an Edwin Strawbridge ballet, *Daniel Boone*: "The soft footed pioneer and Indian dances were lovely and rhythmically tantalizing in their melody."

November 21: Tired after school but "entranced" with the *Woman's Home Journal*: mystery and murder stories.

November 22: Sketching a "jolly old chinese vase" in art.

November 23: Lacking inspiration until Mother suggests an idea: "I produced a story twice as long as my other one, and mother titled it 'Mary Jane's Passport.' It is more or less a character story."

November 24: "This morning my face was so broken-out that mother kindly let me stay home from Thanksgiving service." Practices the viola and types a story, Mother types up an essay on the ballet *Daniel Boone*: "It took a long time, but the finished result didn't turn out too badly at all!"

November 25: All-A report cards for Sylvia and Warren.

November 26: "Miss Frank will be lucky if I ever speak to her again! Honestly! I utterly forgot all about a permission not that is required if you go anywhere for school!" She wanted to go the art museum, "but she smiled a sardonic, implacable smile and said that she would not take all responsibility of me as Mr. Thistle required me to tell her! So M. F. and the four others drove blithely off, leaving me standing forlornly alone."

November 27: Gleeful about publication of two poems, "To Miss Cox" and "October" in *The Phillipian.*

November 28: An ideal Thanksgiving Day: Uncle Frank and Aunt Louise visit for a "delicious dinner"—turkey, rice, squash, gravy, corn, and the "inevitable cranberry sauce," and apple pie for dessert. The phone rings, and Sylvia answers, learning she has won first prize (five dollars) for her *Daniel Boone* essay.

November 29: "Today a miracle took place—I got up early and went in town to 'visit' my dentist, and wonder of wonders I had <u>no</u> cavities—no buzzing drill to painfully writhe under. Ahhh!" [Drawing of girl smiling.]

November 30: Earns two dollars for babysitting, "I then put on my dress, the red velvet one, [drawing of dress] and my real pearls, and my nylons, and my white gloves and we all went to see Marjorie Eaton's wedding to Manuel de Lerno." Good refreshments and eats "loads of cake."

Typescript—"A Morning in the Agora." {PM}

December 1: While babysitting, tries to make popcorn, but "Luckily the kiddies were peacefully slobbering over their soup in another room, and didn't see little me drown the fire!" Earns a dollar.

December 2: Not enough room in her diary to write down all her poems. "From the Memoirs of a Baby Sitter" and "Snowstorms." {a school paper; PM}

December 7: Christmas assembly: wears a powder-blue dress and "looked very nice in it, if I do say so," dances but with no "<u>special</u> boys."

December 22: Relaxes in preparations for a church pageant: Grammy drives her to the event, Sylvia wears a "pale green taffeta costume. . . . I felt strangely excited. The lights dimmed as we walked barefoot down the church aisle, our dresses swished, and our performance was a great success, <u>and</u>, I was so glad to have it over."

December 23: Trims the Christmas tree and turns on the colored lights: "I hardly can wait until Christmas." [Drawing of living room decorated for Christmas.]

December 24: "Dear Diary: I have neglected you sadly in preference for my sleek new diary. You have been a nice comrade for a year, but a time must come when we part. I will fill up as many back pages as I can, and then leave you in a corner of my bookcase to gather dust but not to be forgotten. The empty spaces in here I will cover with clips and bits of my poems."

From the new diary: "Grampy is having Christmas with us, because he has to go back to the club tomorrow." Pleased with her new clothes—a dark green sweater, a red and green plaid skirt, a "marvelous slip," two pairs of socks (red and white), and a "stunning long-sleeved plaid blouse." Warren gets a "bee bee" rifle and sets up a rifle range in the basement with Uncle Frank. "As I dozed off I seemed to hear Santa's reindeer on the roof!"

Edna St. Vincent Millay joins Teasdale as an early influence on Plath's poetry.

December 25: The best Christmas yet: "Perhaps my two favorite gifts were my new diary and box of 58 pastels."

New diary: more gifts—Turkish figs, two dollars from Aunt Hazel, St. Vincent Millay's *Renascence and Other Poems* (1917) from Mother, *Dancing Star: The Story of Anna Pavlova* (1942), and flowered stationery for thank-you notes. Big turkey dinner.

December 26: Spends a day with Prissy Steele admiring their Christmas presents and arrives home for hot cocoa and cookies.

December 27: Margot Loungway visits for the weekend, Sylvia works on a blue vase and rainbow cup in wax crayon: "the best thing I've done so far."

December 28: A walk in the woods with Margot in a blizzard hearing the "ceaseless sifting of the snow through the tree branches." Worries about freezing to death "like some famous explorers, but—no such luck." Chats and plays games at Perry Norton's.

New diary: "Dick Norton (Pant! Pant!) called for me at eight o'clock in his father's car, and we were off!" Sits "cosily around a fire," plays games and puzzles, has ginger ale and oatmeal cookies, Perry takes her home at midnight.

December 29: Sylvia is very sleepy after staying up until midnight, misses New Year's service, very sad but "'bettered my soul' by going up on the big hill and coasting into space with Warren." All to themselves, they have a "glorious time riding on silver runners under a steel blue sky. I felt quite inspired."

December 30: "Today was fit for a poem. The world was etched in frosty lace. The trees wore soft, powdery skirts, and the air was like a crystal breath." A "fragile blue sky," a "far-off sun" that sets "icicles to twinkling like myriads of stars or sparklers."

December 31: A big day—friends visit, tobogganing.

Memoranda in diary includes a stamp budget, detailing purchases, and a record of bank account deposits and interest, camp reports, and clippings of performances and assembly events.

New diary: "What a rush!" Housecleaning in preparation for visit by David Freeman, Wayne Sterling, and Ruthie Freeman who arrive at noon. The boys go to the rifle range in the basement.

1947

Undated: Poems—"Bereft," "Blue shingled rooftops slippery with rain [first line]," "Sorrow," "The Stranger" (first line reads "The stream, from a subterranean"), and "Youth."

January 1: After breakfast, sledding with Ruthie Freeman, works on campaign speech for class secretary.

The next entry is perhaps Plath's first encounter with an English girl and a culture she has only read about in novels.

January 2, 6:45 a.m.: Grammy wakes Sylvia up for first day of school after the break. But it is a snow day. A drive to Natick, Massachusetts, for a sleigh ride, meets seventeen-year-old Mary, who has just arrived from England on the *Queen Elizabeth* for a year in the US. The moon is a "hazy veil" as the horses draw the sleigh through a fog, and "we sang gaily in the night."

January 3: "We had school today—how I hate it." Returns home and finds that "a miracle had happened—WAYNE had WRITTEN ME A LETTER!!!!!! It is quite entertaining, and I was very appreciative, knowing what an effort it must have cost the poor boy!" Reads the "thrilling" *Three Musketeers* (1844): "I can't put in to proper words the way I feel about the enthralling masterpiece. The plot, the super characterization, the excellent, exciting atmosphere of this book transported me to France of the 1600s—Ah! What bliss to live as another person in another romantic world!" [Drawing labeled "D'Artagnan."]

January 5: Walks home with Mary after church, coasting with Warren: "We felt as if we were birds soaring in the blue, blue sky for one brief morning."

January 10: "I just love every minute of my art lessons!"

January 11: Coasting. "I must say that I would have had a more enjoyable time if Pris [Prissy Steele] hadn't demurely removed herself from the sled every time that we neared a tiny bump!"

Letter to Margot Loungway: Describes a "sporty" party, no dancing— "I was slightly greatly grateful because of my dilapidated shoes!" Describes playing forfeits[310] with Ruthie Freeman, David Freeman, and Wayne, who "happened to get the old one 'Bow to the wittiest, kneel to the prettiest, and kiss the one you love the best!' Oh, brother! He sure was funny—his attempts, you know." Says she has no chance in the election for secretary because she is running against the "most popular boy in school," but it has been fun to campaign with posters and 130 tags.

January 14: Rehearsal for campaign speeches tomorrow.

January 15: "Gee! Today was just some big day. . . . As if in a dream I saw the hall fill up with people, and finally I heard my name called." The audience looks like a sea of blurred faces but then she hears her voice fill the auditorium, and she begins: "For my campaign speech I have chosen to represent the different sections of Wellesley as different Indian Tribes" and then begins to recite a parody of Longfellow's "The Song of Hiawatha." Describes herself as a "little stranger / With her quill and writing tablet." She asks the chief "for a trial to / Prove her value as a scribe.'" She is invited to "write about our people / And about their worthy deeds." The poem ends: "If when you go to vote for scribe / You cast your vote for 'good squaw Sylvia.'"

January 16: Voting.

January 17: "I could hardly sleep last night for wondering about the outcome of the election." Loses to Sarah Bond: "I feel very jolly now that the suspense is over." In bed, reads two hundred pages of *David Copperfield*: "Only two hundred more to go now!"

January 18: Reads *Vanity Fair* (1848) by William Makepeace Thackeray, lists her dance partners with descriptions, such as "no glamour," "Tall, dark and m-m-m," "blonde tall and cute," "Tall, dark, adorable nose," "Blonde, kinda wish-washy," "ATOMIC," "Mortimer Snurd-ish,"[311] "redhead, but + entertaining," "Swooper! neat dancer!," "super waltzer," "Perfect dancer (and has adorable black curly hair)." Watches a dance instructor ("hubba!") demonstrate the rhumba. "The man was about six foot four and was like a beautiful dream." Admires his French accent. [Drawing of a couple dancing.]

January 19: Too sleepy for Sunday school, makes a poster for the Unitarian dance.

January 20: "I just adore seeing the rain splatter on the windowpane and washing the whole world with gray reflections."

January 21: "Today certainly contained many freaks of nature." The day darkens with "Snow-hail" from the clouds, the "lacy snowflakes" floating "gently to earth," another snowstorm in the evening.

January 22: "The great day of the Spelling Bee dawned bitter-cold and windy." Tense before assembly begins. The first word is "leisure," which Sylvia spells correctly. Contest narrows down to the top six. Advances to the final three when she spells "toboggan" correctly. Then it is between her and Bill. She hopes he wins since it is "nice to have a boy ahead." She misspells two words, and he spells one of them correctly, taking first prize.

January 24: Working on pastels in art. A poem, "Fireside Reveries," by the fireside with a book of poems in her lap she sees "through the living screen of fire . . . Gold castles in the air / My thoughts to shining fame aspire / For there is much to do and dare." Delights in *Holiday in Mexico* (1946), starring "adorable" Jane Powell, also likes the actors Roddy McDowall, Walter Pidgeon, and José Iturbi "ever 'n ever so much!"

January 25: "Today is the most wonderful Saturday yet. The air is soft, and a mild spring wind wafts the scent of pine-needles. . . . The sky is deep and blue and just now a silver winged airplane is droning overhead." Walks in "the Fells" with her mother where new homes are being built. "I could almost fancy myself standing on the Western plains as I gazed at the rows of boxy 'monopoly' houses." She watches the light play on the pebbles of a brook with "strange shadows."

January 26: Sliding with Warren on Lake Waban on the Wellesley College campus.

January 28: Babysitting, Mother types five poems for a scholastic contest.

January 29: Calls basketball her "favorite sport. It is so exciting when the ball teeters breathlessly on the edge of the basket!" Takes the bus home with Prissy Steele after buying "one of scrumptious, hot, crust, sugary, stuffy donuts, oozing with sweet, sticky ruby-red jelly—m-m-mmm!"

January 31: "I cannot remember any month as long as this one." Christmas seems a "dim dream." Note to her diary: "who knows someday <u>you might be in print.</u> Once I start to write it is so hard to stop. There are so many things that I feel deeply about and want to get written down in here before it is too late and they have slipped away."

February 1: Talks with her mother last night "for ever so long before falling asleep," dreams of climbing a "huge, steep mountain" with Warren and Margot Loungway and "just hanging onto the edge," reaching up to a blue heaven so intense it "hurt to look at it." The howling wind roared a "wild song" as they reached the top. They arrived barefoot in bathing suits on "hard ground" in a yard of an "ordinary brown house." A maple tree with huge roots made bumps in the earth as they looked down on a fishing village, viewing the rigging of sloops "tied up by the weathered old boat house." The rain came down in the form of a "turquoise-blue sulfa gum," the pellets piling up around them as the scene "faded into a misty haze," and Sylvia woke up. Purchases a scrapbook she labels "Sylvia Plath—1947," using India ink and writing in "old English letters." Pastes in a snapshot of herself as a child, her friends, filling up "every empty space" with "a more or less running account of my life history and descriptions of my experiences."

February 2: Sunday school. Sits in front because last time Mr. Rice got annoyed when she sat "way in back" with Beverly Newell and Lizzie. Reads Wanda Gág's diary, *Growing Pains.*[312]

February 3: A lump, "thinking I might have cancer or mumps." Cleans out bookcase and does the homework Warren brings home. Looks over the first chapter of her fairy story, deciding she should "make the happenings seem natural, or marvel on the impossibility of them. I decided on the first, and made a few important changes." Makes an action, "seemingly innocent, take on a deeper meaning. This is quite impossible since I am not that experienced (yet!).”

February 4: “Today everyone in school seems a complete stranger—what a difference one day can make!”

February 5: “I have resolved to sketch as much as I can!”

February 6: Walks to the Nortons’ and takes care of little David William Norton.

February 7: Reads *A Connecticut Yankee in King Arthur’s Court* (1889), skates with Patty Dunne and Betsy Powley, at Dunne’s house in the basement playroom: hot chocolate cookies, peanuts, potato chips, and popcorn. A “super night,” returns home at midnight.

February 8, 1:00 p.m.: Get ups.

A half-hour, boring telephone talk with Wayne Sterling.

February 9: Stays in bed with a head cold, draws and finishes homework, listens to the radio before going to bed.

February 10: A “cemented head cold” means no school. Copies story about a sad Miss Minton carried away into the air. “There was one last moment of bright April sunshine and then total darkness. The earth had opened and had closed over the head of the terrible Miss Minton forever! Since this day the name of Miss Minton has never been heard again. But since we should never forget this awful lesson, this tale was sent to me by some unseen power to tell to you.”

February 11: “I feel so much like writing tonight that I have to stopper my feelings up tight so that they won’t let out because I haven’t enough time to use them.” Composes a poem, “His Majesty, the Ocean,” about the “slap of the waves,” the “bubbling foam,” the “shrill sand pipers,” the “foghorn’s moan,” the “flap of sail,” that “make this glorious symphony.”

February 12: An assembly speaker with a Scotch accent: “The Seven Keys to the Castle of Good Living.”

February 13: Works on her “6th letter,” the “only one in the history of the school that has achieved such an ‘honor.’”

February 14: “Friday at last!” Listens to *People are Funny*.[313] “It was a riot!”

February 15: Comments on boys she danced with: “Popular, Romantic,” “Beautiful, conceited,” “shy, retiring,” “Neat,” “Tall, blonde, sweeping,” “Swell,” “Cute, Loads of fun.” Conclusion: “I really had a wonderful night!”

February 16: “Ho! Hum! I’m sooooo sleepy,” but makes it to Sunday school, finishes *David Copperfield*.

February 17: “What an extraordinary lovely sunset sky tonight—lush layers of bright pink and lavender—more vivid coloring in the west. In fact the dark silhouettes of the trees make the pink seem almost fuchia in hue.”

February 18: "Today was like spring. Time is short," earns forty cents babysitting.

February 19: Mother washes her hair "for the first time in weeks and now it feels wonderful—full of life glowing shining electric and sweetly clean at last!"

February 20: The class takes parts reading *Julius Caesar*. To the book club, she reads some of her favorite pieces by Rudyard Kipling, including the "throbbing rhythm of": "Bloomin' idol made o' mud- / Wot they called the Gret Gawd Budd- / Plucky lot she cared for idols when / I kissed her where she stud!"

February 21: Walks through a blizzard: "Just as I was beginning to feel I was becoming a natural part of the snowdrift, a hulking gray shape loomed out of the swirling storm and stopped beside me. With a frosty sigh of relief, I stepped into the school bus!" Returns home after school to read more Kipling, including *Gunga Din* (1890) and *The Man Who Would Be King* (1888), "a magnificently gruesome, thundery sad story." Quotes her favorite part of *Gunga Din*: "So I'll meet 'im later on / In the place where 'e is gone— / Where it's always double drill and no canteen. / 'E'll be squattin' on the coals / Givin' drink to pore damned souls, / An' I'll get a swig in hell from Gunga Din!" She adds: "pardon the rather coarse language." Pleased to see her publications in *The Phillipian*: a story, "Morning in the Agora," a poem, "Fireside Reveries," and a club report, and her name in a few news items. Warren has a few items too.

February 22: "What a day!" On her own to visit Ruthie Freeman in Winthrop by bus and subway: "foul with the smell of smoke and wetness . . . full of evil-looking men who gazed at innocent me from out of shifty, bloodshot eyes." At the beach, a "grand time balancing precariously on board fences above the deep, sucking green whirlpools of salt-water" at high tide. Tired of reading O. Henry,[314] goes to a party, "Wayne [Sterling] really thinks he's something—poor, mis-informed boy!"

February 23: "What a boring day!" Church, Monopoly, wishing something exciting would happen, takes a "super bubble bath" with Ruthie before bed: "The bubbles just about lifted us up into the air—there were so many." They read themselves to sleep.

February 24: A "super day" in the castle-like Metropolitan Theatre, where she checks her suitcase with a boy looking "so cute in his blue uniform," watches *California*,[315] starring Barbara Stanwyck and Ray Milland, and *Susie Steps Out*.[316]

February 26: With Warren, working on a snow house, works on chapter 3 of "Stardust."

February 27: A visit to Betsy Powley's home in western Massachusetts, skis face-first into a snowdrift, revels in Betsy's "comfy" room with two "soft beds, bed lamps, radio," a good view of the snow-covered hills, they sit around the fire telling spooky stories.

February 28: A mile hike to the Massachusetts-Vermont line, creates a fashion magazine and draws clothes for it with Betsy.

March 1: Listens to *Your Hit Parade*: "the top tune is 'I Love You for Sentimental Reasons!' M-m-m."

March 2: A tedious five-hour drive back to Wellesley through snow and "gales of rain. . . . I was glad to get back to my cozy little house at nine o'clock. Everybody was pretty glad to see me, too!"

March 5: "Today was really exciting! I have the most wonderful news!" Two of three pictures are awarded Gold Keys in the scholastic exhibit. Mother takes her to town and at the exhibit she is "rather disappointed" in her pictures because "I felt that I could do a lot better." She notices a self-portrait of a boy. "I fell in love with <u>him</u>!" An "inspiring time and had a lot of new ideas for future drawings of mine."

March 7: Reads *The Man in the Iron Mask* (1850) by Alexandre Dumas, waiting for Wayne Sterling to arrive. He presents her with "four lovely carnations," all white, that she puts in her hair and on her dress. "I <u>guess</u> Wayne made a good impression on the girls + boys there, and they made quite an impression on him. . . . Warren seemed sweeter than usual—suspiciously angelic—Hmmmm!"

When a boyfriend reads Plath's diary, she learns for the first time the impact of what she writes on those she writes about as well as revealing why it may not be wise to take too seriously any single entry as a reflection of her true state of mind.

March 8: "Wayne was unusually cool to me. In the living room he revealed the horrible truth! He had persuaded my beebee-brained brother to let him have my precious diary last night, and he had read it all in his room while the rest of us were sleeping." He quotes the worst parts about his "shallow character. . . . Mum said later he was really terribly hurt! Heaven knows I write things here that I don't mean two minutes later—but!" A tense day. She is sorry about "hurting anyone's feelings." But Wayne calls up later, they talk, and she is relieved they "sort of made up."

March 10: Wins five dollars for an essay on the songs "Sentimental Reasons" and "You'll Always Be the One I Love" by Dinah Shore.

March 11: Miss Lawson gives her a copy of *Contemporary Verse* (1939). Draws a variety of women's heads with different features, like a Greek nose, "sweeping black eyelashes," a black "shimmering updo," a "heart-shaped face," a "tilted snub nose," "Wide, clear blue eyes that look as if stars had melted in them," "long blond lashes and arched brows," a "page-boy . . . With a pert, black satin bow, large black-flower earrings," a "peaches and cream complexion," "vivid pink lips," with an array of clothing: a "red velvet gown with long sleeves caught tightly at the wrist, a full skirt clasped snugly by a broad gold belt at the waist, and a low, rounded neckline," a "sweeping black satin gown with a sweet heart neckline, cap sleeves, triangular midriff and a trailing skirt," and a "blue high necked evening gown with three-quarter sleeves and a wide skirt caught with a white silver belt."

March 12: A "racking fever," Wayne Sterling thinks it is "funny to have another boy over and call me up, yet do nothing but talk to the other boy while I wait every minute more impatiently. . . . I think he is nauseating, and if he ever reads this again and sees what I think it will serve him right for being so conceited and nosy!"

March 13–16: "Missed school because of talking so long to Little Lord Fauntleroy last night." Too ill to do homework, listens to the radio.

March 17–21: Returns to school but is not especially interested, reads the "thrilling, scientific book" *The Mysterious Island* (1875) by Jules Verne at home.

March 22: Finishes a short story, "One World," for English.

March 23: Mother and Grammy take Warren to Symphony Hall to sing with seventy boys in the Handel and Haydn Society. Grammy tells her about "soil, fertilizers, and composts which was quite interesting, only I don't enjoy the down to earth type of science—only the fantastic theories that would take me soaring up to the moon or Mars with David in one of his space-ships. Well I can dream can't I? Didn't you know I'm going to be the greatest, most entertaining author in the world? Well don't feel badly, I didn't either!"

March 24: Just a "hint of spring in the smell of the rich damp earth wet by an early morning rain."

March 25–31: Feels guilty about not writing in her diary, a weekly summary: Viola lesson, senior class play, shampoo, art lessons, drawings. "Finished reading 'Forty Faces' [by Mary Urmstrom]—punk!"[317] Gets her mother's birthday present. Visits two art exhibits with Grammy at Wellesley College and Hathaway House, gets a new pair of loafers for six dollars.

April 1: Earns money babysitting.

April 2: Enjoys the assembly dramatization of "The Legend of Sleepy Hollow" (1820), reads a socialist paper, declares her strong desire for world peace: "I was gripped by a cold, tense excitement that made me and my ideas an important part of the chaos in the world today." With only the chirping of purple grackles, and the sight of her Grampy cheerfully working with his "treasured compost," she wonders how 'murder and ugly quarrels" could go on in such a "beautiful world." But then a fire engine comes "screeching around the corner."

April 3: "No school tomorrow—Horray!" Listens to the radio: "Gracie Allen sounds so cute! Mum hates murder stories!"

April 4: Tidies up at home, listens to the radio "like a real housewife," reads *The Cuckoo Clock* by Mary Louisa Molesworth,[318] admiring its style, rereads part of her seventh-grade diary, calling it a "scream."

April 5: A "super assembly tonight," dances with a "tall, blonde, drool some guy with an English accent!" Comes home "very much elated (why sho!)."

April 7: Delivers research talk, "Ballads for the People," which went "perfectly smoothly."

April 9: Enjoys "every minute" of a "super assembly," with Edith M. Clark performing upon the "resonant Swiss hand bells, the high keyed French lyre, and the xylophone."

April 11: Lovely art lesson: makes "a sweet copper pitcher, a pewter dish and a little shiny <u>blue</u> plate," brings home plate to her pleased mother [drawing], listens to *The Fat Man*,[319] *The Adventures of the Thin Man*,[320] and *People Are Funny* in Grammy's room upstairs, finishes a water color, "The Music House."

April 12: Awakened by Warren and his friends "galloping around the house," Mother shoos them out so Sylvia can go back to sleep, spends the morning chatting with Mother, dresses in a gray jacket, plaid skirt, and an "adorable new gray felt 'picture hat' with the stiff, rusty, plaid taffeta bows" [drawing], spots one daffodil opened up as they drive to Jamaica Plain. "Margot [Loungway] welcomed me with her usual pitiful, moronic smile." With "Maggot," crosses the street to play with Dickie, "a rather comical, yet pathetic little boy (age 15!)," who is just recovering from polio.

Plath begins correspondence with a German student, Hans-Joachim Neupert, which reflects her already well-developed interest in world affairs and how people in other countries live.

April 13: Shivers like a "living iceberg" under her thin blanket. With Margot Loungway, visits the "dull and dim" Union Congregational Church, and has a Sunday-school class discussion on the Resurrection. She wants to bring up her Unitarian beliefs but holds back. Bored by the sermon that Margot thinks is "marvelous," quotes a little old lady, in tears: "M-my dear, it is so good to see you all you blooming y-young people in church—so fresh and bright it it just touches me!" Receives Neupert's letter wishing to correspond with an American high school student.

Letter to Neupert: She thinks it will be enjoyable to discuss their interests, ideas, and ambitions, wants to know how he lives, describes herself as almost sixteen, in the tenth grade, tall, brown hair and eyes, likes to draw, write stories, and play piano and basketball. What subjects does he study? She has "heard sad stories" but has "never experienced the horror of being bombed." Wonders whether he finds it strange that they can correspond while their countries "wage war and murder," worries that another war would be "fatal." What does he know about America? Describes herself as "far from rich," describes Wellesley: "rolling green hills, shady woodlands, and little White Houses." Wants to know about his reading. When she grows up, she wants to be a "foreign correspondent, a newspaper reporter, or an author or artist," encloses pictures of her house.

April 14: Receives a 100 percent on Latin test.

April 16: A "boring, short play" in assembly, feels a thrill watching a film, *America the Beautiful* (year unknown): "How wonderful it is just to live in AMERICA!"

April 18: Poems, "Sea Symphony" and "Victory," published in *The Phillipian*, works on a Tiffany glass vase with "deep blues, purples, and greens like a butterfly's wing every time you look at it in a different angle," very pleased with the "feeling of the luminosity of the gleaming glass!" Warren is writing poems and drawing pictures for his "Spring Booklet." Both listen to *The Fat Man*, *The Thin Man*, and *People are Funny*.

April 19: "At last vacation has begun! It is a glorious day! Wind-blown and sweet! The grass is fresh green and the blue shingled roof-tops sparkle in the warm sunlight. As yet, most of the trees are bare, but the fluttering old daffodils swaying gently among their spiky green leaves assure us that spring is really here, now! I am so happy!" Wayne Sterling writes on a postcard from Grant's Tomb: "Does Grant's Tomb give you any <u>nice</u> thoughts?" It shows "he really was thinking of me."

April 21–22: "Ah! Vacation is so-o-o relaxing!" Spends the day designing clothes for paper dolls.

April 23: Sees *The Jolson Story* (1946), starring Larry Parks: "It was thoroughly enjoyable, although a trifle labored in places. It was all glittery and dazzling, as show business is on the outside, and the singing was simply glorious—comedy was rich!"

April 24–25: Visits ailing Mrs. Norton, washes dishes, cleans house, looks after baby David William Norton, dead tired after working 9:00 a.m. to 5:00 p.m., earns six dollars, relaxes by designing dresses and listening to the radio.

April 26: "Mother's birthday!" Her gift: "a lovely box of letter paper." Tells Warren he is "ostentatiously, obnoxiously superfluous." Off to Boston with Mother and Warren to see the operetta *The Red Mill*. They sit in the last row of the second balcony, so steep that a trip would land her in the orchestra. But they see and hear everything "beautifully." Her favorite dance: "The Dance of the Moonbeams." "The stage was softly lit with dusky blues and violets, and maidens danced on in clinging blue gowns that swished as they swayed and danced gracefully. Then, at the first rosy glimmer of dawn, they melted to the ground and lay there in little soft curved pools of blue cobwebs. They were so liquid and lyrical that they seemed almost magical!" Comes home after a "thrilling day."

April 27: Warren's birthday with a sky "hung with threatening clouds . . . somewhat eerily, to tell the truth."

April 28: Surprised at how well she is doing in Latin, a "wonderful time" chatting with Ruthie Freeman.

May: Poem—"Interlude." {PM}

May 2: Finishes reading *Ivanhoe* (1819).

May 3: Dances with Dick Durgin in "sturdy, friendly silence," with Frank Irish who talks "very entertainingly," with six-foot-three-inch Bruce Palmer, who is "oooh! So nice," a "super dancer, and it's such fun to have him lead 'cause you know just what he wants you to do!"

May 5: Babysitting.

May 7: A "most-thrilling" assembly about the atomic bomb and radar. The speaker shows sound waves on a "little round screen," turns on a sound machine with clicks that he calls the "voice of God." These are "cosmic bullets."

May 12: Finishes reading *Wind, Sand, and Stars* by Antoine de Saint-Exupéry,[321] sunbathes.

May 13: "Today was a lucky day for me, all right!" Taken into the principal's office to receive "two big certificates, each splashed with a huge gold seal" for two of her pictures sent to Carnegie exhibit and honorable mentions in the National Poetry Contest, rushes home to tell Mother the "wonderful news."

May 14: Enjoys a "super assembly" with an orchestra and audience that "seemed to be only a dark blue of motionless alert faces around me—and only me and the rhythmical music floating around in the dark black void."

May 15: Relieved to turn in her class poem and return home to write a poem about May.

May 16: In art, "Miss Hazelton is stricter than ever about every little speck of color going in the right place."

May 17: Mows the lawn while Mother tidies up the house. "It was pleasant to smell the dewy, sweetness of the new-mown grass. I watered the violets blooming around our birch and put my ear to the ground so I could hear it absorb the water." Writes a poem, "New England Library," with each shelf offering "New worlds to see with ease, / Between the cover of each book."

May 19: A "determined ambition to win recognition in fashion designing, journalism, book-illustrating, or something tied in with my two specialties, and THEN to go on a trip around the world, staying as long at each spot as I wish!"

May 20: Typescripts: poems—"April" and "Finality." {PM}

May 25: Awarded a book on contemporary American verse, and Warren is awarded a book by Henry David Thoreau for perfect attendance at Sunday school, Sylvia starts making a book of all her "bestest poems," along with pictures for every other page, titling it "Sylvia's Scrapbook,"—"Of course I've let out all my silly little jingles!"

Twenty-four typed poems. {PM}

Finishes "Steely-Blue Crags," illustrated with a "magical color photo of some purple cliffs in Bulgaria."

May 30: In art, works in pastels, a "Chinese jug and plate of grapes, cherries, and oranges," her best so far, which she shows proudly to Mother, who is "very pleased."

Writes first line of poem, "I Thought I Could Not Be Hurt." {PM}

June 6: Lots of orchestra rehearsals for senior graduation night, wears a "yellow taffeta dress with the black velvet bows," a gay evening.

June 9: Driving with Grammy, enjoys the "tranquil, complacent atmosphere . . . occasionally shattered by the shouts of little children." At home, listens to *The Inner Sanctum*[322] and *Sherlock Holmes*.

Plath is awarded a copy of the classic anthology Understanding Poetry *(1938), edited by Cleanth Brooks and Robert Penn Warren, a book that advanced her to a new level of appreciating poetry as rendered by a scholar and poet who set a new, high standard for a generation of teachers and students.*

June 11: "Dearest of Diaries," a day "full of surprises." Helps prepare for the jubilee assembly, Warren receives a certificate, and "wonder of wonders, I got the Wellesley Award for the second time.!!!!!!!" The prize is *Understanding Poetry,* "full of delightful poets, many of whom I recognized," a book she has been longing to own. She wins several other awards, "colorful certificates with bold golden seals splashed liberally all over them." Watches a baseball game between all-star girls and boys. "Needless to say, the boys won (26–5)." Dancing afterwards and has to wait out two dances ("felt awful") before she is asked for the next six. At home, she is greeted by her "enthusiastically appreciative family."

June 13: Last art lesson, completes a "picture of a delectable purple eggplant grouped with three red tomatoes on a yellow-bordered plate."

June 14: Gregory Peck is "superbly handsome" as Penny in *The Yearling* (1946). "Jane Wyman was excellent as Roy, and little Claude Jarman was superior as Penny's son, Jody. The technicolor had many sad parts, during which I wept copiously and many happy parts which were so beautiful that I cried also, so you can see that I dampened a considerable number of handkerchiefs with my tear drops." Describes a "lovely little Bostonian garden" near the *Christian Science Monitor* building, at home, eats on the "cool porch. Strange mists were rolling over the earth, and a damp, eerie little wind was blowing up from the ground."

June 15: Father's Day, draws a "little pastel" card with a "bouquet of our iris" for Grampy.

June 17: The last day of junior high school. She gets seventy-five signatures on *The Phillipian* and all As. She is writing a radio play, *The White Mantle Murders*, with "some very mysterious, as well as romantic parts in it."

Just before entering high school, Aurelia Plath presents her daughter with an evening dress, as if to mark an important passage in her daughter's life.

June 18: "THIS IS THE FIRST DAY OF VACATION!" Works on her radio play, on bus to Boston, sees Tommy Duggin: "So, I screwed up my courage and sat down beside him (he has the <u>nicest</u> smile!) We chatted together until he came to his stop. If I could <u>pick</u> my specially [*sic*] favorite 'Boyfriend,' he'd be IT! He's not only tall, handsome, and the athletic type, but talkative and <u>very</u> friendly. Not at all vain or affected like <u>SOME</u> boys I know!" Meets her mother, who buys her an "adorable" thirty-five-dollar evening dress "marked down to $5!!!!!!!!!! . . . It has a snug white brocaded bodice and puffed sleeves of the same material. White net is inserted and brought up to make a high, round neckline. The shirt is of billowing white net also." On the bus, they feel proud of themselves for having had such a "successful day."

June 19: Describes a "fresh blue" sky after a thunderstorm, "little clouds are scudding across before the wind like little wisps of cotton batten flung up into the sky." Watches a robin hop close to her chair, darting its beak in the ground and coming up with a "juicy worm," devouring it, and flying away. "Well, I must get back to my story writing, so I'll say bye-bye for now!"

June 21: After lunch, Ruthie and David Freeman arrive. He is "taller, better-looking, and oh! So much improved (I mean <u>nice!</u>)." They play Monopoly in the warm afternoon sun, eating outdoors, and tanning themselves in their bathing suits. They play baseball until dark.

June 22: Watches boys' swimming stunts, invited by a lifeguard to climb up to the high dive with him as he performs his "fancy dives," refuses his offer of cigarettes, turns red after so much sunbathing.

June 23–25: Terrible sunburn, listens to radio, and designs paper-doll dresses, nose drops for a cold, packs for camp, mentions writing a long letter to Betsy Powley, who is in the hospital.[323]

June 27: Excited about spending two weeks at Vineyard Sailing Camp, feeling tingly last night, like "gingerale bubbles through my veins." Calmer now, "sitting in our green, birch-screened backyard for the last time, enjoying the dewy grass and the sun's warm and caressing light." Imagines the cooling, perfumed morning breezes are "lonely, too, I guess, from wandering around so long without anybody to keep them company except the birds. Upstairs my airy room is just the way I left it, the blinds drawn halfway to temper the golden rays of the sun and the windows all wide open with the breezes blowing the lacey white curtains against the screens." Mentions the rumpled bed: "Of course I'll make the beds! Don't get so indignant—just wait a little while longer!" Grammy drives her to Boston's South Station. After the train, a wait on the dock for the steamer. In a "misty haze of bluish-gray" in salt-wind lands and then travels in a camp truck on a bumpy road. In her tent suffers a "wave of homesickness."

Postcard to "Dear Mother": "Do write me cheery letters." Girls are "nice." The water is a "beautiful shade of briny green . . . cold but refreshing."

June 28: Passes a one-hundred-yard swimming test. Misses Ruthie Freeman and Betsy Powley.

Postcard to "Dear Mummy": She is "fine." Her bike and other items have arrived, in a tent with three girls, food is good, she has a new name, "Sherry."

June 29: Eats supper on the "bluffs overlooking the lagoon," likes to eat until she is "really <u>full</u>": "6 slices of bread filled with peanut butter and ketchup, egg salad, and lettuce and mayonnaise respectively, two cookies, half a pear, an apricot and two cups of milk."

Postcard to "Dear Mother": recounts camp expenses for boat trip and truck ride, "Love, Sivvy."

June 29–30: Postcard to "Dear Mummy": Recounts her prodigious eating. "There is something—an atmosphere—about camp that just can't be got at home. I love it. Xxx Sivvy."

June 30: Postcard to "Dear Mummy": "Shame on you! No letter today." Describes sailing: takes her turn at the halyards and the tiller and gets "really nautical in my vocabulary am I not?!" Mentions keeling over and turning green, the swelling in her toe has subsided, wants her mother to say "happy birthday" to Grammy.

Postcard to Mother: eating everything she "possibly can," a sunburn from sailing, wants her mother to save her postcards for her diary when she returns home, "xxx Sherry."

July 1: A seven-mile bike trip through the countryside to East Chop, in Oak Bluffs, Massachusetts, sailing in the afternoon: "<u>I am having a perfectly wonderful time here!</u>"

July 1–2: Letter to "Dear Mummy": Pooped from her bike trip past houses with "quaint little gables and turrets crowding in at every possible angle of the roofs." Sunburn treated with calamine lotion and Noxzema, the next day a bike ride to West Chop, in Tisbury, Massachusetts, to watch sailboat races, a four-pound gain, totaling 118 pounds: "I only hope I dont loose them with all the exercise I'm getting! . . . I love you very, very much & do miss you just a little." Mentions she has written to Warren and Betsy Powley.[324]

July 2: Describes the twelve-mile bike ride to West Chop, climbing the lighthouse sites, feeling "quite wobbly" but refreshed with a picnic lunch on a warm, sandy beach. Chews gum, relaxes, "letting the pleasant flavor flood my mouth." Another sunburn.

July 3: Sailing. "When it came time for me to jibe[325] I was dreadfully stupid, and accidentally let go of both tiller and main sheet at once. Just in the nick of time Web's quick thinking and acting saved the boom from breaking the mast—did I turn red." After dinner, goes rowing in the glass lagoon with the setting sun making deep purple shadows on the calm water in the "last pinky-green light" vanishing from the "starry western skies."

The first mention of Seventeen, *which began publishing for the teenage market in August 1944, and would become the venue for much of Plath's early work.*

Postcard to "Dear Mummy": Reports she has written postcards to Warren and Betsy Powley. Requests a copy of *Seventeen*, mentions a talent auction in which the girls do stunts and are rewarded with various services from the counselors.

July 4: Gathers wood for evening bonfires, weenie roast, consumes three hot dogs, three rolls, carrots, radishes, onions, two cups of punch, and "when I was through with the dessert of peaches, biscuits and whipped cream I was only moderately hungry." A costume party and then into pajamas around the campfire at twilight, eats ice cream, singing "lovely sad and happy songs" while "watching colored rockets burst in the air across the water." A "perfect evening."

Postcard to "Dear Mummy": Wants to know how her mother is celebrating the fourth. Describes her adventures sailing. Sleeps like a log, dreams of Ingrid Bergman in *Joan of Lorraine* (1946).

July 5: An eight-mile bike ride during which she imagines building a "little white villa," into the ocean, playing games under water, puts on a skit, "I'm Alone in the House," with "special dialogue and gestures." Goes over well with lots of laughter. She ties with another contestant, three helpings of a delicious duck dinner.

Postcard to "Dear Mummy": describes "hilarious" costume ball.

Postcard to "Dear Mummy": Describes long letter from an unhappy Ruthie Freeman who got "awful homesick" at her camp because of "one of the gangs from Wellesley. I know them, and they are very close and snubbish." Writes a long letter to cheer Ruthie,[326] describes the wonderful July Fourth celebration. "xxx Will write more on next card."

Postcard to Mother: sketching the beach, describes swimming with Sally Haven, "an adorable girl" from Newton with "soft light hair and lovely dark eyes—almost as tall as I am, and still has a little girl charm about her."

July 6: Spends the morning writing postcards, visiting day means keeping quiet and demure, resting, and reading to show off "ladylike" behavior.

Postcard to "Dear Mummy": breakfast in bed brought to her because it is the service that she won in last night's talent auction.

Postcard to "Dear Mother": A five-pound gain totaling 119 pounds, eating huge quantities of food and hoping to keep her weight on, already has a "schedule" for her return home, including a shampoo and hot bath, a "nice cool salad and a big dinner (tomato, bacon and cheese sandwiches) If possible! Oh! Boy! I'll be glad to see you again, but I feel awful about leaving camp." Off to Chappaquiddick Island, in Edgartown, Massachusetts, but can't wait to get home. "xxxxxxxxxxxxxxxxxxxxxxxx Sivvy."

July 7: A twenty-mile round trip by bike to Chappaquiddick, on arrival, eats three ham sandwiches, four fig newtons, two oranges, and one bottle of ginger ale, sunbathes for an hour, swims, rides back for a "Do-as-you-please Night" sitting around a campfire listening to sea stories. Describes the bike trip going through "darling little Edgartown" and the "funniest little 'ferry boat,' which was honestly just a chunky little float of wood no bigger than our cabin floor!" Bringing home shells with "their name and date."

July 8: Has her much-anticipated contest reward: a breakfast in bed (orange, oatmeal, and "three delicious pieces of cinnamon toast" and milk), works on stencils for menu covers.

Postcard to "Dear Mummy": expects to arrive in South Station at 11:40 a.m., hopes someone will meet her and will wait on the track until someone arrives.

Postcard to "Dearest Mummy": describes breakfast in bed—"Oh! Heavenly bliss!" Joins campers for photographs.

July 9: Packs two duffel bags for tomorrow's early-morning departure, glad she can avoid long drawn-out good-byes! Sorry to go but happy to return home, reads *Seventeen*, enjoys the campers but finds fault with the "insulting and boisterous" Gloria Marie Caouette, "conceited and boastful," Anne Brown, "sweet but impatient," describes the formal dance at camp at which she wears a "gown of white towels" decorated with roses. In the back of the skirts, she has a shorter towel brought to uniform length with the others by a stylish towel ruffle. Walks out to the bluffs to listen to the waves against the rocks with the light of Vineyard Haven, in Tisbury, gleaming like "a crown of gems on the horizon." Fireflies amid the telling of ghost stories, the "sweet" girls make up a farewell poem: "O quite an actress is our Sherry: / Her, 'Woman, woman women!' Makes us scary."

July 10, 4:00 a.m.: A deluge wakes her up with deafening noise and a hissing wind "like a jet of high-pressure steam through the trees."

6:15 a.m.: On the camp truck, musing: A brief chapter of her life has closed but every moment has been "filled with the glory of <u>real living</u>. I feel inexplicably different inside—a little too old for my outer shell."

Relishes arrival at home, alone with mother for a week: "The house seems dreadfully quiet and the walls seemed to crowd in on me at first, but now I'm used to it all." Feels "wonderful to be spotlessly clean again, and to <u>sleep between</u> crisp <u>white sheets</u>."

July 11: To Betsy Powley's with some sweet William and a dozen plums to "cheer her up" after coming home from a hospital stay, one leg in a heavy cast.

July 12: In Boston, moved by *Cynthia* (1947), starring Elizabeth Taylor as a young girl with watchful parents, and notes that the film "solves many of my own problems." Also watches *The Great Waltz* (1938) about Johann Strauss, "beautifully filmed" with "heavenly" music bringing her to tears as the waltzes bring out the Austrian in her. On the way home, as her bus is stopped, some boys yell, "Hey Blondie!" One of them reaches into the open window and pulls her hair. She blushes red when people on the bus look at her. "NOT that I'm blonde, of course, but it does something to a girl's morale to have even strange boys pay attention to her. I felt very happy about the whole evening!"

July 14: Betsy Powley loans her *Mrs. Mike* by Benedict Freedman.[327] "I enjoyed it so much!"

July 15: "If I had to pick one day of my life to live over, this would be IT!" Supper with Madeline Sheets and her son, sixteen-year-old Redmond, at Steubens: "Oh, Diary! I've never <u>seen</u> such a nice boy!" Very good looking but not conceited "like <u>some</u> people I know." Entertaining talk about the their common interests, Redmond has dark, wavy hair and "astonishingly dark brown eyes." He puts his hand over hers, and she "doesn't mind." Sylvia just loves "the way Redmond looked at me sort of out of the corner of his dark eyes." So "understanding" and "natural." She gets "tingles" running "up and down my veins" and feels "sort of wobbly." Feels she could "faint from sheer happiness! M-m-m!"

July 16: "I just can't stop thinking of how nice Redmond is and wondering what he's doing now and if he's thinking of me!"

July 17: On the way home, in a downpour from her first disastrous piano lesson at the conservatory, the rain stops as she fits the key into the front door, "as if propelled by some unseen and very mocking power! (I'm in love with someone)."

July 18: Piano practice: "<u>I love it so!</u>" Enjoys the "luxuriant and green garden," the tall pines, the bridal wreath bushes, and rose arbor. "Well! I must get back to the mystery story I'm writing." Off to Wellesley College for a performance of *The First Mrs. Fraser*. With her family but pretends Redmond Sheets is sitting with her. "The three act comedy was simply delicious, and Jane Cowl[328] acted wonderfully!"

July 20: Makes plans with Betsy Powley for a summer at the Vineyard, working as waitresses in upstate New York at the Mohonk Mountain House.[329]

July 22: With Mother to Winthrop to visit the Freemans, Ruthie Freeman is at camp, and David Freeman "fills one or two of my needs and requirements, but when I think of Redmond, David seems very lacking."

July 23: "This morning was like a nightmare with a happy ending." Sets off by herself with some anxiety for a music lesson in Boston, accosted by an old woman in a black coat and "battered black hat," who announces she knows about Sylvia's visit to the Freemans' house. Sylvia nods and wonders whether the woman is a "secret FBI Agent," although that seems impossible. She gets away and describes the subway, "dark black tunnels dotted with white, yellow, red and green lights," the masses of "hurrying people," with "varied personalities," as she emerges into the light of day, "shaking, but triumphant." Later David takes her to the movies. She pretends she is with Redmond, is glad David didn't try to hold her hand, which she wouldn't let him do "if he tried, because when he starts getting 'romantic' he's so silly that it's sickening." Watches the far-fetched *Vacation Days*[330] and the "wonderful" *Calcutta*,[331] starring Alan Ladd, "so strong and handsome."

July 24: Buys a new diary for eight-five cents, "thinner and smaller than you are, but the paper is better, if I do say so. You see how I have had to crowd my writing for fear I would run out of space before I got a new diary!"

July 25: "It's good to be able to spread out and stretch again, knowing that I have a new diary waiting." Buys a "dream of a dress" at Filene's, "aquamarine with black bands around the neck, waist and sleepers, and a narrow black-square outline all through the material."

July 27: Mother visiting friends, Warren at camp, Grammy takes Sylvia to the country club for a delicious dinner, including sweetbreads, mushrooms, salad, and Sylvia is so "sufficiently sufficed" that she cannot eat dessert. Notices a "pile of books" on the windowsill beside her and opens one: "To Sylvia Plath from Mr. and Mrs. William Dana Orcutt."[332] She is "really thrilled! To think that a 'really-truly' author had condescended to become my friend and even to send me five lovely art books!" Returns home to Mother and Warren, who has "really changed. His voice is a little deeper, he's very tan, and quite thin."

July 28: Sunbathing and working on a mystery story and a "planet story" called "Mission to Mars."

July 29: Writing and sunning. Recounts a dream of herself as a "beautiful detective-ess who solved the ghastly murder of a young man." In another, she rescues friends from drowning in ice in Antarctica, dreams about Redmond that turns into Wayne ("ugh!") and then David Freeman.

July 30: With Mother, purchases an "adorable cotton dress (blue with white polka dots)" for three dollars at Filene's. Aunt Elizabeth, who had called them, turns up with two "glamorous, richly-styled beautiful materialed swishy evening gowns for ME! Two $40.00 dresses marked down to $2.50."

July 31: Dick Barry visits: "mentally slow and childish and painfully boring. . . . I purposely described him in dead, short sentences, because that is just the way I feel about him."

August 1: At the beach, sunbathing and swimming, walks into the Wellesley Hills, and is whistled at by truck drivers and a boy on the way home, in the evening, at Wellesley summer theater with the family to see *Dear Ruth* (1947) with Joyce Van Patten as "Miriam." She laughs "all the way through it."

August 2: Piano practice, biking, sunbathing after a seven-mile ride, eats her Aunt Dot's homemade ice cream, chased by boys on a motorcycle who ask whether Sylvia and Ruthie Freeman want to "go for a ride with them." They say "no" "in a freezing tone." Relieved and exhausted, they go to the drugstore for ice water, the soda clerk tries to flirt, "but we felt so experienced that we just ignored him, too!"

August 3: Letter to Margot Loungway: spends more time on outdoor sports than reading and reports on her "thrill-packed summer."

August 6: Piano practice, checkers, cards, gossip, other games, the new croquet set has arrived, plays with Grammy and Warren until it is too dark to see the wickets.

August 7: Wakes up after sleep on the porch overnight, goes over to Betsy Powley's, listening to radio while giving each other back rubs, Betsy's mother gives them "adorable" cherry lipsticks. They play cards all evening. Draws a radio with the text "He's stepping on the scales weight—257 pounds! Who is it? The fat man! Fortune—'Danger.'"

August 8: To Morses Pond for swimming, plays thirteen games of croquet with Warren at home: "He won, naturally, 8 to 5, but it was very close in a number of places!"

August 9: Reads the *Reader's Digest* condensation of *In Hazard*.[333]

August 10: Morning croquet with Warren, plays cards in the evening.

August 11: Truck drivers whistle at her.

August 12: Swimming at Morses Pond.

August 13: Sees twins painting a house and remarks, "you go to one side of the house, and there is one painting. You go to the other side, and there he is again."

August 14: Now she can tell the difference between them, even when the twins aren't together. "They keep teasing me about my boyfriends."

August 15: Dreams about Redmond, invited to a "fashionable group. . . . Nothing like a big opportunity!" Talks to the twins, likes Richard better than Roland: "Richard is very nice—a little too fresh sometimes, but then! What those boys talk about! They had me listening to their views on marriage before the day was over." She lets Richard fix her bike. "He is very sweet and all—I got paint over my arm and he wiped it off for me—oh, so gently." They sit in the "coolness of the garage" and talk before lunch.

August 16: Excited about going to see *Gone with the Wind* (1939). "I promised myself to see the picture ever since I was a little girl and read the book five years ago." Transported to the "magic world of the past. I was Scarlett O'Hara—with all my beaus flocked around me." Afterwards, walks out of the "velvet blackness" of the theater worn out after "five hours of exciting drama."

August 17: Plays croquet with Ruth Geisel, Warren joins in.

August 18: Reads the new *Women's Day*, "I now weigh 121 lbs!"

August 19: At Betsy's: "Nora, the Powley's Irish maid, was there, and she certainly is a character! She is absolutely, indescribably funny." The twins have finished painting the house and leave a message for her. "Roland told Warren to tell me goodbye, and Richard just told him to tell me that he was glad he knew my name and telephone number. Oh well!"

August 21: "Oh Diary! I had my hair cut today. Mother told the barber to cut off the tip ends about one inch, and he cut off three or four. My hair came out straight, bushy, not quite shoulder-length, and heartbreaking both to mother and me." Goes home and is in tears: "my long curly brown hair with the gleaming blonde and copper lights in it has always been considered my crowning glory." She feels she has lost a "good part of my 'look.'" Goes over to Powleys', and Mrs. Powley arranges her hair in a "becoming array of soft, turned-under curls." She never realized "true friends . . . Until this crisis in my life." Overjoyed to learn bridge, "since it is a great social asset."

August 23: Plays blackjack at the Powleys', listens to the radio as they give each other back rubs: a "fun-packed time."

August 24: After a stay over at Powley's, they read the paper and enjoy a "yummy breakfast." Grammy picks her up for a country-club dinner. The menu: cold potato soup, lobster salad, blueberry muffins and butter, apple pie à la mode, and milk. "I always feel very 'corpulent' when I'm through eating there, but I can eat ever and ever so much without gaining any appreciable weight!"

August 25: Plays bridge at the Powleys': "Mr. Powley and I won the rubber 990 to 390."

August 26: "Oh! DIARY!" Redmond's mother calls, and Sylvia confesses that "I never knew anyone affected me that deeply." Then she hears on the radio "Wanting you, wanting, you, no one else in this world will do." She dances up and down. Over to Aunt Dot's to see her adopted baby, Nancy, "a plump little darling. I held her in my arms for a while and the sweet little thing fell right asleep then and there." Reads stories by Poe before going to bed.

August 27: Relaxes in the sunshine.

August 28: Enjoys her lunch and "lovely chat" with Mrs. Powley at Howard Johnson's before going to the hospital to pick up Betsy.

August 29: A last piano lesson at the conservatory and a visit to Aunt Dot's for shampoos and baths because their hot water tank is out of order.

August 30: Prepares for a date with Redmond, spending "all morning getting ready," putting on her blue dress with the "airy white polka dots and frothy ruffles, my white socks, brown loafers, shiny silver aluminum bracelet, white beads," and a white gardenia pinned in her brown hair, "brushed until it fell into a soft curly page-boy with coppery lights gleaming in the brown waves." With Warren and Mother, travels to Boston by bus, wonders, Did Redmond change or did she? "He is not as interesting or talkative as before." On a boat ride, they sit together, and he puts his arm around her shoulder. They see *Thunderbolt*[334] and *Great Expectations* (1946), which "wasn't at all as I had hoped it would be, but I enjoyed myself nevertheless."

August 31: A family reunion to celebrate Uncle Joe's birthday: "I never knew we had so many distant friends and relatives on that side of the family. So many rich ones, too. . . . I could have kissed Bea when she asked me if I went to college. She said she thought that I was at least seventeen or eighteen years old!"

September 1: Bikes to Wellesley College with Ruth Geisel for canoeing with Ruthie Freeman on Lake Waban, enjoying the "sound of the canoe as it glides through a field of flat lily pads." Followed by some boys, Ruthie (Freeman?) buys a package of cigarettes to impress them and offers one to Sylvia, who puffs away, feeling "very guilty and wobbly-at-the knees." She discovers that she can fake inhaling. "I had vowed never to smoke for dozens of reasons, but the desire to impress the world over-came me for a short while." The boys yell, "Ohh! Smoking!" She drops the cigarette, feeling "very cheap and ashamed."

September 2: Plays checkers and honeymoon bridge[335] with Ruthie.

September 3: Takes Warren canoeing: "I enjoyed giving him the pleasure, for I knew he liked the ride."

Sometimes Plath uses her diary to mark a new stage in her education and life.

September 4: "Today I commenced with school once more." In senior high, taking English, math, French, Latin, art, gym, and orchestra. All the teachers are men except in gym and French. "The men are indeed a welcome change! I am really almost glad to get back to the old grind."

September 5: With three other girls, bikes over to the Sunshine Dairy for ice cream cones—"We got along beautifully, and we also realized that we four made a nice group: Mary's a redhead, Sonya, a blonde, Ruthie has black hair, and mine is light brown."

September 6: Canoeing with Ruthie on Lake Waban. As they walk home, a "good-looking man leaned out and asked us the way to the lake in a debonair way." Impressed with the driver and his handsome companion, the girls point the way to the lake. They are disappointed when a second car pulls up and the driver is an "elderly gray-hair man" asking for directions.

September 7: Mother leaves for a minor operation at Carney Hospital. "How I hated to see her go!"

September 8: Letter to "Dearest Mummy": Misses her, reports on her activities, including playing cards with Ruthie, doing homework, including a paper on Matthew Arnold that Mr. Wilbury Crockett calls "well said." She "just about" bursts with pride. Half the class drops out. "It seems we've had quite a desertion," says Mr. Crockett, smiling. Nineteen left, which "makes it nice." Mr. Crockett tells them they are a "likely lot" with "a knack for our subject." Also enjoys art class and working in characters: "From your very own Sylvia-girl With love and best wishes."

September 9: Letter to "Dearest Mother": Not much news, her complexion is showing "signs of improvement." The "big red spots" are "drying up." Latin and French going well. English: "I could sit and listen to Mr. Crockett all day." He asks the class which paper is best, and one of the students says, "Sylvia's," and Mr. Crockett replies "I decidedly think so." Says Warren misses her more than she does. "I fool myself into not having time to miss you by planning what I'm going to do in every minute of my time so I'll never have any moment left to 'be lonesome' in." Ends with "I pray for you every night."

Hearing the recording of Edna St. Vincent Millay in class may well have contributed to Plath's later development of her own voice and delivery, especially in her BBC recordings.

September 11: "My English course is so stimulating. Today Mr. Crockett played 'Renascence' and 'The Ballad of the Harp-Weaver' on the recorder, spoken by the author. They were both so beautiful that I could hardly keep from crying." She writes a poem, "City Streets,"[336] one of her best, that begins, "Alone and Alone in the Woods Was I," and another poem, ending with "These are the wan gray shreds of the tattered day." Feels like she is pouring out her soul. "I'm full of love and exuberance for everyone in the world." Mother returns home weak from her hospital stay.

September 13: Canoeing and sharing of confidences with Ruthie Freeman.

September 15: Tries out for the *Cynthia* contest,[337] talks on the phone with Ruthie, Nancy, and Betsy Powley.

September 16: Worn out from canoeing with Ruthie.

September 19: Decides not to run for any school offices: "I want to insure my popularity before opening myself to anymore malicious attacks. It was good to sit on the sidelines for once, after being so active in the ninth grade."

September 20: Enjoys herself at a football game with Warren, pointing out a "few of the principals while the game went on."

September 27: Accompanies Arden Tapley to Boston to see *Man and Superman* (1903): "Arden is such a light, breezy influence and it's nice to have a pretty, blonde friend that's taller than I." Loves the play's "witticism and excellent scenes and humor."

October: Poems—"In Memoriam" and "October."

October 1: After a music lesson at the conservatory, she spots Bill Mac-Gorty with the "cutest six-footer imaginable!" She gives Bill the "most dazzling smile he has probably ever received." Bill includes her in the conversation, and as the "handsome stranger" gets off the bus, he casts a "long look" at her, and she responds with a "little smile." She wonders why she couldn't just say, "I like you and let him know." She was sure he wanted to meet her, but "it wouldn't be 'proper' to pick up a 'chance acquaintance' like that, no matter. How nice it would seem to be."

October 2: Joins the feature staff of *The Bradford*, assigned to do a profile of Mr. Colette, the school's new art teacher.

October 3: Roaring up Paine Street with Bob and Arden Tapley in a "baby blue Ford with the red trimmings, called Henry." They are joined by two more girls and two more boys. "How we got to Arden's house in one piece, I don't know." They play tag and blow plastic bubbles, and she returns home having learned "new jokes and card tricks."

October 4: Worried about an icebreaker and whether any boy will dance with her. Enter Perry Norton, who dances every dance with her. Perry is "almost lyrical," saying her hair smelled "sweetly shampooed" and that she had a "charm that no other girls had." What a simply "heavenly time." At midnight, he walks her home. Not even the ghastly death of a kitten, crushed by a speeding car, seems to disturb her bliss.

October 10: With considerable trepidation, presents her poems to Mr. Crockett, who reads them in class, saying she has a "lyric gift beyond the ordinary." She is "overjoyed" but doubtful that poetry will make her more popular. Ventures by bus to Boston for a stay at Margot Loungway's, in her "Victorian guestroom," she writes: "Somehow, at her home I feel I could write my best stories—there is just enough uncertainty in the air, a little mystery, and quite a supply of homey, country-influence to get my imagination working."

Plath questions certain "truths"—another sign of her disengagement from childhood.

October 11: Reads *Seventeen* with Margot in bed in the morning, bikes to the "fall splendor of Jamaica Pond." Confesses that "lately I have acquired the discomforting habit of questioning those truths which my life had been based upon—such as religion, human nature, and other others. I am also able to see the 'other person's side' so clearly and understandingly in its own light, that I am sometimes swayed by surges of doubt." Expresses her reluctance to accompany Margot to see *Cynthia* again and that she has a "dread of concentration camp films."

October 17: Mentions her crush on a junior, a perfect artist's model: "tall, handsome and sturdily quiet." Invited to the Powleys' farm, enjoys the ride there with the whole family.

October 18: Revels in a "happy jumble of rustic country delights," gazing at the hills, eating a neighbor's apple pie, quilt making with "real country-folk," an artist's studio, and a late-night card game of their own fashioning with pieces of paper.

October 19: Pancakes, homemade maple syrup, sunbathing, returns home "happily to bed."

October 25: Watches Wellesley "shellak" Hingham 34–12, enjoys ride home with friends, who blow hard on their thumbs twenty times to see if they would faint: "I had a super time."

October 27: Staying home from school with a cold on her birthday. Lists all her presents, including "a striking red-and-black wallet" (from Warren), a brush and comb set (from Aunt Dot and Uncle Joe), long green socks (from Uncle Frank and Aunt Louise), a dark-brown over-arm bag, a black scarf (from "Mum"), a ten dollar bill (from Mum and Grammy) to buy a new dress, shoes, a yellow silk scarf (from Betsy Powley) and "adorable stationary from Ruth [Freeman]."

October 30: Finds just the right dress in Boston with "sales ladies about me like a chorus line; exclaiming with suitable gestures: 'Oh, how becoming!' and 'My! How sweet!' and 'What a dear child!'" At five foot, eight inches, she finds it hard to imagine herself as a "dear child," but: "Maybe some tall dark MAN might think so some time." Shopping for shoes, an elevator boy eyes her in the full-length mirror and is flustered when she catches the "amused look of one of the salesmen."

October 31: Observes that the rain and gray clouds against a "ghostly pale moon" create a "perfect setting" for Halloween.

November: Poem: "Reverie." {PM}

November 1: Describes different partners at the "first formal assembly," regrets that the "only bright spots were when I danced with <u>dreamy Tommy Duggin</u>" [drawing of a heart with an arrow through it]. Creates a scene when Bruce tries to cut in on her dance with Dick, who leaves "in a huff" and goes outside for a smoke. He returns for the last dance with her, departing with the "romantically thrilling words, 'See you next time!'"

November 5: A "strenuous afternoon" of beginner's tennis.

November 7: Attends a football game with Ruthie Freeman in Winthrop, spends time at the piano with Dave Freeman, playing little pieces, including "Chaconne" and "Barcarolle," letting loose with the "Whiffenpoof song." Sees ("ugh!") *Jack London*[338] and *Nob Hill*[339] in technicolor.

November 9: So tired that she almost misses her subway stop on the way home from the Freemans' house. On the bus, she is accosted by an Asian man, who begins asking her personal questions. He grabs her hand, she snatches it away, and he gets off the bus. At home, she reflects that "strain of the day proved a little too much for my delicate (ha!) constitution."

November 12: A rainy, snowy day, on the way to school, wreckage of three cars: "a total smash-up!!"

November 13: "Sweet" Bob Winslow makes her heart "give a naughty thump" whenever she sees him, a senior in her art class. She hides her admiration by joking with him, and that seems to amuse him. But then he grabs her wrists and tells her to "Get away." On the crowded bus home, he blows smoke rings with his pipe as she laughs and wrinkles her nose in "mock horror at his odiferous tobacco." Prays she will be invited to the football dance.

November 17: No one calls about the dance.

November 18: Still imagining and hoping to be asked to the dance.

November 19: Jeanne Woods tells her it is still not too late to be asked to the dance.

November 20: Tempted to say Perry Norton is taking her to the dance, a relief when Perry calls and he actually asks her to the dance. "When I had informed mum that I was invited her eyes were starry and she was overjoyed. . . . Oh, Joy!"

November 21: Dresses in her "velvet and plaid number" for the dance, Perry arrives and has to wait five minutes while she finishes dressing. He manages "an appropriately admiring 'Gosh!'" An evening of "perfect fun," out on the cold porch both Perry and Frank Irish put their arms around her so that she won't "freeze to death." She walks home with Perry, who "kept his arm around me all the way home (his hand must have about frozen off) and we talked about weighty matters as usual." At her house, they have cocoa and "little orange-iced cakes by the dim light of the stove lamp." Then, at 1:00 a.m., Perry rides home on his bike.

November 22: Gets ready for another dance in her "new blue dress with the peplum and the scarlet flower at the waist." The dance goes well with various boys cutting in on her partners. She avoids Bruce, turning him down and saying she would rather sit it out than have to dance "his pump-handle shuffle." She believes she is a better dancer than last year when the boys would try her out, but she "couldn't follow well enough. . . . Now, by some dreamy magic, the more I dance with boys . . . The better I dance and the more they ask me."

November 23: Sees John Pollard at Thanksgiving service, he asks her whether she has "recovered yet." She laughs and answers "NOT quite."[340]

November 25: In art, Winslow parks his desk next to hers and rudely says she likes him. She splashes his ear with red paint. She still hopes he will ask her out. "Once or twice he's tried to attract my attention, but now he's playing my game, and we're both succeeding in ignoring each other only too well!"

November 27–30: Thanksgiving vacation summed up in "one phrase— 'English assignments.'"

December 1: "Pooh to Mr. Crockett." He admits their assignment is not "humanly possible" and postpones it until just before Christmas vacation. But they still have to prepare a ten-minute oral report. "The duffer ruined my Thanksgiving vacation—NOW THIS."

December 6: Off to the library to work on an oral report.

December 7: The day passes "like a dream" working on her "oral topic."

December 8: Oral reports begin. "I had the awful feeling that he might make a mistake and call upon little unprepared-me!" John Pollard calls her up for her "first real <u>date</u>! (Not to a school dance or anything!)"

December 9: Finishes writing her report and memorizing it in an "amazingly short time." She has nightmares about forgetting her talk.

December 10: Stage fright: cold, damp, and clammy hands. When Mr. Crockett closes the door, she feels like a trapped animal. When he calls on her, she says, "charmingly": "Mr. Crockett and classmates. . . . From there on I had the class in my power. No one stirred. . . . I even fancied that I heard Mr. Crockett laugh appreciatively at one of my scathing remarks concerning the climax of my novel." He "takes exception" to some of her points, but she is sure he enjoyed her "oratory."

December 13: Tense about her first date, but she feels "suddenly powerful and confident" in her "plaid and black velvet dress." Her date is six foot, three inches. They drive to a ballroom with a carpeted path to "circular tiers of divans that circled down and down like a sort of amphitheater surrounding the circular dance floor." Two huge mirrors make the dance floor seem larger than it really is. "The more we dance the closer John [Pollard] grabbed me and it made me feel a peculiar sort of distaste toward him. I really think he's a drip—I don't like him . . . he thinks he's so wonderful." She finds him "nauseating." She avoids "parking" with him, saying she is not hungry, and gets home thinking of it as "opportunity for meeting other boys and letting everyone know how much fun I am"—hoping, of course, to be asked out again.

December 14: Listens to Mr. Rice minister at the Charles Street jail and describes criminals awaiting trial: thieves, murderers, gunmen, a prostitute, and a traitor who had broadcast over Radio Berlin. Describes the barred doors and how she will "never forget the huge room, three stories high, that confronted us—late Bostonian sun streamed in through the high, dusty streaked windows, thin railed cobwebs of iron stairways clung to the walls and narrow iron walks high above bordered the three stories of cell blocks." They are not allowed to speak to the prisoners. Sylvia spots a handsome, tall boy, jailed for a holdup, looking at her as she keeps her eyes on the floor. In the chapel, women prisoners whisper and giggle, supervised by "two matrons in stiff starched white uniforms." She hears one prisoner say, "Haven't they ever seen a <u>prisoner</u> before." Sylvia thinks the pretty African American with a "very curvy figure" is the prostitute. During Mr. Rice's sermon, the men are quiet and the women "gossipy"—"what language they used!" They visit the prison kitchen, a "musty old food storeroom," another building with padded and solitary confinement cells, "pitch black" with no windows or benches and a slot to slide through the bread and water. The warden "playfully" shuts them up in solitary. "It was awful!" The highlight of the trip is to a prisoner's cell that features his two-foot-high church built out of wooden matchsticks with an interior of "tiny carved pews and an altar with two wee gold candlesticks." He accepts their compliments with "proud embarrassment" and wishes them a merry Christmas.

December 20: Dress rehearsal for Sunday-school Christmas pageant. John Pollard invites her on another double date. He nauseates her, but she agrees.

December 21: Ruthie Freeman drops in from Winthrop to borrow a dress for her "Rainbow Dance." Dresses up in her "yellow taffeta with a black velvet bustle" for the church pageant.

December 22: "Oh! Joy! I just finished dressing for the assembly tonight and look positively angelic and Chrismassy in my frothy evening dress with the billowing white net skirt & the line brocaded satin top." She puts two little red poinsettias in her hair with a "long red velvet bow" at her waist that, along with her "dark brown wavy hair," make her look "really glamorous in the colored lights of our gay Christmas tree." Perry Norton picks her up, and she enjoys the dance, with various boys cutting in on Perry and Perry cutting back. "I never had such fun in my life. (PS. We had a hilarious conga line)."

December 23: Wakes up "dazed, tired, happy, and my head feeling like a cotton cannon ball." A foot of snow for a white Christmas.

December 24: "Colored Christmas lights and window candles gleamed mellowly through the dusk, and there was an expectant 'waiting' feeling in the air."

December 25: Gets up early with Warren to open their stockings. Her gifts: "swirly navy blue ballerina skirt; a cabled red sweater; a wool plaid blouse; a frothy, lacy, sheer Gibson girl blouse; two pairs of cobweb nylons; a pair of silver dancing slippers. . . . Three adorable lipsticks in a little gold case; a silver football pin; a pair of white wool socks knit by Ruthie [Freeman], a book of A. E. Housman's poems; Stephen Benet's Pocket book; black velvet ribbon; a box of candy, and $3.50 in cool cash! Not bad, eh?!!"

December 26: Snow is two feet high with six-foot drifts.

December 29: Housecleaning before Ruth and David Freeman arrive, coasting in the afternoon with Ruthie, Perry Norton comes over for supper and gets along well with David, who is over six feet tall now and, like Ruthie, "getting better looking all the time." They play "telepathy games, question games, drawing games, and pulled molasses candy till eleven."

December 30: Shovels sidewalk, coasts with Ruthie, purchases an "adorable plaid taffeta dress for tomorrow night's part for $2."

December 31: Out on a double date with John Pollard, Jack Hoag, and Elizabeth. At the Maugus Club,[341] she has to "hold back my hatred" of John's "loose-jointed" ways. Just before twelve, "everyone started blowing horns and acting like fools." In the deafening noise, Sylvia and Elizabeth were "ready to scream for everything to be quiet." Eager to get home and refuses John's wish to stay out longer, commenting "it's hard for me to be very nice to someone I think is a dope." She expects he will tell all the boys that she is "prissy and unresponsive." But she says she doesn't care.

1948

Undated: Poems—"Earthbound," "The Farewell," "Fog," "The Grackels," "Have You Forgotten?," "I Have Found the Perfect World," "I Reach Out," "Let the Rain Fall Gently," "Obsession," "P. N.,"[342] "Patience," "Portrait," "Recognition," "Reflection," "Riddle," "Song of the Daydreamer," "Spring Again," "Summer Street," "Tulips at Dawn," "Song of the Wild Geese," "In This Field We Wander Through," and "The Mistake."

Drawings—ballerina on verso and self-sketch (both pencil). {PM}
Stories—"Heat," "The Attic View," and "The Brink." {LWM}

January 1: Works with Warren on a snow house.

January 2: A blizzard: Watches flakes float down landing on the "black, skinny angular branches" of birch trees "softened with fairly-puffs of snow." The "lumpy heaps shoveled from sidewalk and driveway are molded to even, sculptured white curves by the ever shifting wind and the ceaseless falling snow. It is indeed inspiring weather."

January 9: Reading over diary, she concludes, "I must have a one track mind—as Margot puts it (sadly)—I'm 'boy crazy.' Well I can't help that! . . . It is boring, I admit, to read over my accounts . . . when I've changed to someone else, but then! It helps to write it down."

January 17: A "super time" with Betsy Powley and Prissy Steele.

January 25: With Betsy, spends the afternoon on Grammy's bed, "reading aloud to each other some spicy parts from two nasty books I received a while ago, when a car honked outside. I ran to the window and saw a car (driven by a handsome guy) ramming into the snow banks outside our front walk." It is the "athletic John Hall!!"

January 27: Midyear exams: "I did very well or flunked completely."

January 30: At a thrilling basketball game, sits with Betsy behind the team and almost chokes "to death—that awful smell! Ugh! But we had a wonderful time drooling over J. Hall."

January 31: A triple date arranged by John Pollard, loads of fun, home "safe and sane I think."

February 1: As if in a dream: "Who should get on the bus (alone) but handsome, magnificent, drooly, superb, wonderful TOMMY DUGGIN!" He gives her a "darling smile." He walks her home, and she is careful to walk slowly. Some mean conversation ensues about Pollard. Even though Tommy Duggin seems full of himself, she still likes him.

February 2: All As in Latin, math, French, and English. "I am still in a daze."

February 6: "Gay Nineties Scrap-Book in High School tonight."

February 7: An assembly dance. Why does Tommy Duggin dance with Louise Pullen and cut in on Barby? "Darn! I'm a lot nicer than she is."

February 15: A "horrible shock": sees Tommy Duggin kissing Betsy Powley. "When she recognized me she let out a surprised 'Sylvia' and the look of mingled feeling on that girl's face I shall never forget! I greeted them non-chalantly and they just sat there on the bench making no room for me to sit down or anything. I could have cheerfully murdered all three of them then and there. . . . Now sometime later, I can see the humor of it all." At home, she bursts into tears. "If only it weren't Betsy! I'll get Tommy yet, even if it is for another girl! Despair!"

February 20: Hopes Perry Norton will take her to the junior prom so that she doesn't have to accept John Pollard's invitation, Perry blushes and asks her to "make up my mind" about whether she really wants to go with him.

February 21: "The Attic View." {PM}

February 22: At the movies to see *Killer McCoy*,[343] "starring the NEW Mickey Rooney," and *Her Husband's Affairs*.[344] "A very fresh group of three men sat next to me, and the one nearest tried to start a conversation in the middle of the movie." He asks whether she lives in Wellesley, about where she goes to school, and tries to hold her hand. She turns away and loses herself in the "bloody boxing bouts" of *Killer McCoy*.

February 23: Coasting in the morning with Ruthie Freeman: "I love that girl."

Quite aside from Plath's attendance at Unitarian Sunday school, she showed a deep and abiding interest in religion in her course work at Smith, during her employment for a Christian Science family, and in her studies at Smith College and Cambridge University.

February 25: Enjoys talking to Don Woodward about religion, dancing in the evening: "He is a bit too effeminate (or something) for me but I learned a lot from him. He's 18 and a senior which gives me a lot of prestige." Returns home after a "sobering (heaven knows why) evening."

February 26: Shopping with Mother after a "good piano lesson."

February 28: Says everyone has the "best time of their lives" at the assembly dance, lots of cutting in and changing partners, enjoys chatting up some new partners, picks Tommy Duggin for "Ladies' choice," who keeps holding her "tighter and tighter" until she is almost breathless. "I'm just so 'in love' with him that it hurts." His chin against her cheek, "so manly and rough where he had shaved. I was just in dreamland. . . . Betsy [Powley] can be kissed by him everyday and twice on Sunday but <u>I've had this one triumphant night!</u>"

February 29: Still thinking about Tommy Duggin, who is taking someone else to the junior prom, hopes he will get tired of his date.

March 4: "The Mistake." {PM}

March 5: "Oh, horror of horrors!" Dreading her junior-prom date with John Pollard, annoys him by paying attention to Bob Talley, who "acted as if he'd just come to realize I existed."

March 7: "Room in the World" (a play), "Sarah." {PM}

March 8: More fun with Talley at the Gold Key art awards in town.

March 13: A good time square dancing after a trying time babysitting three obstreperous boys, she dances with everyone.

March 14: Perry Norton: "pure and wonderful. It just seems unnecessary to talk when we're together because our thoughts run along the same lines.

I feel so natural and perfect when I'm with him . . . I feel as if I'm walking on an elevated plane and that there is no need for the little surface boy-girl chatter . . . I can be happy as long as Perry is alive." She thinks others are laughing at her "awkward predicament" about Tommy Duggin: "it isn't every day that a girl makes such a fool of herself by running after a boy!"

March 16: An "excited joy ride" with schoolmates in Bob Tapley's car to Overbrook, Massachusetts, and then to Weston, Massachusetts, Bob decides to show off while driving and playing a harmonica and rams a snowbank: "Just call me a snowplow," he exclaims.

March 18: Off with friends after school: "This is the first time in my life that I haven't told mother exactly where I went." Another joy ride with the boys in the front saying "nasty" things. They turn around to see if the girls heard them.

March 22: Back to school after being sick all weekend because of the "Thursday escapade" in the car.

March 25: In art, begins a pastel of her friend, Arden Tapley.

March 27: Poems—"The Traveller," "Youth's Appeal for Peace," and "The Visitor." {PM}

April: In *The Bradford*, publishes a front-page article, "The Atomic Threat," expressing her pacifist ideas. {HC}

April 16: Poem: "Joy." {PM}

April 17: Poem: "Persecuted." {PM}

May 13: Begins work in English with classmates, writing and producing three radio plays, an adaptation of Poe's "Monsieur Bon-Bon," a play about World War II, and "an original play" by Sylvia in collaboration with Mary Ventura, titled *The Island*. {EB}

Spring: Junior prom.

June 14: Writes to Hans-Joachim Neupert: Calls his writing "remarkably nice," praises his command of English, hopes they can exchange visits. College-bound students study hard, but others are "carefree and jolly, thinking only of parties and fun." Explains that her father was born in Germany and came to America as a boy and became a professor of German and biology at Boston University and wrote a book about bees. Her father is dead, so her mother teaches. She earns money by babysitting. Asks about the stories and poems he reads, hopes to hear more about Germany and his "ideas about religion, war, or life or science," provides a map of her part of Massachusetts, likening Wellesley to a "country-like" town but with the shops found in cities, thanks him for the map and mentions she could follow the course of the Rhine River to his home in Grebenhain and has marked it with a star to show where he lives. She likes his photograph. "I look so forward to your next letter!"

June 21: Poem: "Carnival." {PM}

July 1: Returns to the Vineyard Sailing Camp in Oak Bluffs, Massachusetts.

July 2: Letter to "Dear Mother": Shocked to learn about a girl who won't write home to her mother, calls herself, Betsy Powley, and Anne Brown, "the three musketeers," mentions a long conversation with three sailors on another boat, swimming tests and sailing on the first day of camp. "I'll never get homesick—I love it here . . . don't expect more than a post card each day."

July 3: Letter to "Dear Mother": Complains about a noisy Betsy. "If she wakes me up again—I'll conk her with my suit case. . . . Love Sherry."

"Dearest Mum": Refreshed after swimming. "I live to go sailing! I feel a sort of thrill go through me when I'm at the tiller thinking 'This is me sailing the boat,'" looks forward to bike trips.

"Dear Mum": "Here I am again. At this rate I'll use all my post cards up in a week." She is eating and eating but only weighs 122 pounds.

July 4: Letter to "Dear Mum": Four miles of biking to Methodist Trinity Church with a "lovely dome for the roof and open-sides." Hopes for a visit on the eleventh and suggests bringing some fruit.

July 5: Letter to "Dear Mummy": A swimming meet this afternoon, complains about charges for transportation—"Things are so gypsy here." Not enough sailing and just occasional bike trips—"sometimes things get so dull."

July 6: Letter to "Dear Mum": draws two pictures of sailboats to show how the "boat was perpendicular to the waves" so that her face was almost in the water.

"Dear Mum": "I can't wait to see you Sunday." Dreads the "overnight hike . . . sleeping on the coooold cold ground!"

July 7: Letter to "Dear Mum": Skimpy servings of mostly salads and soups, so she fills up on bread and butter. Memorizing a skit. She has received more mail than anyone else in her tent. "Keep up the good work!"

July 8: Letter to "Dear Mummy": A sore throat and backache, so the nurse won't let her swim, wears flannel every night and is very thankful. Asks her mother to give her address to friends, including Wayne Sterling. Getting too old for camp, except as a counselor, but the counselors dislike "our whole tent," signs herself "Love to all, from your very own me Sherry."

July 11–12: After a visit from Mother, "Naughty, naughty mother, Honestly I simply could die when I think of you running up and down that damn old hill." Hopes her mother can write and says: "honestly that you are fine and rested and suffer no ill effects from your silly run! I don't know how you'd get along without me, really." Looks forward to returning home to write poems and stories, feels an "emotional purge" after her mother's visit, "all my pent up feelings let go when I cried, and I feel so much better," singing hymns around the campfire also helps.

July 13: Letter to "Dear Mummy": No more sore throat, but she has a bloodshot, watery eye. Complains that Ruth Freeman is a pain in the neck—"At times like this I long for my very own mummy. I miss our piano, too, but I'll cheer up."

July 14: Letter to "Dear Mum": dramatizes "Snow White," playing Snow White and Ruth as the wicked queen, looking "stunning in a draped rose bathrobe—I wore a lacy white blouse and a blue silk skirt."

"Dear Mum": Writes the letter during "rest hour." Relieved to hear her mother is well and happy after her "little run." Feels better herself: "A stomach full of food [bananas and a tin of molasses cookies] puts me in a very contented mood!"

"Dearest Mum": "so happy here I'll cry when I come home."

July 15: Goes out rowing and is enjoying herself.

July 15–16: Details of counselor training—"In my way of thinking just about the whole camp is getting to know me!" Looks forward to some free time to sunbathe, she is told she has an "inborn sense of balance and design" in pottery. Describes the "iridescent moonlight . . . like a clear, silver wash over the trees and it shines through the leaves and into our tent, touching everything with a quiet, hushed radiance."

July 17: Letter to "Dear Mum": a quick note to say her "emotional thermometer is stationed permanently at 125 the 'Highly Happy mark.'"

July 18: Letter to "Dear mummy": exhausted after a very long bike ride (thirty miles).

July 19: Letter to "Dear Mum": Her eyes are better now that she is using sunglasses. A dull sermon in church, rejects a belief in the trinity. "Give my special love to Grammy & grampy. These two weeks are flying by on wings of jam and cheese."

"Dearest Mum": "My thermometer is rising a little more even. Lots of hugs & kisses."

"Dear Mum": too much starch in the camp diet.

July 20: Upset because Betsy Powley and Ruth Freeman have gone sailing and she is left behind, cheers herself up with sketching. "I'm getting tanner—so watch out."

Letter to "Dear mummy": hopes her mother received the last two postcards—"I just had to blow off steam to someone, and now I feel much better."

"Dear Mum": feeling even better, happy to meet a girl whose brother knows Wayne Sterling. PS: "I had about the most fun today as I have had yet. The morning was very calm and we sailed across down the lagoon to a boat-building place."

July 21: Letter to "Dear Mum": After overcoming "petty jealousies, found myself . . . filled with complete serenity" and grateful for "cheery little cards which have arrived so faithfully!" Happy to get a card from Mrs. Freeman and Wayne Sterling's letter.

July 22: Letter to "Dear Mum": Works on a jam pot in pottery, a little lopsided since she did it by hand. "Don't expect too much."

July 23: Letter to "Dear Mummy": Loves her lopsided jam pot. Describes the process of drying, firing, soaking, glazing, painting, and "heating again!" Three-hundred yards of swimming: "50 crawl, 50 inverted breast stroke, 50 sidestroke, 50 breast stroke, 50 dog paddle." Draws portraits of "just about the whole camp," a demand for pictures: "That's where everyone's vanity crops up!—They all want self-portraits."

July 24: Letter to "Dear Mum": "Boy! Do I have an earful to tell you!" Relates what she hears in the infirmary while getting nose drops, a cook confesses she doesn't know how to make the camp food.

August 10: Postcard to "Dear Mum": Arriving at South Station at noon on Thursday noon, with midge bites and a tan from sailing. "I was glad to get your letter! I am lucky!! I love you lots & realized how lucky I am to have you for a mother."

September 24: Letter to Hans Joachim Neupert: Happy to have a letter from her "entertaining correspondent" after a return home from school. Mentions the "special place" in her heart for the ocean: "I like the way the water changes from one mood to another—from high waves on dark, stormy days, to tranquil ripples on sunny days." She realizes how complacent life could be for people not suffering. "Perhaps when I get out of school and into the business world, that will change." Even an event as colossal as the war hardly seems real, even though she is quite aware of it. In the eleventh grade, she has not yet decided between "commercial art or journalism (writing)." Dreads the atomic bomb and wishes that all nations could "forget their differences and work toward a common goal." She has many questions about the way Neupert lives, his hometown, and how young people think.

October 27: Sixteenth birthday.

Ca. October–December: Writes a poem, "Neither Moonlight nor Starlight," about her desire to write, acknowledging a voice that rages within her that can never be still, writes a series of poems—"Obsession," "Recognition," "Reflection," "Earthbound," and "Tulips at Dawn"—about the "mysterious nature of identity, the fear of self-knowledge, and the sinister nature of seemingly normal everyday existence." {AW}

December 2: Makes the honor roll. {EB}

December 20: Letter to Hans-Joachim Neupert: Wants to know what he eats and whether it is similar to the cold cereal she has for breakfast. American cooking can be "tasteless, but she is "very fortunate to have an Austrian grandmother who cooks good European dishes for us." Describes window shopping for Christmas, singing carols, and other holiday customs and sports, like skiing, children demanding stories about Santa Claus while babysitting. Traveling to Europe is one of her "far off dreams."

1949

Undated: Drafts—"Adolescence," "The Dark River," "Humoresque," "I Put My Fingers in My Ears," "In Passing," "Lonely Song," "Question," "Wallflower," "Among the Shadow Throngs," "East Wind," "The Green Rock," "Place: A Bedroom, Saturday Night, in June." {PM}

January 29–February 6: Letter to Hans-Joachim Neupert: Describes Christmas customs and Thanksgiving, mentions completing her twenty-five-page thesis on Mormonism, prefers classical music to bebop, but she can play boogie-woogie on the piano. Dreads the idea of a third world war and considers war as "disastrous & unnecessary." Realizes her views are idealistic, wishes more younger people would become active in politics for a better world.

March: Writes an anti-war poem, "Seek No More the Young," inspired by World War I poets Wilfred Owen and Siegfried Sassoon, evoking the "eyes glazed blind" and "the eyes of those alive—alone!"

March 11: Works on poem, "Seek No More the Young." {PM}

February 17: Makes the honor roll. {EB}

March 15: Letter to Professor Irwin Edman of Columbia University on behalf of English class 31, challenging his article, "A Reasonable Life in a Mad World."[345] He leaves out the "spiritual element." Humankind cannot rely on the self for guidance. Acknowledging an "omniscient power, man may view his problems and his goals in a less distorted relationship with the rest of the universe."

April 14: Letter to Hans-Joachim Neupert: "It must be extremely difficult for you to study without any books—I find it hard enough to study with them!" Plans to play tennis during Easter break even though she is not a good player, mentions her piano practice, love of music, including German composers Beethoven, George Frideric Handel, and Wolfgang Amadeus Mozart, a favorite: "Moonlight Sonata." Claude Debussy is one of her "ideal composers—his music is so clear-cut and dreamy," mentions "La mer," "La fille aux cheveux de lin," "Deux arabesques," and "Clair de lune." Discusses religious groups who prophesize the end of the world, shares his love of dancing—a good way for members of the opposite sex to learn about one another, corrects some of his English expressions while noting she has the same problem writing in French. She is planning a painting excursion with a friend. Wants him to describe what she would see if she met him. "PS. do you have big fat robins that come in the spring? There is one bold fellow eating a worm on our lawn right this minute!"

June 10: Works on poem, "To Ariadne." {PM}

June 26: Sails on the "Kiboko" to Star Island, New Hampshire, attending a Unitarian youth conference. {PKS}

June 27: Letter to "Dear Maman [mother]": she is "fine" and enjoying meeting new people.

June 28: Letter to "Dear Mum": Plays tennis and dances at a costume ball "feeling perfect." Wants news about the family. "John Pollard is here—what an odd thing he is."

June 29: Worries in her diary about a "dateless evening," smiles at Eddie Mason, and "he came running, and I knew I had a date for 'le banquet.' . . . I hope I can stand him tomorrow night. I can never relax, when I'm with him, because he's always leering into my face, trying to attract my attention all the time, which gets mildly horrible after a while."

July 1: Attracted to Hank, she turns to Eddie Mason, who flashes his "weak little grin with a veritable Aurora Borealis. 'You won't mind, will you?'"

July 4: Letter to Hans-Joachim Neupert: Looks forward to the long days ahead now that school is over, taking art lessons and doing watercolor sketches, describes July Fourth celebrations—fireworks are "burning bouquets of light," evoking a "huge sigh of awe" from the "crowd of thousands." Describes the Unitarian youth conference—one hundred girls and sixty boys, an invigorating, even spiritual experience with "painted sunsets, or the first rosy light of dawn across the ocean," ten groups discuss various problems, swimming, dancing, costume party, movies. Asks about his projects and plans for the next school year.

July 9: The verdict on John Hodges: "He always leaves me up in the air; without ever making another date. He makes me so mad."

July 16: First alcoholic drink: "No, lightening didn't blast me on the spot, and I didn't turn purple! It tastes good, sort of, but it burns like a fire inside."

July 22: "I am awful. I actually wanted to go parking." Worries about her reputation and boys losing respect for her: "Why is everyone so embarrassed & secretive about physical differences & intercourse, etc.? Maybe if we could talk without such inhibitions, sex problems would be easier to solve."

August: "As for reflections on this summer," she "could stand to gain a few pounds, and my complexion could be better, not to mention my personality." But she has "assets to balance my major failings," including her considerable experience "avec les garçons"—those she has loved and lost. But "there's always another one around the corner." Lists the twenty-one boys she has had dates with since the fall of 1948, giving a "*" to three memorable occasions and "**" to three memorable guys.

The above is another example of how Plath uses her diary to mark important junctures in her life and reflect on the nature of her existence.

August 24: Letter to Hans-Joachim Neupert: Feels "wistful and nostalgic" as the new school year approaches. "This has been my last summer of really carefree youth—next summer I will get some sort of job and earn money in preparation for college." She prefers to go away and live on campus but may have to accept a Wellesley scholarship. The town has a "very wealthy class of people here, and in my school almost all my acquaintances come from well-to-do homes." Speaks of conquering her fear of heights by climbing a water tower. She has sent poems and stories to magazines, and all have come back as rejections but also with a few "notes of encouragement" from editors. She will keep trying. Asks whether he ever wonders about "why you are you and not someone else . . . it sounds silly to say it, but it is absorbing when you think of it." How much of her is environment, how much inherited? "I think that many of our opinions are not really our own but rather ideas that we have unconsciously borrowed from other people."

The entry below is perhaps the first time Plath articulates the idea of a bond with a man that would function as a kind of circuit of feeling that would complete herself.

August 30: A trip to Cape Cod with John Hodges: The sun burns through, and the sky gets bluer as they cross the "exuberant height of the far-flung bridge" down to the "sea of green pine trees threaded with a colorless ribbon of roadways. And suddenly, there was the ocean—my own special ocean!" They play tennis with another couple. Then swimming—"I was surprised and happy to find out that John does not swim especially well. I was relieved, because I am no Esther Williams." Thrills to the idea of a "physical complement—someone who understands, I get the feeling of a thrilling current of joy flowing. . . . Not just a single flash of perception and delight, but a continual feeling of motion, of answer to a question; of response to a seeking—a complete circuit of electric, tingling happiness." They drive into Falmouth, Massachusetts, "tan and radiant" in their bathing suits. "Today was a basis for our companionship that I will never forget!"

August 31: Plays tennis with John Hodges, and they talk about marriage. He tells her how two of their friends have "intercourse practically every week, like a couple of dogs." Sylvia reads *The Townsman*'s terse announcement about the couple's sudden marriage with only the immediate family present. She is heartened that John's opinion of her has improved. They agree that sex has to be beautiful and not misused.

Fall: Aurelia preserves a lock of Sylvia's hair. {PM}

September 15: Publishes "High School Highlights" column in *The Townsman*. {EB}

October 10: Letter to Hans-Joachim Neupert: Asks whether bodies are still buried under German ruins. She regrets she cannot take a European trip that a teacher is organizing for young people next summer. She needs to save all her money for college. Explains the different kinds of poems she has written, mostly in traditional rhyme, such as "White Phlox," "Gone Is the River," "The Farewell, "The Stranger," and "City Streets." She has a "strong kinship for anything German . . . the most beautiful language in the world." Meeting people with German names or traits excites a "sudden secret warmth." Recommends books for him to read: *My Ántonia* (1918), poems of Robert Frost, plays by Eugene O'Neill (*Strange Interlude* [1928], *Great God Brown* [1926], *Emperor Jones* [1920]), *Gone with the Wind*—worthwhile expressions of "various sections & eras of American culture."

October 28: Boards a train to Williamstown, Massachusetts, for a week-end with John Hall[346] at the college—a Friday night pep rally, Saturday's football game, and a house party. {PA}

November 7: Sends her letter of application to Smith College. {PA}

November 13: "As of today I have decided to keep a diary again—just a place where I can write my thoughts and opinions when I have a moment. Somehow I have to keep and hold the rapture of being seventeen. Every day is so precious I feel infinitely sad at the thought of all this time melting farther and farther away from me as I grow older." She considers this the "perfect time" of her life, with the "tragedies and happiness . . . All unimportant now." Describes how she has made her own room suited to her "tailored, uncluttered and peaceful" with subdued colors "peach and gray, brown-gold maple—a highlight of maroon here and there," with the "quiet lines of the furniture—the two bookcases filled with poetry books and fairy-tales saved from childhood." At present, she is "very happy, sitting at my desk and look out at the bare trees around the house across the street—the chilly gray sky like a slate of icy marble propped up against the hills. The leaves lie in little withered heaps, blown in place orange piles in the gutters." She wants to share her existence in a "wry, humorous light—and mock myself as I mock others." She dreads the idea of growing older and marrying. "Spare me from cooking three meals a day" and the "routine and rote." She wants to be free, to travel the world, to learn about "morals and standards" other than her own. "I want, I think, to be omniscient—and a bit insane." She thinks of herself as "the girl who wanted to be God." This is a "terrible egotism," she confesses, and yet she worries that she has been "too conditioned to the conventional surrounding of this community." What vanity and what a craving for pretty clothes she has. Would she face herself at last and overcome her fears of the "big choices" looming up in her life: which college, which career? She is reluctant to forsake her mother's protection, yet she wants to devote herself to a cause.

November 24: Breaks it off with John Hodges who does not share her interest in art and books, she watches him leave and then sees him sobbing in his car. She shuts the door "slowly, sick inside. I had done this—so much more hurtfully than anything John Hodges had done to me. If I could only start over again—going out." She wonders about what will happen when others hear about the breakup, from "what quarter the reverberations will come. I know I managed this whole thing pretty brutally. But one emotion I can't fake is love." She prefers "light friendships with a lot of boys! I don't want to settle down yet!" So, another chapter has ended. She gets some "disgusted looks in my direction" and is without dates. "First I had five boys going out with me—now all of them are strangely silent!"

November 26: Goes out to a local dancehall, the Totem Pole, and everyone is drunk, and she is in a "rather gay mood myself, since I created quite a sensation (my ego cropping up again)." A good-looking blond boy ambles over to her and asks her name and says that Poe "wrote a sonnet to Sylvia once. May I kiss you?" She describes girls pretending to be happy with the boys they hate, boys leaving their dates and flirting with other girls— "bottles, bottles everywhere, and the high, nervous laughter. Even I found myself laughing—at myself for being part of all that. For even I was playing a part." She feels like screaming because she could not express herself.

Letter to Hans-Joachim Neupert: A greeting card wishing him a Merry Christmas and happy New Year. Describes her life as "very happy." Mentions she is editor of the school newspaper. Writing a thirty-page term paper on Thomas Mann[347] and asks for his advice.

December 19: "Today I met Patsy [O'Neil] and was, as usual, caught up in a senseless babble of words. Talk, talk, talk. That's all we do."

December 20: "Today was much better." A calm visit from a boyfriend, Bob Reideman, a "companionable time."

December 21: Bob drops her off at home. "I felt let down somehow."

December 22: "I have this whole asinine book I've been writing in. What I call writing doesn't deserve the name." She feels like she is just "wallowing."

December 23: A complicated time sorting out her feelings for Bob Reideman and John Hodges.

Boston from Winthrop, Massachusetts, the site of Plath's early childhood home. Courtesy of Gail Crowther.

Johnson Avenue, Winthrop, Massachusetts, the site of Plath's early childhood home. Courtesy of Gail Crowther.

Winthrop School in Winthrop, Massachusetts. Courtesy of Gail Crowther.

Otto Plath's grave.
Courtesy of Gail Crowther.

The house of Plath's grandparents
(the Schobers) in Point Shirley in
Winthrop, Massachusetts. Courtesy of
Gail Crowther.

Point Shirley in Winthrop, Massachusetts, where Plath's grandparents lived and a place she commemorated in one of her poems.
Courtesy of Gail Crowther.

Plath's home at 26 Elmwood Road,
Wellesley, Massachusetts. Courtesy
of Gail Crowther.

Elmwood Road bedroom.
Courtesy of Peter K. Steinberg.

Elmwood Road interior and fireplace.
Courtesy of Peter K. Steinberg.

Martha's Vineyard, Massachusetts, where Plath spent two weeks in the summer of 1947 at Girl Scout camp. Courtesy of Gail Crowther.

Plath's scout uniform.
Courtesy of Gail Crowther.

Wellesley High School.
Courtesy of Gail Crowther.

Lookout Farm, where Plath worked the summer before she entered her freshman year at Smith College. Courtesy of Gail Crowther.

Arden Tapley

Tall, friendly and quiet (sometimes) . . . Artistic . . . Good student . . . Remember "Henry" (her old Ford) . . . "Air raid!" . . . Another "calorie counter" . . . Raw carrots . . . Has a nice singing voice . . . That naturally curly, blonde hair . . . Hates food . . . Sense of humor.

John Stenberg

Sten . . . Tall, thin, and good-looking . . . A Yearbook editor . . . Basketball captain . . . Has a good word for everyone . . . Seen with Duck . . . Lots of fun . . . Oh, those Cape parties . . . Drives a green Graham . . . Television enthusiast . . . "Good Time" . . . Ping! . . . From God's country.

Frank Irish

Skeek . . . Lots of fun anytime . . . Always out front with Perry in the cross country meets . . . "Life, life, I love it so—" . . . If it squeeks it might be "Skeek" . . . He can get an "A" from any teacher — in high school . . . College? Time will tell.

Bruce Mansfield

Manny . . . Excellent athlete . . . Yes, he's been on the varsity football and baseball teams for three years! . . . Personality plus . . . Oh, that grin! . . . Friendly . . . Versatile . . . "Where's Joe?" . . . Good looking . . . What DOES he have that the girls like? . . . Another curly head . . . Well liked by all . . . Football Co-Captain.

Wellesley High School yearbook photographs. Courtesy of Peter K. Steinberg.

Patricia O'Neil

Patty . . . Friendly . . . Pleasing voice . . . Always has a smile . . . Doing devotionals again this week, Patty?? . . . Always full of wim, wigor, and witality . . . Excels in basketball . . . Bradford editor . . . Where'd she get those great, big, beautiful eyes? . . . Vive la France! !

Louise Giesey

Small and dark . . . Vivacious . . . Prominent voice in the Senior Class . . . Editor of the Yearbook . . . Member of the Student Council . . . Girls' sports editor of the Bradford . . . Writer of Highschool Highlights . . . What happened to the mailbox? . . . One of the Sub Debs . . . Reissue on Southern Accent.

Dorrit Licht

Marilyn Fraser

Quiet and studious . . . Musical . . . Famed for her violin selections . . . Has taken many prizes for the presentations of speeches written by herself . . . She's artistic, too . . . Her ambition will get something out of life for her . . . Art editor of Yearbook.

Wellesley High School yearbook photographs. Courtesy of Peter K. Steinberg.

Elizabeth Jane Powley

Betts . . . Cute, petite, and popular . . . Has a knack for designing (?) and making her own clothes . . . One of the Yearbook editors . . . One time Student Council member . . . Never a dull moment when Betsy's around . . . Oh, those hen parties . . . Gully-Gully . . . Good time! . . . Let's play inch-me, pinch-me!

Perry Norton

Norty . . . A good friend for anyone . . . National Honor Society member . . . "Hi ya, champ!" . . . Captain of Cross Country team . . . Track star, too . . . Clarence DeMar and Gil Dodds better watch out . . . Likes to swim off Cape Cod and travel by thumb . . . The medical world has a good man in its future.

Jeanne Woods

"Jeannie with the light brown hair" . . . Those beautiful hand-knit sweaters . . . Excels in field hockey, tennis and basketball . . . Bradford . . . Student Council . . . Came from Philadelphia . . . Always ready with a smile . . Beaming personality . . . Good worker.

Thomas Duggin

"Where's Liz?" . . . One of Wellesley's "sparkling" ends . . . "Hey, Dug!" . . . An "active" sense of humor . . . Performs wonders with his model A . . . Seen often with "Gately", "Powley", "George" Norcross, and "x" . . . Track enthusiast . . . Friendly and well liked by ONE and all.

Wellesley High School yearbook photographs. Courtesy of Peter K. Steinberg.

Sylvia Plath

Warm smile . . . Energetic worker . . . Co-Editor of Bradford . . . Bumble Boogie piano special . . . Clever with chalk and paints . . . Weekends at Williams . . . Those fully packed sandwiches . . . Basketball and tennis player . . . Future writer . . . Those rejecticn slips from *Seventeen* . . . Oh, for a license.

Wellesley High School yearbook photographs. Courtesy of Peter K. Steinberg.

Haven House, where Plath spent her first year at Smith College. Courtesy of Gail Crowther.

Haven House porch, where Plath met some of her dates during her first year at Smith College. Courtesy of Gail Crowther.

The Belmont Hotel, where Plath waited tables in the early summer of 1952 before she became ill and returned to Wellesley. Courtesy of Gail Crowther.

The Cantor home in Chatham, Massachusetts, where Sylvia worked during the summer of 1952. Courtesy of Gail Crowther.

Plath's dorm room in Lawrence House, where scholarship students stayed at Smith College. Courtesy of Gail Crowther.

One of Plath's journals.
Courtesy of Gail Crowther.

Sage Hall at Smith College, where Plath attended meetings and lectures. Courtesy of Gail Crowther.

Neilson Library at Smith College, where Plath spent many hours studying. Courtesy of Gail Crowther.

Smith College infirmary, where Plath was often treated for sinusitis and other ailments. Courtesy of Gail Crowther.

Smith College waterfalls, where Plath went with Gordon Lameyer on October 1, 1954. Courtesy of Gail Crowther.

Paradise Pond at Smith College, where Plath spent time with her dates. Courtesy of Gail Crowther.

Rahar's, a Northampton, Massachusetts, restaurant that Plath frequently patronized. Courtesy of Gail Crowther.

Le Veau d'or, in New York City, where Plath dined with Richard Sassoon. Courtesy of Gail Crowther.

Bloomingdale's and other New York City department stores, where Plath shopped during her *Mademoiselle* summer. Courtesy of Gail Crowther.

The Barbizon Hotel, where Plath and other *Mademoiselle* editors lived in the summer of 1953. Courtesy of Gail Crowther.

Entrance to *Mademoiselle*, one of the magazines that published Plath's fiction and poetry. Courtesy of Gail Crowther.

Mademoiselle offices, where Plath worked as a guest editor in the summer of 1953. Courtesy of Gail Crowther.

Aurelia Plath. Courtesy of Helle
Collection, Smith College.

Aurelia Plath and Warren
Plath. Courtesy of Helle
Collection, Smith College.

Sylvia Plath in her backyard, 1947.
Courtesy of Helle Collection, Smith College.

Undated: Typescript drafts—"Class Song," "Elizabeth in April," "Family Reunion," "The Invalid," "Midnight Snow," "Slow, Slow the Rhythm of the Moon," "First Date," and "The New Girl." {PM}

No longer a devoted listener to radio programs, and eager to begin a new phase of life, Plath began to turn away from Wellesley and look forward to attending Smith College.

January 2: Letter to Hans-Joachim Neupert: "I am so tired of all the young girls here who think of nothing but party dresses and of boys who care for nothing but money and pretty faces." She decries the parties with the "same empty faces with painted smiles," deplores the crudity of television and radio: "Forgive me for being so vehement!"

February 20: Letter to Neupert: Thanks him for material about Thomas Mann for a term paper due in April. Studying now for college board exams, tells him about the letter she wrote with a friend protesting the hydrogen bomb, mentions attending a winter carnival at the University of New Hampshire and a formal dance at the "Stardust" in Maine.

Plath maintained a steadfastly pacifist position throughout her life.

March 16: The *Christian Science Monitor* publishes "A Youth's Plea for World Peace," coauthored with Perry Norton.

May 10: The director of admissions at Smith sends a letter of acceptance. {PA}

Plath could have attended Wellesley on a scholarship and eased her family's financial worries. Her decision to attend Smith, and her mother's support of that decision, are remarkable, setting up, however, a complicated, conflicted mother-daughter relationship, as Sylvia struggled to be her own person, and her mother struggled to respect her daughter's independence even as she exercised a degree of concern that bedeviled her daughter.

May 30: Letter to Hans-Joachim Neupert: Joyful about acceptance to Smith College, she did well on her term paper, read to the class part of his letter about Mann, which the students enjoyed "very much! . . . You may be amused to know that I feel my German background very strongly. I noticed a sort of patriotic pride when I read Mann." Working on a farm this summer to earn money for college expenses.

June 7: Receives diploma from Gamaliel Bradford Senior High School. {PM}

July: Farm work: "Now I know how people can live without books, without college. When one is so tired at the end of a day one must sleep, and at the next dawn there are more strawberry runners to set, and so one goes on living, near the earth."

Plath's journals begin to take on a meditative tone, casting her own experiences in a historical dimension that will eventually culminate in her mature poetry portraying the self and the world that includes but also transcends her own ego.

August: "And Summer Will Not Come Again" published in *Seventeen* magazine.

She loves people like a stamp collector loves his collection: "Every story, every incident, every bit of conversation is raw material for me." {PJ}

"Nothing is real except the present, and already, I feel the weight of centuries smothering me." {PJ}

Her cheeks burn as she is teased with a singsong "Oh, Sylvia," as she accompanies Ilo Pill, her Estonian coworker on the farm, to the barn to see one of his drawings. In the dim light of the barn, she climbs a ladder to see the picture but senses trouble and says she has to go. "And suddenly his mouth was on mine, hard, vehement, his tongue darting between my lips, his arms like iron around me." She cannot remember whether she screams or whispers in her struggle to break free. He lets her go and smiles as she cries. "No one ever kissed me that way before, and I stood there, flooded with longing, electric shivering." Ilo gives her a glass of water to calm her. Outside everyone seems to know about the assignation as she is called "cutie pie" and "angel face." She smiles, "as if nothing had happened." {PJ}

Describes the sensation of gas entering her body at the dentist's office as she stares at the light and it quivers, breaking into "little iridescent fragments" that swing in a "rhythmic arc, slow at first, then faster, faster." Dreams of a pirate ship and then hears the dentist and sees the sunlight bursting into the room through Venetian blinds. {PJ}

On a date with a Wellesley boy, Emile George de Coen III, dancing at Ten Acres,[348] describes herself as the "American virgin, dressed to seduce." But "we play around and if we're nice girls, we demure at a certain point." She likes the "strong smell of masculinity which creates the ideal medium for me to exist in" and notes the "hard line of his penis taut against my stomach, my breasts aching firm against his chest." Later when he tries to embrace her, she tells him: "You don't give a damn about me except physically." He departs after successfully getting in a long, sweet kiss. She wants him and remarks that after "fifteen thousand years——of what? We're still nothing but animals. . . . God only knows what *he's* thinking." {PJ}

Thinks about the "hints of evolution suggested by the removal of wisdom teeth, the narrowing of the jaw no longer needed to chew such roughage as it was accustomed to." Muses on the "prolonged adolescence of our species; the rites of birth, marriage and death; all the primitive barbaric ceremonies streamlined to modern times." {PJ}

The children across the street put petunias in her hair: "And all my hurts were smoothed away. Something about the frank, guileless blue eyes, the beautiful young bodies, the brief scent of the dying flowers smote me like the clean quick cut of a knife. And the blood of love welled up in my heart with a slow pain." {PJ}

"I like people too much or not at all. I've got to go down deep, to fall into people, to really know them." {PJ}

Letter to Eddie Cohen: "It's getting so I live every moment with terrible intensity." She fears a world war will end everything, with her kid brother never getting a chance to fulfill all his "potentialities in the line of science."

She envies boys who can "dispel sexual hunger freely" while she drags out from "date to date in soggy desire, always unfulfilled . . . so much hurt in this game of searching for a mate, of testing, trying." Without sex organs, she wouldn't waver on the brink of nervous emotion and tears all the time. Seeking a man "physically magnetic and personable." {PJ}

August 1: A hot, steamy day, tempted to write a poem.

The correspondence with Eddie Cohen initiates a new phase of self-assertion and self-criticism that is hastened by Cohen's astute observations of Plath's character and accomplishments.

August 3: Cohen writes to congratulate Sylvia for her story that is more subtle than what usually appears in *Seventeen*.

August 6: Replies to Cohen, gamely accepting his challenge to correspond and to hear from a "critic." She describes her suburban house and environment. She mentions the fifty rejection slips before her first *Seventeen* acceptance and her work on a truck farm: "I just smile when my white collar acquaintances look at me with unbelievable dismay as I tell them about soaking my hands in bleach to get them clean."

August 11: Letter to Cohen: "I wasn't aware that anyone quite like you existed." Describes herself as tall, tan, and thin and "mercurial," her early years as difficult because she was "too individual," until she became interesting to boys, describes her brother and father and mother.

The *Christian Science Monitor* publishes "Bitter Strawberries."

August 12: Letter to Neupert: Hopes that she can get to Europe during her junior year of college, regards the conflict in Korea as futile, the word "communism" is "blinding. No one knows exactly what it means, and yet they hate everything associated with it." She quotes Thomas Hardy: "You shoot a fellow down / You'd treat if met where any bar is, / Or helped to half a crown."

September: In new clothes and has a new set of luggage, embarks for Smith College, in Haven House.

September 11: Letter to Eddie Cohen: Recounts her fear "for myself . . .
the old primitive urge for survival," dreads the "great ultimate destruction"
of atomic war—"our nerve reactions can convey worry about the future,
until the fear insinuates itself into the present, into everything." So, she lives
"every moment with terrible intensity . . . I get stared at in horror when
I suggest that we are as guilty as Russia is, that we are war-mongers too."

September 24: First letter to "Dearest Mummy" from Smith: Thinks
the girls are "wonderful" at a cider social. "Gosh, to live in a house with 48
kids my own age—what a life!"

September 25: Letter to "Dear Mum": has fun decorating her room in
Haven House.

September 26: Letter to "Dear Mother": Lots of party girls in her house
but a few seem interested in literature, faculty advisor is a "darling," who
says, "people had written nice things about me, and Smith could expect a
lot." He tells her "Keep liking all your courses" and "have a good social life."
Sylvia has subscribed to the Sunday edition of the *New York Herald Tribune*.

"Dear Mummy": the "whole house is just the friendliest conglomera-
tion of people imaginable."

September 27: Letter to "Dear Mother": "How could I ever be homesick?" So "many openings—so many groups, so many girls." Lisa Powell is
a good housemate, doesn't smoke, knits, and plays bridge, "very steady &
self-willed." At college assembly, she comes close to crying when seeing the
professors "resplendent with colors, medals & emblems, march across the
stage . . . I still can't believe I'm a Smith girl!"

September 28: Postcard to "Dear Mummy": "I shall do my best to keep
a tight budget."

3:30 p.m.: Passes hygiene exam.

Postcard to "Dear Mummy": Excited about a senior who has picked
out a boy for her who writes poetry—"I just sat there burbling inarticulately
into my coffee." Eats "two helpings of everything."

September 30: Letter to "Dear Mother": Physical exam—height five
foot, nine inches; weight 137 pounds. She has "good alignment" but is told
"you are in constant danger of falling on your face." Mentions letters from
her mother, Eddie Cohen, and Bob Humphrey, a trip to the chapel to see
a first communion—"Beautiful ceremony, but nothing I could ever believe
in." After supper, reveling in the camaraderie, singing around a piano for a
"good hour" with a group of girls, befriends Ann Davidow, a "free thinker
. . . very attractive—almost as tall as I, freckle-faced, short brown hair and
twinkling blue eyes" with "a palomino named Sylvia." Shows Eddie's letters
to Ann, and Ann says he is "wonderfully socially conscious."

October: An upsetting fire alarm—"So this is what we have to learn to be part of a community: to respond blindly, unconsciously to electric sirens shrilling in the middle of night. I hate it. But someday I have to learn—someday—." {PJ}

Feels ugly and unable to attract males and wonders why she ever thought she was desirable. She has lost her sparkle and self-assurance. "I think I am mad at times." She fears she is a "knot of nerves, without identity." {PJ}

October 1: Letter to "Dear Mother": Her first blind date with a senior at Amherst College is a relief since he is six feet tall, slender, and neat looking. He surprises her by noting points of her personality that she has usually kept hidden. They dance, and she tells him that he reminds her of Warren. At Haven House, they watch couples kissing, and he says, "some people just don't have any inhibitions" and then briefly kisses the tip of her nose, saying she lives hard and is histrionic, talking sometimes like a schoolgirl reporting a theme with a "southern accent!"

October 2: Postcard to "Dear Mother": Delighted with another date with the Amherst senior, who "comes back for more of my scintillating peculiarities."

October 3: Letter to "Dear Mother": Grateful for her mother's "utterly fascinating" letters. Ilo Pill[349] and Eddie Cohen have also written to her. A heavy course load in art, botany, English, French, and history, "which floors me."

October 4: Postcard to "Dear Mother": Struggling with reading for history. "Oh, what joy to have no studies & to bike to the mountains."

Postcard to "Dear Mother": asks for socks and *Seventeen*.

10:15 p.m.: Postcard to "Dear Mum": "Don't worry that I'm sacrificing valuable time. These cards take only a second. Just before I hop to bed." Sends a "snatch of verse" about "Gold leaves" shivering in "this crack of time" that ultimately end in "dull pools of gold."

October 6: Letter to "Dear Mother": Asks for all her issues of *Seventeen* for use in an art course. History is her Waterloo.

October 8: Letter to "Dear Mother": Writing on a Sunday morning in her pajamas, bath robe, wool socks, and slippers, a feverish weekend, and trip to the doctor's office to get nose drops and cold pills. She no longer feels attracted to Bill Gallup, just as Eddie Cohen predicted. "Eddie as he often does, hit the nail on the head." Meets a boy who reminds her of Perry Norton, "enchanted by his open-ness." Stays in bed, waiting for her sinuses to drain, regrets missing the "acquaintance dance between 4 men's colleges. Damn."

October 9: Letter to "Dear Mummy": "As comforting as it would be to crawl sniffly into your arms and have you tell me what to do, relieving me of all responsibility, I realize that now is the time for me to learn to be master of myself." Mentions that Eddie Cohen and Ilo Pill are "writing very encouragingly and sustainingly. I love them both."

October 10: Thanks her mother for sending two packages. Still attending to her cold. "History is going to require a lifetime of study." Thinks of coming home for a day if her mother cannot visit her.

Postcard to "Dear Mother": "curled up in my cozy room" recovering from her cold and wondering how the girls can play bridge all night.

Postcard to "Dear Mum": Tuesday night—"These postcards are getting to be a habit." Proposes a visit home on October 21 to see "that favorite person of mine for a while (You, of course)."

October 12: Postcard to Mother: Delighted with her mother's "cheerful letter," still getting treated for her cold, now expects to arrive by bus October 20. The short stories in English are "terrific."

October 15: Postcard to "Dear Mum": still in the infirmary, working on an English paper.

October 16: Postcard to "Dear Mum": Released from infirmary, can't wait to get outdoors—"Smith is the most beautiful college on earth."

Postcard to "Dear Mum": "1 PM . . . Can't seem to stop dropping my favorite person postcards." English is her favorite course, enjoys the outdoors, learning the names of trees for botany, mentions two other girls who also write and send out material to *Cosmopolitan*, *Coronet*, and children's magazines. She wants to do the same thing but that will have to wait until vacation.

Finishes "The Golden Season," with instructor's comments.

October 17: Letter to "Dear Mum": no way can she afford a visit home before Thanksgiving with all her work and pleasure in the company of girls, chatting at meals and learning about their activities.

October 18: Letter to "Dear Mum": "I'm almost 18! I get a little frightened when I think of life slipping through my fingers like water—so fast that I have little time to stop running. I have to keep on like the White Queen, to stay in place."

October 19: Postcard to "Dear Mum": "It's heaven! Love, Sivvy."

Postcard to "Dear Mum": turning in at ten, the only teacher to complain about is in art, a "foggy bumbling man."

October 20: Postcard to "Dear Mummy": Practicing her tennis backhand, "Paradise [Pond] is reflecting russets & bronzes. Wellesley never had such hills!" She bikes everywhere, "coasting from class to class."

Friday night postcard to "Dear Mummy": Exhausted after a strenuous week, she has gained a pound, requests Toll House cookies, which she will eat before bed with milk. Wants to learn bridge[350] and knitting, "nice 'small' ways of conforming."

October 23: Describes a weekend of dating and the "futile" system at Amherst—"The boys take their dates up to their rooms, usually to drink," the couples wander around to the fraternity parties. Her date, Bill Gallup, is like the other superficial boys she has encountered. She dozes off at a party. Vows to stay home next weekend, wonders whether she will "ever meet a congenial boy."

Postcard to "Dear Mum": Weekend bike trip with Betsy Whittemore, a tall freshman in Haven House. The countryside reminds her of a Rembrandt painting. Now five foot, nine inches and 140 pounds, "perfect weight, said the nurse, according to my chart. I should have orthopedic & posture treatment, however." Mentions the delectable cookies.

Postcard to "Dear Mum": drowsy, no more Sunday-night dating, shocked to get a B- on an English paper, feels "slightly sick" but is told the teacher is a "hard marker. . . . Love from your mediocre child."

October 24: Postcard to "Dear Mum": "Time ticks by relentlessly. Am I queer, or is it normal that I am so snowed by being a microcosm here that I don't yet get the feeling of going to Smith?"

October 25: Postcard to "Dear Mum": Feels heroic over refusing a Friday-night date with "faithful old Bill [Gallup]." Studying for history hangs over her.

October 26: Postcard to "Dear Mum": "Touched" by her birthday package—cake, dates, a scarf, a maroon blouse, cards from Ilo Pill and Aunt Hazel. She's told not to let studying "blot out" her social life.

October 27: Celebrates her birthday with a pizza at Joe's in Northampton, Massachusetts. {HC}

October 28: Postcard to "Dear Mum": happy about speaking with her mother last night, flustered but happy when her botany professor acknowledges her in a coffee shop "are there any colleges other than Smith?"

3:00 p.m.: Postcard to "Dear Mum": prepares to "plunge into history," refuses all date invitations, but treats herself to a ticket for a Thursday performance of *A Streetcar Named Desire* (1947) for three dollars and sixty cents.

October 29: Postcard to "Dear Mum": Hopping into bed at 11:00 p.m., her head jumbled up with "empires, centuries & trends." Undecided about accepting a date with a freshman from Dartmouth. "What do you think?"

October 30: Postcard to "Dear Mum": Outlines her answer to a question about church and state in the eleventh century. She is shocked at how many students are more intelligent than she is. Doing well in botany, an English paper is due soon—"If I get another B- I'll scream. . . . Your moronic offspring—Sivvy."

October 31: Letter to "Dear Mother": Meets with her scholarship advisor, almost in tears while sharing her enthusiasm for Smith and Haven House.

The advisor recommends resuming weekend dates so as not to "go stale." Excited over $850 scholarship from Olive Higgins Prouty, who wants to hear about Smith's impact on her and about her future plans. Boys are "secondary" right now.

November: Publishes "Ode to a Bitten Plum" in *Seventeen*.

November 1: Postcard to "Dear Mum": reading assignments—*All the King's Men* (1946) by Robert Penn Warren and *The Mayor of Casterbridge* (1886) by Thomas Hardy, the Prouty scholarship has given her "a lift in my heart."

November 2: Postcard to "Dear Mum": midsemesters soon—"If you find any examples of Chinese brush drawing, sculpture pictures or pictures of lithographs & woodcuts, send 'em along."

November 3: Postcard to "Dear Mum": Describes reaction to a performance of *A Streetcar Named Desire*: "dynamic . . . poetic bestiality." Notes the "jagged nervousness of the heroine" and her straightforward sister.

November 4: Postcard to "Dear Mum": wonderful lot of mail—four letters and a postcard, a good time at Amherst watching a vaudeville show.

November 5: Postcard to "Dear Mum": working on a twelve-hundred-word paper.

November 6: Postcard to "Dear Mum": Eddie Cohen has sent a "lucid criticism" of her poem in *Seventeen*: "Thinks I overdid the first part too lushly (which I did) but likes the second about the history inside the stone." She shows his letters to a varied reception: "Mainly envy & awe of him —'terrific writer'—'lots of drama in my life' etc. etc." She thinks he is a "little too sure of his philosophy of life & his infallibility in analyzing others. Oh, heck—he's only 23—give him time."

Finishes "Atmosphere in the Short Story," with instructor's comments. {PM}

November 7: Postcard to "Dear Mum": all day in the library.

November 9: Postcard to "Dear Mum": looks forward to Thanksgiving break, a little hollow eyed, but a good night's sleep at home will remedy that, mentions an advanced course with Mary Ellen Chase, whose marking standards align with *Harper's* and the *New Yorker*.

Plath's comments on suicide vary a great deal in tone, although her interest in it is clear and frequent, even if not always applicable to herself.

November 10: Postcard to "Dear Mum": advises Ann Davidow "never to commit suicide because something unexpected always happens."

November 11: "Dear Mother": Enjoys working on a block print in art, with the aim of understanding the "relief method of printing."[351] Looks forward to a quiet evening reading *The Mayor of Casterbridge*. "Oh, mummy, I'm so happy here I could cry! I love every girl & every blade of grass."

November 13: Letter to "Dear Mother": In the library with "all the comforts of home"—good reading lamps, "cushioned easy chairs," and a window seat looking out on the "Holyoke range . . . purplish in the Sunday dusk. And all the while the carillon bells are chiming out hymns and college songs."

November 14: Letter to "Dear Mother": attends a guest lecture: "Sex before Marriage."

November 16: Postcard to "Dear Mother": taking her books home with her for the Thanksgiving holiday.

November 17: Postcard to "Dear Mother": One of her "asset" days with two cards from her mother and a "fat letter" from Eddie Cohen, thrilled with her A in botany, the boathouse lights on Paradise Pond, "reflecting in the glassy water & the lavender-blue twilit hill in the distance," remind her of a Chinese painting. A frank talk with Ann Davidow, "a wonderful girl—I love her witty spontaneous temperament & evidently the feeling is mutual."

November 18: Postcard to "Dear Mum": an entertaining letter from Warren, one from Ruth Geisel, setting her up with a "gorgeous blond hunk," and one from Bob Humphrey, who wants to take her to another performance of *A Streetcar Named Desire*, but she doesn't think she can "sit through it twice!"

November 19: Postcard to "Dear Mum": expects to come home exhausted after all her socializing and studying.

November 20: Postcard to "Dear Mumsy": Enjoys freshman friends who share confidences with her about their dates—"It's so nice to live a few other lives beside your own."

Finishes her third English theme: "'Character Is Fate.'"[352] "If I had to hazard three words to sum up my philosophy of life, I'd choose those." Ann Davidow saves her from the "grim fate" of a weekend without a date by arranging one who accompanies her to a Mardi Gras celebration, and she enjoys "renewing myself in the public eyes of various strategic people. . . . All I need to do is keep my judgment, sense of balance, and I'll be fine. If character is fate, I sure am adjusting mine under my lucky star." {PJ}

November 22: Finishes "Character Is Fate," with instructor's comments.

November 26: Returns to Smith feeling homesick and lonely, only three or four girls are in Haven House, but she has snapped out of her depression—her first since arriving at Smith, and she realizes family is important for all her "brave talk" of self-sufficiency.

Describes Thanksgiving-return home, "smaller than when I left, with the spots on the darkened wallpaper more visible." In her Haven House room, she realizes "no matter how enthusiastic you are, no matter how sure that character is fate, nothing is real, past or future, when you are alone in your room with the clock ticking loudly into the false cheerful brilliance of the electric light. And if you have no past or future which after all, is all that the present is made of, why then you may as well dispose of the empty shell of present and commit suicide." Yet "there is always the turning, the upgrade, the new slant." {PJ}

November 28: Letter to "Dear Mum": "I'm almost famous"—a clipping about her and other Smith girls "in the news" on a bulletin board in College Hall. "History is becoming rather vital and fascinating," especially when her teacher quotes German.

The first snow at Smith: A "white world," is what she imagines after a nuclear holocaust, "nothing will matter much." She thinks of the terror throughout history, the Spanish Armada, the Black Death, and her own "dark age" of "quick desperate fear, the ticking clock, and the snow which comes too suddenly upon the summer." She is living "on the edge, looking over, looking down into the windy blackness." {PJ}

November 29: Letter to Prouty: Recounts her first exhilarating impressions of Smith, which is like the door to reality, with everything she has dreamed of. Leaving home is the only way to lead a "fuller life." She feels a "sense of belonging" after having been immersed in the "sea of personalities." She relishes the "stimulation and competition. . . . I don't think I've ever been so conscious of the dignity and capacity of women." Explains her desire to write and the writers who have inspired her, mentions her many rejections before she was published in the August issue of *Seventeen*. "I just want you to understand that you are responsible, in a sense, for the formation of an individual. And I am fortunate enough to be that person."

November 30: Postcard to "Dear Mum": worries about a weekend without a date but another classmate gets her a blind one.

December 1: Postcard to "Dear Mum": studying history in the library, As in French, history, and botany; Bs in English and art.

December 3: Letter to "Dear Mother": Up until 2:30 a.m. studying history, overwhelms a date by asking him to talk about what has hurt or bothered him. He is so taken with her interest that he "seemed to think we should have intercourse." She strongly rejects the idea. Should she see him again?

December 4: Postcard to "Dear Mum": talks over her last date with "some of the girls, and most of them had something similar happen to them."

December 5: Postcard to "Dear Mum": annoyed at a B+ on her third English paper.

Postcard to "Dear Mum": a dull evening of homework.

December 7: Postcard to "Dear Mum": Thrilled to get a letter from Prouty, who says she has "a gift for creative writing." Wants to see some poems and extends an invitation to tea.

Postcard to "Dear Mum": Frustrated with a work in sculpture, attends a life class. "So I sit here in house meeting, hoping that I can make it to Xmas vacation without going completely insane—you know that sort of morbid depression I sink into."

December 8: Letter to "Dear Mum": somehow, she escapes the food poisoning that has spread around Smith like the "Black Plague or something. . . . here's hoping I don't drop dead in the next 12 hours."

December 10: Letter to "Dear Mother": Has to study but would rather ride her bike, her friend Ann Davidow confesses she cannot keep up with the work at Smith—"I got scared when she told me how she had been saving sleeping pills and razor blades and could think of nothing better than to commit suicide. Oh, mother, you don't know how inadequate I felt!" Ann's mother "couldn't see how incapable the poor girl is of thinking in this state . . . If you were her mother, she would be all right."

December 11: Letter to "Dear Mother": Ann seems better. Some disappointing dates with males who simply want a good time and have no idea of her low opinion of them.

Postcard to "Dear Mum": new hope for a "very promising fellow—tall (6' 2") nice-looking, doesn't smoke or drink and is very conscientious (from what Ann says) about his work."

Letter to Guy Wilbor: mentions inviting him to a Christmas dance at Haven House: "This is just to make things official—and to say how glad I am that the answer was yes—Sincerely Sylvia."

December 12: Postcard to "Dear Mum": not sure about attending a high school reunion.

December 13: Letter to "Dear Mother": feels better after cutting three classes and finishing an English paper, looks forward to Christmas celebrations.

December 15: Letter to "Dear Mum": "Today we had just the right amount of snow to make things Christmassy and white." Several weekend parties, last days of tests—"I have reached the saturation point."

December 18: Finishes "The Agony of Will," with instructor's comments. {PM}

December 24: Letter to Hans-Joachim Neupert: Writes from home to acknowledge his letter and "wonderful picture!" Describes Smith and how happy she is there, mentions the parties and socializing, "but this war-scare bothers me so much that I can never completely forget myself in artificial gaiety. . . . I think of us as of the Roman Empire and feel that this is the fall, perhaps, of our new and bright civilization."

1951

January: Observing the Smith campus from her window. "I think I am worthwhile just because I have optical nerves and can try to put down what they perceive. What a fool!" Sees her childhood as a fairy-tale world blighted by an awareness of "school. . . . marriage, sex, compatibility, war, economics, death and self." In a "stream of consciousness" passage, she catalogues the grim realities but also her love of Marcia Brown and her exuberance. {PJ}

Records the "nasty little tag ends of conversation directed at you and around you, meant for you, to strangle you on the invisible noose of insinuation. You know it was meant for you; so do they who stab you." {PJ}

January 4, 9:00 a.m.: Winter recess ends.

Letter to "Dear Mum": returns to Smith still recovering from a sinus infection.

January 5: Postcard to "Dear Mum": the doctor has told her to rest, still stuffed up but doing well in botany.

January 6: Bells.[353]

January 7: Postcard to "Dear Mumsy": slept nine hours but still not the "peppiest creature in the world," penicillin and nose drops have helped.

Postcard to "Dear Mother": concentrating on history and resting.

Letter to Ann Davidow: Still a little wobbly from her sinus infection and cough medicine—"I swear the stuff is half alcohol." Feels lost without Ann, thinking about taking up bridge to connect with "Haven House humanity." Mentions Eddie Cohen responding to a letter she wrote in a "careless mood" that has "evidently hurt the poor guy's masculine pride." Confesses a part of her wants to remain a sheltered child because her mother's purpose is to see her and Warren "happy and fulfilled," Sylvia feels compelled to "pretend to her that I am all right & doing what I've always wanted," confessing she went through an "awfully black mood during vacation," but now she is "not quite so close to going utterly and completely mad." Worries about Ann's state of mind: "you're one of the most admirable characters I've ever met."

January 9: Letter to "Dear Mother": reports receiving an A- on an English paper.

January 10: Makes a note to see college physician.

Postcard to "Dear Mum": pronounced in good condition in her checkup and is "eating like a pig," writing an essay on Thomas Mann.

7:00 p.m.: Bells.

January 11: A botany quiz.

5:00 p.m.: Bells.

Postcard to "Dear Mum": looks forward to another trip home after her exams, hopes to hear from Ann Davidow.

January 12: Marks her calendar "<u>wait</u>."[354]

Letter to Ann Davidow: At her desk, "having a good little cry and feeling very sorry for myself." Lonely with no close friends now that Ann is gone: "What made me sparky & giddy was the friction of us two banging together & giving off electricity." She has won a one-hundred-dollar third prize in a *Seventeen* short-story contest. "Maybe I'm silly, but if I'd had you to scream to about it, it would have been something."

January 13: Letter to "Dear Mother": "Am seriously thinking of spending a few days in New York this spring—la-de-dah!"

Postcard to "Dear Mum": announces she has found a new friend in Marcia Brown.

January 14: Postcard to "Dear Mother": taking notes on two books about Thomas Mann, a still-life assignment in art, sees *All About Eve* (1950).

January 15: Postcard to "Dear Mum": hard at work on a history paper.

January 16: Postcard to "Dear Mum": doing well in botany and still dreading her performance in history.

January 17: Finishes "The Dualism of Thomas Mann," with instructor's comments. {PM}

Letter to "Dear mum": with all the pressures still feels "remarkably happy," loves experimenting with flat areas and color in her art class.

January 18: Letter to "Dear Mum": seeks out other freshmen to take Ann Davidow's place.

January 19: Postcard to "Dear Mother": "Got a stiff little postcard from Warren in response to my news about the $100—not even a word of congratulations!!!! Oh well—."

January 20: To the movies and waitressing.

January 22: 9:00 a.m.: English.

10:00 a.m.: Gym.

2:00 p.m.: History.

10:30 p.m.: Letter to "Dear Mum": relaxing on Sunday, writing in her notebook, mentions "amusing" fraternity party last night at University of Massachusetts.

Sunday evening: Letter to "Dear Mum": A walk before dinner with Marcia Brown "who is the dearest girl. She is so alive, and we were shouting out our opinions about life while striding along into the bitter wind and antiseptic sunlight."

January 23, noon: All artwork is due.

January 24: Midyear examinations begin with French at 10:30 a.m.

January 25: Cleans her room.

January 26, 8:00–11:00 p.m.: Sees Bob Humphrey.

January 27: At a dance with Bob Humphrey.

January 28: BW.

January 29: Letter to "Dear Mummy": "Thank you for putting up with me for 4 and a half days—for feeding me good meals, baking me my favorite desserts, buying me perfume, and stockings, letting me sleep late, keeping the house quiet and . . . other thoughtful little favors."

January 30, 9:00 a.m.: "After two donuts, orange juice, rhubarb, milk, and two cups of coffee, I am ready to face the world." Going to the library feeling rested and ready for work.

January 31, 10:30 a.m.: Botany, asks Bessie McAlpine, Nancy Seelye, Nancy Rosenfeld, Bobby Matthews to supper.

Postcard to "Dear Mum": Acknowledges her mother's "cheerful letter," trouble sleeping after reading for ten hours a day, taking sleeping pills until exams are over.

February 1: Postcard to "Dear Mum": "It is now after supper, and in 24 short hours I will either have hung myself with typewriter ribbon or joined the A. Anonymous Society." Distressed over the "hundred Philips and Johns and Henries and Charlies of the various Empires," worried that the questions "will involve some obscure angle I never studied."

February 2: Midyear examinations end with history at 2:30 p.m. Then to Francestown,[355] New Hampshire, with Marcia Brown.

February 3: Letter to Ann Davidow: Happy to get Ann's letter. "It's funny—but the two people I spill over most to are now both writing irretrievably from Illinois."[356] Sizes up Eddie Cohen's philosophy of life and his comment that "'two people of such sensitive & emotional natures' would no doubt get hopelessly involved—and he actually confessed he would fall for me." But dating and marriage is out of the question, he says, because of her "tender age." His words make her "feel rather good inside" but also "pretty sad when a girl has to rely on typewritten words from a guy she's never met (and no doubt would not get along with if she did) to send a little shiver of excitement and tenderness up her spine." Describes her unsatisfactory dates, dismisses the American male's view of woman as a "combination of mother and sweetheart."

Letter to "Dear Mother": describes visit to Marcia Brown's aunt's house in Francestown, talking all the time and relaxing, shopping in Peterboro, and hiking in "bitter air."

February 4: Reports to her mother from Francestown about skiing on a "modest little gently rolling hill" for the first time—"I never have been so thrilled in my life!"

February 5: Postcard to "Dear Mum": Sees the "whimsical" *Harvey* (1950)—"I enjoyed crying in spots." Awaits the results of exams.

February 7: Pearl Primus.[357]

February 8: Cleans her room.

Letter to "Dear Mother": concerned about grades now that she knows other girls are getting straight As, but one of the girls in another art section says to her, "Oh, Sylvia they showed your work in class today as an example of a promising Freshman."

February 10: Out with Marcia Brown to a concert.

Postcard to "Dear Mum": freezing at night even with sweater, bathrobe, and wool socks, sends thank-you note to Grampy for his gift of twenty-five dollars.

February 11: Postcard to "Dear Mum": Listens to records and knits with Marcia Brown—"Both of us hate women en masse. But individually they are nice."

February 12: Supper at Morrow House[358] on Smith campus.

February 13: Supper with Bessie McAlpine.

February 14, 4:00: Tea at Alumnae House.

Letter to Ann Davidow: Hearing from Ann is like getting a "shot of personality in the arm." If Davidow feels adventurous, she should contact Eddie Cohen. Dating is a little better now. Dick Norton—"a med student, good-looking, intelligent!"—has asked her to visit him at Yale. She is going to room with Marcia Brown next year. But no one can replace Davidow.

Postcard to "Dear Mum": An A on her history midyear exam. The cookies and mittens have arrived. "It seems I have hit a midwinter slump. Ever since I've come back from Francestown I haven't been able to work or study."

February 15, 9:30 a.m.: A hair appointment.

February 16: A botany test.

7:00 p.m.: Bells.

February 17: "Yale!" Thinking of trip to see Dick Norton.

February 18: Makes a note to get someone to wait tables for her while she is at Yale.

February 19: English paper due.

Letter to "Dear Mother": Enjoyed her Yale weekend with Dick Norton, wants to learn more, with Warren's help, about physics, chemistry, or math so as to keep up with Dick. "Poetry & art may be the manifestations I'm best suited for, but there's no reason why I can't learn a few physical laws as to hold me down to something nearer truth."

9:00 p.m.: Bells.

February 20: Letter to "Dear Mother": looks forward to hearing diplomat Ralph Bunche speak and the freshman dance, worries about her mother's ulcer, enjoys meeting Dick Norton's classmates, mentions that he has memorized some poetry although he "does not credit emotional expression as valuable without scientific knowledge . . . or something."

February 22: "RALLY DAY."[359]

Postcard to "Dear Mother": Delighted to get a six-page letter from Dick Norton, her "favorite man." All As except for a B+ in English ("damn").

Letter to "Dear Mother": "I do feel I must have told you, mummy. You have the same weakness I have—getting cross at people who show up the inadequacies of someone we love." Impressed with Bunche's talk about "living by democracy as well as swearing by it—of putting all efforts into helping Africa and Asia medically, economically, etc." through the United Nations. Attributes a certain weakness to having her "first regular period for five months."

February 24: BW, considers going to the movies at 7:30 p.m.

Postcard to "Dear Mum": Mentions an article posted on the College Hall bulletin board, "BORN TO WRITE! Sylvia Plath, 17, really works at writing," calls her "the little Wellesley, Mass blonde," Sylvia comments, "All this effusive stuff appeared in the *Peoria Illinois Star* on January 23."

February 25: Sees Bob Humphrey, goes to vespers, Reinhold Niebuhr lecture at 7:00 p.m.[360]

February 26: Finishes "Modern Tragedy in the Classic Tradition," with instructor's comments. {PM}

February 28: Postcard to "Dear Mum": she does not feel successful— "Every minute is taken up trying to keep my head above water as far as my courses are concerned."

March: Reads her diary of 1949. "What I dreamed of once has become reality, and I have cast off that reality like a pair of old shoes." {PJ}

After reading Anatole France's *Penguin Island* (1908), wonders, "after the fashion of the eternal female, what man would someday be by my side. . . . How lovely it is to be a virgin—with all the dreams and longings for passion just stirring in one's flesh. I long for the blind burning irresponsible delight of being crushed against a man's body. I want to be ravished . . . to hear a man groan hoarsely, for in that moment I am the victor. In that moment, only the man becomes a child, while I, yet conscious of the stars, of the twilight, possess the wisdom of Eve, before abandoning myself to the lovely flame that eats at my insides with warm, spilling heat." {PJ}

March 1: Postcard to "Dear Mum": "I think I shall start a new scrapbook about myself, what with all my little attempts at writing being blown up rather out of proportion. Imagine one awestruck girl greets me yesterday with 'I hear you're writing a novel. I think that's just wonderful.'"

March 2: Botany and a written French exam.

March 3: Letter to "Dear Mum": Reports she is fine and does not have the flu. "Could I be as presumptuous to say you sounded a wee bit frantic?" Explains the burden of work will slow down the flow of letters, thinking about a summer job on the Cape.

March 4: Works on a paper for English.

Postcard to "Dear Mum": "All I can see is exams, exams, exams."

March 5: Letter to Ann Davidow: A fun Yale weekend, "if you look at it in one way, and frightening, if you look at it in another." Describes her outing with Dick Norton, handsome, intelligent, well built, and athletic, she feels intimidated and has difficulty talking to him, but he relaxes her by going to a swim meet, biking, and dinner in a Chinese restaurant. "I never felt so shallow in my whole life." He is the logical scientist; she has only the "slippery shifting basis of liberal arts." Wonders whether Ann or Eddie Cohen had anything to do with the Peoria, Illinois, newspaper article about her.

Postcard to "Dear Mum": apologizes for not telling her mother earlier about the dates with Dick Norton who, she thinks, is "just doing it to be nice."

March 6: Postcard to "Dear Mum": Disappointed to get a B- on an English paper. "He says I did a superficial job—and although he may be partly justified, I certainly am going to have a talk with him if I don't get a good mark on the paper I'll pass in tomorrow."

10:00 p.m.: Postcard to "Dear Mum": Going to bed even though the work ahead is "Herculean." Looking forward to seeing a dramatization of Arthur Koestler's novel, *Darkness at Noon* (1940).[361]

March 8, 4:00 p.m.: Hair appointment, BW.

March 9: A test on bacteria in botany, looking forward to Yale's junior prom.

Appreciates her mother's "morale boosting letters," assures her she is in bed by 11:00 p.m. every night.

Finishes "A New Idiom," with instructor's comments. {PM}

March 10: At Yale.

"Hello Mother": After two pages written by Dick Norton, Sylvia calls the "cooperative letter-writing affair . . . quite fun." This week she will do a "'full painting in analytical cubism, employing advancing, receding and transparent planes and color and equivocal line.' How's that for a mouthful? . . . I'll write after I pass through this week. Either that, or you will receive a little ink bottle full of ashes. Please scatter them on the waters of the ocean I loved so well in infancy."

March 11: At Yale.

March 12: Written exam in history.

March 13, 8:00 p.m.: Visits English professor, Robert Gorham Davis at home.

March 14: BW.

March 15: French midsemester exam.

March 15–16: Letter to Ann Davidow: Describes herself in high school as a "gawky mess" and an "outcast of sorts," only the past two years have seemed a success. Praises Ann's honesty about herself. Both Davidow and

Eddie Cohen have stimulated her as "deep companions." She confesses to "one of those spells where I think I won't live till vacation." Thrilled with her romance with Dick Norton after the Yale junior prom.

March 16: Describes walking with Dick Norton on a raw March evening, hearing the dry leaves in the rushing wind: They kiss but say nothing. In her room, in bed, indulges in the "luxury of the dark. Still the blood and relish of me were electric and singing quietly" giving way to sleep that she later links to her earlier thoughts about death and finality, a finish to human life. {PJ}

March 17, 7:15 p.m.: With Guy Wilbor at Amherst freshman prom.

March 18: Bells.

March 19: Postcard to "Dear Mum": Work piling up, still getting Bs in English, "All I need is a shot of vitamins & a week's sleep."

Midnight: Postcard to "Dear Mum": finishes scrubbing her room from top to bottom, with Marcia Brown writes a "sarcastic essay" on boys.[362]

Finishes "The Tragedy of Progress," with instructor's comments. {PM}

March 20, 3:00 p.m.: Appointment with Albert Madeira, English professor.

BW.

March 21, 3:50 p.m.: Spring recess begins.

March 22: To the movies with Tony Stout.

March 23: Babysitting with Dick Norton.

March 24, 8:00 p.m.–12:30 a.m.: Out with Dick Norton.

March 26, 9:30 a.m.: In Wellesley, with Ruth Freeman.

March 27: Out with Abner Wheeler.

March 29, 1:00 p.m.: Biking with Perry Norton.

"It's funny, but now I'm home, and no matter how many mansions I will see, I won't care about the shabbiness of this dear little house." {PJ}

March 30: With Marcia Brown in New Jersey.

March 31: A visit to New York with Marcia Brown and friends.

April: "Outside it is warm and blue and April. And I have to digest Darwin, Marx, and Wagner." Records her reactions to classes: the "astringent wit" of Professor George Cohen in art, the "slow tedium of rusty scalpels scraping clumsily on moss" in botany. {PJ}

April 1: In New York.

4:00 p.m.: Return train home.

April 2, 8:00 p.m.: Sees Perry Norton.

April 4: Out with Abner Wheeler.

5:00 p.m.: On bus back to Smith.

April 5, 7:00 a.m.: BW.

9:00 a.m.: Spring recess ends.

Dishwashing

7:00 p.m.: Bells.

April 6: Meets with Lisa Powell for supper.

April 8: Letter to "Dear Mum": "It will be a long pull till June 2. Could you—if you have a minute—sort over 'my cottons' (skirts & blouses) & whatever else & send them up sometime soon. No hurry really."

April 9: Needs to check her gym schedule.

5:00 p.m.: Art committee meeting.

April 10: BW.

Letter to "Dear Mum": "If you get cards from me with frightening irregularity just put it up to a sudden access of papers and meetings. . . . Saw a brief Dali shock movie—my one free act for the rest of the year. Keeps my morale up!"[363]

Describes the Dali film in detail, noting the treatment of lust and the sexual symbolism. {PJ}

April 11: Tennis, meets Professor Albert Pierpont Madeira for supper.

April 12: Botany quiz, purchases tennis balls, fixes her bike.

4:30 p.m.: Hair appointment.

Postcard to "Dear Mother": still getting Bs in English.

April 13: Tennis 7:30?

Meets Dick Norton.

April 14: Out with friends and Dick Norton.

April 15: Writes English paper, out with Dick Norton.

Letter to "Dear Mother": exhausted after weekend with Dick Norton biking, ping-pong with Marcia Brown, and her blind date, badminton.

April 16, 7:15 p.m.: Art meeting.

April 18: English theme is due.

4:30 p.m.: Studio (art) club.

Letter to "Dear Mummy": Not sure about next year's course schedule—"Sometimes I wonder whether or not I should go into social work.'" She could earn a living, or "you could get me started secretarial next summer." Should she plan for a career? "I hate the word," or should she freelance? "If I ever catch a man who can put up with the idea of having a wife who likes to be alone and working artistically now & then?" Considering the possibility of babysitting in Swampscott, Massachusetts. She is upset that Dick Norton is not paying more attention to her on their dates.

Finishes "The Imagery in Patterns," with instructor's comments. {PM}

The arrival of Eddie Cohen at Smith shocked Plath, who had said in letters she thought of their intimacy as an epistolary one. But why she treated him so coldly she never quite explained. His arrival upset her enjoyment of a correspondence that she could manage according to her own timetable and concerns.

April 19: Botany quiz.

    2:15 p.m.: Job interview.

    4:00–5:00 p.m.: BW.

Works on sophomore poster, attends class meeting.

    7:15 p.m.: Eddie Cohen shows up.[364]

April 20, Noon: Tennis.

April 21, 6:45 p.m.: Babysitting.

Letter to "Dear Mother": Reports her happiness at getting a summer babysitting job along with Marcia Brown. "I imagine life will not be a bed of roses, but my wish to have an incentive to learn to cook has come true." Being a "mother" will be a "new challenge." Mentions Warren's "delightful long letter in response to mine. He's the dearest boy I know!"

April 23: History paper due.

    Lunch with Mrs. Clara Ford.[365]

    Postcard to "Dear Mother": first A- on an English paper.

April 24, 1:00 p.m.: House picnic in the Franklin King House at Smith.

    5:45 p.m.: Meets Nancy O'Connell, attends a step sing.[366]

April 25: Supper with Enid Epstein and an appointment with Professor Madeira.

Letter to "Dear Mother": anticipating a "delectable" weekend with Dick Norton, also expecting Bob Humphrey who has a "most dear sense of humor."

April 26: Notes her mother's birthday on her calendar, cleans her room.

    1:00 p.m.: Hair appointment.

    7:00–10:00 p.m.: Works on decorations for freshman prom with Sydney Webber, Betty Hancock, and Bobby Matthews.

April 27: Warren's birthday.

    7:00–10:00 p.m.: Works on decorations for freshman prom.

Letter to "Dear Mother": dinner with Marcia Brown to celebrate their summer job plans, they sat and talked over cocktails that put Sylvia in a "mellow mood."

April 28: BW.

    1:30 p.m.?: Dick Norton.

    9:00 p.m.: Bob Humphrey.

April 29: Bob Humphrey.

    7:00 p.m.: Bells.

April 30: Supper with Enid Epstein.

May 1: Nancy O'Connell.

Letter to "Dear Mother": Asks her not to worry about an illness that sent her to the infirmary. She will miss Warren this summer, needs to learn about babies, asks Mother to show her how to mend socks as part of the domestic skills needed for her summer job. Dick baffles her and seems like two different people. She wonders whether his oiliness isn't a coverup.

May 2: Works on theme for English.

Letter to "Dear Mum": describes the beautiful spring campus.

May 3, 7:00 p.m.: Meets Pat Woodridge at Lawrence House.

May 4: Botany exam, BW.

With Marcia Brown, publishes "In Retrospect: A Plea for Moderation" in the *Princeton Tiger*.

May 5: Shopping.

May 6: Letter to "Dear Mum": Relays Eddie Cohen's critique of her work, pointing out "something that I had never thought of." Describes her new clothing—"I have outgrown the frilly high school stage, tra la la."

May 8, 3:00 p.m.: Meets with Miss Mary E. Mensel.[367]

Letter to "Dear Mother": Explains an accident—a slip resulting in a badly sprained or broken ankle (awaiting X-ray results). Finds Dick Norton the "most stimulating boy I've ever known," does not understand how an athletic boy like Dick can "bear a girl as uncoordinated as I am."

May 9: Letter to Ann Davidow: Describes spring sinus attack, slip resulting in a sprained ankle that will complicate her date with Dick Norton, meeting Eddie Cohen, who offers to drive her home for spring break—"I just couldn't get used to the idea that this physical stranger was the guy I'd written such confidential letters to." She admits she was rude and did not invite him into her home fearing her mother's reaction and then is surprised that her mother is cross about her "lack of hospitality." Admits to being "rather shaken and surprised by the whole unexpected encounter. The thing that makes me maddest at myself is that I just ignored the fact that he'd driven night-and-day from Chicago without stopping. So I just let him drive back." Mentions his letter to her complaining about cold New Englanders, but they are writing "as if nothing had ever happened."

Postcard to "Dear Mum": confirms the badly sprained ankle, but she will be able to hobble through her date with Dick Norton, feels good after finishing a nine-page paper on Edith Sitwell.[368]

May 10, 10:00 a.m.: Phi Beta Kappa meeting, BW.

4:00 p.m.: Hair appointment.

May 11, 2:54 p.m.: Train to New Haven, Connecticut, to visit Dick Norton and attend performance of *The Skin of Our Teeth* (1942) by Thornton Wilder.

May 12: Sachem's Head[369] picnic with Dick Norton.

May 13: Breakfast with Perry Norton at Lighthouse Point in Plymouth, Massachusetts, a lamb chop dinner with Dick.

May 14: Letter to "Dear Mother": Article about blind dates written with Marcia Brown gets a "big spread" in the *Princeton Tiger*. News about John Hodges, Bob Humphrey, and Ilo Pill—the boys she has dated and have taken an interest in her, performance of *The Skin of Our Teeth* "delightful—loud & obvious, but fun."

Attends Dick Norton's class in contemporary events with a "stimulating instructor," plays volleyball, reads Ernest Hemingway with Dick on a "rocky shore."

Next day, breakfast with Perry Norton, out on the rocks with Dick: "I think I am curing him of his jovial mask which made me so cross." A "straight A (!)" on her Sitwell paper. {PM}

May 15: Letter to "Dear Mother": She just had to write about the "green and fragrant liquidity" of the pink and white dogwoods and the "subdued murmur of twilight birds," appearing as "leafy silhouettes of treetops." Works on her last assignments, cuts some classes, spends time on the Haven House sun porch, reports Dick Norton's comment on her African American features.

May 16: BW.

Letter to "Dear Mum": thinking about next year and beyond, wondering whether she could somehow afford to take her junior year abroad.

May 17: Sewing with Betsy Whittemore. Botany quiz, washes hair.

May 18: Studio (art) club, picnic.

May 19, 2:00 p.m.: Betty Hancock.

9:00 Humphrey, Float Night.[370]

Letter to "Dear Bruvver" (Warren): Encloses a poem about her "grungy" old closet and the old jeans she wears since she cannot afford spring fashions. Slacking on schoolwork and tanning herself.

May 20: A drive with Nancy Wiggins, canoeing with Bob Humphrey, tennis with M.[371]

Letter to Ann Davidow: considers Ann's college applications and the possibility of a return to Smith, the important thing is to make a fresh start, not necessarily at Smith, mentions her own unpopularity at Smith because she does not socialize and play bridge and never stays up late to gossip.

5:00 p.m.: Postcard to "Dear Mum": reports spending the morning writing letters on the sun porch, out driving and canoeing with Bob Humphrey—"I do feel like a playgirl."

May 21: Studying for exams.

10:00 a.m.: Art.

11:00 a.m.–1:00 p.m.: Botany.

2:00–3:00 p.m.: History.

4:00 p.m.: Tennis.

5:00 p.m.: Swimming.

May 22: Studying for exams, BW.

4:00 p.m.: Tennis.

Swimming.

May 23: Studying for exams, chapel.

10:00 a.m.–noon: Sewing.

Noon: Gym.

Senior dinner.

Letter to "Dear Mum": packing up, preparing for her mother to drive her home.

May 24: Exams, "Study!!"

May 25, 2:00 p.m.: Botany exam.

Mother, "call Dick?"

May 26: To Harvey Wheaton's,[372] overnight with Dick Norton.

May 27: Wheaton's.

6:00 p.m.–midnight: Dick Norton.

Study.

May 28, 1:30–4:00 pm.: Dick Norton.

Driving lesson.

May 29, 1:30 p.m.: Dick Norton.

Driving and tennis.

Letter to Marcia Brown: Reports on a trip to Swampscott to look at the grand home where she will be babysitting—"Methinks I shall arrive in a coach-in-four with a diamond tiara titled casually over one eye. Impressed? I'm still gasping."

May 30, 1:30 p.m.: Dick Norton.

May 31: "Pick up Art!" History: maps, "afternoon & night."

June 1, 8:00 a.m.: History.

11:00 a.m.–1:00 p.m.: French.

June 2, 8:00 a.m.: French.

"Emancipation Day!" Home with Dick Norton and Perry Norton.

June 3: Plays piano, mows lawn, cleans her room, unpacks, writes to her brother, Warren, and to her summer employer, Mrs. Mayo.

June 4: Plays piano, tennis, mows lawn, and shops for records and books.

June 5, 1:30 p.m.: At the Gardner Art Museum.

Reads Dick Norton's sociology reports.

June 6: Finishes mowing lawn.

2:00 p.m.: Meets Pat O'Neil.

Works on scrapbook.

Letter to Hans-Joachim Neupert: Feels her first year of college has sped by. Describes summer job taking care of three children (ages two, four, and six) of a "wealthy doctor's family," discusses his reading of Upton Sinclair, assures him there is more to America than money.

Letter to Marcia Brown: Encloses a poem beginning "She clasps the sun oil with hooked hands; / Close to the sun in backyard lands, / Ringed with azure halter, she stands."[373] At home, mowing the lawn while Dick Norton and his brother Perry are off for a week in Maine, Sylvia purchases several books, including titles by Knut Hamsun, John Steinbeck, and William Faulkner: "Some of the covers are a bit lurid—but Hemingway & Faulkner aren't the coolest babies in the literary game, after all."[374] Meets up with Phil McCurdy, five years her junior, described as her "protegé" and a "cutie. . . . A handsome, athletic and brilliant baby doll"—and a high school junior she "maternally" pats on the back. Visits the Gardner Museum, "browsing through old Eric's [Gill] and letters to the Great Isabella [Isabella I of Spain] from everybody from [Fyodor] Dostoievsky to Herbert Hoover."[375]

June 7: Writes letters, plays tennis, piano, shops, reads aloud with her mother.

June 8: Washes hair, bike riding with Ruth Geisel.

June 9: Shops, plays tennis with Phil McCurdy, and babysits with Dick Norton.

June 10: At Yale, Baccalaureate Class Day, at Savin Rock[376] with the Nortons.

June 11: Yale graduation with Dick Norton.

June 12: Calls "Mr. C.,"[377] reads *The Tales of Hoffmann* (1881), double dates with Ruth Geisel.

Letter to Marcia Brown: Tries to sunbathe but "big glossy clouds" intervene, days with Dick Norton, attends his Yale graduation, enduring small talk at headmaster's house, with a "sweet girlish smile" frozen to her face. "I felt like drowning myself in the iced tea."

June 13: With Ruth Geisel and Ann Davidow, tennis with Dick Norton, bakes date-nut bars.

June 14: At the Cape with Dick Norton and Perry Norton.

June 15: Warren calls.

For the first time in her writing Plath thinks about her dead father and the portent of her past.

"I am in my old room once more for a little, and I am caught in musing—how life is a swift motion, a continuous flowing, changing, and how one is always saying goodbye and going places, seeing people, doing things. . . . The film of your days and nights is wound up tight in you, never to be re-run—and the occasional flashbacks are faint, blurred, unreal, as if seen through falling snow." She fears she hasn't done "well enough." Thinks of her father: "somewhere in you, interwoven in the cellular system of your long body which sprouted from one of his sperm cells uniting with an egg cell in your mother's uterus." She remembers she was his favorite and how she made up dances for him. Does his absence explain her craving for male company? She is frightened by hearing her mother's voice within her. She wants to anchor herself in her brother: "You fought with him when you were little, threw tin soldiers at his head, gouged his neck with a careless flick of your iceskate . . . and then last summer, as you worked on the farm, you grew to love him, confide in him, and know him as a person . . . and you remember the white look of fear about his mouth that day they had all planned to throw you in the wash tub—and how he rallied to your defense." {PJ}

June 18: Leaves for Swampscott job.

June 19: Letter to "Dear Mother": Homesick and trouble sleeping, feels "cut off from human kind," tending to three very young children, dishwashing, housecleaning, and laundry are exhausting, with no time to read or write, uncertain how to discipline children, seems to have lost her sense of humor, and her face has broken out, her tan has faded, her "eyes are sunken."

June 20: Letter to Marcia Brown: writes fantasy newspaper crime story about a babysitter who kills the children, puts one down the kitchen sink, broils another in the oven, with one percolating in the coffee pot— "Seriously, Marty, I thought I would never live through my first day."

June 21: Letter to "Dear mater": her sense of humor has returned after a trip to the beach and an encounter with a "young blade slicking a comb through his hair approaching," expects to get used to the household routine.

Letter to Marcia Brown: notes that her room overlooks sun and sea, embarrassed about not being able to cook, family dog has bitten her, awaits a visit from Dick Norton.

June 22: Letter to Melvin Woody: sunning herself on a "big private porch overlooking the sea," calming her "uneasy questionings and self-searching," writes to him about Yale, which he is to attend in the fall.

June 25: Paid fifty dollars for her job.

June 26: Letter to Ann Davidow: Thrilled to hear Ann's voice on the phone the other night, describes her arduous daily routine working in a "beautiful big white mansion on a big grassy green hill overlooking the water." She is trying to learn how to cook, and her hands are covered in cuts. By the end of the day, she feels "most unattractive. Sex appeal—wow!"

June 28, 8:00 p.m.: Home.

July 1: Bakes cookies.

Letter to Marcia Brown: Buoyed by a visit from Warren and a break from her babysitting job. Describes her luxurious surroundings, "living in the lap of it!" Learns to cook a little, turning out a batch of Toll House cookies.

July 2: An evening with Joanne "Joey" Mayo and Alice.

July 3: Cleans up after a cocktail party.

July 4: Fireworks.

July 5: At the beach at Galloupes Point in Swampscott with "kiddies." Marcia Brown arrives.

July 6: A rainy day off, a walk with Marcia in Swampscott.

Letter to Ann Davidow: pleased to hear about Ann's admission to art school, has to stick out her tiresome babysitting job to earn money, work is in spurts from 7:00 a.m. to 9:00 p.m., Dick Norton, on the Cape waiting tables, has not found "anyone quite like me," misses boys and compliments, no one cares how she looks, wants to hear more about Ann's boyfriend, Jim.

Letter to "Dear Mummy": Envies Marcia's setup, babysitting older children she can swim with, describes her reactions as "primarily blind and emotional—fear, insecurity, uncertainty, and anger at myself for making myself so stupid and miserable." Battling the customary problem with her sinuses, gets her first fifty-dollars-a-week check, mentions fan letters from *Seventeen*: "I laughed a bit sadistically, and take them out to read, whenever I think I'm a worthless, a gifted lummox—some gal by the name of Sylvia Plath sure has something—but who is she anyhow?"

Ca. July 6: Rebels against the "children's tantrums," the "daily chores," and "living always in the shadow of the lives of others." Marcia, "in tears," also agrees to leave her job. Sylvia plans to call her mother the next day. But after taking care of the children again, she cannot abide by the idea of giving up on the job nor what she has done to herself: "You are a prisoner of sorts, and yet you have made yourself so, accepted this job for what you could make out of it." She tells herself it is better to leave with "a sense of accomplishment." {PJ}

July 7: At the beach with Joey Mayo.

July 8: "The day that shook the World."

July 9: "Ditto."

July 10: A day off with Marcia Brown at Castle Point in Boston, Massachusetts. A picnic, swim, then supper.

July 11: Ironing.

July 12: Bakes a cake.

Letter to "Mother dear": "A brief note to tell you and grammy just how I much I love you both!" Looks forward to a day off, sketching at Marblehead, Massachusetts, requests her mother's sponge cake recipe: "Mechanics bother me. Like how to get a layer cake right side up & together after cooling face down with out breaking or crumbling. Do you use a spatula? Hands?"

July 13: At the beach club for one and a half hours, tennis and swimming, washes hair, stays in for the evening and irons.

July 14: An hour off for sunbathing.

July 15: One and a half hours playing tennis and swimming.

July 16: A day off in Boston with Dick Norton, a picnic on Lake Waban, and dinner with Mr. Norton, Dick's father.

July 17: Rides back to Swampscott with Warren and Rodney Holt (a friend of Warren's) in time for lunch, meets Elaine McIntyre and other friends.

July 18: Sunbathing at the beach, a bike ride with Joey Mayo.

9:45 p.m.: In bed.

Letter to "Dearest Mother": Settled in now in a lovely room, hearing the sound of the sea and feeling a "proprietary air about it now." She laughs at her "former moanings." She could never be sad living by the sea. She has had fun driving around with Marcia Brown and friends.

July 19, 2:00 p.m.: Rain and ping-pong, the first big storm Sylvia experiences in Swampscott, watching the sea "angry with white foam, the crackling blasts of sheet lightning and the immediate whip cracks and rattling, banging, ear splitting burst of thunder," and then running from room to room closing all the windows with sills "wet with puddles, and the water . . . collecting in streams along the floor." {PJ}

July 20: An hour at the beach in the morning.

2:00–3:00 p.m.: Free time for tennis, sunbathing, later a cocktail party.

July 21, 11:00 a.m.–7:00 p.m.: A trip on the *Mistral*.[378]

July 22: Stays in the house on a hot day, sees Marcia Brown.

July 23: At the beach club in the morning on another hot day.

July 24, 10:30 a.m.–3:30 p.m.: At Children's Island in Salem, Massachusetts, on a day off, picnic supper on Castle Rock in Marblehead with Arthur Gordon Stanway.[379]

July 25, 11:45 a.m.: Eastern[380] with Stanway.

July 26: An hour at the beach in the morning, boating with Joanne Mayo and others.

Letter to "Dear Mother": sunbathing and letter writing, enjoys a day on a yacht, bikes on her day off with Marcia Brown, socializes with friends.

July 27: Mostly a free day, Hodges visits.

July 28: Marcia Brown's birthday, reads *The House of the Seven Gables* (1851), out with Arthur Gordon Stanway.

July 29: Stays home all day.

July 30: At beach club, paid fifty dollars for her job, afternoon with Joanne Mayo and Marcia Brown.

July 31: A day off, cookout on Castle Rock.

August: A "wet gray August morning" and the awakening to consciousness of a woman who stretches wearily and yawns, thinking "No, not another day beginning." {PJ}

August 1: "Blodgetts[381] 70th birthday," dishwashing with Elaine.

11:30 p.m.: Does not want to sleep, she would lose "a part of my integrity" without writing, but she is dissatisfied with the results, which are too self-absorbed. These notes, "disjointed and meaningless," are not enough and do not equate with creating characters and plots. "It is only when these bits are woven into an artistic whole, with a frame of reference, that they become meaningful and worthy of more than a cursory glance. Therefore, think and work, think and work."

August 2: Drives to the beach and has a talk with Lane and Marcia Brown.

August 3: A beach party with Bob Michael.[382]

August 4: A day with Esther "Pinny" Mayo at the beach.

Letter to "Dear Mum": Describes a beach party in Marblehead, double dating with Marcia Brown, a great time with an athletic "good-looking male," mentions drinking two beers in the course of an evening, which she can handle: "What think you?" She envies the boys who "love so much harder than girls, and they know so much more about life. Learning the limitations of a woman's sphere is no fun at all."

August 5: Draws and reads in the afternoon.

August 6: Cooking in the morning, then ironing and laundry.

7:30 p.m.: A ride home.

August 7: A day off in Boston with Marcia Brown, shopping, then off to Wellesley.

9:00 p.m.: Returns to Swampscott.

August 8: Rainy morning at the Blodgetts' house, makes cookies in the afternoon, and reads *Catcher in the Rye* (1951).

August 9: A muggy morning of housework, ironing, dinner, a swim.

Letter to "Dear Mummy": expresses her delight in home after a short break from her babysitting job.

August 10: A "HOT" day, making applesauce and Jell-O in the morning, followed by an hour at the beach club.

August 11: Foggy, a letter from Dick Norton, morning housework, washes hair after dinner, and makes blueberry muffins.

August 12: Fog, blueberry muffins, apple cake, afternoon at the beach.

August 13: Ironing, beach with Joey Mayo, with Marcia Brown in the afternoon around the house.

August 14: Sun and fog on a day off, tennis, a trip to Nahant, Massachusetts, with Grammy and Mary.

August 15: Irons in the morning, piano in the afternoon, followed by pastel portraits, an evening walk with Freddie Mayo until 8:35 p.m.

August 16: Morning ironing, draws Freddie in the afternoon, then Joanne Mayo, reads poetry while it rains.

Letter to "Dear Mum": expresses her comfort now in taking care of the children and the amusement she derives from their care.

August 17: Morning housework—changing beds, out in the afternoon with Lane and Marcia Brown, works on a charcoal drawing, getting to bed late.

August 19: Morning housework.

11:00 a.m.–noon: Beach.

A "nice day with Marty [Marcia Brown] & Lane & Joey [Mayo]," makes applesauce and date-nut bars.

August 20: A day off with Dick Norton, rain and a picnic at Lane's house, bikes to Castle Rock, supper on the road, a night swim.

Letter to "Dear Mum": describes a day with Dick Norton—"Even a regular cadence of weekend dating provides enough male friction or magnetism, taken in small doses, at a distance."

August 21: "FOG," morning housework, Joanne Mayo's birthday party in the afternoon.

August 22: Morning housework, then the beach, cleans up playroom, spends the rest of the afternoon sunbathing with Marcia Brown, followed by a night swim.

August 23: Morning housework, spends part of the day with Marcia while watching the kids.

7:30 p.m.: To bed.

Letter to "Dear Mum": Looking forward to a relaxed routine now that her employers, the Mayos, are on a cruise, leaving Sylvia with two younger docile charges and, in the words of her journal, the "thoroughly therapeutic company of children."

August 24: Cruise in the morning with Joey Mayo and Helen, does a big wash, supper with Mr. Brown and Marcia Brown.

August 25: Morning housework and taking care of Joey.

1:30–4:00 p.m.: Tennis, swimming, makes supper.

August 26: Sits in the morning sun with Joey.

2:00–4:00 p.m.: Sunbathing and writing on the roof.

4:00–7:00 p.m.: Takes care of Joey.

Late to bed.

August 27: Has the morning to herself, then takes care of Joey and Pinny Mayo, cooks dinner.

1:00 p.m.: An hour of sun with Pinny at the beach.

6:30 p.m.: Puts the children to bed, writes.

August 28: Sick in the morning, rests in the sun.

1:00–3:00 p.m.: Naps, reads in living room.

6:30 p.m.: Writes in bed.

August 29, 10:00–11:00 a.m.: Out on terrace.

1:00–2:30 p.m.: Sunbathes on porch, the beach in the afternoon, a return home to read.

August 30: At the beach in the morning.

1:00–2:00 p.m.: Sunbathes.

1:45 p.m.: Anticipates the return of the Mayos from their cruise, on the sun porch with her poetry books: "I have felt the intangible steel cord of subservience loosened from my intestines." She has played the piano, gone swimming, doing what she liked. She wonders: "Where is the girl that I was last year? . . . Two years ago? . . . What would she think of me now?" Smith had seemed nearly an out of reach choice and now that choice seems inevitable. "Yet had I gone to Wellesley, I could only hazard about what might have appeared inevitable." {PJ}

Midnight: Hears what might be a prowler on the porch.

Plath's sense of her destiny is revealed in the following entry.

August 31, 10:30 a.m.–noon: At the beach with Joey and Pinny Mayo, the Mayos return home from cruise, Sylvia begins packing.

8:00 p.m.: In bed, opens her calendar and realizes tomorrow is September: "God! All the quick futility of my days cascaded upon me, and I wanted to scream out in helpless fury at the hopeless inevitable going on of seconds, days, and years." Records her goodbyes to her fellow workers and friends, describing their features and stories, she yearns to wrap her summer around herself like a cocoon as she prepares for "the next great phase—my sophomore year." {PJ}

September: Mulls over options, presuming that she will have to decide in three years to find an eligible man and a marriage that will permit her to fulfill her writer's ambitions, if that is even possible. She speculates on what it might be like to marry Dick Norton and become a doctor's wife. Would it be a "massacre" of herself? {PJ}

September 1: Cold, wet, rainy, and a late breakfast. Makes cookies and lunch. Talks with Monty in the evening.

8:00 p.m.: Puts the children to bed.

Writes her first poem in a year, "April Aubade," a sonnet, which ends: "Again we are deluded and infer / that somehow we are younger than we were." {PJ}

September 2: Laundry, ironing all morning, cooks dinner, mostly free in the afternoon.

September 3: Works as usual in the morning.

11:00 a.m.: Arrives home and plays the piano.

September 4: Plays piano, reads, irons, bakes two batches of cookies.

September 5: Picnic on a Cape beach, swims with Perry Norton, a talk with him in the evening.

September 6: Drives to Harding Beach in Chatham, Massachusetts, for a walk with Richard "Rit" Newell, Dick Norton, "et al.," at Crowley's restaurant.

September 7: Reads in the sun, swims with Dick Norton, an evening talk among the stars.

September 8: Dick Norton comes for breakfast, rests and reads, a picnic on the canal, a swim with Dick before the drive home from the Cape.

September 9, 9:00 a.m.: Reads, sunbathes all day.

September 10, 11:00 a.m.: At the dentist.

Types all her manuscripts.

September 11, 10:00 a.m.–1:00 p.m.: shopping, washes hair, types letters to Eddie Cohen, Marcia Brown, and Dick Norton.

Letter to Marcia: Enjoys the sensuality of shopping for clothes but deserves to be "kicked for such horrible and mercenary afflictions of wishful thinking." A visit to Plymouth Rock in Plymouth and a lecture by Mr. Norton ("Uncle Bill"), enjoys talking to the brotherly Perry Norton, "a sort of alter ego of mine, on the male side." Not sure about Dick Norton, who thinks she has lost interest in him.

September 12: Cleans house.

Noon: Meets Ruth Freeman for lunch, sunbathes in the afternoon, an evening stroll.

Letter to Ann Davidow: She is sorry to have missed Ann's visit to New York City and the opportunity to invite her to stay at her home at 26 Elmwood Road. The summer has taken a toll on her since she has had few dates with men. Mentions the previous evening when she had a "truth talk" with Dick Norton, straightening out some of their problems. He does not propose but suggests marriage is a possibility: "I'm just not the type who wants a home and children of her own more than anything else in the world."

September 13: Shops with Ruth in the morning and writes letters in the afternoon.

September 14, 12:30 p.m.: Meets Mary,[383] makes note to call Mr. Crockett, plays tennis in the afternoon.

September 15: Driving in Wilmington, Massachusetts.

September 16: Driving in Framingham, Massachusetts.

September 17, 11:00 a.m.: Driving test, gets license, plays tennis with Warren, goes to a Young Voter's meeting with Dick Norton.

September 18: A day with Dick.

8:00 a.m.: A walk in Boston along the wharves and into the subway. A picnic in an old park, cleans her room, plays tennis.

11:00 p.m.: After a supper at Dick's, a "great talk."

September 19: Sleeps until 10:00 a.m., plays piano.

5:00–6:30 p.m.: Writes speech, plays tennis.

8:00–10:00 p.m.: A walk and talk with Phil McCurdy.

September 20: Plays piano, types part of a story, reviews her speech.

4:30 p.m.: Tennis with Dick Norton, "supper & wonderful home evening."

September 21, 3:00–5:00 p.m.: Smith Club tea.

Picks up Louise Giesey and Patricia O'Neil,[384] reads and recovers in the afternoon.

September 22: Shops with Mother, tennis with Dick Norton and his family, supper and evening with Dick.

September 23: Church, tennis with Dick, meets Mr. Crockett.

8:30 p.m.: Sunday night Unitarian church date with Don Arrowsmith.[385]

September 24: Sleeps until 11:00 a.m., packs, sees Mrs. Aldrich.

Phil McCurdy comes over.

September 25: Sees Mrs. Olga Ditiberio, a Wellesley neighbor, in the morning, goes to the bank.

3:45–6:30 p.m.: Drives to Smith with Grammy and Mother, supper with them.

September 26: Sophomore meeting, shopping, a walk with Marcia Brown.

September 27: Religion class, sees Patsy O'Neil, washes hair, house meeting.

Letter to "Dear Mother": Describes her new room, shared with Marcia. Looking for a "long narrow print of Georgia O'Keeffe," takes a religion course with a paper due on Albert Schweitzer,[386] expects to write her mother twice a week, signs herself "your Smith girl."

September 28: Bells.

3:00–5:00 p.m.: Bike ride with Marcia.

7:00 p.m.: BW.

September 29: Religion paper due.

10:15 a.m.: Edith Hirsch.[387]

Freshman Day, Sydney Webber.

October 1: In classes until 4:00 p.m.

4:00–5:00 p.m.: shopping.

Writes Dick Norton in the evening.

Postcard to "Dear Mum": Biking with Marcia Brown, meets a junior at Wesleyan (Don Arrowsmith), "an amazing creature—makes up his own lyric songs, has his own car, & sang his lyrics to me all night."[388]

October 3: Studio (art) club.

October 5: Unitarian supper.

October 6: "Constantine! Plato! Eric!" A supper dance at Maureen Buckley O'Reilly's.[389]

October 7: Sleeps until 11:00 a.m., brunch at the Buckleys', returns to Smith.

5:00–10:00 p.m.: Bells.

October 8: Summary due for English paper, supper at Wiggins "gigantic and beautiful house"

BW.

Letter to "Dear Mother": Describes her dazzling time in Sharon, Connecticut, driving through the hilly countryside and arriving at "The Elms," the home of the Blodgetts, sharing a room with Marcia Brown with a "big double bed & bath to ourselves in a room reminiscent of a period novel, with balconies, gold drapes, and an astounding view, a buffet at the Sharon Inn "reminding me of Scarlett O'Hara before the ball." A chauffeur takes them to the Buckley estate, with girls in taffeta, satin, and silk, swishing up the stone steps under the "white colonial column," to attend a dinner dance in honor of the Buckleys' daughter, Maureen Buckley O' Reilly. Sylvia describes her surroundings in great detail to her mother, portraying herself as standing "open mouthed, giddy, bubbling . . . I am sure you would have been supremely happy if you had seen me. I know I looked beautiful. Even daughters of millionaires complimented my dress." They are announced at 9:30 p.m. She dances with several attractive and accomplished men from Yale and meets Maureen's brother Fergus. She meets Constantine Sidamon-Eristoff, son of a Russian general, a Princeton senior, and a wonderful dancer, and then Plato Skouros, son of Spyros Skouros, head of Twentieth Century-Fox. He points to a Botticelli Madonna over the fireplace and says, "You remind me of her." She is dazzled by his conversation filled with allusions to Greek myth. "There is a sudden glorying in womanhood when someone kisses your shoulder and says, 'You are charming, beautiful, and, what is most important, intelligent.'" The next day, a one-o'clock brunch served in great copper tureens—"scrambled eggs, bacon, sausages, rolls, preserves, a sort of white farina, coffee, orange juice! Lord, what luxury!" At 3:00 p.m., a chauffeur drives them back to school. When she thinks of Constantine, it seems like a dream "conjured up in moment of wishful thinking." She composes a rough "bit of free verse": "The bronze boy stands kneedeep in centuries, and never grieves, remembering a thousand autumns, with sunlight of a thousand years upon his lips, and his eyes gone blind with leaves."

October 9, 8:00 a.m.: Lecture.

Postcard to Dick Norton: She lists "entertainment desires"—"Your presence. Visit to art gallery, tennis court, wildlife" and whatever else "weather and inclination direct."

October 10: "MOUNTAIN DAY."[390]

Noon: Bells.

5:00 p.m.: Press board.[391]

October 11, 5:00 p.m.: Press board, supper at Chapin House on Smith campus.

October 13, 9:15 a.m.: Hair appointment.

2:30 p.m.: Expecting Dick Norton's arrival.

At Joe's pizzeria, a walk, a talk with Dick.

October 14: "Wait for Pris" (Prissy Steele?).

5:00 p.m.: Bells.

Letter to "Dear Mother": expects a grueling week, describes a visit from Dick Norton and fixing up a date for his friend Ken Warren, canoeing with Dick on Paradise Pond, located on Smith campus, talking with Lisa Powell[392] about the "dilemmas of womanhood," finishes a story for *Seventeen* and a paper for English.

October 15: English paper due.

7:15 p.m.: Movie.

October 16: To the infirmary.

8:00, a.m.: BW.

October 17: "MARY [Mort]," studio (art) club, in the infirmary with a "nobody-loves-me" feeling and worried about an interview with a *Mademoiselle* staffer. She has no "matching accessories." She has made her mother and Dick Norton unhappy: "Sinusitis plunges me in manic depression." {PJ}

October 18: Press board article due.

Letter to "Dear Mum": Reports that the nurse says she looks wonderful. Mentions a fan letter about her story "Den of Lions" and how much work she has to do to catch up. "Dick has been very understanding." Mentions getting a letter from "Dear old Eddie [Cohen]," Constantine Sidamon-Eristoff has invited her to Princeton, and she is weighing the pros and cons of an "arduous and expensive" trip, although she has spent no money on her social life, and he represents "an experience, an emancipation, a new world." He seems like the only alternative to Dick. Or will she be disillusioned with Constantine?

October 19, noon: Out of the infirmary, worries over catching up with course assignments, press board, and working at a mental hospital. "I'm torn by a desire to really get to know the girls in my house—and chat and play bridge now & then." But she has the "terrible responsibility of being an A-student." How to keep up her "front"? And then there's making time for Dick. "Now I know why Ann [Davidow] left."

6:00 p.m.: Soaring after getting a letter from Constantine Sidamon-Eristoff: "Will I be the wife of a handsome dark haired Russian oil magnate-to be??" But she also thinks of Plato Skouras, "the blond Greek god cutting cadavers in the heart of Boston." Reports a long discussion with a nurse in the infirmary who talks about nursing school and her boyfriend and his brother's suicide and is told "Some people can take just so much and no more." {PJ}

October 20: Religion, "Work!"

Letter to "Dear Mother": scared "blue" about English literature exam—"I have no real grasp of the subject," asks for help on the Romantics.

October 21: Writes "The Estonian."

Letter to "Dear Mother": "Wisdom has won the day," and she has decided not to visit Constantine Sidamon-Eristoff at Princeton, even though "everybody is urging me to go—maybe I'll marry into Russian society, etc." She is trying to balance between "possibilities of future life, or present tasks." Still recovering from sinusitis, which has made her feel like a "depressive maniac"—it feels like a renaissance just to breathe again.

Letter to "Dear Constantine": Still dealing with her feeling that he is only a dream, "sad and apologetic" about having to refuse his invitation but hopes he will extend another invitation, hopes he is not cross with her and that he will tell her about Princeton.

October 22: Sets tables.

October 24, 8:00 a.m.: Lecture.

BW.

October 26, 1:00 p.m.: Home, sees Alison Prentice Smith, a Smith College friend, Dick Norton for supper.

October 27: With Dick Norton, visits Boston City Hospital clinic, followed by lunch, a birthday supper at the Nortons', a long talk with Dick.

October 28: Attends high mass before returning to Smith College.

October 29: English paper due, press board meeting, lecture by William F. Buckley Jr.

Letter to "Dearest woman . . . whoops! I mean Dear Mother": Full of news about all the boys who are interested in her, including Eddie Cohen, who is going to send her a prose poem signed by Nelson Algren, and Ilo Pill, the farmworker immigrant she met during her summer of work before Smith. The News Office loves her tryout articles. Mentions going to hear the Buckley talk about his book, *God and Man at Yale* (1951).[393]

October 30: Supper at Chapin House.

Finishes "The Latvian," with instructor's comments. {PM}

October 31, 9:00 a.m.: English 211.

8:00 p.m.: Lecture.

8:20 p.m.: Welcomes "take-ins" for Alpha Phi Society, Sophia's circus.[394]

November 1: Press story, BW.

    3:00–5:00 p.m.: In News Office, "Press Board Party?"

    7:15 p.m.: Seminar.

November 2: Press board.

    12:00–1:00 p.m.: Bells followed by "Tea."

Letter to "Dear mother": encloses a sonnet, "To Eva: Descending the Stair"—"likening the mind to a collection of minute mechanisms, trivial and smooth-functioning when in operation, but absurd and disjointed when taken apart."

November 3, 1:00 p.m.: Meets Edor Nelson.

Letter to "Dear mum": Describes a date with Nelson, who had been two years ahead of her in high school. He is studying poultry genetics, she accompanies him to the stock yards and later to a horticultural show.

November 4, 11:00 a.m.: High mass.

    BW.

November 5: BW.

November 6: English 211 written exam.

November 7, noon: Government written exam.

    8:00 p.m.: Lecture.

November 8: Religion written exam, press board tea, shopping, supper with Edor Nelson.

    6:00 p.m.: Letter to "Dear Mum!": relieved to be done with three written exams, tells her mother to buy November 6 and 7 issues of the *Christian Science Monitor* for her article "As a Baby-Sitter Sees It."

November 9, 3:45 p.m.: Press board tea.

    7:15 p.m.: Church.

    BW.

November 10, 10:00 a.m.: Shopping.

    4:00 p.m.: A walk with Eric Lane Wilson, then dinner at Rahar's (a pizzeria), a movie at Sage Hall, dancing at Rahar's.

November 11: English paper.

November 12: Art painting due, supper at Chapin House.

November 13: English essay.

Letter to "Dear mother": Purchases a "beautiful pair of red leather pumps . . . matching lipstick and a red belt" with the fifteen-dollar check from the *Monitor*, discusses recording of T. S. Eliot's *The Cocktail Party* (1949)[395] at a Unitarian Young People's meeting, watches "the great Greta Garbo" in *Anna Christie* (1930),[396] "extremely interesting, if over dramatized." Encloses "Sonnet to Time" about the "mechanical age as versus the natural world."

November 14: Episcopal communion, meets Herbert Tovey.

    8:00 p.m.: Lecture.

November 15, 9:00 a.m.: Press board meeting, English paper due.

11:00: Bells.

Finishes "Suburban Nocturne" and "Somebody and We," with instructor's comments. {PM}

November 16, 8:15 a.m.: Press board.

3:45 p.m.: Tea.

5:30 p.m.: Bridge.

10:00 p.m.: Bed.

November 17: Shopping, laundry, letter writing, BW.

7:15 p.m.: Movie in Sage Hall.

Letter to "Dear mum": working on a fifteen-hundred-word paper on Unitarianism, asks for books or pamphlets her mother can line up.

Letter to Hans-Joachim Neupert: Describes the season at Smith—"I am now nineteen, and suddenly I am struck by the fact that I have been living for almost twenty years." Wonders whether her brother and their generation will be able to live a normal life span or "will be killed, and the land destroyed." She is disgusted with the stalemated peace talks in Korea and wants Neupert to tell her what Germans think. "I think about you often, and wonder how your work is coming." She wants to know about his government's plans to reunify Germany. Tells him about her babysitting summer, hopes they will never stop writing each other "even if there are long spaces of silence in between our letters, which I hope there won't be . . . Thank you for being such a delightful correspondent."

November 18, 2:00 p.m.: Art.

Letter to "Dear Aunt Marion"[397]: thanks her for writing about the *Monitor* article, comments on how beautiful and happy Ruthie Freeman looks.

November 19, 4:00–6:00 p.m., 7:00–10:00 p.m.: Studying for government course.

November 20, 7:00–10:00 p.m.: "Wash hair?" Packs.

November 21, 1:00–4:00 p.m.: Rides home with Edor Nelson, dance in Boston with Dick Norton.

November 22: Thanksgiving—rides to Exeter, New Hampshire, with Warren, who attends Phillips Exeter Academy.

November 23: Drives into town to get a paper notarized, lunches at Harvard Medical School, observes a dissection.

"Revelation—King Lear God."

November 24: Shopping in town.

2:00–4:30 p.m.: Talks and reads with Phil McCurdy.

Mrs. Freeman, Dave Freeman, and Dick Norton for supper.

November 25: Church.

8:00–11:00 a.m.: Edor Nelson drives her back to Smith.

November 26: Letter to "Dear Mother": a safe and easy trip back to Smith in spite of the slush.

November 28: Studio (art) club.

8:00 p.m.: Denton Snyder.

November 29: Dinner, dishwashing, sees Ann Hogan and Sydney Webber (in Sylvia's history class).

November 30: English paper due.

8:15 a.m.: Press board.

7:15 p.m.: Young People's (Unitarian) meeting.

December 1, 2:00 p.m.: Works on decorations for sophomore prom.

5:00 p.m.: Bells.

Dinner at Rahar's, sees *Oliver Twist* (1948) with Eric Lane Wilson.

December 2: Postcard to "Dear Mother": Shut up all day working on a religion paper. "For some reason, life seems very depressing at present. No doubt it is because I have so much plodding work to do ahead of me that I can't really be free a minute without feeling guilty. Also, am rather worn. Ah me."

December 3: BW, supper with Kathy Grimes.

December 4: Press board article due.

December 5: English written exam.

Noon: Bells.

Supper at Chapin House

Letter to "Dear mother": Lack of sleep and grinding study routine but letters keep her going, serves on committees for the house dance, charity ball, sophomore prom, reports a conversation with a date about his visit to a prostitute. He tells Sylvia: "'You know, you aren't like other girls. You understand, and aren't shocked or anything.' At that point I burst into silent laughter at the irony of the affair." To her surprise, she has heard again from Constantine Sidamon-Eristoff. She is still attracted to Dick Norton but Constantine is "promising." She wants to see whether he "stands up under the test of daytime wear." Asks her mother's advice.

December 6, 9:00 a.m.: Gym.

11:00 a.m.–noon: Cleans room.

3:00 p.m.: "Review Sec-Gov."[398]

Dinner, dishwashing.

December 7, 8:00 a.m.: Press board meeting.

December 8: Religion paper due.

9:00 a.m.: Press board meeting.

Letter to Constantine Sidamon-Eristoff: Feels the Christmas spirit in spite of the "iced slush," tells him about her courses and creative writing teacher, a "compelling, ugly, dynamic character—quite a challenge to slave under." She will be visiting in South Orange, New Jersey, and can travel to New York City to meet him. She wants to explore their rapport, she tells her "gallant Georgian."

Finishes "Unitarianism: Yesterday and Today," with instructor's comments. {PM}

December 9: Church, "Gina Stark?"

Letter to "Dear mum": Excited about the prospect of visiting Marcia Brown and going to New York to see *Don Juan in Hell* (1952), hopes to meet Constantine Sidamon-Eristoff in a Russian restaurant, mentions Mrs. Freeman's box of fudge, cookies, and brownies: "Her card bore the pious quote: 'The home is woman's paradise.' No doubt she considers herself a missionary converting the wayward."

December 10, noon: Government written exam.

Supper with Louise Giesey.

8:00 p.m.: Bells.

December 11, 7:45 a.m.: Press board meeting.

9:15 a.m.: "Tuesday meeting Davis Art model?"

7:15 p.m.: Movie.

December 12: "Dishwashing—Fran—."[399]

December 13: Dinner, dishwashing, house meeting.

Letter to "Dear Mother": Just finished a fifteen-page story for a creative writing class and thinking of returning home with more work to do but also time out for friends and rest. "It is really frightening to see days chopped into frantic segments, with a dozen alternative choices for work crying to be done." Does some Christmas shopping—"There were so many little luxuries I would have liked to get for you, and Marcia [Brown]!" She is amused at a Christian Science lecture about "transcending the 'falsities of the flesh.'"

December 14: English paper due.

Publishes "'True Health' Lecture Topic at the College," in *Daily Hampshire Gazette.*

December 15: Decorates all morning (for sophomore prom), paints windows, house dance with Dick Norton.

Letter to Constantine Sidamon-Eristoff: Looks forward to meeting his parents but urges him not to worry about entertaining her, she is the "sort of character who can sit for hours and meditate on the ocean in great content."

December 16: A day with Dick Norton, a good-morning kiss at breakfast, talk in the sun, a drive, a lamb-chop dinner—"It has been a dream."

7:00 p.m.: Dick Norton leaves.

December 17: Art project due.

3:30 p.m.: Hair appointment for Christmas party.

December 18, 12:50 p.m.: Winter recess begins.

"Snow, snow, snow" at Grand Central Station in New York City with Marcia Brown for a visit to Marcia's New Jersey home.

December 19: In New York with Marcia and her mother to see *Don Juan In Hell*—"magnificent," Fifth Avenue bus ride, trip to the automat, an evening with Mr. and Mrs. Brown at home.

December 20: Shops with Marcia and with Smith classmate Carol Pierson, a trip to New York City to meet Constantine Sidamon-Eristoff for lunch, a dinner at his family home, an outing to the Russian bar Two Guitars to drink Moscow mules and listen to a gypsy orchestra.

3:00 a.m.: Arrives at home.

December 21: Trip to New York City, lunch at the restaurant Child's, visit to the Museum of Modern Art, Brentano's bookshop, a ride back to Boston with a Korean War veteran.

December 22, 8:30–10:30 p.m.: An evening with Dick Norton.

December 23: Sees Perry Norton and Dick Norton, Gerry (Marjorie Clarke, a Smith student), and several unnamed others, sees Carol Pierson, a party at the Braces, sees Dick Norton in the afternoon, supper at his home.

December 24: In bed with sore throat.

December 25: Dick Norton comes on Christmas for a brief visit.

December 26: Supper with the Nortons and Sandra Peters, Christmas cotillion.

December 28: In bed with cold.

December 29: Dick calls.

December 30: Dick visits in the afternoon, supper at the Nortons'.

December 31: New Year's Eve, home with Dick Norton.

1952

Undated: "Jilted." {PM}

January 1, 2:00–6:00 p.m.: A long walk and talk with Perry Norton, cocoa and apple cake by the fire in the evening, Bob Humphrey and Dick Norton call, Sylvia reads for English class, writes "Aunt" Marion Freeman a thank-you for Christmas gifts and the "delectable box of goodies" sent to Smith. In bed for a week with a "nasty sinus infection."

January 2, 9:00: In Boston with Dick Norton, visits art museum, lunch.

5:00–6:00 p.m.: Jim Kellam.

7:30 p.m.: At the movies with Philip Brawner.

January 3: Drives back to Smith with Dick Norton and Warren, Eric Lane Wilson calls.

January 4: Press board meeting.

Letter to "Dear Mum": recovering from sinus infection with nose drops, "Marcia [Brown] is supremely well—plans to get married in 1954," enjoys Marcia's gift of Ezra Pound's *Pisan Cantos* (1948).

January 5: Finishes studying for government and religion courses.

January 6: A walk with Marcia Brown and works on English paper.

January 7: Works on English paper.

January 8: English paper due, Adrienne and Edor Nelson for supper? Types English paper in the afternoon.

 7:00–10:00 a.m.: Government.

January 9, 4:00–6:00 p.m.: Religion?

 8:00 p.m.: Required lecture in religion.

January 10: Cleans room before breakfast.

 11:00 a.m.–noon: College Hall.

 3:00–6:00 p.m.: Studies for religion class.

 7:00 p.m.: Washes hair and shaves.

 8:15 p.m.: Meeting at Davis Center.[400]

 House meeting.

January 11, 8:00–9:00 a.m.: Press board meeting, College Hall.[401]

 9:00–11:00 a.m.: Finishes government "sign cards."

 3:00–6:00 p.m.: Meets with Miss Mensel.

 7:00–10:00 p.m.: "Gerry Brace Sportsman."

January 12: Works on English paper in the morning, into town for vitamins, shampoo, lemon juice.

 2:30–10:30 p.m.: With Eric Lane Wilson at Rahar's.

January 13: Works on English paper in the morning.

 2:00–9:00 p.m.: Art.

 Bells.

January 14, 2:00–6:00 p.m.: Finishes English paper, begins work on government.

 7:30 p.m.: Lecture in Sage Hall, meets Bobby Matthews.

Letter to "Dear Mum": too much studying and her room is a mess, in the gym to relieve stress, owes lots of letters.

January 15, 9:00 a.m.: Press board assessment due.

 2:00–6:00 p.m.: Government.

 7:00–10:00 p.m.: Supper with Prentice Smith, includes a sonnet in her journal "Van Winkle's Village": "Agape, they marvel at the alien's / Archaic jargon; with mockery they plague / His puzzled queries."

January 16, 12:30 p.m.: Semester conference with Professor Evelyn Page, lunch with Mother.

 2:30 p.m.: Meets with Miss Mensel.

 4:00–6:00 p.m.: Meeting with Professor Cohen?

5:00 p.m.: Sherry and blue cheese.

7:00–10:00 p.m.: Supper with Vera Meader, "re Joe Staples."

January 17: Cleans room.

3:00–6:00 p.m.: Studies for religion class.

7:00 p.m.: Washes hair.

January 18: English paper due.

8:00–11:00 a.m.: Finishes work for government class.

4:30 p.m.: Tea at Tenney House.[402]

January 19: Catches up in English 211 work.

4:00 p.m.: Shops for skirt, sweater, loafers, Kleenex. "Poetry techniques—Stuart."

January 20: English 211 work. "Get art organized mounted?"

January 21: "Wed classes c'est tout!"

4:00 p.m.: BW.

9:00 p.m.: Bells.

January 22: 8:00–10:00 a.m.: Art.

10:00–11:00 a.m.: Mails book to Marcia Brown.

12:00–1:00 p.m.: A walk with Goodie (Anne Goodkind).

5:30 p.m.: Government, current events, etc. in College Hall.

8:00 p.m.: Bells.

January 23: Buys stamps.

8:00 a.m.–1:00 p.m.: Final essays and prepares questions for English.

2:00–3:00 p.m.: Squash with Mary Mort.

January 24, 8:00 a.m.–1:00 p.m.: "Sabine," latest notes, Marcia Brown's mail.

2:00–6:00 p.m.: At the library, washes hair.

7:00–10:00 p.m.: Current events.

January 25: 10:30 a.m.–12:50 p.m.: Government.

2:00–4:00 p.m.: A walk with Anne Goodkind, shops, buys a skirt.

7:00–10:00 p.m.: Washes hair, irons, cleans room.

January 26: Shops in the morning for a jersey, purchases stamps, sews her skirt, religion class, meets Dick Norton at art museum, walks on hill, visits Prentice Smith and Patsy O'Neil.

2:00 p.m.: English 211

2:00 p.m.–midnight: "Dick!" Reads poetry aloud with him.

January 27: With Dick Norton on a hillside, prepares questions for English 211, dinner.

January 28, 8:00–9:00 a.m.: Studies for English 211.

January 29, 2:30–4:50 p.m.: English 211, BW.

5:00 p.m.: Religion.

January 30, 11:30 p.m.: Bells

January 31, 8:00–10:20 a.m.: "Religion 14."

11:00 a.m.: Home on bus, sees Smith classmates Betsy Whittemore, Charlotte Kennedy, Joan Dutton.

8:00 p.m.: Calls Dick Norton.

Dick Norton, studying to be a doctor, took Plath with him to witness various medical procedures and operations.

February 1, 9:00–11:00 a.m.: "BOSTON LYING IN—9–11 BABY BORN!"

Lunch at Harvard Medical School, subway to Scollay Square in Boston for macaroni lunch.

3:00–5:00 p.m.: Cancer clinic at Jimmy Fund Building,[403] "Tom—blood tests," with Dick Norton in Boston to see *Lady's Not for Burning* (1948),[404] hitchhikes home.

February 2: At the Nortons' for dinner, "E. Williams—Dickens black velvet suit," "Dick [Norton], Kerr, Carol [Pierson],—Theater."

February 3, 3:00–5:00 p.m.: A walk with Dick, a visit to the Nortons', Fitzwilliams.

7:00–11:00 p.m.: Bus back to Smith.

February 4, 8:00 a.m.: Writes up Reinhold Niebuhr lecture, "Phone to S. Union by 11 pm."

Letter to "Dear Mum": Marcia Brown has measles.

February 5, 8:30 a.m.: Niebuhr article due, shops in afternoon, BW, "bring letter."

7:00 p.m.: Davis Hall "—Soph Rome—name? Under-Sea."

Washes hair.

February 6: BW.

3:00–6:00 p.m., 7:00–10:00 p.m.: Reading for government class.

5:00 p.m.: Art club.

"Mrs. B—call."[405]

Letter to "Dear Mum": still thinking about employment in a mental hospital, *Springfield Union* publishes her account of the Niebuhr lecture.

February 7: In chapel, buys religion notebook.

12:00–1:00 p.m.: Government class.

3:00–6:00 p.m.: Studies for religion class, supper with Prentice Smith.

7:00–10:00 p.m.: More work for religion class.

February 8:15: Davis Hall, "Anne Horner?"

8:30 a.m.: Press board meeting.

10:00 a.m.–1:00 p.m., 3:00–6:00 p.m.: More work for government class.

7:00 p.m.: Young People's meeting—Anne Mirserean, Gina.

Postcard to "Dear Mum": "I am working on re-orienting my life about my own potentialities—much better & secure that way. Only I feel dateless as hell." Mentions a letter from Constantine Sidamon-Eristoff that says she charmed his mother.

February 9: Finishes art poster, reads *Villette* (1853) by Charlotte Brontë, writes English paper, studies for government.

February 9–11: Postcard to "Dear Mum": church sermon about love before marriage.

February 10: Church.

10:30 a.m.: Anne Mischou, Gina, Mary Mort, works on poster, reads *Villette*, applies for an Elks scholarship in which she describes activities in high school, honors in literary contests, journalism published in the *Christian Science Monitor*, poems in *Seventeen*, art in the national exhibition at Carnegie Institute, participation in orchestra in high school, senior play, summer farm job with Black people, displaced persons, and college students, babysitting and governess work for three young children, and how she enjoyed "every minute of it," won the "Son of the Revolution Prize" in history, and likes working with people.

February 11, 9:00 a.m.: Press board article due.

3:00–5:00 p.m.: People's Institute[406] on Gothic Street.

5:00–6:00 p.m.: Sophomore prom meeting.

7:00 p.m.: "Harlow case?"[407]

February 12: BW.

1:30 p.m.: Laundry.

3:00–6:00 p.m., 7:00–10:00 p.m.: Reads for government, set tables.

5:00–6:00 p.m.: Bells.

Supper with Mary Mort in Albright House on Smith campus.

February 13: Feature write-up on kaffeeklatsch due.

3:00–6:00 p.m.: Finishes government paper on "to secure these rights."

7:00–10:00 p.m.: Case briefs.[408]

February 14, 9:30 a.m.: House meeting.

11:00 a.m.: Meets with Miss Mensel.

3:00–6:00 p.m.: Religion.

7:00–10:00 p.m.: Supper with Louise Giesey.

February 15, 8:15 a.m.: Press board, finishes work for religion.

6:00 p.m.: English paper due.

February 16: Drawing in Scott Gymnasium for charity ball.

4:00 p.m.: Double date at Williams College with Carol Sameth, a Smith classmate, "Party—dinner at ??," "jazz concert," "dance at Beta."

February 17: "Read—Pat."

Plath's letters, calendar entries, and journals reflect her exhilarating and exhausting activities, marked by frequent colds and sinusitis.

February 18: BW, English paper due, "Eider house council rep NSA due 8:30."

3:00 p.m.: People's Institute.

7:00 p.m.: Sophomore meeting.

Letter to Ann Davidow: Sinus infection has prevented her from writing a long overdue letter—"a full month of penicillin shots, misery, and cocaine nose packs to make me breathe again." Describes a visit with Dick Norton to a maternity ward. "I had the queerest urge to laugh and cry when I saw the little squinted blue face grimacing out of the woman's vagina—only to see it squawk into life, cold, naked and wailing a few minutes later." She has been shocked to learn that Dick, her "blond god" is not a virgin. Admits her envy of males—"their ability to have both sex (morally or immorally) and a career." She fears pregnancy and getting "trapped in an early marriage." Prefers dating tall guys, her devotion to art, study, and writing is a sublimation of sexual energy. Relays news about their Smith friends and adds, "I think I could understand and love anything you told me, just as I can spill over to you without reserve." Longs for spring break—"Smith is a damn, heartless, demanding machine at times!"

Letter to "Dear Mum": takes her mother's advice to go on a blind date—rather dull but she enjoys a two-hour drive to Williams College, a free dinner, and a great Dixieland concert.

Letter to Constantine Sidamon-Eristoff: Compares her life now to one "in a state penitentiary." Her maternity ward visit, "life in the raw," will make excellent material for stories. She has enough rejection slips to wallpaper several rooms, but they have only made her more determined. Mentions a "great curiosity about mental Asylums" and wants to work in a hospital. She loved meeting his family and losing her heart to his mother, "who is one of the most delightfully stimulating women I have ever met! Do remember me to her, please." Wants to hear about the life of a "suave Princetonian gentleman" and "enchanting Georgian!"

February 19: Brings poster to Sally Rogers, a Smith classmate.

3:00–5:30 p.m.: Works in Sage Hall on decorations for sophomore prom, setting tables, supper with Marcia Brown.

February 20, 3:00–4:30 p.m.: Religion.

4:30 p.m.: "Marks—Seelye [Hall]."

5:00–6:00 p.m.: English lecture.

9:00 p.m.: Studio (art) club.

February 21: "Local lead due See [Miss] Mensel."

1:30 p.m.: Press board office.

3:00–6:00 p.m.: "Decorate hall for PINES."[409]

7:00–10:00 p.m.: "Mother."

February 22: "Mother."

10:00 a.m.: Working on decorations in John M. Greene Hall.

2:00–6:00 p.m.: Haddock, BW.

7:30 p.m.: "M. [Marcia] Watrous."

8:00 p.m.: Rally Day.

February 23, 9:00 a.m.–1:00 p.m.: Decorating, charity ball with Dick Norton.

Dines at the Whale Inn with Prentice Smith, Mary, Mike, Carol, and Ken.

February 24: BW.

9:00 a.m.–3:00 p.m.: A walk across snowy fields to the Connecticut River, eats a cheeseburger, "Hamp-library,"[410] Sunday supper.

9:30 p.m.: Reads in bed.

February 25, 3:00–5:00 p.m.: People's Institute, finishes *The Mill on the Floss* (1860) by George Eliot.

Letter to "Dear mum": studying without veering to "sally forth, knapsack on back, for unknown hills over which . . . Only the wind knows what lies."

February 26, 2:00–6:00 p.m.: Rewrites and types a story.

7:00–10:00 p.m.: Supper with Louise Giesey, Vicky Boyle, Patsy O'Neil, Buddy, and Greta.

February 27: Sends David[411] a birthday card.

3:00–6:00 p.m.: Religion.

5:00 p.m.: English meeting.

7:00–10:00 p.m.: "Publishing biz."

Letter to "Dear Mother": Weekend assignment—read two novels for a total of nine hundred pages, and four hundred pages for a government class, "write a story, paint a still life, and spending all Friday norming & night & Saturday morning over at the News Office! What a life!" A $150 increase in room and board. "Just as we thought we had things in hand, too!" She will try to get an adjustment. Pleased that her journalism would bring in a "sizeable sum." She thinks that if her mother taught her shorthand and typing, she might get a job in some aspect of publishing—secretarial, publicity, or editorial.

February 28, 9:00 a.m.–1:00 p.m.: Cuts morning classes in religion and government and gets class notes.

3:00–6:00 p.m.: Supper with Prentice Smith, house meeting.

February 29, 8:15 a.m.: Press board meeting.

10:00 a.m.: Meets with Miss Mensel at scholarship office.

3:00–6:00 p.m.: Art.

6:00 p.m.: Revision of story due.

8:00 p.m.: Child development lecture.

Finishes "The Estonian," with instructor's comments. {PM}

March 1: Lecture cover due, press board morning meeting.

9:00 a.m.: BW.

3:00–6:00 p.m.: "Art, Gov?"

March 2: Reads *Far from the Madding Crowd* (1874) by Thomas Hardy, writes story.

2:30 p.m.: "Call for gov. book."

5:30 p.m.: Government.

6:00–7:00 p.m.: Radio.

8:00 p.m.: Bells. "Finish Art."

March 3, 3:00–5:00 p.m.: Ballet rehearsal, "Call Cole."[412]

7:15 p.m.: "Cover Struick lecture" in Browsing Room.

March 4, 9:00 a.m.: Lecture cover due.

3:00–6:00 p.m.: "Finish religion."

7:00–10:00 p.m.: Reads *Lord Jim* by Joseph Conrad (1900).

8:00 p.m.: Bells.

Postcard to "Dear mum": Puts off a trip to Princeton, worried about getting another winter cold. She has worked out a fifty-dollar adjustment on the $150.00 rise in room and board. "Of all the crazy things—money is worst."

Finishes "Marie," with instructor's comments. {PM}

March 5, 8:30 a.m.: Chapel, "Call [William Graham] Cole."

3:00–9:00 p.m.: Government.

March 6, 8:00–8:30 a.m.: Cleans room.

9:00 a.m.: "Vespers advance due."

11:00 a.m.–1:00 p.m.: Cleans room and types a story.

3:00 p.m.: Works on press board story.

7:00–10:00 p.m.: Government.

Letter to "Dear Mother": She has refused all weekend dates, listens to a "fascinating" lecture by a Communist from MIT. Her account appears anonymously as "Heresy Hunts," mentions Enid Epstein, a good friend whose stories are "terrific." Amazed that she has been nominated for president of her house: "Knowing how I am 'loved' by various & sundry I smile. So much for my political career."

March 7, 8:15 a.m.: Press board meeting.

10:00 a.m.–1:00 p.m., 3:00–6:00 p.m., 7:00–10:00 p.m.: Notes for government course from Louise Giesey, English notes from Patsy O'Neil.

March 8: Reads English reference books, finishes paper for government, "Newspapers[413]— afternoon."

11:00 a.m.: Bessie McAlpine, "press board advance," BW.

March 9, 9:00 a.m.–1:00 p.m.: Studies for exam in government.

2:00–5:00 p.m.: "Newspapers Constitution."

7:00 p.m.: Works on vespers cover in John M. Greene Hall.

March 10: Government written exam.

Noon: Vespers cover due.

3:00–5:00 p.m.: People's Institute.

7:00–10:00 p.m.: English.

March 11, 9:00 a.m.: English written exam.

3:00–6:00 p.m., 7:00–10:00 p.m.: Studies for religion exam, "Miss [Professor] Page?"

3:15 p.m.: Washes hair.

Postcard to "Dear Mother": feeling the strain of so much reading, which has to be fitted into a demanding class schedule, exams, and other activities, publishes in *Daily Hampshire Gazette*—"Misery of Man Is Due to His Defects," a report of a talk by Reverend John M. Green.

March 12, 8:30 a.m.: Chapel.

2:00–4:00 p.m.: Religion.

4:00–6:00 p.m.: Studies for religion exam.

7:00–10:00 p.m.: Massimo Salvadori lecture.

March 13, 9:00 a.m.: Lecture cover due, cleans room.

10:00 a.m.: Religion written exam.

4:30 p.m.: Tea in Davis Hall.

7:00–8:00 p.m.: Bells.

8:00 p.m.: Faculty show, house meeting.

March 14, 8:15 a.m.: Press board meeting, cuts religion class.

11:00 a.m.: Bus home.

3:00–10:00 p.m.: In Boston, meets Dick Norton, they discuss Hemingway

Finishes "Though Dynasties Pass," with instructor's comments. {PM}

March 15: Plays the piano and irons.

5:00 p.m.: Cocktails with Tom deCornfeld, dance with Dick Norton at Harvard Medical School followed by dinner, more discussion of Hemingway, meets Felix Loeb, Eddie Harris, Tom Gabazda, George Cobb, and Adam Chabanian at dance.

March 16: Church.

3:30 p.m.: On bus, returning home, talks with a passenger, Bill, about life, destiny, and hypnotism followed by supper, coffee, and a walk.

Letter to "dearest-mother-whom-I love-better than-anybody": reports reading Hemingway aloud with Dick Norton for "seven solid hours—without even eating." Next day, out for dinner and dance, where she meets "all sorts of lovely" African Americans, Africans, Armenians, and Americans.

Church on Sunday, meets a "lanky, tall and attractively nice looking" young man on a bus, they talk "solidly for the rest of the trip." He is a PhD student in entomology at the University of Massachusetts. She tells him about Warren, her summer jobs, "destiny, hypnosis, dream significance, chance, future plans." They go to a restaurant, talk another hour over sandwiches and coffee: "It dawned on me during the course of conversation that daddy majored or taught entomology." It turns out he knows Otto Plath's book about bees. "Life seemed too strange for words . . . his name was Bill something-or-other, and for a few hours I told him about most of my life and ideas and I think I loved him for talking to me. It just shows what wonderful people an uninhibited girl can run across."

Dinner with Dick Norton and his father.

March 17, 8:30 a.m.: Chapel.

3:00–5:00 p.m.: People's Institute, studies for government class, washes hair, supper with Bessie McAlpine.

10:15 p.m.: House meeting.

Letter to Constantine Sidamon-Eristoff: looks forward to spring as a "pagan sun-worshiper," suggests several dates for their meeting—"This is just to convince you I am not busy every weekend for years in advance."

March 18, 3:00 p.m.: Press board? BW.

4:00–6:00 p.m., 7:00–10:00 p.m.: Religion, supper with Marcia Watrous.

March 19, 8:00–9:00 a.m.: Religion.

9:00 a.m.: Gym.

10:00 a.m.: Press board meeting.

11:00 a.m.: Cleans room in the afternoon and checks gym schedule.

3:00 p.m.: Haddock.

4:30 p.m.: Studio (art) club.

Supper with Prentice Smith, Barbara Ward lecture, finishes packing.

March 20, 9:00 a.m.: Gym.

10:00 a.m.: Religion.

Noon: Government.

3:00 p.m.: Religion.

5:00 p.m.: Bus home for spring vacation, calls Dick Norton.

March 21, 12:00–5:00 p.m.: Writes letters, walks with Warren.

8:00–9:30 p.m.: Dick Norton visits, they read Dylan Thomas.

Letter to Ann Davidow: Wishing her a happy spring, wants to know all about her boyfriend and whether she is going to marry him. "Maybe your family is amazed at your surge of independent individualism—but all I can say is, more power to you!" Mentions her own wariness with Dick Norton, she does not want to become "a victim of my passions." But the attraction is very strong. She has applied for a waitressing job on the Cape. Mentions crying over Thanksgiving about Dick's "salacious past," describes her moving encounter with the young entomologist, a "glimpse of complete happiness," but he was going to start work and live in Connecticut. "I know I'll never see him again."

Letter to Hans-Joachim Neupert: Resting during spring break at home with her brother, who has returned from preparatory school—"our little family is together at last." Hopes for a scholarship abroad, mentions her opposition to Dwight D. Eisenhower's call for universal military training— "You know what a pacifist I am!" Describes her volunteer teaching of painting to little children in a settlement house, enjoys living in a dormitory but confesses her yearning for a "comforting hand. And a motherly or fatherly shoulder to comfort me." A summer waitressing job will help pay for room and board.

March 22, 1:00 p.m.: Hair appointment, supper at Harvard Medical School.

8:30 p.m.: In Boston, attends a performance of *Swan Lake* (1875–1876) with Dick Norton, observes the lit-up city, the "leaping water" (fountains?), and the trees in Fenway.

March 23: Dinner with Dick Norton, Rit Newell, and Bev Newell in Newton, Massachusetts.

1:00 p.m.: Out with Phil McCurdy for supper and conversation, works on sketches.

March 24: Dick calls. "Poems for May 1 rewritten & typed."

March 25: Begins a story about the Mintons,[414] starts reading D. H. Lawrence's *Women in Love* (1920).

March 26: Dick Norton calls as she cleans house, finishes *Women in Love*.

2:00–3:00 p.m.: Walks with Warren to Elephant Rock in Wellesley.

March 27: Begins writing "My Studio Romance."

2:15 p.m.: On bus with Patsy O'Neil and Louise Giesey, spends an afternoon at Mr. Crockett's with Miss Walton and Miss Dora E. Palmer, a Wellesley High School English teacher.

March 28: "TRUE STORY—'My Studio Romance' typed."

March 29, 8:00 a.m.: On bus with Dick Norton, attends a physiology lecture on the gastrointestinal tract, learns about secretion and absorption, lunch at Aunt Mildred's (Norton), a bike trip, up a hill to a lookout, a farm with an aqueduct.

March 30, 8:30 a.m.: Drives down to the Cape with Dick Norton in the warm sun on a "blue day," passing a "deep blue-green canal," the Belmont Hotel in west Hardwick, Massachusetts, lunching at the Pine.

6:30 p.m.: Arrives home and calls Phil McCurdy about his Yale trip.

March 31, 5:00 p.m.: Supper, studies with Dick Norton at Harvard Medical School, an hour of tennis.

10:00 p.m.: Meets Milton Viederman and Al Sandler, Harvard medical students.

April 1: "Cong. On trial?[415] Finish?" Shops for a record for Warren, "Kaar Kainen," Dick calls, Phil (McCurdy?) brings over a picture, a talk with Mother.

April 2: Returns to Smith with Patsy O'Neil, supper at the restaurant Jack August's with Marcia Brown.

April 3, 9:00 a.m.: Vacation ends.

Gets appointment with Miss James.

3:00–6:00 p.m.: "Hobbies," "do Kaar Kainen."

9:00 p.m.: Bells.

Letter to "Dear mum": gathering information about a waitressing job.

April 4, 8:15 a.m.: Press board.

10:00 a.m.–1:00 p.m.: Finishes work for religion.

3:00–6:00 p.m.: Types paper.

7:00–10:00 p.m.: Works on government class.

April 5: Morning shopping.

10:30 a.m.: News office, finishes artwork, English paper in the afternoon, "Dick's date with Nancy."

Postcard to "Dear Mum": Justifies purchase of a thirty-four-dollar sweater to wear all year round, anticipating talks by Robert Frost on April 9 and Senator Joseph McCarthy on April 10—"What an opportunity."

April 6, 9:00 a.m.–1:00 p.m.: Works on English paper.

2:00–6:00 p.m.: Art and religion.

7:00–10:00 p.m.: English paper.

April 7: "$1.62 Anne Roesing."

3:00–5:00 p.m.: Teaches at People's Institute.

7:00–10:00 p.m.: Works on story about the Mintons.

April 8: BW.

1:30 p.m.: To the bank.

3:00 p.m.: Press board, works on Minton story.

7:00–10:00 p.m.: Maury Longsworth for supper, types story.

April 9: Lecture cover due.

Noon: Press board?

3:15 p.m.: Miss James.

4:00–6:00 p.m.: Mass meeting.

8:00 p.m.: Robert Frost.

Letter to "Dear mum": continues to get As in her classes, including one written for the "august Elizabeth Drew,"[416] sending a story, "Sunday with the Mintons," to *Mademoiselle*, writing two poems and working on her journalism.

April 10: Lecture cover due.

  Noon: Press board? "<u>Shopping</u>."

  3:00–6:00 p.m.: Works on government class.

  8:30 p.m.: Senator McCarthy.

  House meeting.

April 11, 8:30 a.m.: Press board meeting, press board banquet—two dollars and sixty cents, works on government in the morning, washes hair after lunch.

  6:00 p.m.: English paper due.

  7:00 p.m.: Bells.

  Finishes "The Dead," a poem with instructor's comments. {PM}

April 12, 9:00 a.m.–1:00 p.m.: Studies for government class.

  10:00 a.m.: Press board meeting.

  5:00 p.m.: Supper with Dick Norton and Marcia Brown at Northampton diner.

  7:30 p.m.: "Italian movie," "walk to hill," "reading poetry at White House."[417]

April 13: "$1.30 cleaner."

  Dick Norton on vacation visits Northampton.

  9:00 a.m.: Bike trip to Mount Tom near Holyoke, Massachusetts, a walk in the rain to Bray Tower overlooking a valley.

  "Cheeseburgers, Don Juan in Hell, Dylan Thomas etc.—at 'Old Mill,'"[418] supper at Haven House and then studies in the library.

April 14: Calls Miss William, Miss Graham, and Lee Spencer, to the shop Albert's about a sweater, waitressing at lunch, works on reports for astronomy and English with Dick Norton, writes astronomy report.

  3:00–5:00 p.m.: Teaching at People's Institute.

  6:00–8:00 p.m.: Press board banquet.

  8:00–10:00 p.m.: Studies government.

April 15: Sees Spencer.

  9:00 a.m.: "Miss Gill due."

  "Dick & Miss Drew!"

  1:30 p.m.: Meets with Gene at press board.

  5:00–6:00 p.m.: English lecture at Seelye Hall.

  7:00–10:00 p.m.: Studies government with Dick Norton in the library.

April 16: Calls Alice

  8:20 a.m.: Chapel.

  "March in—Soph Prom."

10:00 a.m.–noon: Studies in Sage Hall.

Noon: Written exam in government.

Shops at Albert's.

3:00 p.m.: Press board meeting and studies religion.

4:00 p.m.: Sees Marcia Brown.

6:00 p.m.: Lobster dinner with Louise Giesey at Jack August's "Eng. Majors?"

April 17, 12:00–1:00 p.m.: Press board junior prom story.

3:00 p.m.: At press board meeting and shopping at Albert's.

Washes hair and studies for religion class.

April 18: "Buy record for Warren's birthday."

8:30 a.m.: Sophomore meeting.

10:00–11:00 a.m.: Press board meeting.

11:00 a.m.: Bus home.

"Call Dick [Norton]—Grover Cronin's [a bar]—Dick & Dave," buys pajamas and pants for Dick, scrapbook for herself.

April 19: "Bring back books," note to write to The Pines and Eddie Cohen.

10:00 a.m.: Tennis and boating with Dick, dinner at the Nortons', dancing in their kitchen.

April 20: Tennis in the morning, dinner at home, forest fire, "sun on rocks & black smoking trees," on bus with Phil (McCurdy?).

April 21, 8:00 a.m.: Meeting with Maria Canellakis Michaelides, a Smith classmate, calls Elizabeth Drew, BW.

2:00–3:00 p.m.: Press board meeting.

3:00–5:00 p.m.: Teaching at People's Institute.

"Enid [Epstein][419]—Story," "bike ride—Alison [Prentice Smith]—Florence—ice cream."

Postcard to "Dear mum": Earning ten dollars a month from her journalism.

April 22: "Call Jack August—7 couples," sets lunch tables.

3:00–4:00 p.m.: Press board meeting.

4:00–6:00 p.m.: Religion.

Supper with Prentice Smith.

April 23, 8:30 a.m.: Chapel.

12:00–1:00 p.m.: Press board meeting.

2:00–5:00 p.m.: Religion.

5:00 p.m.: Studio (art) club, sophomores meet in Sage Hall.

7:00–10:00 p.m.: Studies for religion class.

April 24, 8:00–9:00 a.m.: Cleans room.

1:30–4:00 p.m.: Press board meeting.

BW, Bells, washes hair, house meeting, "poster?" "Marty's [Marcia Brown] guest table."

April 25, 8:15 a.m.: Press board meeting.

10:15 a.m.: Gym.

Works on English paper, shops (camisole, stamps, lemon juice, a canvas for Carol).[420]

3:00–4:00 p.m.: Press board meeting.

April 26, 9:00 a.m.: Step sing, BW.

10:30 a.m.: Professor Eleanor Terry Lincoln.

A call from "Spizzwinks" and Dave Sanderson.

7:00 p.m.: Jack August's for dinner.

Sophomore prom with Dick Norton.

April 27: Studies for government class, works on sketches for art.

Letter to "The morning-after-the-night-before Dear mum": still in pajamas, describes last night's dance accompanied by Dick Norton, buys a summer outfit for just twelve dollars.

April 28: "Get [Robert Gorham] Davis permission—rel. assignment."

10:00 a.m.: Professor Maria Schneiders.

10:30–noon: Press board meeting.

Cuts English class

1:30–4:00 p.m.: Art.

4:00–6:00, 7:00–10:00 p.m.: Government.

April 29, 3:00–5:00 p.m.: Press board meeting.

5:00–6:00 p.m.: Government.

"Course cards due."

7:15 p.m.: Movie in Graham Hall.

April 30: "Poems for contest? Call Maureen [Buckley?]," "Call Mrs. Taft re cards & Phy Sci."

12:00–1:00 p.m.: Press board meeting.

1:00 p.m.: "Picture for House."

2:00–6:00 p.m.: Studies religion in the sun and gets assignment sheet.

8:00 p.m.: Reports on Frederic Ogden Nash appearance.

Letter to "Dear Mother": "You are listening to the most busy and happy girl in the world." She has just been elected to Alpha-Phi Kappa Psi, an honor society for the gifted in dance, drama, literature, music, or painting. Reports on five lectures in the next four days: Ogden Nash, three lectures on European students, and a Friends of Smith meeting about "fascinating Smith alums with great book collections." She gets these assignments because she works fast and has an "angle." Looks forward to W. H. Auden's[421] course in creative writing next year. "Honestly, mum, I could just cry with happiness—I love this place so, and there is so much to do creatively, without having to be a 'club woman.'[422] The world is splitting open at my feet like a ripe juicy watermelon."

May 1: Turns in book contest list.

 8:00–9:00 a.m.: Cleans room.

 9:00 a.m.: Miss Rochon.

 2:00–4:00 p.m.: Press board meeting.

 4:00 p.m.: "Browsing Room—cover."

"<u>Carol's</u>[423] <u>birthday</u>," washes hair.

Springfield Union publishes "Ogden Nash's Rhyming back Makes Up for His Talent Lack."

May 2: BW

 8:15 a.m.: Press board meeting.

 10:00 a.m.–noon: Gym and a movie.

 4:00 p.m.: Browsing Room cover.

 7:30 p.m.: Writes religion paper.

Daily Hampshire Gazette publishes "Ogden Nash Is Speaker."

Postcard to "Dear mum": mentions all her academic activities, summer job at the Belmont Hotel, "What a double life I lead!"

May 3, 8:00–9:00 a.m.: Tennis with Marcia Brown.

 9:00–10:00 a.m.: Press board meeting.

Types religion paper.

 2:00 p.m.: Browsing Room.

In the evening, writes for *Campus Cat*.[424]

Finishes "Religion as I See It," with instructor's comments. {PM}

May 4: Types English paper in the morning.

BW.

 2:00–5:00 p.m.: Sketches for art class.

 7:00 p.m.: Bells.

 8:30 p.m.: Honor Board.

Note to cover Ward's lecture.

May 5: Makes an appointment with Mrs. Sherk.[425]

 1:30–2:30 p.m.: Press board meeting.

 5:00 p.m.: "Miss [Esther Cloudman] Dunn—English" (Shakespeare).

Publishes "Smith Library Displays Fanny Fern Collection" in *Daily Hampshire Gazette*.

Letter to "Dear Mother": Discusses participation on Honor Board, offenses committed by students, the proper punishment. One case involves a student ripping out articles in a library magazine, another comes back late to college, plagiarizing a poem. "As you can see, I find my job exciting! Lots of ideas for stories! God! I'll have to start studying psychology!" Fixes up three dates for Dick Norton's friends.

May 6: At the Library, BW, note to get an appointment with Kenneth Sherk, BW, "SET TABLES!"

    1:30–2:30 p.m.: Press board meeting.

    3:15 p.m.: <u>Maria's room.</u>[426]

    4:00–6:00 p.m., 7:00–10:00 p.m.: Fanny Fern Collection.

    Supper with Bobby Matthews at French House.

May 7: 8:30 a.m.: Chapel

    12:00–1:00 p.m.: Press board meeting.

    4:00 p.m.: *Campus Cat* meeting.

    Supper with Joan Dutton.

    Postcard to "Dear mum": awaiting confirmation for her Belmont Hotel job.

May 8: A meeting with Professor Sherk and Professor Page about senior personals.[427]

    1:30 p.m.: "Push—Davis WAIT—TABLE 1."

    3:00–4:00 p.m.: Press board meeting.

    4:00 p.m.: Bells.

    Supper with Janet Salter, a Smith classmate.

    6:00–8:00 p.m.: Required government lecture in Sage Hall, house meeting, washes hair.

May 9: Meets with Professor Sherk in Stoddard Hall.

    8:30 a.m.: Press board meeting.

    English Paper due.

    3:00–6:00 p.m.: Religion.

    7:00–10:00 p.m.: Personals.[428]

May 10, 9:00 a.m.: Coffee shop.

    9:00 a.m.–1:00 p.m.: Religion paper due.

    Press board meeting, supper in Haven House in a "gray cotton dress" with Dick Norton, Prentice Smith, Milton Viederman, Nancy Teed, and Ben Whitehill.

    "Anne Goodkind—Al Sandler paradise" (Paradise Pond?).

    7:15 p.m.: Movie in Graham Hall.

May 11: Note to ask Professor Page to dinner.

    10:00 a.m.–1:00 p.m.: Paints woodwork at Mrs. Brown's.

    "Rain Picnic!"

    7:00 p.m.: Honor Board meeting.

    Letter to "Dear Mother": Sunbathing, attends a talk by Patrick Murphy Malin, head of the Civil Rights Commission, the "handsomest, kindest, most tolerant, creative man," the "antithesis to Senator McCarthy's 'guilt by association and hearsay' lecture." Describes the dates of Dick Norton's friends, time with Dick, an outing for a cookout on the mountain range, Belmont Hotel job has been confirmed—"I am leading a glorious

country-clubby life, in spite of my work. I have at least gotten thinner &
you should see my tan!"

May 12, 9:00 a.m.: Note to get press board assignment to News Office.

"Press Board finish," finishes senior class personals, Phi Beta Kappa
formal dinner.

8:30 p.m.: Coffee with Betsy Whittemore.

May 13: Religion notes, reading period begins.

2:00 p.m.: Meeting with Professor Sherk.

3:00–6:00 p.m.: Press board meeting.

May 14, 8:30 a.m.: BW, meets with Mrs. Margaret Pratt Shakespeare,
Haven House mother, before lunch.

4:00 p.m.: Story due for *Campus Cat* meeting.

May 15: "Wash hair?"

3:00–5:00 p.m.: Press board meeting.

5:00 p.m.: Fulbright meeting in Seelye Hall.

7:00–10:00 p.m.: Supper with Janet Salter.

*The following passage is from one of the periodic journal entries in which
Plath takes stock of her progress.*

"I will still whip myself onward and upward (in this spinning world,
who knows which is up?) toward Fulbright's, prizes, Europe, publication,
males. . . . From the inactive (collegiately), timid, introvertly-tended individual of last year, I have become altered. I have . . . directed my energies in
channels which, although public, also perform the dual service of satisfying
many of my creative aims and needs." Reflects on what it means to have
sex and to mate and to achieve balance rather than domination, wonders
if Dick Norton's assertiveness is part of a "mother complex." Cites Philip
Wylie's book on momism, *Generation of Vipers* (1943), mentions Dick's "rul-
ing matriarch," his desire to "assert his independent virile vigor." Resents his
"superiority complex," which she has as well, but his "patronizing attitudes"
are "extremely offensive." His comments about family life inhibiting her
creativity is a fear he is seeking to implant in her. She considers a vow not to
marry, "*JAMAIS, JAMAIS!*" Desires a man without fear: "How many men
are left? How many more chances will I have? I don't know. But at nineteen
I will take the risk and hope that I will have another chance or two!" {PJ}

May 16, 1:00 p.m.: Picnic at the Field House on the Smith campus.

5:00 p.m.: Bus home with Prentice Smith.

May 17: Dance at Harvard Medical School with Dick Norton.

May 18: Write-up on sophomore prom.

11:30 a.m.: Brunch.

3:30 p.m.: Returns by bus to Smith, supper at "Snow's," writes Honor
Board "stuff."

May 19, 8:00 a.m.–noon: Art.

Noon: Last government lecture.

2:45 p.m.: Conference with Professor Page.

Dinner at the Wiggins.

Postcard to "Dear Mum": After spring break, confined to a "rigorous schedule again." Thrilled to get an invitation to tea from Professor Drew.

May 20, 10:00 a.m.–1:00 p.m.: Art, BW.

8:00–11:00 p.m.: Honor Board.

May 21, 8:30 a.m.: Chapel prizes.

9:00–10:00 a.m.: Honor Board "Write ups."

10:00 a.m.–1:00 p.m.: "ART DUE."

"Maria—after lunch."

2:00–6:00 p.m., 7:00–10:00 p.m.: Finishes *Big Democracy* (1945) by Paul H. Appleby.

May 22: "Free Day." "Study gov Newspapers, etc."

May 23, 8:00 a.m.: Government exam.

11:00 a.m.–1:00 p.m.: Bells.

Writes Honor Board letters, "soph prom thing."

7:00 a.m.–9:00 p.m.: Bells.

May 24: Tennis with Janet Salter.

8:00 a.m.: Meets Maria at Davis Center.

BW, sees Marcia Brown.

6:00 p.m.: Dinner at Brown's.

May 25: "Rain," "Study English."

May 26, 8:00 a.m.: English exam.

11:00 a.m.–1:00 p.m.: Honor Board reports delivered to press board. BW, "coffee."

Postcard to "Dear mum": studying for exams with a "great clot of memorized poetry in my head—I do love memorizing."

May 27, 9:30 a.m.: Meets with Miss Mensel, picks up religion paper.

10:00 a.m.–1:00 p.m., 2:00–6:00 p.m., 7:00–10:00 p.m.: Religion.

Publishes "15 Area Girls to Graduate from Smith" in *Daily Hampshire Gazette*.

May 28, 8:00 a.m.: Religion exam, "Press Board," "art—supplies & paintings," "HOME!"

May 29, 11:00 a.m.: Dental appointment.

Noon: Mrs. Norton.

3:00–10:30 p.m.: At Harvard Medical School with Dick Norton.

Tennis, bull session.

May 30, 9:00 a.m.: At the Cape with the Nortons, picnic lunch.

3:00–6:00 p.m.: nap.

Picnic supper, "pinecones & bat with David [Freeman?]," "walk with Rit [Newell] and Perry [Norton]."

May 31: A tour of the Belmont Hotel with Leo Driscoll, a picnic "at cabins," goes to Sheep Pond in Brewster, Massachusetts, with the Nortons, reads before bed.

ca. June: Letter to Claiborne Phillips: "I want you to know also that if ever things look black and ominous, I am always here, wanting you to come visit or stay any time at all (if I'd been sure of someone being 'there' any time I wanted, I might have not felt so frightfully isolated last summer)." {HR}

June 1: Returns home, dinner at home with the Nortons, raining, cleaning her room, unpacking,

Dick Norton visits, "bull session" with Mother afterwards.

June 2, 10:00–11:00 a.m.: Washes hair, reading *Orlando* (1928) by Virginia Woolf in the sun.

12:00–1:30 p.m.: Lunch with Patsy O'Neil.

Reads & sunbathes, Dick calls, starts packing.

June 3: Shopping, sunbathing, writing "The New Day."

June 4, 10:00 a.m.–2:00 p.m.: Shops in Wellesley, outfitting herself for her summer job at the Cape.

3:00–6:00 p.m.: A nap and boating with Dick Norton.

8:00 p.m.–midnight: Packing at the Nortons', thunderstorm.

June 5, 11:00 a.m.–2:00 p.m.: Shops for a bathing suit, crinoline, other items, and rewrites "The New Day" in the evening.

June 6, 10:30 a.m.: Hair appointment, "sun-washed hair," types stories.

June 7: Lunch with Eddie Cohen and his friend Marty (Marcia Brown), on Lake Waban at Wellesley College, a trip to Sunshine Dairy, a car wash, dinner with Louise Giesey in Boston, sees *The Man in the White Suit* (1951), a British comedy, "Savoy Coral[429] convert—moon—top down," bull session.

June 8: Sunbathing while reading *Three Lives*,[430] sees Louise (Giesey?), roast beef dinner, packs.

June 9: "Stories notarized."

11:00 a.m.–2:00 p.m.: To the Cape for job at the Belmont Hotel and a picnic.

Unpacks during a rainstorm, drives in convertible to get ginger ale, "supper—zoo."

The telegram from Aurelia announcing Sylvia's prize and first publication in Mademoiselle *is a momentous event after so many rejections of her work. It is, in effect, a Cinderella story since the telegram arrives while she is cleaning hotel tables.*

June 10, 7:15 a.m.: "Breakfast TELEGRAM Re Mme [*Mademoiselle*]."

8:00 a.m.–noon: Scrubs furniture, washes dishes, silver, other items, fills sugar bowls, pepper shakers.

3:00–5:00 p.m.: On the beach with boys, Perry Norton visits.

8:00 p.m.–midnight: Writes letters, talks on the porch to Perry, they go for a walk.

Letter to "Dear Mum": Scrubbing Belmont Hotel tables when her mother's telegram announces she has won a $500 *Mademoiselle* prize for her story "Sunday at the Minton's." Wants her mother to buy some "pretty clothes," she will buy a winter coat and an "extra special suit." Scared stiff about Thursday when she begins waitressing, balancing "trays on one left hand." Plenty of "cute guys," a "cute note from Dick. . . . So it's really looking-up around here, now that I don't have to be scared stiff about money."

June 11, 7:00 a.m.: Breakfast, shops in Dennis Port, Massachusetts.

11:00 a.m.–4:00 p.m.: Sets up tables, chairs, silver, dishwashing for lunchroom, waitresses in the side hall for supper.

8:00–11:00 p.m.: Has a "gab session with girls."

June 12, 7:00 a.m.: Breakfast, waitressing in the side hall.

10:00–11:30 a.m.: "Bed."

12:00–2:00 p.m.: Waitressing in "lunch side hall."

2:00–5:00 p.m.: Reads and fixes up her uniforms.

8:00 p.m.: A walk with Kay and Pat, beach party with Ralph.

Works "like a dog . . . moving and dusting tables, putting on cloths, silver, glasses, plates (all of which we had to wash & wipe first)." Vows to be just as boisterous as the Irish Catholic employees. She is in the side hall because of her inexperience. Speculates on why her story took hold at *Mademoiselle*, wonders whether Dick Norton will recognize "his dismembered self! It's funny how one always, somewhere, has the germ of reality in a story, no matter how fantastic." But she is also proud of creating a character, Liz, who "isn't always ME—and proved that I am beginning to use imagination to transform the actual incident. I was scared that would never happen—but I think it's an indication that my perspective is broadening." Thinks of applying for a *Mademoiselle* guest editorship next year. {PJ}

June 13: Waitressing in the side hall.

9:30–11:30 a.m.: At the beach, writes to Marcia Brown.

12:00–12:30 p.m.: Waitressing in the side hall.

3:00–4:00 p.m.: At the beach.

5:00–7:00 p.m.: Waitressing in the side hall, "yanked out to librarian's convention in main dining room—drunk men, etc."

10:30 p.m.: Meets with Dick Norton and Perry Norton and Bill[431] for ice cream.

June 14: Breakfast, waitressing in the side hall.

At the beach.

4:00 p.m.: Betsy Whittemore's wedding.

2:00–5:00 p.m.: A swim with Dick Norton.

5:00 p.m.: In Brewster.[432]

"Supper & walk with Uncle Bill [Norton]."

June 14: Letter to "Dear mother": confesses to being homesick and lonely, encourages her mother to write letters because she is in a "very dangerous state of feeling sorry for myself."

June 15: Still shaky, can't seem to "adjust to new situations involving a lot of people my own age." Feels stuck in the side hall, watching the more experienced waitresses in the main hall, hopes to hold on to until at least July 10, asks her mother whether it is cowardly to quit after a month.

June 15: Sleeps till 10:30 a.m., writes letters.

12:00–2:15 p.m.: Waitressing in the side hall.

2:30–3:30 p.m.: Swimming.

5:00–7:00 p.m.: Waitressing in the side hall.

10:30 p.m.: A date with Lloyd Fisher, Dartmouth student and bellhop, at Souwester (a restaurant in Chatham) for beer, cheeseburgers, a trip to the lighthouse, coffee, a walk.

June 16: Washes dress, apron skirt.[433]

7:00 a.m.: Waitressing in the side hall.

9:30–11:00 a.m.: Beach.

12:00–2:00 p.m.: Waitressing in the side hall.

2:00–4:00 p.m.: At the beach.

6:00–8:00 p.m.: Waitressing in the side hall.

8:00–10:00 p.m.: A talk with "Ray, Ella, Pat etc."

10:30 p.m.: A date with Lloyd at Cape Town club, they walk home, talk.

Letter to "Dear Mum": On the beach, feeling better even though she is not "loved by all the girls." One good date, a Dartmouth student: "The characters around here are unbelievable, and I already have ideas churning around in my head."

June 17, 7:00–9:00 a.m.: Waitressing in the side hall.

10:00–11:30 a.m.: Rests.

12:00–2:00 p.m.: Waitressing in the side hall.

3:00–4:00 p.m.: Walks in warm fog with Dick Norton, attends "Show for Harvard."

9:30–11:30 p.m.: "Bed!"

June 18, 7:00–9:00 a.m.: Waitresses in the side hall.

9:00–11:30 a.m.: At the beach swimming, sunbathing.

12:00–2:00 p.m.: Waitressing.

3:00 p.m.: Meets Dick, Mrs. Norton, Mrs. Bertocci, brief drive to Herring River[434] with Dick Norton.

5:30–7:30 p.m.: Waitressing in the side hall.

10:00 p.m.: Meets Dick Norton.

Letter to "Dear mother": "I do so appreciate your very thoughtful letters which have been arriving every day."

June 19, 7:00–9:00 a.m.: Waitressing in the side hall.

9:00 a.m.: Washes hair.

9:30–11:00 a.m.: At the beach.

11:30 a.m.–1:30 p.m.: Waitressing in the side hall.

2:00–4:30 p.m.: Nap.

5:00–7:30 p.m.: Waitressing in the side hall.

"Talked avec gals," Dick calls.

June 20, 7:00–9:00 a.m.: Waitressing in the side hall.

9:00–10:00 a.m.: Washes clothes.

10:00–11:30 a.m.: At the beach for a swim with "Clark W" (James Clark Williams), Sylvia's roommate arrives.

12:00–2:00 p.m.: Waitressing in the side hall.

2:00–4:30 p.m.: At the beach swimming with Jerry, "motor boat tow."

10:00 p.m.: Date with Dick Norton, walk on a starry night, to Dennis Port for ice cream.

June 21, 7:00–9:15 a.m.: Waitressing in the side hall.

10:00–11:00 a.m.: Writes letters.

11:30 a.m.–2:30 p.m.: Telephone convention.

4:00–6:00 p.m.: Rests and talks.

6:00–8:30 p.m.: Waitressing in the side hall.

Talk with Raymond Wunderlich, bed.

Saturday, 10:00 a.m.: Letter to "Dear mother": Now considering working for two months. "What do you think?" Her roommate, Polly LeClaire, "a very sweet girl," reminds her of Ruthie Freeman. Wants to write a story, "Side Hall Girl," for *Seventeen*: "The ending would be very positive and constructive." Swam with a "beach boy life guard," another visit from Dick Norton. "I just don't care what people think about me as long as I'm always open, nice, & friendly."

June 22, 7:00–9:30 a.m.: Waitressing in the side hall.

10:00 a.m.–noon: Rests

12:00–2:00 p.m.: Waitressing in the side hall.

2:00–5:00 p.m.: Writes letters and naps.

6:00–8:00 p.m.: Waitressing in the side hall.

9:30 p.m.: Birthday party for Jimmy at Sand Bar in Chatham, with Clark Williams who reads aloud from T. S. Eliot's work in the starlight.

June 23, 7:00–9:30 a.m.: Waitressing in the side hall.

9:45–11:30 a.m.: At the beach for a swim with Polly LeClaire.

12:00–2:00 p.m.: Waitressing in the side hall.

2:00–5:00 p.m.: A twelve-mile bike ride to Long Pond in Lakeville, Massachusetts, and a boat ride with Dick Norton and Perry Norton.

5:00–8:00 p.m.: Waitressing in the side hall.

8:00–11:30 p.m.: Irons, writes letters.

Letter to her mother: Pleased to hear about Warren's job. "Your Side-hall philosopher," at a party of about forty at the "Sand Bar" last night, meets a "dear" first year Harvard law student. They go out to the beach, and he produces a volume of Eliot's poetry, which she reads to him with his head in her lap. "Most nice!" Mentions outings with Dick Norton and Perry Norton on Monday afternoon, and "generally having a lot of fun." Waitressing is tiring. "In spite of everything, I still have my good old sense of humor and manage to laugh a good deal of the time."

June 24, 7:00–9:30 a.m.: Waitressing in the side hall.

10:00 a.m.–noon: Naps.

12:00–2:00 p.m.: "Worst lunch—tempers etc."

2:00–5:00 p.m.: At the beach.

5:00–7:15 p.m.: Waitressing in the side hall.

7:15 p.m.: Walks along a foggy beach with Polly LeClaire.

8:30 p.m.: "Ice cream in DP [Dennis Port] with Pierre, Swanee, etc."

June 25, 7:00–9:30 a.m.: Waitressing in the side hall.

9:30–10:30 a.m.: Rests, Dick Norton calls.

10:30–11:30 a.m.: Trip to Dennis Port with Polly LeClaire—money order of twenty-five dollars.

12:00–2:00 p.m.: Waitressing in the side hall.

2:00–3:00 p.m.: Washes hair and showers.

3:00–5:00 p.m.: At the beach with Art Kramer, "etc."

6:00–8:00 p.m.: Waitressing in the side hall.

8:00–10:00 p.m.: At the beach, conversation and ice cream.

Letter to "Dear Mother": "I'm just not the beer-brawl type." Wants to leave her job August 10 with one week's notice.

June 26, 7:00–9:00 a.m.: Waitressing in the side hall.

9:00 a.m.–noon: Writes letters.

2:00–5:00 p.m.: At the beach for a swim.

5:00–8:30 p.m.: Side hall orchestra arrives.

8:30–10:30 p.m.: Writes letters.

June 27, 7:00–9:30 a.m.: Waitressing in the side hall and cleans her room.

10:00 a.m.–noon: "Coma."

12:00–2:30 p.m.: Waitressing in the side hall. "[Leo F.] Driscoll's offer."[435]

2:30–5:00 p.m.: Writes letters and relaxes.

5:00–8:00 p.m.: After waitressing in the side hall, takes a shower and writes.

Letter to "Dear mother": Fatigue and a heat wave, she turns down an extra job of handing out linen. It would add to her schedule for a total of seventy hours a week, long walk with Raymond Wunderlich, "a dear boy."

June 28, 7:00–9:30 a.m.: Waitressing in the side hall.

9:30–11:30 a.m.: Writes.

12:30 p.m.: Lunch, "MEAL OFF!"

12:30–5:00 p.m.: Dozes.

5:00–8:00 p.m.: Waitressing in the side hall.

8:30 p.m.: Date with Philip Brawner at Mill Hill Club, banjo player, dancing, "swinging—ginger ale."

June 29: Sore throat, rain, "Phil [McCurdy], Weasel, Rodger Decker, beer."

5:00–8:30 p.m.: "Back to Wellesley laughter by the sea with Phil."

June 30: In bed at home with sinus infection.

July 3: First day up.

July 4: "Fatal call—Belmont."

Letter to "Dear Dickie [Dick Norton]": Writes about returning home with a sinus infection, does not plan on returning to the Belmont Hotel.

July 5: 3:30–5:00 p.m.: Tennis with Phil McCurdy.

7:30 p.m.: "Kind Hearts & Coronets" and "Quartet" at Kenmore with Phil McCurdy.

July 6: Washes hair, reads *National Geographic* magazine.

9:00 a.m.–noon: At the Sheraton in Copley Plaza in Boston with Phil McCurdy. "Scotch & soda-merrygoround conversation."

"To look at her, you couldn't tell much: how in one short month of being alive she has begun and loved and lost a job, made and foolishly and voluntarily cut herself off from several unique friends, met and captivated a Princeton boy, won one of two $500 prizes in a national College Fiction Contest and received a delightful, encouraging letter from a well-known publisher who someday 'hopes to publish a novel she has written.'" She is "laughing and crying, at her own stupidities and luckinesses, and at the strange enigmatic ways of the world which she will spend a lifetime trying to learn and understand." {PJ}

July 7: Packs in the morning and cleans her room, then reads and rests.

Describes a powerful revery of a movie date and the impact of motion pictures on the masses. {PJ}

July 8: Reads and writes letters.

3:00–4:30 p.m.: "Backboard tennis."

9:00 p.m.: Dancing with Phil McCurdy at Ten Acres, a cocktail lounge outside of Boston, drinking ginger ale, conversation, music, "etc."

Letter to Harold Strauss, editor in chief at Knopf: Responds to his "encouraging letter" about "Sunday at the Mintons." With schoolwork and writing for a newspaper, she is not in a "position to concentrate on any sustained writing project as yet." She will contact him when she can devote her time solely to writing.

Letter to Marcia Brown: Describes her summer work and getting sick, lonely summer at home in the "warm, stagnant calm of a deserted Wellesley." She blames herself for starting out the summer so well and then collapsing: "I aimed terribly high, and exacted too much living capacity for my physical frame, and now anything, no matter how good in itself, seems calm and quite tasteless in comparison."

July 9, 10:30 a.m.: Interview with Mrs. Frank Williams, a real estate agent.[436]

"Janice Cort & mother 45 Brook St." (a real-estate property).

Trips to Wellesley, lunch with Mrs. Williams, visits two house with Mrs. Williams at Carver Street ($20,500) and De Marco Collari builders ($12,900).

4:30 p.m.: Returns home, meets Uncle Bill (Mr. Norton) at a diner, then to bed.

July 10: Washes hair, irons dresses, cleans room all afternoon, writes letter to Polly LeClaire[437] and Gloria, writes in her notebook, describes with epithets people she worked with at the Belmont Hotel. On arrival home, greeted happily by her mother who tells her that last night Grammy dreamed she was coming home. "As Frost said, Home is where when you go there, they have to take you in!" {PJ}

July 11: "SEVENTEEN acceptance $25!" Writes letters. Tedious recuperation with penicillin shots but elated at deciding not to return to the Belmont but regrets not going back to the beach and seeing the friends she has made, compares her current state to the "lifting a bell jar off a securely clockwork-like functioning community, and seeing all the little busy people stop, gasp, blow up and float in the inrush, (or rather outrush,) of the rarified scheduled atmosphere—poor little frightened people, flailing impotent arms in the aimless air." She begins looking at want ads and finds a promising listing in the *Christian Science Monitor* for a "neat, intelligent college-age girl of pleasing personality" to look after two children—"Sounds great. That's me." She calls to make an appointment. {PJ}

July 12, 1:30 p.m.: Meets Uncle Bill (Norton) at a Shell gas station on the south side of "Cape Bridge" on the way to the Norton summer cottage in Brewster, moonlit boat ride with Dick Norton among shooting stars and an orange moon.

Letter to "Dear mum": "If jolly old Phil should just happen to call, say very brightly — 'Oh, Sylvia was having such fun down the Cape that she decided to make a long weekend of it. Won't be back till Tuesday.' Yuk — Yuk—."

July 13: In Brewster for a late breakfast, meets Connie Lampreys.

2:00 p.m.: Interview with Mrs. Margaret Cantor at Bay Lane for a job taking care of three children, Billy (three), Susan (five), and Joan (thirteen).

3:00–5:00 p.m.: Swims at Saints Landing Beach in Brewster with Dick Norton.

Evening at Otha's[438] with beer, storytelling, and other African Americans.

July 14: In Brewster, "Dick's Day OFF," bike ride to Pleasant Bay near Cape Cod in bathing suits, picnic, swimming, sunbathing, talk, green stinging flies, home to a steak dinner, evening at Dennis Playhouse to see *The Glass Menagerie* (1944) by Tennessee Williams with Dana Andrews, a talk over orange sherbet and then to bed.

July 15: In Brewster, writes to Art Kramer, Marcia Brown, Mickey, Phil McCurdy, and Hans-Joachim Neupert.

11:00 a.m.–3:00 p.m.: Drives back to Wellesley with Aunt Mildred and David Freeman, rests and writes.

9:00 p.m.: Marcia Brown calls.

July 16: First draft of "Initiation."

Letter to Marcia Brown: Announces new babysitting job for the Cantors, a Christian Science couple, enjoys herself with the Nortons and other friends before she begins her new work. Mentions a party with several African Americans: "a new experience for me, being in the 'minority' group temporarily."

July 17: Second draft of "Initiation," packs up for summer job, listens to recording of the composer Francis Poulenc.

7:30 p.m.: Esplanade concert with Jim McNealy, a Yale student, walks over old streets

Midnight: Watermelon at midnight in Louisburg Square in the Beacon Hill neighborhood of Boston.

July 18: Types "Initiation," notarized at the bank, types "White Phlox," twilight riverside reverie hearing voices in the fog, all packed up for summer job in Chatham, listening to the gently falling rain, submits "Aquatic Nocturne" to the *Christian Science Monitor*.

July 19: Dick Norton calls, Grammy and Grampy go to Falmouth.

9:00 a.m.: Departs for Chatham job at Cantors', takes care of Billy Cantor, ice cream float at Howard Johnson's.

12:00–1:00 p.m.: Beach picnic.

2:00–3:00 p.m.: Arrives at Cantors', unpacks.

3:00–5:00 p.m.: Beach outing, a bath for Billy, serves supper to the kids, lobster dinner.

10:30 p.m.: In bed, Dick Norton calls.

July 19–20: Letter to "Dear Mother": describes break-in period in "new surroundings," unpacking, meeting the children, parents "very gracious."

July 20: 8:00 a.m.: Makes breakfast, dishwashing, laundry.

10:00 a.m.: Makes Jell-O and Billy Cantor's lunch.

10:00 a.m.–12:30 p.m.: Helps with dinner of fruit drinks, steak, egg salad with Roquefort and lemon, tomatoes, lettuce, and red cabbage, salad oil, salt, pepper, and radishes.

4:00–6:00 p.m.: At the beach with the kids, attends to their supper and dishwashing.

9:00 p.m.: In bed when Art Kramer calls.

July 21: Art Kramer and Dick Norton call, a note to write "Phil McCurdy, Louise G. [Giesey], Enid E. [Epstein], Mary B. [Bonneville?], Barb M. [McKay], Hans-Joachim [Neupert], Mrs. F. Polly."

7:30 a.m.: Serves Billy Cream of Wheat.

10:30 a.m.: Gets the newspaper, cleans kitchen, washes dishes. Outing to Oyster Pond in Chatham, lesson, shopping.

4:00–5:00 p.m.: At the beach.

5:30 p.m.: Dick Norton visits, Sylvia cooks supper, washes dishes, puts kids to bed, Art Kramer calls.

July 22: Washes hair, Dick Norton calls, scrubs bathroom, dusts, washes dishes.

10:30 a.m.–noon: At Oyster Pond Beach with the kids for a sandwich lunch.

Scrubs kitchen floor, washes clothes and hair, shaves, manicure, irons dresses, dinner with Lobbly sisters, resulting in "great mounds of dishes."

July 23: A day off after preparing breakfast, washing dishes.

10:00–10:30 a.m.: Explores Chatham.

10:30 a.m.: Swims and sunbathes.

1:30 p.m.: Out with Art Kramer, wears white shorts with a V-neck jersey, Dick Norton calls.

5:00 p.m.: "Conversations—Blossoms,[439] B, Ruth."

5:00–7:00 p.m.: Plays tennis, takes a bath, changes for dinner.

8:30 p.m.: Dinner at clam bar, a walk, and a drive to Orleans, Massachusetts, with more talk until 12:15 a.m.

The following is one of Plath's first explanations of her need to leave home.

July 23–24: Letter to Marcia Brown: "Life as in the rarified atmosphere under a bell jar all according to schedule." Fitful meetings with Dick Norton who bikes over from his job to the "charming" Cantors. Describes the children, the food, and her domestic routine. Mrs. Cantor asks, "And where did you meet all these boys?" Sylvia wants to ask: "What the hell do you think I am? Red Riding Hood?" Asks herself why she took the job and admits "I think I did it to get away from mother & Wellesley, as much as I hate to admit it. I love her dearly, but she reverberates so much more intensely than I to every depression I go through. I really feel she is better without the strain of me and my intense moods—which I can bounce in and out of with ease."

July 24, 7:30 a.m.: After breakfast, washes towels, defrosts icebox, fixes Susan Cantor's hair.

10:15 a.m.–noon: Oyster Pond, alone in a beach wagon, visit to an egg farm.

12:30 p.m.: Lunch.

1:30–2:30 p.m.: Writes letters.

3:00–5:00 p.m.: At Chatham Bars Inn's beach, "supper & dishes—kids baths."

8:30 p.m.: "Finis."

10:30 p.m.: Reads the *New Yorker* in bed.

Letter to "Warren, old boy": She is sunbathing and writing to her "favorite Kid Kolossus." She is enjoying driving the Cantors' Chevy station wagon with an automatic transmission. Learning about politics from Art Kramer, a twenty-five-year-old West Pointer and Yale graduate. "All in all, I am quite happy here."

July 25, 7:30 a.m.: After breakfast, changes sheets, dishwashing, mops, washes two loads of sheets.

10:15 a.m.–noon: At Oyster Pond, with lunch picnic. LeClaire visits.

5:00–6:00 p.m.: Dick Norton calls for picnic at Crystal Lake.

6:30 p.m.: A drive to Brewster.

8:00–9:00 p.m.: Band concert. Dishwashing.

10:30 p.m.–midnight: "Dick [Norton], Rit [Newell], Bev [Newell]."

July 26, 7:30: After breakfast, hangs out wash, dishwashing, sweeps kitchen.

10:00 a.m.–1:00 p.m.: Susan Cantor's lesson at Oyster Pond, purchases corn and squash in Mr. Michael Cantor's car, at Andrew Hardings Beach in Chatham—"Bill's [Cantor] lunch."

1:00 p.m.: Corn on the cob for lunch, dishwashing, rest.

2:45 p.m.: Letter to "Dear Mother": A sunbathing "siesta," preparing for an excursion to Nauset Beach (in Orleans). She has never been "so happy." Misses her mother and Warren but is "glad to be in this lovely environment. . . . I love your dear letters." Mentions talking to Art Kramer about Whittaker Chambers and his autobiography, *Witness* (1952).

3:00–8:30 p.m.: Stays around the house, hamburger cookout, kids have their bath.

8:30–9:00 p.m.: Art Kramer calls for a "long intellectual discussion."

Describes her fascination with Christian Science, which is all about "mind over matter." Sees contradictions in the way Christian Scientists live, such as going to the dentist, calls herself a "matter worshiper," believes in objective truth, even if individuals see only a "fragment of this whole truth," noting that "objective reality" is transmuted into "something quite personal (Like the death of My Father = tears, sorrow, weeping . . . certain areas of sensation and perception about the stream of life moving about one . . .). Hence, 'Thinking makes it so.'" {PJ}

July 27, 7:30 a.m.: Breakfast, washes dishes, washes Susan Cantor's hair.

11:30 a.m.: Christian Scientist church.

12:30 p.m.: "Soloist—readings—summer dresses."

1:30 p.m.: Roast duck dinner, dishwashing, puts Billy Cantor to bed, afternoon reading in a rainstorm.

6:00–8:00 p.m.: Supper, dishwashing.

8:00–10:00 p.m.: Types Kathy Cantor's letters.[440]

Susan is sick.

July 28, 9:00 a.m.: After breakfast, writes Phil McCurdy.[441]

10:00 a.m.: Takes Susan, Joan, and Billy (the Cantors) to Oyster Pond.

11:30 a.m.: Shops in Chatham.

At Chatham Bars Inn's beach until 1:00 p.m.

Borscht and dishwashing.

5:00 p.m.: Chatham Bars Inn's beach, fresh bread and egg supper.

7:45 p.m.: Out with Dick Norton in aqua dress to see "Ballet Variante."

Art Kramer calls.

July 29, 6:30 a.m.: Breakfast, cleaning day—dishwashing, dusting, vacuuming.

10:00–11:30 a.m.: To Oyster Pond with Susan Cantor.

Lunch, dishwashing, washing and waxing floors, Dick Norton calls.

3:30–4:30 p.m.: Andrew Hardings Beach for a swim.

5:30 p.m.: Supper, dishwashing, ironing, puts kids to bed.

8:30–9:14 p.m.: Long talk with Art Kramer.

July 30: "Shave bath?" A day off, picking out bathing suit, gray jacket, "look for <u>Mlle</u>" (*Mademoiselle*), "Sc. Book?"

10:00 a.m.: Dick Norton visits with Grammy and Grampy, drive to Brewster, picking up the issue of *Mademoiselle*.

11:30 a.m.–2:30 p.m.: Swims alone, a picnic, walk on beach in "knee high warm water—seaweed—sand ridges."

2:30–4:00 p.m.: Tennis with Rit Newell and Beverly Newell at Alex Stabins.

Reads, listens to music, steak supper.

11:30 p.m.: "Blanket fight."

July 31, 7:30 a.m.: Breakfast, shopping trip, dishwashing, lunch.

3:00 p.m.: Writes letters.[442]

4:00–5:30 p.m.: Swims at lake in Orleans.

"Flash supper."

8:15 p.m.: "Kids in bed."

Washes hair, manicure.

8:30–9:00 p.m.: Art Kramer calls.

August 1: Writes "Grammy, Mick, Jan S., Cal R."[443]

7:30 a.m.: Billy Cantor's breakfast, dishwashing, shopping in town with Joanie, Bill, Susan (the Cantors).

"Lunch and tennis at Chatham Bars Inn."

"Val Gendron[444]—Book Mobile."

7:45 p.m.: Band concert with Art Kramer.

"Sat in swinging Basket Park."

Beer at Souwester.

12:15 a.m.: Drives home.

Letter to Marion Freeman: Describes her happy work at the Cantors. "My day is a full and busy one—from seven in the morning till after 8 at night." She has been able to enjoy herself with friends too.

August 2, 7:30 a.m.: Billy Cantor's breakfast, gets the newspaper.

9:00 a.m.: "Our breakfast."

Writes Kathy Cantor,[445] shopping trip, blueberry muffins and soup.

10:45 a.m.: Sees Dick Norton.

Lunch and dishwashing, with Billy and Sue at the Chatham Bars Inn.

Supper, dishwashing, "2 baths & Sue's shampoo."

Letter to "Dear mother": Delighted with visit from Grammy and Grampy who bring with them the issue of *Mademoiselle* with her prize-winning story. Already feels she has "outgrown" the story, which has a "great many errors, artistically," thinking about doing a "tremendous job" on the next one, welcomes Art Kramer's critique of her story and suggestions for improvement, loves his lawyer's attention to wording, fascinated with pulp writer Val Gendron. "I plan to haunt her every Friday if I get a minute. . . . She really has been through the mill, I guess."

Letter to Enid Mark: Describes summer at the Belmont Hotel, "getting along with all types of peculiar professional people . . . all kinds of grotesque character types." Explains how she got sick and then got a job with Jewish Christian Scientists in Chatham, looks forward to "being academic again" and "hearing in detail" about Enid's summer.

August 3: 8:00 a.m.: "Up for Billy's breakfast—bikes for paper—gets corn—second coffee—dishwashing."

11:30 a.m.–12:30 p.m.: Christian Science Sunday school with Bob Cochran, dinner.

Dishwashing, reads in backyard until supper, roast duck, dishwashing, "danced to records."

9:30 p.m.: Chatham Bars Inn with Joanie Cantor.

Handwriting analysis at the Chatham Lighthouse.[446]

August 4, 7:30 a.m.: "Huge breakfast—melon, eggs, bacon, kippered herring, muffins, bread, jam, coffee.

Five loads of laundry, lunch, packs for picnic.

3:30 p.m.: Shops for fruit, drives with Cantor children to Brewster for a picnic with Dick and Perry Norton.

8:00 p.m.: Returns home, washes hair.

Letter to "Dear mother": Long and varied and happy days, describes going to Christian Science Sunday school, enjoys asking and answering questions. The "rather dumb blonde woman" teacher thinks "I was an old veteran! . . . I plan to go every Sunday I'm here." At the Chatham Bars Inn, Sylvia is told by a handwriting analyst that she is "the most intuitive person she'd had that night—also that I was very artistic—had a flair for color, pattern & line. Not bad, for a starter."

August 5, 6:30 a.m.: Breakfast, cleans house—kitchen, etc., to "South Pacific."

10:00 a.m.: At Oyster Pond with Cantor children.

11:30 a.m.: A talk about Christian Science.

1:00–3:00 p.m.: An afternoon at Mrs. Berg's, "swimming—Xenia, etc.," "great house overlooking Pleasant Bay."

A steak supper.

8:00 p.m.: Kids in bed.

8:30 p.m.: Art Kramer calls, looks up "epigonous."

August 6: Day off, picks out her clothing for the day, in rain, drives to town for mail.

10:30 a.m.–1:30 p.m.: Writes letters to Betsy Whit and others,[447] reads.

1:30 p.m.: With Art Kramer at the Belmont Hotel.

2:00–3:30 p.m.: Changes clothes.

4:00–6:00 p.m.: Tea with the Blossoms, dinner at the Coonamessett Inn in Falmouth, and sees the play *The Gypsies Wore High Hats* (1952) with Sylvia Sydney.

"Must read up on the neural theories," thinks about how abstract concepts like "love" are actually experienced through the senses. {PJ}

Undated: "Is everything we do an attempt to choose between the lesser of two evils? Is man in this sense, born in original sin?" {PJ}

August 7: Dick Norton calls.

8:00 a.m.: Brings Mrs. Cantor's breakfast to her in bed.

Dishwashing, lunch, to Sail Loft clothing store, dishwashing.

2:00 p.m.: Naps.

4:00 p.m.: Walks to town with Bill Cantor, gets mail, checks on bus to Boston.

6:00–8:30 p.m.: Supper, dishwashing, kids in bed.

8:30–9:30 p.m.: Writes letters.[448]

August 8: Mrs. Cantor is in Boston, Art Kramer calls, Dick Norton calls.

8:00–10:00 a.m.: Breakfast, dishwashing, washing floors.

10:30 a.m.: Susan Cantor's lesson, trip to egg farm for four dozen eggs. Washes hair, arranges flowers.

1:00 p.m.: A tuna fish lunch, dishwashing, flower arrangement.

3:30–4:30 p.m.: Christian Science.

5:00–6:00 p.m.: "Val Gendron Bookmobile."

A bath, chicken supper.

7:45–10:00 p.m.: Kids in bed, reads.

As it rains, she remembers earlier Augusts in the rain—at the Mayos' babysitting, with Dick Norton on a beach in Marblehead, two years earlier with Ilo Pill in his loft, bruised by his kiss, rain outside the car where she sat with Emile George de Coen III, thinking of her summer that would not come again and the story she published in *Seventeen*. She calls the month an "odd uneven time." {PJ}

August 9: A ten-dollar acceptance from *Seventeen*, changes beds and towels in Billy's and Susan's (the Cantors) rooms.

7:30–9:30 a.m.: Breakfast, dishwashing.

Drives to get corn with Marcia Brown, fixes Billy's lunch, dishwashing, ironing in the afternoon, prepares for lobster and corn dinner.

7:00 p.m.: Dances in kitchen, washes dishes.

11:00 p.m.–midnight: "Dick! Lovely short visit and talk in fog outside."

After dropping off the children, "I felt an evil sense of victory and freedom. I was going to see Val Gendron in the Bookmobile and I did." Listens to her advice. "I will be no Val Gendron. But I will make a good part of Val Gendron part of me—someday. . . . She has said I may visit her: a pilgrimage—to my First Author." {PJ}

August 10: Five-dollar gift.

8:00 a.m.: Billy's and Susan's breakfast, then hers.

10:30 a.m.: Dishwashing, gets dressed.

11:30 a.m.–1:00 p.m.: Christian Science Sunday school with Bob Cochran.

1:00–3:15 p.m.: Lobster bisque dinner, dishwashing.

3:15–5:00 p.m.: Writes letters,[449] studies science.[450]

7:00 p.m.: Supper, dishwashing.

9:00 p.m.: Kramer calls, Sylvia washes her hair.

"Ride in the sun crashing light victorious or hold back your rain. Cry in anger or in sorrow at the lost world, the mistaken ones. They are working. They will have you yet in harness." {PJ}

3:30 p.m.: Letter to Warren: "Dear Fellow-Spirit": The Cantors' twenty-two-year-old cousin Marvin Cantor flirts with her in the kitchen. Dick Norton visits and the Cantors approve. Feels devilish in Christian Science Sunday school, meets Bob Cochran there, who is seventeen or eighteen and a "precocious character," mentions that Val Gendron will help her with her work and recommend Sylvia to Gendron's agent.

August 11, 8:00 a.m.: Makes breakfast for Cantors, gets newspaper and mail.

10:00 a.m.–Noon: Drives to town, walk on the beach.

12:00–2:00 p.m.: Lunch.

2:00–3:00 p.m.: Scrubs kitchen floor.

Art Kramer calls, Sylvia waxes floor, works on supper, washes dishes.

8:30 p.m.: Walks on beach in Chatham to lighthouse, a sailboat visible against the "orange half moon" and conversation with Art—"oh! Life oh world, oh time."

August 12, 7:00 a.m.: Cleaning day, breakfast, dishwashing, dusting.

10:00 a.m.: Vacuuming, fixing Susan Cantor's hair.

10:30 a.m.: At Oyster Pond.

11:15 a.m.–12:15 p.m.: Marketing at the "A & P" with Bob Cochran.

12:30–1:30 p.m.: Lunch, dishwashing.

2:00–3:00 p.m.: Rest.

3:00–5:00 p.m.: At Crystal Lake in Orleans.

6:00–9:00 p.m.: Supper, dishwashing.

9:00–11:15 p.m.: Rides to Wellfleet, Massachusetts, with Bob Cochran in his red MG, beer, potato chips, "song & laughter, etc."

Describes long night's ride in MG with Bob who tells her she's "got it." What, exactly, he cannot say. She resists his advances, thinking: "It is much better . . . this way because of how now I am on the top directing both of us." {PJ}

August 13, 7:30 a.m.: Breakfast, dishwashing, a fruit cup, laundry, marketing, preparing luncheon for eight people: "Borscht, salad, French bread, fruit drink." "Joan Salisbury—Newton."

3:00–3:30 p.m.: Dishwashing.

3:30–4:30 p.m.: "Chatham Bars Inn crowd" with Joan Cantor.

5:30–8:30 p.m.: Bath, supper, dishwashing, ironing.

8:30 p.m.: Art Kramer calls, Dick Norton calls.

August 14, 8:00 a.m.: Breakfast, dishwashing, washes hair, packs for a day off.

10:30 a.m.: Dick Norton picks her up, in Brewster, eating cantaloupe in the sun.

11:30 a.m.–2:00 p.m.: A walk to the beach, out on sand flats, a visit to a cemetery, luncheon.

2:30–5:00 p.m.: Bikes with Dick to tennis courts and swimming.

5:00–8:00 p.m.: Return to the Cantors for supper and dishwashing.

8:00 p.m.: Out with Bob Cochran in his MG to the Hyannis Music Circus, sees *Die Fledermaus* (1874), followed by a hamburger and milk.

August 15, 8:00: a.m. Breakfast, dishwashing, fixes Susan Cantor's hair.

10:30 a.m.: Sue's lesson, a trip to the egg farm, drives to Andrew Hardings Beach—"cold clear water," drops off a copy of *Mademoiselle* with her story in it for Val Gendron.

1:00 p.m.: Lunch, dishwashing, silver polishing.

6:00–8:00 p.m.: Writes to Marcia Brown, Agnes, Fran, and Bobby.[451]

8:00–9:00 p.m.: Dinner, dishwashing, band concert.

10:30 p.m.: In bed.

Letter to "Dear Mum": Describes her week, including outings with Cochran, who has given her the "germ of a central character for a short story." She also mentions other writing projects, including a series of "descriptive nature articles about the Cape." Totals up earnings from writing—$700 in three years.

August 16, 8:00 a.m.: Breakfast with Billy Cantor in a "temper," fixes Susan Cantor's hair, washes dishes.

10:15 a.m.: Meets Everett, takes Cantor children to Oyster Pond, shops at Sail Loft clothing store, Atwood's farm, and Newman's.

4:00–4:30 p.m.: Dishwashing, tennis with Fran.

6:30 p.m.: Lobster dinner for eight, including apple pie à la mode.

9:30 p.m.: Dishwashing

10:30 p.m.: In bed.

August 17, 8:00 a.m.: Breakfast, dishwashing, dresses Billy, makes the children's lunch.

11:15 a.m.–12:15 p.m.: Betsy and Bob MacArthur visit, Sylvia gives them "Mexican glasses."

1:00–3:00 p.m.: Dinner, dishwashing.

10:30–11:00 p.m.: A ride with Art Kramer.

Listening to a band concert: the young and old in the "sea of music skipping over time, and the feeling in you very warm and it is our town, we all together, very sweet, all summer light, sometimes almost tearful because it is so moving all the time." So much is subject to change. "Delude yourself about printed islands of permanence. You've only got so long to live. You're getting your dream. Things are working, blind forces, no personal spiritual beneficent ones except your own intelligence and the good will of a few other fools and fellow humans. So hit it while it's hot." {PJ}

August 18, 8:00 a.m.: Breakfast, dishwashing, defrosts icebox, laundry.

10:00 a.m.: Prepares for "gigantic picnic," changes beds, "etc."

12:00–5:00 p.m.: A drive to Nauset Beach in Orleans: swimming, picnic, "wonderful walk—blue blue & great surf—quiet supper."

8:00 p.m.: In South Dennis, in Dennis, Massachusetts, on Center Street, for coffee and cake.

Midnight: With Val Gendron, eating grapes, watching her cats, Prudence and O'Hara, and four kittens as they talk.

August 19, 6:30 a.m.: Breakfast, dishwashing, cleans up living room.

11:30 a.m.: Hangs laundry in her room, scrubs and waxes kitchen floor, makes a picnic, "a glimpse" of Bob Cochran in Chatham.

12:00–4:00 p.m.: Nauset Beach, swimming, picnic, nap, long walk, meets Jerry Dewing, Camp Tonset[452] boys—Crystal Lake.[453]

5:30 p.m.: Cube steak and rice supper.

6:30 p.m.: Dishwashing, puts the children in bed.

7:15 p.m.: A bath, writes to Mother.

9:00 p.m.: In bed.

1:00 a.m.: "Face it kid, you've had a hell of a lot of good breaks. No Elizabeth Taylor, maybe. No child Hemingway, but God, you are growing up." {PJ}

Undated: Val Gendron's shack: "I walk in, feeling big and new and too clean." Describes the cluttered, disheveled surroundings, piles of manuscripts, the cats, the "three hunks of cake" she eats—"I am a pig"—talk of agents, Gendron's stories. She has "lived sold, produced. And how much she has already begun to teach me." {PJ}

August 19–21: Letter to "Dearest mum": Describes a perfect afternoon on Nauset Beach "(over 20 miles of pure white sand and powerful bluegreen surf, low dunes) . . . the most beautiful place on the Cape," a visit to Val Gendron "like a dream of an artist's Bohemia." Sylvia is "browner and healthier than ever." A date with Bob Cochran, biking, a picnic lunch, reads Mary Baker Eddy's *Science and Health* (1875).

August 20, 7:30 a.m.: Breakfast of cantaloupe, blueberry muffins, bacon, dishwashing, sweeping.

10:00–11:00 a.m.: Irons clothes.

11:00 a.m.–noon: Makes picnic lunch.

12:15–1:00 p.m.: Bikes three miles to Cochran's.

1:00–2:00 p.m.: Mrs. Ednah Shepard Cochran serves tea and shows Sylvia around the house.

Walks with Bob Cochran to Ryder's Cove in Chatham and sails across the bay for a picnic on North Beach, reads *Science and Health*.

7:00 p.m.: A calm sail back and picked up by Aunt Mildred and Uncle Bill.

10:00 p.m.–12:30 a.m.: A late supper with Dick Norton at the Chatham Lighthouse.

"I am an outlet." {PJ}

August 21, 8:00 a.m.: Breakfast, dishwashing, a story, fixes Susan Cantor's hair.

10:00 a.m.–11:30 a.m.: Susan's lesson, prepares "big picnic."

Noon: Drives to Truro, Massachusetts, through Wellfleet and rolling hills, picnic, swimming, reading, drives back, stopping to pick beach plums.

6:00 p.m.: Supper, dishwashing, washes hair, bath.

8:00 p.m.: Bob Cochran calls

8:30 p.m.: Postcard to "Dear mum": expecting a visit from Grammy, hopes Mother and Warren can visit, picnic in Truro and a swim.

9:00–9:30 p.m.: Kramer calls.

9:30–10:00 p.m.: A talk, reads about Christian Science.

1:30 a.m.: A Christian Science reverie, a scene with Cochran: "Head on her stomach he lies back, she running long tenderly moving fingers through his hair, cut short, soft. Carefully rapacious and hungry her fingers move along his cheek. They read aloud then from 'Science and Health' about marriage and spirit, she wondering inside at the paradox of delusion: how he can deny matter and flesh as real when one can make such healthful beauty out of them—how he can be inconsistent and admire beauty of flesh, calling her cream and honey because of her skin and white bathing suit." {PJ}

August 22, 8:00 a.m.: Breakfast, dishwashing, vacuums floors.

11:00 a.m.: With Joan Cantor and the other children to Merrythought.[454]

At Bob Cochran's house, gets vegetables, flowers, arrives home for lunch.

2:30–5:00 p.m.: Browses in Val Gendron's bookmobile.

Supper after shopping.

8:00–9:00 p.m.: Band concert with Bob Cochran.

9:00–10:30 p.m.: Horan's house for tea.

11:00 p.m.–midnight: A drive with Bob Cochran "in wind and wonderful talk at Chatham light!"

"For him [Cochran], perfection with the name Sylvia exists. And so she is." {PJ}

August 23, 8:00 a.m.: Breakfast, dishwashing.

Packs "great pork chop picnic" for trip to Nauset.

1:00–5:00 p.m.: Walks up beach with Attila Kassay, Joan Cantor, and Susan Cantor to "our Dune!"

At home for supper, dishwashing, wears black dress for dance at Chatham Bars Inn, fun with Attila dancing, a float at Snack Shack, talks with Attila under the stars.

August 24, 8:00 a.m.: Up for Billy Cantor's breakfast.

10:00–11:00 a.m.: "Our breakfast," dishwashing.

11:30 a.m.–12:30 p.m.: Dresses for church.

Sunday school with Cochran. Billy Cantor's dinner: roast beef and Yorkshire pudding—"yum!," dishwashing.

3:30 p.m.: Swimming with Attila Kassay, Joan, and the other children.

5:00 p.m.: "Talked with guys."

"Dictaphone—farewell."

8:30 p.m.: Billy in bed.

9:00 p.m.: Out with Cochran in his MG.

Writes letters.[455]

Letter to "Dearest mother": Reports juggling dates with seventeen-year-old Bob Cochran, twenty-five-year-old Art Kramer, and twenty-two-year-old Dick Norton: "Imagine—there have been only 4 days so far when I haven't either been called or dated by one or more of my 3 pets!" Beach picnics in Truro and Nauset are part of her work, a dance that the Cantors invited her to—"I must modestly admit I was a knockout—my hair bleached a light blonde, my tan golden brown, my black dress & dark eyes: everybody was wonderful to me." Mentions Attila Kassay, a suave Hungarian she is sure her mother would enjoy talking to in German.

Undated: Describes Attila Kassay, a graceful and athletic Hungarian. She learns from him about the Communist regime his family has escaped. She feels their emotional bond, their "*blutbrüderschaft.*" They are dancing after dinner, and Mrs. Cantor remarks to Attila: "You are holding her too close." Sylvia comments, "There is the rhythmic leading of your legs with mine, my body against yours, suddenly very comfortable; we still being strangers; dancing gives us, in society, this strange prerogative of studiedly casual embrace." {PJ}

August 25, 8:00 a.m.: Up for breakfast, Susan Cantor's lesson.

Shopping at Atwood's farm, "got tomato preserves."

Noon: Sandwich lunch for the Cantor children.

12:30 p.m.: "Wonderful hamburg & salad lunch out in the sun—gingerale & icecream."

2:00 p.m.: Dick Norton arrives.

3:00–5:00 p.m.: A swim at Chatham Bars Inn.

Children's supper, steak dinner with Dick Norton, children in bed, writes Kathy Cantor.[456]

10:30 p.m.: In bed.

"The guy grinned. 'You know' with a laugh, 'I'm awfully glad to hear you can take care of yourself with me. Because I've been out with a lot of girls who sure as hell couldn't.'" {PJ}

August 26, 6:30 a.m.: "Cleaning day," changes beds, makes breakfast, cleans kitchen, defrosts icebox.

10:30 a.m.: Oyster Pond.

Shops at the egg farm, Atwood's, lunch, scrubs kitchen floor, hangs out wash, washes hair.

3:00–5:00 p.m.: "Corn supper—ironed."

"Got belt!"

Reads about Christian Science until 11:30 p.m.

August 27: A day off, a reminder to take Tampax and curlers.

8:00 a.m.: Breakfast, dishwashing, gets the newspaper.

10:30 a.m.: Dick Norton and Bruce Elwell arrive.

11:00–11:30 a.m.: Beverly Newell arrives, they drive to "Old Mill" by "Herring Run."

In Brewster, sketches until 2:00 p.m.

3:30–4:00 p.m.: Lunch under trees.

Tennis at Alec's (Goldstein?).

5:00–8:00 p.m.: Reads *The Story of My Psychoanalysis* (1950) before supper.

10:00 p.m.: "Run to Bev's [Newell]—drive home."

Midnight: In bed.

Publishes "White Phlox" in the *Christian Science Monitor*.

August 28, 8:00 a.m.: Up for breakfast, dishwashing.

Dick Norton calls and Bob Cochran arrives.

10:30 a.m.: Gets mail.

"Bob [Cochran] with us to Oyster Pond," shopping, makes borsht and salad lunch with Bob, dishwashing, makes picnic, shops.

3:30 p.m.: Boat with Chuck Dudley,[457] Joan, Bob Cochran, a ride to Monomoy Point Lighthouse in Chatham for a picnic and swim.

"Built fire—dangerous takeoff."

8:00 p.m.: Arrives home, a bath.

10:30 p.m.: "Talk."

10:30 p.m.: Postcard to "Dear Mum": Mentions a wild boat ride and picnic, a sketching trip, tennis with Dick Norton, "my agonies over losing the Belmont job were a blessing in disguise! I never have felt so happy, rich (spiritually) and loving—chance is strange—one feels afterwards that it must have been destiny."

August 29: Types Kathy Cantor's letters, says goodbye to Val Gendron, Dick Norton calls.

8:00 a.m.: Breakfast, dishwashing, cleans downstairs.

10:30–11:00 a.m.: Oyster Pond and "talk with Barbara Stevens (U of M)."

11:00–1:00 p.m.: "Lunch (Richard)."[458]

2:00–3:00 p.m.: "Got flowers in Harwich," Massachusetts.

3:00–5:30 p.m.: Fixes flowers, talks to Chuck Dudley, washes hair.

6:30 p.m.: Supper, dishwashing, Chuck arrives.

8:00 p.m.: Band concert with Chuck, joined by Bob Cochran in a beret.

August 30, 8:00 a.m.: Breakfast, dishwashing.

10:00–1:00 p.m.: Types fifteen pages of Kathy Cantor's letters.

1:00–2:00 p.m.: Lunch, dishwashing.

2:00 p.m.: Types and talks to Chuck Dudley.

6:30–7:30 p.m.: Supper and dishwashing.

8:00 p.m.: Bob Cochran arrives and a visit with Mrs. Bernard.

8:30–11:00 p.m.: Monomoy Theater for *French for Love* (date unknown)—also Sydney Webber.

11:00 p.m.–midnight: At Souwester for coffee and a cheeseburger.

August 31, 6:30–8:00 a.m.: Up, packing, breakfast, dishwashing, cleans room, "got check."

11:30 a.m.–1:00 p.m.: "Church—Bob [Cochran] gave me books, etc."

1:00–1:30 p.m.: "Ham lunch before leaving."

1:30–2:00 p.m.: "Brewster? With Chuck [Dudley] and Joan [Cantor]."

2:00–8:00 p.m.: Supper and "chat with Bev [Newell]—p.j.'s—icecream." "Float with Dick Smythe,[459] Perry [Norton] & Sandy [William Lynn III]."

1:30 a.m.: Revels in the woman's "art of subtle power! As long as men have ideals, as long as they are vulnerable, there is this power to create a dream for them." Enumerates the boys she has dated and their qualities, Dick Norton "the recurring main theme." All have contributed to the "rich full orchestration" of her life. {PJ}

September 1: A late French toast breakfast with Dick Norton.

10:00 a.m.–1:00 p.m.: Sailing with Dick Smythe, Perry Norton, and Dick Norton, and Smythe's brother and fiancée.

2:00–2:30 p.m.: A sandwich lunch with Dick and Perry.

3:00–5:00 p.m.: "Nap with Perry."

3:30–7:30 p.m.: Dinner at Sandra Keery's.

8:00 p.m.: To the movies to see *O. Henry's Full House* (1952).

11:00 p.m.–1:00 a.m.: In Hyannis for a "Bohemian party" in a cabin with "wine, cheese, candlelight.

"Dick, Perry, Sandy [William Lynn III], Dick Smythe, Betsy Webber."

September 2: Sleeps until 10:00 a.m., a late breakfast in the sun.

11:30 a.m.: Grammy, Warren, Aunt M.,[460] and Mum arrive, lunch.

2:00 p.m.: Visit to Cantors.

5:00–6:00 p.m.: Swimming at Andrew Hardings Beach.

6:00–9:00 p.m.: Drives back to Wellesley, washes hair.

11:00 p.m.: In bed, exhausted.

September 3, 8:00 a.m.: Wakes up, finishes unpacking, cleans room, including bookcase, desk.

12:00–1:00 p.m.: Bank deposit, watch repair.

1:00–5:00 p.m.: Finishes cleaning room, makes supper.

7:00–9:00 p.m.: Studies science.[461]

7:30 p.m.: Irish calls.

8:30 p.m.: Attila Kassay calls.

September 4, 9:00–10:00 a.m.: Breakfast.

10:30 a.m.–noon: Reads about science outdoors.

12:00–2:00 p.m.: Relaxes after lunch.

2:00–4:00 p.m.: Studies science.

4:00 p.m.: Snack.

6:00–7:00 p.m.: Relaxes after supper, Jim McNealy calls.

7:00–10:00 p.m.: Studies science.

10:00–11:30 p.m.: Relaxes after another snack.

Finds it difficult to study her science program at Smith on her own, succumbing to distractions—magazines, "nervous eating"—while trying to maintain her seventy-page-a-day quota. Gets diverted with story ideas and the urge to revise poems, considers which brother to marry (Dick or Perry Norton), looking for any reasonable excuse to break off her studies. Mentions the "conflicting wills that make up my psyche." {PJ}

Undated: Mulls over her platonic romance with Perry, the "proverbial boy next door!" Feels more competitive with Dick, whose sexual experience bothers her. "But I'll show you I can beat you in other ways." To sum up: "Will I ever fling myself into the multitudinous perils and uncertainties of life with a passionate Constantine [Sidamon-Eristoff]; a witty and sardonic and tempestuous Attila [Kassay]; a proud, wealthy aristocratic Philip [Brawner?] They enchant, they fascinate: I could carve myself to the new worlds they imply. But is it not the tragedy of man to be the reactionary, the conservative, and to always choose the certainty of daily bread above the light airy inconsistencies of foreign pastries?" {PJ}

September 5, 9:00 a.m.: Breakfast.

10:30 a.m.–noon: Studies science, covers twenty-five pages.

3:30–6:30 p.m.: Sails on Charles River with Philip Brawner.

8:00 p.m.: A talk with Irish and an ice cream cone.

September 6, 10:00 a.m.–noon: Sends poems to the *Christian Science Monitor*.

12:00–2:00 p.m.: Lunch, washes hair.

2:00–6:00 p.m.: Studies science.

8:00 p.m.: With Attila Kassay at the Totem Pole for dancing, sees Warren and Ann Keddee, who quotes from *Cyrano de Bergerac* (1897) in Hungarian.

September 7: Sleeps until noon, writes to Prentice Smith, Joan Cantor, Mrs. Cantor, and Dick Norton.[462]

3:00–6:00 p.m., 7:00–11:00 p.m.: Studies science.

Letter to Mrs. Cantor: "I want to tell you how infinitely much it's meant to me to become part of your wonderful family for the last month and more! How can I ever express the multitude of thanks for everything—all the trips, and picnics and companionable times . . . I don't know when I have been so completely happy and full of the simple and miraculous joy of living."

September 8, 11:00 a.m.–1:00 p.m.: Studies science.

1:00–4:00 p.m.: "Go over clothes," "decision."

September 9: Sunbathes, writes.

Publishes "Riverside Reveries" in the *Christian Science Monitor*.

September 10, 8:00–11:00 a.m.: Earns one dollar and fifty cents babysitting for Mrs. Aldrich.

Sunbathes, writes to Dick Norton.[463]

1:00–2:00: p.m. Withdraws $398 from bank.

Writes "The Summer Band Concert."

8:45 p.m.: Attila Kassay calls.

September 11: Shops.

2:00–5:00 p.m.: A walk to Phil McCurdy's house for a talk and tennis.

8:00 p.m.: Party at Lou Pullen's with Elizabeth Burdoin and Frieda.

Midnight: Talks, eats date-nut pie, and reads *The Caine Mutiny* (1951) until 3:00 **a.m.**

September 12, 11:00 a.m.: Wakes up, sees Mrs. Aldrich, Uncle Leo.

Noon: Lincoln Art Museum with Jim McNealy, a picnic in Concord, Massachusetts, canoeing upriver,

Ten-dollar acceptance from *Seventeen*.

September 13: "Get: Dick's card, present, lipstick."

Cleans house, dinner with the Clarkes.

8:00 p.m.: Dressed in a black taffeta shirt and long-sleeved white blouse, meets Attila Kassay for a trip to the movies in Boston to see *Carrie*[464] and *Don't Bother to Knock*,[465] a talk in Fenway with Attila about the "Siege of Budapest, etc."

September 14: Makes a cake, drives Warren to Exeter, eats dinner in "Kurt e's diner," finishes frosting a cake.

September 15: Dick Norton's birthday.

9:00 a.m.: Marcia Brown arrives.

11:00 a.m.: Shops, sees Dick.

4:00 p.m.: The Cantors visit.

8:00 p.m.–1:00 a.m.: With Dick Norton, "apples—rain—etc."

September 16: Morning shopping, browsing, lunch, reading in the sun, walks around Wellesley College.

9:00–midnight: "Boating on Morses Pond in New Boat with Dick."

September 17, 10:00 a.m.–2:00 p.m.: Shops in town, buys suit and Bermuda shorts.

3:38 p.m.: Marcia Brown's bus.

Washes hair.

9:00 p.m.–midnight: Jim McNealy's party with popcorn, marshmallow, "Heavenly Hash,"[466] milk, and music.

September 18: Wakes up.

11:00 a.m.–noon: Sees Patsy O'Neil.

12:00–4:30 p.m.: Cleans room, puts away summer clothes, starts packing.

4:30–6:00 p.m.: "Boating with Dick [Norton] & Dave [Freeman?]."

7:00–11:00 p.m.: Finishes putting away clothes, cleaning her room, writes speech for Smith College tea.

September 19: Shops, writes speech all morning.

3:00 p.m.: Smith tea speech "great success."

4:00–6:00 p.m.: Visit and chat with Dick Norton.

8:30 p.m.: Sees Attila Kassay, drives to Weston to see a movie.

September 20: Writes letters in the morning.[467]

3:00 p.m.: A visit and chat with Mr. Crockett in the backyard.

5:30 p.m.: Dinner at the Nortons': swordfish with sour cream, hollandaise, and broccoli, grape pie, port.

"Lovely" evening at home with Dick reading Hemingway and e. e. cummings by candlelight.

"My absurd overflowing enthusiasms . . . I want desperately to be liked." She tends to idealize people and then finds fault with some of them. {PJ}

Undated: After a long talk with Mr. Crockett, thinks of graduate study in England—Cambridge or Oxford. England will be her "jumping-off place" for travel on the continent. She will study philosophy, write stories, and a novel. Although she feels she is in love with both Norton brothers, she considers the idea of falling in love and having "an affair with someone over 'there.'" {PJ}

September 21, 11:00 a.m.: A "rendezvous" with Mr. Wheeler at church. Home for dinner with "Sarge Nichols," a World War II veteran, and an Amherst College student, walk with Perry Norton to "Playfield" after lunch, a church picnic, talk about the future, a drive to Waltham, Massachusetts, supper at the Nortons', where Dick and Perry read aloud from the Mary Poppins series.

10:45 p.m.: In bed.

September 22: Washes hair, reads *Atlantic Monthly*.

Noon: On bus to Harvard Medical School, lunch with Carol Pierson and Ken.

2:30–3:30 p.m.: Talks with Carol about Europe, bus home with Dick Norton.

Finishes packing.

September 23: Packs, loads car in the morning.

2:30 p.m.: Drives to Smith with Dick.

6:00 p.m.: Picnic at Quabbin Reservoir.[468]

10:15 p.m.: Party for juniors, unpacks.

September 24, 9:00 a.m.: Meets Marcia Brown at registration and in chapel.

11:00 a.m.: Juniors meet in Sage Hall.

Noon: Honors meeting.

12:30–1:45 p.m.: BW.

Bells, shopping.

10:15 p.m.: House meeting.

September 25: 9:00 a.m.: "Science."

10:00 a.m.: Bells.

12:30: p.m. BW.

2:00 p.m.: "English."

3:00 p.m.: "Art 11."

4:00: p.m. "Mr. [Professor] Patch."

Letter to "Dear mother": Courses begin "full force" tomorrow. Settling into her new room, she requests several items from home. Now in Lawrence House, where—like other scholarship students—she is required to work an hour per day as part of her room and board, waitressing at lunch. Mentions a complimentary letter from Olive Higgins Prouty who is helping to fund her studies. Her course work for the year will include creative writing, medieval literature, modern poetry, John Milton, physical science. Decides to drop art because of her heavy schedule, mentions a letter from Eddie

Cohen who plans to marry a divorcée with a two-year-old son. "What a wonderfully sordid life."

September 26, 8:15 a.m.: Press board meeting.

   9:00 a.m.: Science.

   2:00 p.m.: "CW."[469]

   3:00 p.m.: Art.

   5:00 p.m.: *Smith Review* staff meets in Davis Hall.

   Supper, evening at Albright House—a residence hall, washes hair.

September 27: Science in the morning, shopping, into the News Office, working on a story about freshman day.

   12:30 p.m.: BW.

   2:00 p.m.: Sees Sally Rosenthal, paints furniture, supper with Enid Epstein.

   7:30 p.m.: At the movies.

September 28, 9:30 a.m.: Meets Enid Epstein and Margie, "dinner at Jack."

   3:00 p.m.: Meeting with Sally Rosenthal.

   5:25 p.m.: BW.

   Plays bridge.

   Postcard to "Dear mum": feels more confident after dropping art and renewing her dedication to working on the *Smith Review* and the press board.

   Letter to Warren: Responding to his postcard, confesses she was scared her first days at Smith and meeting all the new faces in her house. Awed by studying English with Professor Davis, whose review of *The Old Man and the Sea* (1952) was on the front page of the *New York Times Book Review*. Wants Warren to come for a weekend.

September 29, 8:30 a.m.: "Mass meeting," press board meeting, sees Maria Schnieders, a German professor.

   3:15 p.m.: "Chase Berger—RA Center."[470]

   5:30–6:00 p.m.: With Marcia Brown.

September 30, 9:00 a.m.: "RA write up due."

   10:00 a.m.–noon: "Carrell" assignments in library.

   4:00 p.m.: Meeting with Professor Patch.

   Supper at Haven House.

October: *Seventeen* publishes "The Perfect Setup."

October 1, 11:00 a.m.–12:30 p.m.: Press board meeting.

   BW.

   5:00 p.m.: Meeting in Davis Hall, "Phi. Sci."

   7:00 p.m.: "Radio broadcast."

October 2, 8:00 a.m.: At the Green Room.[471]

9:00 a.m.: Science.

10:00 a.m.: Bells.

11:00 a.m.–12:30 p.m.: Press board meeting.

2:00 p.m.: English.

3:00–5:00 p.m.: Working on English paper.

October 3, 8:30 a.m.: Press board meeting.

9:00 a.m.: Science.

10:00 a.m.–12:30 p.m.: Press board meeting.

"Wash hair bath."

October 4, 9:00 a.m.: "Phy-sci."

Shopping in the morning, finishing a story for the press board.

2:00 p.m.: A walk in the country with Goodie.

6:00 p.m.: Supper with Marcia Brown and her husband, Mike Brown.

7:30 p.m.: "Sage Movie?"

October 5: *Seventeen* "second prize!" In the morning, types paper for English 245.

5:25 p.m.: BW.

9:30–11:00 p.m.: At Joe's pizzeria for beer with Marcia Brown, Mike Plummer, and Charlie Gardner, an English major at Trinity College—"much talk and fun."

Letter to "Dear mother": announces she has won a *Seventeen* second prize for her story "Initiation," a boost to what had been her faltering self-confidence, appreciates her mother's last "morale building letter" and all she has done for her and Warren, turning down dates from old boyfriends in favor of her studies, anticipating a visit from Dick Norton.

October 6, 8:00 a.m.: At the Green Room.

9:00 a.m.–12:30 p.m.: Geoffrey Chaucer, "get films developed."

2:00 p.m.: Press board meeting.

Springfield Daily News publishes "Faith Groups Open Center for Students."

October 7, 8:30 a.m.: Reads Chaucer.

12:30–2:00 p.m.: Press board meeting.

3:00–5:00 p.m.: Studies science.

Edor Nelson for supper.

October 8, 8:30 a.m.: Works on "chapel cover," "Pick up film."

11:00 a.m.: "Enid?"[472]

2:00 p.m.: "Pictures taken."

Creative writing paper due. Supper with Perry Norton and Charlotte Kennedy. *Daily Hampshire Gazette* publishes "Central Spot for Religion Groups."

October 9, 10:00 a.m.: Bells.

4:00 p.m.: "Photographers."

5:00 p.m.: *Smith Review* meeting.

October 10, 8:30 a.m.: Press board meeting.

4:00 p.m.: "Patch unit paper due."

5:00–6:00 p.m.: Davis Hall talk with Maury Longsworth.

Friday night: Letter to "Dear Mother": Her new roommate, Mary, is working out fine, although they do not have the rapport that Sylvia had with Marcia Brown. Mentions a delightful dinner at Joe's, "a colorful local beer and pizza place with red-checked table clothes and a gay atmosphere," with Marcia and Mike Plummer and Charlie Gardner. She is working hard on an article for *Springfield Daily News*, with feature stories that get "full picture spreads."

October 11, 9:00 a.m.: "Science."

10:00 a.m.–noon: Press board meeting, "Smith mobile."

2:00–4:00 p.m.: Canoeing with Jean Francis.

A steak supper with Dee Neuberg,[473] including pomegranates, at a Chinese restaurant.

October 12, 9:00 a.m.: Breakfast with the Browns at Florence Diner.

Biking to Mount Tom, "Clams, Apples, cheese, cider, cookies."

3:00–4:30 p.m.: Bells.

5:25 p.m.: BW.

Dinner with Dick Norton.

October 13, 9:00 a.m.–12:30 p.m.: "Library look up Faculty Club."

2:00–3:00 p.m.: Press board meeting, "clip Sunday paper."

3:00–6:00 p.m., 7:00–10:00 p.m.: Reads Chaucer.

October 14, 9:00 a.m.: "Write up on Outing Club due."

9:00–12:30 p.m.: Reads Chaucer.

2:00–3:00 p.m.: Press board meeting.

3:00–6:00 p.m., 7:00–10:00 p.m.: Reads Chaucer.

October 15, 8:20 a.m.: "Take ins."

9:00–10:00 a.m.: Science.

11:00 a.m.–12:30 p.m.: Press board meeting.

3:00–6:00 p.m.: Reads Chaucer.

Supper with Professor Lincoln.

7:00–10:00 p.m.: Reads Chaucer.

Postcard to "Dear Mother": a restful weekend with Dick Norton, reads letters from readers of her stories.

October 16, 8:00 a.m.: *Smith Review* meeting.

4:00 p.m.: "Unit—paper due."

Supper with Professor Page.

October 17, 8:15 a.m.: Press board meeting.

9:00 a.m.: Science.

11:00 a.m.: "Bus."

October 18: "Write Either Eng. paper or Chaucer paper," "Shopping?" Halloween show, a walk with Maury Longsworth.

October 19: Dinner at the Nortons', drives back to Smith with Dick Norton.

5:25 p.m.: supper.

Coffee with Perry Norton and Charlotte Kennedy.

10:15 p.m.–midnight: "Late bells."

October 20, 8:00 a.m.: Tennis.

9:00 a.m.–12:30 p.m.: Reads Chaucer.

BW.

2:00–3:00 p.m.: Press board meeting.

3:00–5:30 p.m.: Reads Chaucer.

Supper with Marcia Brown.

8:00–10:00 p.m.: Reads Chaucer.

Postcard to "Dear Mother": finished a Chaucer paper and contemplating a weekend in Princeton.

October 21, 9:00 a.m.–12:30 p.m.: Reads Chaucer.

2:00–3:00 p.m.: Press board meeting.

3:00:-6:00 p.m., 7:00–10:00 p.m.: Reads Chaucer.

October 22, 8:30 a.m.: Chapel.

11:00 a.m.: Studies science.

11:00 a.m.–12:30 p.m.: Press board meeting.

2:00 p.m.: "Creative paper due."

3:00–6:00 p.m.: Studies science.

October 23, 8:00 a.m.: *Smith Review* meeting.

9:00 a.m.: Science.

10:00 a.m.: BW.

11:00 a.m.–12:30 p.m.: Press board meeting.

4:00–6:00 p.m.: "Unit paper due."

7:00–10:00 p.m.: Studies science.

House meeting.

October 24, 8:30 a.m.: Press board meeting.

9:00 a.m.: Science written exam.

2:00–6:00 p.m.: Shopping.

Washes hair.

8:15 p.m.: Letter to "Dear Mother": Draws a picture of her new outfit purchased at Filene's, encourages Aurelia to vote for Adlai Stevenson, mentions witch-hunting Republican Senator Joseph McCarthy, the "southern snobbery" of Senator William E. Jenner, the "reactionary foreign policy of

[Robert] Taft." Stevenson is sound on civil rights. Tomorrow night she will see *Rashomon* (1950).

October 25, 9:00 a.m.: Studies science, does laundry, press board meeting. Attila Kassay is in Florida for three weeks.

7:00 p.m.: Sees *Rashomon.*

10:00–11:00 p.m.: Calls "Warden,"[474] gets bike.

October 26, morning: Postcard to "Dear Mummy": Praises the cake her mother sent and the birthday party of ten girls who enjoyed it: "how did you ever make it heart shaped!" Delighted that Ilo Pill remembered her birthday with a card, a "beautiful pen-and-ink sketch."

5:25 p.m.: Supper.

October 27, 9:00 a.m.–noon: Bells.

2:00 p.m.: Press board meeting.

3:30 p.m.: "X-RAY infirmary."

5:30 p.m.: Supper with the Browns.

7:30 p.m.: "Honor Board Pic—Davis." Meets Miss Mensel at scholarship office.

9:00 p.m.: "Write Play—Jan."

Springfield Daily News publishes "Smith Girls Will Get Chance to Jeer Faculty," a report of a student-faculty soccer game. *Daily Hampshire Gazette* publishes "Cheers, Jeers Promise for Smith Game."

Postcard to "Dear mum": Describes a birthday dinner, her "perfect presents"—"a Van Gogh book of reprints, a chunky pottery Italian Plate, and a new Modern Library book of Franz Kafka's short stories." Two "fat letters" from Dick Norton.

October 28: "Miss [Cynthia S.?] Walsh."[475]

8:00 a.m.: *Smith Review* meeting.

10:45 a.m.: Meets with Miss Mensel.

2:00 p.m.: Press board meeting.

7:15 p.m.: *Smith Review* meeting.

Postcard to "Dear Mother": describes her new outfit of coat, shoes, and bag, totaling her prices and her "sensible" purchases—"I really feel a bit frivolous, going to Princeton & spending the train fare but I figure it'll probably be my only invitation this fall, so I'll make the most of it & thus never say 'I wish I'd gone.'"

October 29, 8:30 a.m.: Chapel.

10:00–11:00 a.m.: Studies science.

3:00 p.m.: Meets Miss Walsh.

Postcard to "Dear mum": Disagrees with her mother's letter about reasons to vote for Eisenhower. Enjoys Lawrence House: "The girls are all wonderful! Wish me luck at Princeton."

October 30, 9:00–10:00 a.m.: Studies science, cleans room.

10:00 a.m.–12:30 p.m.: Press board meeting.

Halloween supper party.

October 31, 8:30 a.m.: Press board meeting.

9:00 a.m.: Science.

1:10: p.m. Train to Princeton.

Dinner, dance.

November 1: Princeton-Brown game, score 39–0. Dance, "Rodger Decker[476] 10 South Dodd Hall."

November 2, 9:30 a.m.: Train from Princeton to Grand Central, where Sylvia lunches.

Postcard to "Dear Mum": back from Princeton, tired but impressed with the college's beauty, even if her date was "intellectually stupid . . . I cannot abide dumb rich boys."

November 3: Contemplates the urge to commit suicide. {PJ}

November 4: Writes feature on writing clinic.

November 5, 8:30 a.m.: Chapel.

9:00–10:00 a.m.: Science.

10:00 a.m.–12:30 p.m.: Press board meeting.

2:00 p.m.: "Creative paper due."

2:00–3:00 p.m.: Professor Davis's class.

3:00–6:00 p.m.: "Chaucer—Chart—critical."

7:00–10:00 p.m.: "Final e's."

November 6: Cleans room.

9:00–10:00 a.m.: Science.

10:00 a.m.–12:30 p.m.: Press board meeting.

4:00–6:00 p.m.: "Unit."

House meeting, "Sandy's Table."

Letter to "Dear Mummy": An anti-Eisenhower letter. "Stevenson was the Abe Lincoln of our age." Feeling keen competition with the best students in her Chaucer course. Professor Patch, is the "most brilliant man I have ever known" and Chaucer the "most rich and rewarding of writers." Thinking of Harvard summer school.

Letter to "Dear Warren": impressed with Princeton's library and Gothic cathedral: "Most of the boys were Republicans because, of course, they came from wealthy families."

November 7, 8:30 a.m.: Press board meeting.

4:00–6:00 p.m.: Goodie.

November 8, 8:30 a.m.: Laundry.

9:00–10:00 a.m.: Science.

10:00–11:00 a.m.: Press board meeting.

11:00 a.m.–noon, 2:00–6:00 p.m.: Studies science.

Reads Chaucer's *Troilus and Criseyde* (ca. mid-1380s).

6:45–8:00 p.m.: "Sat bells."

November 9, 9:00 a.m.–noon: Reads *Troilus and Criseyde*.

12:00–1:00 p.m.: "Sun."

2:00–5:30 p.m.: Reads *Troilus and Criseyde*.

7:00 p.m.: Supper with Marcia Brown.

November 10, 8:00 a.m.: *Smith Review* meeting.

"Chaucer paper Minor poems."

November 11: Mr. and Mrs. Norton visit.

Letter to "Dearest mummy": thinks her mother works too hard and that she ought to give up teaching Sunday school, "amazing" that she has not had a cold so far.

November 12, 8:30 a.m.: Works on "chapel cover."

9:00–10:00 a.m.: Press board meeting.

10:00–11:00 a.m.: Science.

11:00 a.m.–12:30 p.m.: Press board meeting.

2:00–3:00 p.m.: English.

3:00–6:00 p.m.: Science.

7:00–10:00 p.m.: Studies Chaucer.

November 13, 8:00–9:00 a.m.: Cleans room.

9:00–10:00 a.m.: Science.

10:00–11:00 a.m.: Bells.

11:00 a.m.–12:30 p.m.: Works on press board speech.

2:00–3:00 p.m.: English.

4:00–6:00 p.m.: "Unit—minor poems."

7:00–10:00 p.m.: Washes hair, studies science.

November 14, 8:30 a.m.: "Press Board Speech."

9:00–10:00 a.m.: Science.

10:00–11:00 a.m.: Press board meeting.

11:00 a.m.–12:30 p.m.: Studies science.

2:00–3:00 p.m.: "English tea-? Haven?"

8:00–10:00 p.m.: Supper with Marcia Brown.

Admits she has "broken down and cried" over the diagnosis of Dick Norton's tuberculosis, but she also seems to reject him as his mother's "spoiled pet." With Marcia, she lets the "tight mask fall off," and the "bewildered, chaotic, fragments pour out." She felt so integrated rooming with Marcia, "one of the most vital experiences of my life . . The passionate discussions, the clear articulate arguments." Now she is putting up with a roommate who whines and stumbles, "eyes drooping, mouth drooping. God!" {PJ}

November 15, 9:00–10:00 a.m.: Science.

10:00–11:00 a.m.: Press board meeting.

2:00–6:00 p.m.: "Start eng paper wait supper."

November 16: "CW paper," "Eng paper."

6:00–8:00 p.m.: "Supper at Davises."[477]

November 17, 4:00 p.m.: "Tea at alumnae house with Marybeth Little."[478]

Letter to "Dear mum": takes phenobarbital to get to sleep after a dinner at the house of the "great critic," Professor Davis.

November 18: Supper with Bessie McAlpine.

"You have forgotten the secret you knew, once, ah, once, of being joyous, of laughing, of opening doors." {PJ}

Like her former roommate Ann Davidow, Plath felt the pressures to perform at the highest level in college, and like other Smith students, she felt the need to seek professional help.

November 19, 8:30 a.m.: Chapel.

9:00–11:00 a.m.: Science.

11:00 a.m.–12:50 p.m.: Press board meeting.

2:00–3:00: p.m. "Creative paper due."

4:00 p.m.: "Press board pic."

Letter to "Dear mother": Eager to get home for rest. Alludes to a "very frustrated mental state." Worried about her science course. "I have practically considered committing suicide to get out of it." She considers seeing the school psychiatrist.

November 20, 9:00–10:00 a.m.: Science.

10:00–11:00 a.m.: Bells.

11:00–12:30 p.m.: Press board meeting.

2:00–3:00 p.m.: Professor Davis's class.

4:00–6:00 p.m.: *Troilus and Criseyde* paper.

7:00–10:00 p.m.: Studies science.

10:15 p.m.: House meeting.

November 21, 8:30 a.m.: Press board meeting.

9:00–10:00 a.m.: Science.

10:00–11:00 a.m.: Press board meeting.

2:00–3:00 p.m.: Professor Davis's class.

7:00–10:00 p.m.: Supper with Marcia Brown. "Ice cream."

November 22, 9:00–10:00 a.m.: Science.

3:00 p.m.: Meets Charlie Gardiner. "Chaucer books due."

November 23: "Chaucer paper."

November 25, 8:00 a.m.: *Smith Review* meeting.

"[Katherine] Mansfield books due."

November 26, 8:30 a.m.: Chapel.

10:00–11:00 a.m.: Studies science.

12:50 p.m.: Thanksgiving vacation begins.

"Write: Olive Higgins Prouty, MLLE, Eddie [Cohen], Hans [Neupert], Davidow, M. Watrous, Alison [Prentice Smith]."[479]

November 27: Attila Kassay's birthday.

"Thanksgiving dinner—Pooch, Mother, Warren."

5:00–11:00 p.m.: Drives Warren to Exeter with Cindy Morrow.

November 28, 3:00–6:00 p.m.: Visits the Cantors.

6:00–10:30 p.m.: Dinner at the Nortons' with Perry Norton, Myron Lotz, and Bob Cochran.

November 29: "MLLE off," studies Chaucer, "Dick MacKey" (?) calls.

November 30: "Prouty letter—science."[480]

3:30 p.m.: Returns to Smith.

Writes Dick Norton and Myron Lotz.[481]

December: *Seventeen* publishes poem, "Twelfth Night."

December 1, 8:30 a.m.–12:30 p.m.: "Chaucer or Dante."

2:00 p.m.: Press board meeting.

2:30–6:00 p.m., 7:00–10:00 p.m.: Dante.

December 2, 8:30 a.m.–12:30 p.m.: "Science & chemistry."

11:00 a.m.: Postcard to "Dear mum": in the library reading Dante, Thanksgiving has restored her, she is looking forward to seeing Myron Lotz.

"Dante & science."

2:00 p.m.: Press board meeting.

2:30–6:00 p.m.: "Science."

7:00–10:00 p.m.: Studies for final exams.

December 3: Chapel.

10:00 a.m.: Studies science.

11:00 a.m.–12:30 p.m.: Press board meeting.

"Prepare lunch."

2:00 p.m.: "English."

5:00 p.m.: Works on *Smith Review* speech in Davis Hall.

7:00–10:00 p.m.: "Science for Thurs Start beat."

December 4: Cleans room.

9:00 a.m.: Science.

10:00 a.m.: Bells.

11:00 a.m.–12:30 p.m.: Press board meeting.

2:00–4:00 p.m.: Studies for English and final exams.

4:00–6:00 p.m.: "Chaucer Unit—TEST."

7:00–10:00 p.m.: Studies science.

Letter to "Darling mother": Dick Norton has sent her a story—"bless the lad for trying."

Letter to "Dear Warren": confesses trouble with understanding her science course, mentions a thrilling meeting with Myron Lotz, tall, handsome, grinning, and also a "brilliant scholar," her promising *New Yorker* rejection, and her pride in her "tall handsome brilliant brother."

December 5, 8:15 a.m.: Press board meeting.

9:00 a.m.: Science.

10:00 a.m.–12:30 p.m.: Press board meeting.

2:00 p.m.: English.

3:00–6:00 p.m., 7:00–10:00 p.m.: Studies science.

December 6, 9:00 a.m.: Science.

10:00 a.m.–12:30 p.m.: Press board meeting.

2:00–6:00 p.m.: A walk with Marcia Brown.

"Read for unit," "Shop for dress?" "Xmas gifts?"

7:00–10:00 p.m.: Dinner dishes.

11:00 p.m.–12:00: Bells.

December 7, 9:00 a.m.–1:00 p.m., 2:00–5:00 p.m., 7:00–10:00 p.m.: "Read for unit," "Eng paper."

December 8, 9:00 a.m.–12:30 p.m.: "Science review temp etc."

2:00 p.m.: Press board meeting.

3:00–6:00 p.m.: Supper at Gillett House on Smith campus.

December 9, 9:00 a.m.–12:30 p.m., 3:00–6:00 p.m., 7:00–10:00 p.m.: Studies science.

2:00: Press board meeting.

Postcard to "Dearest mum": her mother's letter has given her a boost, announces she is going to tea with Olive Higgins Prouty, and is happy about letters from Dick and Perry Norton, and a card from Elizabeth Drew inviting her to tea.

December 10, 8:30 a.m.: Chapel, writes to Dick Norton.[482]

10:00–11:00 a.m.: Studies science.

11:00 a.m.–12:30 p.m.: Press board meeting.

2:00 p.m.: Reads Dante.

3:00–6:00 p.m., 7:00 p.m.: "Review science."

December 11, 9:00 a.m.: Studies for science exam.

10:00 a.m.: Bells.

11:00 a.m.–12:30 p.m.: Press board meeting.

2:00 p.m.: English.

3:00 p.m.: Meets Professor Lincoln in the library.

4:00–6:00 p.m.: "Chaucer unit, wash hair, do nails, get clothes, read."

7:00–10:00 p.m.: "Science for Friday."

December 12, 8:15 a.m.: Press board meeting.

9:00 a.m.: Science.

10:00 a.m.–12:30 p.m.: Press board meeting, "shop," "turn in course cards," "call photo."

2:00 p.m.: English.

3:00: p.m. "Science for Sat."

7:00 p.m.: "Myron [Lotz]—vespers."

10:00 p.m.–midnight: "Joe's—pizza—conversation."

Finishes "Mary Ventura and the Ninth Kingdom," with instructor's comments. {PM}

December 13, 11:00 a.m.–3:00 p.m.: "Ride into country with Myron [Lotz]—Snowstorm, pictures, conversation."

4:00–5:00 p.m.: "Walk to Mental hospital."

5:00–6:00 p.m.: "Cocktail party."

6:00–9:00 p.m.: "Dinner & conversation."

"House Dance 1am Myron Lotz 14 hrs."

Letter to "Dear Mother": Describes her hectic day—creative writing, appointment with honors advisor, Chaucer class, shopping, and various social outings with Myron, Perry Norton, and others.

December 14, 9:30 a.m.: "Ham & eggs at Northampton Diner."

A four-mile walk into the country, at the airport, "tomato soup with pilot," airplane ride over Pioneer Valley, relaxes and reads in Lawrence House, club sandwich at Rahar's, returns to Lawrence to listen to music until 10:15 p.m.

Plath's interest in abnormal psychology emerges in her second year at Smith and continues throughout the rest of her life.

December 15, 8:30 a.m.–12:30 p.m.: Out with Marcia Brown.

2:00 p.m.: Press board meeting.

2:30 p.m.: "DOCTOR [Marion] BOOTH" at the infirmary.

Supper with Jan and Sybil.

Letter to "Dear Mother": Outings with Perry Norton and Myron Lotz, including a drive into the country, a walk past a mental hospital hearing people screaming, "a most terrifying holy experience, with the sun setting red and cold over the black hills . . . I want so badly to learn about why and how people cross the borderline between sanity and insanity!" Describes her first half-hour flight in a two-seater plane at the invitation of the pilot while Myron waits on the ground. She watches the mountains "reeling up into the sky" and the clouds floating below as the pilot does a "wing-over." "Never have I felt such ecstasy!" The pilot allowed her to take the stick and make the plane climb and tilt. She is suffering from insomnia and has an appointment with the psychiatrist, Dr. Marion Booth, about her science course.

December 16, 11:00: a.m. Meets with Mary Ellen Chase.

    2:00 p.m.: Press board meeting.

December 17, 8:30: a.m. Chapel.

    10:00 a.m.: Studies science.

    11:00 a.m.–12:30 p.m.: Press board meeting.

    2:00 p.m., 3:00–6:00 p.m., 7:00–10:00 p.m.: Studies English. "Pick up pictures."

December 18, 9:00 a.m.: Science.

    10:00 a.m.: Bells.

    11:00 a.m.–12:30 p.m.: Press board meeting.

    2:00–3:00 p.m.: English.

    4:00–6:00 p.m.: Supper with Marcia Brown.

    7:00–10:00 p.m.: "Pack, etc."

December 19, 9:00–10:00 a.m.: Science.

    11:00 a.m.: Home with Warren.

    12:50 p.m.: Winter vacation begins.

December 20: Writes Christmas cards and New Year's letters.

    5:00 p.m.: Tea with Olive Higgins Prouty.

    An evening with Perry Norton.

December 21: John Hodges visits, Dick Norton returns home.

December 22: Supper at the Nortons', a talk with Warren "till late."

December 23: The Nortons visit the Plaths for dinner, party at McNealy's.

December 24: Morning dental appointment, lunch with Dick and Perry Norton and George Harper.

    3:30–5:00 p.m.: The Cantors visit for the afternoon.

    Reads the *Atlantic Monthly*.

December 25: A walk with Warren, a visit to Phil McCurdy, supper at Aunt Dot's, packs, washes hair, manicure.

December 26, 7:00 a.m.: Train to Saranac Lake Sanitarium for Christmas cotillion and to see Dick Norton.[483]

    Dinner at Bill Lynn's.[484]

December 27: Skiing at Mount Pisgah in Northborough, Massachusetts.

December 28: "BROKE LEFT LEG."

December 28–29: Telegram to Mother: Announces she has fractured her fibula skiing. Jokes that it is not painful but "just tricky to manipulate while charlestoning."

December 29: Knee X-ray, reads Lynn's book.

December 30: "Home?"

    8:30 a.m.: Train from Saranac to Framingham.

December 31: At the Nortons' to see Perry, snow, New Year's Eve party with Philip Brawner.

1953

January 5: Returns to Smith.
January 7, 8:30 a.m.: Chapel.
    10:00 a.m.–12:30 p.m.: Studies science.
    2:00–6:00 p.m., 7:00–10:00 p.m.: Studies English.
January 8, 9:00–10:00 a.m.: Science.
    10:00–11:00 a.m.: Bells.
    2:00–3:00 p.m.: English.
    4:00–6:00 p.m.: "Unit."
Letter to "Dear mother": hobbles to the library and her classes, still worried about her science course, concerned that Myron Lotz will forget her in her crippled, exhausted state, hopes to work on a creative writing paper.
January 9, 8:15 a.m.: Press board meeting.
    9:00–10:00 a.m.: Science.
    3:15 p.m.: Meets the Schnieders.
Letter to "Dearest mother": walks to science class in drifts of snow, hopes to be able to just audit her science class next semester.
Letter to Myron Lotz: Comments on the "lucid anatomizing of the issues" in one of his essays. This sentence strikes her "forcibly" and with "mental elation": "in this amphoteric position man is constantly yearning to attain a condition of complete happiness, which the earth obviously cannot provide him but yet constantly thwarted by the realization that the attainment of this condition in heaven (which is itself but a conjecture) involves the destruction of the physical form which would realize this pleasure." Describes the feeling of a "brief eternity" as she plummeted down a hill before breaking her leg, mentions meeting a doctor,[485] who shows her his Joycean novel. Lotz's letter reminds of her lines from a favorite poem, "Rubaiyat of Omar Khayyam": "I sent my soul through the Invisible, / Some letter of that After-life to spell: / And by and by my soul returned to me, / And answered "I myself am Heav'n and Hell." She is excited about W. H. Auden's arrival next semester, reports getting to know Professor Davis, developing a "reverence for the lofty genius of some of the professors here."
January 10, 8:00–10:00 a.m.: Science.
"SHERK," note to get Thomas Carlyle book and one about Gerard Manley Hopkins by Professor Vida Dutton Scudder.[486]
Eddie Cohen believes she needs psychiatric help.[487] But she thinks she just needs more sleep, "a constructive attitude, and a little good luck." Describes her strong attraction to Myron Lotz, her realization that she could never live with Dick Norton because of their competitive, "passionate

jealousies." She no longer desires him. But she wants to "go easy on the sexual part" with Myron, not wanting to "rush it" but to build a creative life with "someone like him." {PJ}

January 11, 10:00–11:30 p.m.: Bells, writes *Piers Plowman* paper.

January 12: Reads "Holy Grail,"[488] gets library books, and washes hair.

Vows to socialize more, meet and renew acquaintances in various Smith campus houses as well as getting to know faculty better, looks forward to spring, removal of her cast, and to "dance along greening leaves into the sexual sunlight." {PJ}

Seventeen publishes "Initiation."

January 13: "Read for Holy Grail" and write paper.

4:00 p.m.: Coffee with Mary Ellen Chase.

January 14, 8:00–10:00 a.m.: "science."

11:00 a.m.–1:00 p.m.: Types Grail paper.

2:00–6:00 p.m., 7:00–10:00 p.m.: Studies science.

January 15, 9:00–10:00 a.m.: Science class.

10:00–11:00 a.m.: Bells.

11:00 a.m.–1:00 p.m.: Studies science.

2:00–4:00 p.m.: Studies science.

4:00–6:00 p.m.: "Unit—bring Troilus [*Troilus and Criseyde*], book to sign."[489]

7:00–10:00 p.m.: Studies science.

January 16, 9:00 a.m.: Written exam in science.

2:30 p.m.: "Warden" (an Honor Board meeting).

Letter to "Dearest of mothers": Welcomes a respite from studying "stultifying science" now that the exam is over. Goes through all her academic assignments, noting Professor Patch's comment on her work on *Piers Plowman* (ca. 1377): "That was a brilliant paper." Complains that she has nothing in common with her "pitifully inarticulate" roommate, Mary, describes her delightful coffee with Mary Ellen Chase, the "dearest woman."

January 17, 9:00–10:00 a.m.: Science class, starts creative writing paper, talks with Sheila Saunders, a Lawrence House classmate, and Claiborne Phillips.

January 18: Finishes creative writing paper.

6:30 p.m.: "MYRON [Lotz]!"

Sunday night supper with Marcia Brown.

10:15 p.m.–midnight: Bells.

Letter to "Dearest mother": Celebrates her successful petition to audit her science class. Now she can concentrate on a new Milton course, creative writing, get some rest, relax, mentions her excitement at getting a call from Myron Lotz who says he is in Northampton. He visits her at

Lawrence House. The "MOST WONDERFUL BOY IN THE WHOLE COLLEGE," invites her to Yale's junior prom.

"The nadir is passed. I know that now. . . . I have gone through my winter solstice, and the dying god of life and fertility is reborn. . . . I realized now that I was really more crippled, mentally, all last fall, than I am, physically, now." The call from Myron has the "final crowning touch," sending her into ecstasy. She realizes there is a range of men beyond Dick Norton, and even if Myron does not pursue her, he will have "served, to heighten me." {PJ}

January 19, 10:00 a.m.: Science, creative writing paper due, supper with Marcia Brown and then to the Dublin Players production of *The Importance of Being Earnest* (1895) by Oscar Wilde.

Vows to work hard in the seven weeks leading up to her junior prom appearance with Myron Lotz, which she compares to "living on a slide ruler of calculated dream fantasies." Describes how she hugged Myron impulsively when he asked her to the junior prom, the words bubbling out like "colored lanterns." The girls congratulate her—"One nice thing about living with a hundred girls—excitement shared is multiplied a hundred times!" {PJ}

January 20: Sees *Bell, Book, and Candle* (1958).

January 21: Bells.

Letter to Dick Norton: asks him to make what he can of her two religion class papers—"Religious Beliefs" and "Religion as I See It."

Letter to "Dear mum": Includes her story, "Mary Ventura and the Ninth Kingdom."[490] Didn't like the production of *The Importance of Being Earnest* but loves *Bell, Book, and Candle* performances by Zachary Scott and Joan Bennett in a "heavenly humorous tale of modern witchery." Announces she will be going to the junior prom with a "rather magnetic male" and upholding the "aristocracy of the intellect." {PJ}

January 22, 9:30 a.m.: Appointment with Dr. Marion Booth.

10:00 a.m.: Bells.

2:30 p.m.: Honor Board meeting.

"I have been deprived of sexual activity for long unnatural months now and it is only normal that I transfer my daily and nightly sex fantasies to the one male I have been seeing lately." Cautions herself that Myron Lotz is unaware of the role she is casting him in: "Take it slow, please. He is to be no engine for your ecstasy. Not yet, anyway." But it is not just sex but rather Myron's combination of "loving gentleness . . . athletic good cleanness" and his towering mind that makes him a composite of the other men she has been involved with and with none of their defects. "Do I want to crawl into the gigantic paternal embrace of a mental colossus? A little maybe. I'm not sure." She looks forward to the possibility of a "creative marriage now as I never did before." {PJ}

January 23: Works on cartoon for *Mademoiselle*.

January 24: "Write health article" for *Mademoiselle*.

10:00–11:00 a.m.: Bells.

Reading, quoting, and feeling like Gerard Manley Hopkins: "The world is charged with the grandeur of God. . . . How to keep . . . Beauty, beauty, beauty . . . From vanishing away?"

January 25: "Study science," writes Dick Norton.[491]

7:45–9:15 a.m.: Bells.

Postcard to "Dear Mum": Discusses her mother's appointment with Miss Mensel. "Love Lawrence [House] more every day—girls are all great—so happy here!"

Psyches herself up for passing the science exam that will allow her to audit the course. "God I am beginning to sound like [William Ernest] Henley: 'I am the master of my fate; I am the captain of my soul.'"[492] Comments on her journal: "I think this book ricochets between the feminine burbling I hate and the posed cynicism I would shun." Spends a long passage on the pleasures of nose picking. "God, what a sexual satisfaction!" {PJ}

January 26: Describes the ruckus of winter—"damned if I'm going to be raped by the North wind." She is writing to put off studying. Thinks of graduate school in philosophy or psychology since she has done so much work in English at Smith or employment in publishing or in an office or a Fulbright to England, a year of graduate school perhaps at Columbia, Radcliffe, or Johns Hopkins, a job, marriage, regrets summers of reading young girl's novels rather than "more purposive lasting books." {PJ}

11:00 a.m.: "Still going on, ignoring science, peering out the window for mail." Thinks about writing about her childhood.

January 27: Meets with Marcia Brown.

January 29, 10:30 a.m.: Science exam.

1:00 p.m.: "DONE with Science!"

"Buy books: W. H. Auden, Elizabeth Drew, 'Golden Bough' [1890, by Sir James George Frazer]."[493]

2:30 p.m.: Miss Mensel.

Reads *Ulysses* (1922) by James Joyce: "semantically big . . . mind cracking, and even webster's is a sterile impotent eunuch as far as conceiving words goes."

January 30: Writes Honor Board reports.

January 31: With Myron Lotz, supper, talking at Rahar's.

February 1: Myron for dinner in Lawrence House, reads, listens to music with Lotz, out to coffee shop, "Rahar's till 12."

February 2: Letter to "dearest mother": Looks forward to modern poetry taught by Elizabeth Drew and supper with Enid Epstein, "writer-artist-and friend," fun with Marcia Brown and her family, Myron Lotz's Saturday and

Sunday visits during which he opens up about his family, how he got to Yale, working all the time on studies and road crews, living in a neighborhood with African Americans, immigrants, "and all kinds of people." Still in her cast, Myron carries her around very easily. Worried about her writing—"I deserve a couple of hundred rejections, now" to make her work "madder and harder." She is happy about Dick Norton's acceptance to medical school and his publication about William Carlos Williams. But she is reluctant to join him for the Middlebury Winter Carnival.

Compares Perry Norton and Myron Lotz, the former wanting to be loved and to have his glory reflected, the latter more concerned with establishing himself, not with what a woman could do for him. "I think I am a good deal more experienced in varieties of kisses than he [Myron] is: I better be careful I don't shock him or make him think he needs more experience, because I like him this way, and perhaps subtly I can let him know how other ways I like to be kissed." She wants a "Giant, Superman: mental and physical." {PJ}

February 3, 8:00 a.m.: *Smith Review* meeting.
10:00 a.m.: Audits a course on James Joyce with Professor Drew.
2:00–4:00 p.m.: "Carrel ass [assignment?]."
Dinner with Professor Patch and six other students at Wiggins Tavern.
February 4, 10:00 a.m.: Audits Elizabeth Drew's class on Joyce.
2:00 p.m.: Professor Davis's class.
3:00 p.m.: Milton class.
8:00 p.m.: Meets Gordon Lameyer for the first time at Lawrence House.

Writes to her mother making sure they have their stories straight about why she does not want to join the Nortons on their trip to Middlebury. "I am becoming an expert in the polite expedient white lie. Ugh." Quotes Professor Patch as saying he "thought all smith girls he knew were beautiful, compared to the other women's colleges he taught in. Nice, what!"

February 5, 9:00 a.m.: Audits science class.
10:00 a.m.: Bells.
11:00 a.m.–1:00 p.m.: "[William Butler] Yeats."
2:00 p.m.: Professor Davis's class.[494]
3:00 p.m.: Milton class.
Letter to "Dear Mother": describes Gordon Lameyer "the most hand-some, tall, lean, curly brown-haired boy," a senior at Amherst majoring in English whose mother attended Plath's Smith Club talk, he looks "most promising."

February 6, 8:30 a.m.: Press board meeting.
9:00 a.m.: Audits science class.

10:30 a.m.: An X-ray of her broken leg.

2:00 p.m.: Professor Davis's class.

3:00 p.m.: Milton class.

Letter to Mother, "dearest of favorite people": Accepting more invitations to dinner at "other houses with gusto now." Enthuses over Myron Lotz's five-page letter full of ideas and his confession that "I can think much more clearly while away from your biological magnetism." But then there is the "new Gordon [Lameyer], whom I still can't believe is coming: all the girls want to be around to see this handsome creature when he comes! I just know it will be fun."

February 7, 9:00 a.m.: Audits science class.

1:30 p.m.: With Gordon at Amherst, reading aloud from Joyce, talking about religion.

Letter to Myron Lotz: suggests walking might be a better way of thinking than sitting, "cramped upon manmade boxes—so stultifying!"

February 9, 10:00 a.m.: Audits Elizabeth Drew's class on Joyce, reads a short paper on Yeats.

2:30 p.m.: "Cook—Honor Board."

Supper at Haven House.

February 10, 10:00 a.m.: Audits Elizabeth Drew's class on Joyce.

Letter to "dearest maternal image": Expresses her hopes for Warren doing well in last year of high school. Gordon Lameyer, a "Joyce fanatic," is "utterly lush." Likes his saying he is a "renegade unitarian," so she can say anything to him. He favors manual work but looks like a "lean handsome country-clubber." Mentions Myron Lotz's continuing attention: "those french ladies have nothing on me! ho ho."

February 11, 10:00 a.m.: Audits Elizabeth Drew's class on Joyce.

2:00 p.m.: Professor Davis's class.

3:00 p.m.: Milton class.

5:00 p.m.: "Class—meet."

Supper at Wallace House.

February 12, 8:00: a.m. Audits science class.

2:00 p.m.: Professor Davis's class.

3:00 p.m.: Milton class.

Pleased with sharing "eclectic ideologies" with Myron Lotz, and her "therapeutic amherst Saturday with Gordon, considers Myron her best option after rejecting Dick Norton and feeling that Perry Norton knows her too well, there is no room left for "discovery." Among other attributes, Myron offers "power." Others like Bob Cochran and Phil McCurdy seem like puppies she would have to mother. Discards the idea of marrying a writer or artist: "I see how dangerous the conflict of egos would be—especially if the wife got all the acceptances! . . . so I undertake my journeyings into the ways of vulnerability again, and of what I define as love." {PJ}

February 13, 9:00 a.m.: Audits science class.

    2:00 p.m.: Professor Davis's class.

    3:00 p.m.: Milton class.

    Supper with Marcia Brown.

February 14: Audits science class.

February 15: Marcia Brown's party.

February 16, 10:00 a.m.: Audits Elizabeth Drew's Joyce class.

    7:30 p.m.: "Modern poetry."

February 17: Audits Drew's Joyce class, "Mick—supper," "MLLE—summer ideal."

February 18, 10:00 a.m.: Audits Drew's Joyce class.

    2:00 p.m.: Paper due for Professor Davis's class.

    3:00 p.m.: Milton class.

Letter to "dear mother": asks her mother to type an assignment for *Mademoiselle*, fed up with her cast and wants it off even though the doctor says she won't be able to put weight on her left leg for "days and days," pleased with her grades—all As, awaiting Myron Lotz's arrival in his new Ford.

"'Oh, I would like to get in a car and be driven off into the mountains to a cabin on a wind-howling hill and be raped in a huge lust like a cave woman, fighting, screaming, biting in a ferocious ecstasy of orgasm. . . .' That sounds nice, doesn't it? Really delicate and feminine," impatient for Myron's arrival.

February 19, 9:00 a.m.: Audits science class.

    10:00–11:00 a.m.: Bells.

    2:00 p.m.: Class with Professor Davis.

    3:00 p.m.: Milton class.

    "DOCTOR CAST OFF," washes hair.

February 20, 9:00 a.m.: Audits science class.

    2:00 p.m.: Professor Davis's class.

    3:00 p.m.: Milton class.

    4:00 p.m.: Infirmary for whirlpool treatment.

February 21, 11:15 a.m.: Infirmary for whirlpool treatment.

Sends the poems "Villanelle: Doomsday" and "Villanelle: Mad Girl's Love Song" to the *New Yorker* and *The Atlantic*.

Letter to "dear mum": Disappointed because Myron Lotz's car has not yet been delivered, worries that her leg has not mended and she will have to wear another cast, vows to live in a southern climate, bicycle, swim, eat mangoes, mentions the villanelle as a "rigid French verse form" that she attempted for the first time, and which made her feel "a good deal better."

February 22: Reads Yeats.

1:45 p.m.: Infirmary for whirlpool treatment.

Describes cutting off the cast: "The corpse of my leg lay there, horrible, dark with clotted curls of black hair, discolored yellow, wasted shapeless by a two-month interment." She requires whirlpool therapy and feels weak, "mentally and physically," thinking about intercourse in Yeatsian and Swedenborgian terms." {PJ}

February 23, 8:15 a.m.: Infirmary for a whirlpool bath, "RALLY DAY," supper with Marcia Brown.

Letter to "dearest of mothers": Whirlpool treatments are improving her "range of motion and ankle rotation." Doing bicycle exercises, claims that "Christian science has subconsciously developed my mental attitude, I think, all in all." She is now hopeful about dancing at the junior prom, happy that Myron Lotz is, at last, on his way to see her.

February 24, 10:00 a.m.: Audits Elizabeth Drew's Joyce class.

6:00 p.m.: Rides with Myron in his new car in the moon, the ice, the snow.

February 25, 10:00 a.m.: Audits Drew's Joyce class.

2:00 p.m.: Professor Davis's class.

3:00 p.m.: Milton class.

4:00 p.m.: Infirmary for whirlpool treatment.

Letter to "dear mother": Mentions a visit from Art Kramer, who is disgusted at her curt reception of this summer lover, Dick Norton's "pathetic letter," carefully extricating herself from his claims on her. Too much to do with studies, and mentions some friends will visit Dick, who, she fears, will try to get her and Dick's relationship started again. "I've controlled my sex judiciously, and you don't have to worry about me at all." Describes an "unbelievably lush" night with Myron Lotz, driving through woods by the lake talking.

The agony of waiting four hours for Myron to arrive, their drive and, by turns, tender and rough sex play. {PJ}

February 26, 9:00 a.m.: Audits science class.

10:00–11:00 a.m.: Bells.

Cleans room.

2:00 p.m.: Professor Davis's class.

3:00 p.m.: Milton class.

4:00 p.m.: Infirmary for whirlpool treatment.

"MLLE."

February 27, 9:00 a.m.: Audits science class.

10:00 a.m.–1:00 p.m.: "WROTE MLLE."

2:00 p.m.: Professor Davis's class.

3:00 p.m.: Milton class.

4:00 p.m.: Infirmary for whirlpool treatment.

February 28: Purchases a formal dress for the Yale junior prom, Myron Lotz arrives, they drive to Vermont, stopping along the way at Mount Tom and, in the moonlight, return to pizza at Joe's pizzeria.

Letter to "dearest mother": Loves her "superlative" mother's long letter. "I have always felt I can be completely honest with you and want more than anything to make you proud of me so that some day I can begin to repay you for all the treats you've given me in my two decades of life." Describes her new dress, the enjoyable drive with Myron, her work on a story for *Mademoiselle*, and her reasons for not wanting to marry Dick Norton. Myron is planning trips for them in his car. Hopes to continue making money with her press board work and to write more in the summer.

March 1, 7:15 a.m.: "Electoral Board," "Laura Scales Smoker."

Describes her prom wear and concludes, "I want to be silverly beautiful for him: a sylvan goddess. . . . I can't stop effervescing." Her ecstatic drive with Myron, who carries her back to the car after a maple syrup stop, asking "How high shall I toss you?" She replies, "To the moon." He quotes Shakespeare. It has been seven months since she has felt "the good black tides of lust drown and bathe me into relaxed slumbrous quiescence."

March 2, 10:00 a.m.: Drew's class on Joyce.

11:00 a.m.: "Hair."

"Drew Unit paper written."

7:30 p.m.: "Modern poetry."

Letter to Mother, "dearest one": Reports her activities on the electoral board, mentions prom dress "hanging up in my window in all its silver glory," her long hair trimmed into a "smooth pageboy," a visit from Gordon Lameyer—"by far the handsomest, tan physical specimen I've ever gone out with."

March 3, 10:00 a.m.: Elizabeth Drew's class on Joyce, "New Yorker rejection," sends more poems to the *New Yorker* and *Harper's*.

7:15 p.m.: Electoral board meeting.

March 3–6: Letter to "dear mother": Mentions encouraging rejection letter from the *New Yorker*, which prompts her to send more work, models her dress for the Lawrence House girls, enjoying their good company and academic motivation that is higher than other houses, enjoys her work on the electoral board, emphasizes that Myron Lotz is a good driver and they are behaving like a sensible couple, plans to submit work in the summer to *Ladies Home Journal*.

March 4, 8:30 a.m.: Chapel.

10:00 a.m.: Elizabeth Drew's class on Joyce.

2:00 p.m.: Paper due for Professor Davis's class.

3:00 p.m.: Milton class.

7:15 p.m.: Electoral board meeting.

March 5, 9:00 a.m.: Audits science class.

10:00–11:00 a.m.: Bells.

2:00 p.m.: Professor Davis's class.

3:00 p.m.: Milton class.

"Pack."

March 6, 11:00 a.m.: Aboard train to New Haven for junior prom, "sunset West rock[495]—roast beef dinner—prom—moonlight w. Rock 5am."

March 7: "Lunch—T. D.," a drive to the beach: "sun—flat clean colored houses—apple sider—dinner—music—bed—Greenes livingroom."

March 8: Breakfast with Myron Lotz.

11:00 a.m.: Returns by train to Smith.

2:00 p.m.: Electoral board meeting.

4:30 p.m.: "<u>W. H. Auden—Browsing Room</u>."

Letter to Dick Norton: Writes about the death of William Sanford "Sandy" Lynn III (1948–1953)—"still we persist in hopefully, faithfully, bringing forth children into the world. I loved that boy sandy, and all the sprouting of goodness and fineness in him."

March 9, 10:00 a.m.: Elizabeth Drew's class on Joyce.

11:00 a.m.: Coffee at Toto's with Marcia Brown.

7:30 p.m.: "Modern Poetry."

Letter to "dear mother": Very tired after Yale weekend and a ten-hour electoral board meeting. She could dance without "much trouble" and saw many of her Yale friends at a "legendary extravaganza." Disgusted at Perry Norton and Shirley Baldwin necking: "I would vomit if any boy hung over me like that all the time: I like my integrity, and feel that a mature relationship isn't a complete all-smothering thing where two people can't be whole when they're apart." Myron Lotz agrees on a "balanced partnership . . . facing life together instead of blinding each other by excluding the rest of the world." Hopes for just a brief, painless meeting with Dick Norton.

March 10, 10:00 a.m.: Elizabeth Drew's class on Joyce.

11:00 a.m.: Press board.

"STUDY FOR MILTON."

7:15 p.m.: Electoral board meeting.

March 11, 9:00 a.m.–1:00 p.m.: Studies Milton.

2:00 p.m.: Report for Professor Davis's class.

3:00 p.m.: Milton class.

4:00–6:00 p.m.: Naps.

7:15 p.m.: Electoral board meeting.

March 12, 9:00 a.m.: Audits science class.

   10:00–11:00 a.m.: Bells.

   11:00 a.m.: Press board meeting.

   2:00 p.m.: Professor Davis's class.

   3:00 p.m.: Milton exam.

March 12–13: Letter to "dear mum": Decides not to run for office after long meeting of the electoral board so that she can devote herself to classes and to writing, hopes to write a senior thesis on Joyce after auditing Elizabeth Drew's class, praises Warren's achievements, pleased to be back at work in the press board office, worried about all the competition for a *Mademoiselle* summer guest editorship. She plans to flood the market (*New Yorker*, *Ladies Home Journal*, *Seventeen*, and *Mademoiselle*) with her poems and stories. Only by being prolific, she feels, will she make the breakthrough into publishing. Signs off "your rejected daughter, sivvy."

March 14, 9:00 a.m.: Audits science class.

   2:00 p.m.: Drives with Myron Lotz along the Connecticut River headed to the hills in Holyoke, reads from his book on abnormal psychology, a delicious dinner of "baby beef" for three dollars and eight cents, listens to new car radio under the stars and trees and the dark.

March 15, "T. S. Eliot," "Enid [Epstein?]—S Review [*Smith Review*]."

   9:15–10:15 a.m.: Bells.

Letter to "Dear mother": describes her drive with Myron Lotz, wants Warren to visit her.

March 16: X-ray on her leg, which still pains her.

   2:00–4:00 p.m.: "Unit."

   BW.

Letter to "dear mum": Describes all her "businesses" involving class meetings, a petition to take psychology next year, an interview with her thesis supervisor, securing a recommendation for Harvard summer school (she is intent on taking Frank O'Connor's short story course), expects to earn $200 for articles in *Hampshire Gazette*.

March 17, 8:00 a.m.: *Smith Review* meeting.

   1:30 p.m.: Press board meeting.

Letter to "dearest progenitor": "I feel violets sprouting between my fingers and forsythia twining in my hair and violins and bells sounding wherever I walk." Happy to report the X-ray showed no problems with her leg, happy about her "good warm friends," Myron Lotz, and the "promising Raymond Wunderlich," a check from the *Springfield Daily News*, purchases books, including the basic writings of Sigmund Freud, letter from Mr. Norton about a visit means she will finally "get it over with."

March 18, 8:30 a.m.: Chapel—"AUDEN."

"Rejection <u>Atlantic</u>."

1:30 p.m.: Alpha.

2:00 p.m.: A paper due for Professor Davis's class.

3:00 p.m.: Milton class.

4:00 p.m.: "Mass meeting."

March 19, 9:00 a.m.: Audits science class.

10:00–11:00 a.m.: Bells.

2:00 p.m.: Professor Davis's class.

3:00 p.m.: Milton class.

7:15 p.m.: House meeting.

March 20, 8:30 a.m.: Press board meeting.

9:00 a.m.: Audits science class.

10:00–11:30 a.m.: Press board meeting.

2:00 p.m.: Professor Davis's class.

3:00 p.m.: Milton class.

5:30 p.m.: Supper with Marcia Brown.

7:15 p.m.: "Usher."

March 21, 9:00 a.m.: Audits science class.

"Laundry."

2:00–6:00 p.m., 7:00–10:00 p.m.: Works on Edith Sitwell paper.

Letter to Warren: Mentions twenty-five-page paper on Sitwell, describes Auden speaking in chapel, the picture of a "perfect poet: tall, with a big leonine head and a sandy mane of hair, and a lyrically gigantic stride . . . a wonderfully textured British accent, and I adore him with a big Hero Worship." Imagines presenting him with a poem: "I found my God in Auden." Looks forward to Warren's visit, advises him to "tell the girl on bells youre my Brother." After a good dinner and "collegiate atmosphere," they will return home with Marcia Brown. A "million things" to talk about since she hasn't written him "for a long time," and he is still her "VERY Favorite Person!" Tells him all about Myron Lotz who wants to meet Warren, brings him up to date on her publications and rejections.

March 22, 6:30–10:00 a.m.: BW.

March 23, 8:30–9:00 a.m.: "Mass meeting."

9:00 a.m.–12:30 p.m.: "Finish paper begin typing."

2:00–6:00 p.m.: "Finish typing paper."

Supper—Ruth Ullmann.

7:30 p.m.: "Modern poetry."

March 24: Press board meeting.

9:00 a.m.–12:30 p.m.: "RELAX."

2:00–6:00 p.m.: Honor Board, News Office.

7:00–10:00 p.m.: "Pack."

Tries to write a true story, a confessional. {PJ}

March 25, 8:30–9:00 a.m.: Chapel.

    9:00 a.m.–12:30 p.m.: Packs, cleans her room.

    2:00 p.m.: Professor Davis's class.

    3:00 p.m.: Milton class.

    3:50 p.m.: Spring vacation, drives home with Warren and Marcia Brown.

March 26: "Marcia [Brown], Steve, Warren."

March 27: "Forbidden Games," goes to Boston with Steve.

March 28: "Walk to new school."

    11:00 a.m.–1:00 p.m.: Shopping with Marcia Brown.

March 29: "WRITE AND TYPE MLLE ASSIGNMENTS."

March 30, 8:00 a.m.: Ray Brook.

    5:00 p.m.: "Snow rain, sleet."

    "Cabin, in pines."

March 31: "Roast beef dinner at Saranac Lake [New York]," "Bridge with Geena, Dick, Mr. N[orton]."

April 1, 10:00 a.m.–noon: A drive with Dick Norton to Saranac.

    9:00 p.m.: "Home—Middlebury[496] Perry [Norton] & Shirl [Shirley Baldwin]."

April 2: Cleans her room and begins "recuperating."

April 3: Reads *True Confessions*[497] while sunbathing.

April 4: Types thirty pages of "I Lied for Love" while sunbathing, Chinatown for rice and sweet and sour pork dinner, sees *I Am a Camera* (1951) by Christopher Isherwood, meets the Cantors, fruit juice at Mrs. Frances Bragg's, talks with Betsy Bragg about Harvard summer school plans.

April 5: Finishes first draft of "I Lied for Love." {PM}

    8:00–11:00 a.m.: Reads works by Hans Christian Andersen, watches "water bird movie" with Jim McNealy.

April 6: Begins final draft of "I Lied for Love."

    4:30 p.m.: Dental appointment.

April 7: Finishes typing fifty-one-page draft of "I Lied for Love."

    11:30 a.m.–1:00 p.m.: The Nortons visit.

    Shops, calls Mrs. Bragg, packs.

April 8, 3:30 p.m.: Returns to Smith, unpacks.

April 9: Audits science class.

    10:00 a.m.: Bells.

    11:00 a.m.: Press board meeting.

    12:30 p.m.: "Waitress."

    2:00 p.m.: Milton class.

    3:00 p.m.: Professor Davis's class.

4:00–6:00 p.m., 7:00–10:00 p.m.: Studies Milton.

"In spite of reams of papers to be written life has snitched a cocaine sniff of sun-worship and salt air, and all looks promising." {PJ}

April 10, 8:00 a.m.: Press board meeting.

9:00 a.m.: Audits science class.

Noon: X-ray.

3:00 p.m.: Milton class.

8:00 p.m.: Auden lecture in Sage Hall, meets Gordon Lameyer afterwards.

April 11, 9:00 a.m.: Audits science class.

Works on "Dialogue En Route."

Noon: Meets Myron Lotz for a drive in the country in the twilight, a baby beef dinner, party at Art Fleisher's.

Letter to "dearest mother": Waiting for verdict on publications in "empty silence!" Encloses a draft of poem "Dialogue En Route" trying to perfect a "rollicking" rhythm, looks forward to seeing Myron, excited about the round-trip train ticket to New York City that Ray Wunderlich has sent her, describes going out with Gordon Lameyer after Auden lecture—the "great god Gordon" with "movie star" looks has asked her to a dance.

April 12: Types "Dialogue En Route."

10:15 p.m.–midnight: "Late bells."

Seventeen publishes "Carnival Nocturne."

April 13, 8:15 a.m.: Fills out class cards.

Press board meeting, laundry, writes letter to Harvard summer school,[498] supper with Marcia Brown.

Noon: House meeting.

April 14: "Ransom analysis."[499]

11:30 a.m.–12:30 p.m.: Press board meeting.

2:00–4:00 p.m.: Works on modern poetry report.

8:00 p.m.: John Mason Brown lecture.

April 15, 8:30 a.m.: "Chapel cover" due.

10:00 a.m.–12:30 p.m.: Studies Milton.

2:00 p.m.: Professor Davis's class paper due.

3:00 p.m.: Milton class.

4:00–8:00 p.m.: "Pinning party."

8:00–10:00 p.m.: Studies Milton.

April 16, 9:00 a.m.: Audits science class.

Infirmary (sinus infection).

2:00 p.m.: Professor Davis's class.

3:00 p.m.: Milton class.

Washes hair.

April 17, 9:00 a.m.: Audits science class.

Infirmary.

2:00 p.m.: Class with Professor Davis.

3:00 p.m.: Milton class.

4:00 p.m.: Miss Siipola-Pierce.

April 18: Audits science class.

7:30 a.m.: At Amherst College, crew race with Gordon Lameyer. "Guys and Dolls Dance."

April 19: Infirmary (sinus infection).

April 20: "SALE."

2:00–3:00 p.m.: Press board meeting.

3:00 p.m.: Miss Siipola-Pierce.

7:30 p.m.: "Modern poetry.

April 21: Appointment with Professor Lincoln, supper with Marcia Brown.

April 22, 8:30 a.m.: Chapel.

2:00 p.m.: Class with Professor Davis.

3:00 p.m.: Milton class.

"Auden—dinner!"

Sends Mother poems to type "if you have nothing to do (ho ho!)."

April 23, 9:00 a.m.: Audits science class.

10:00 a.m.: Bells.

11:00 a.m.–1:00 p.m.: Press board meeting.

2:00 p.m.: Professor Davis's class.

3:00 p.m.: Milton class.

4:00 p.m.: Archibald MacLeish.

5:00 p.m.: "Davis <u>Mlle</u>."

8:00 p.m.: Symposium, "Art and Morals" with Gordon Lameyer.

April 24, 8:30 a.m.: Press board.

9:00 a.m.: Audits science class.

10:00 a.m.–12:30 p.m.: Press board.

"Harpers acceptance $100."

2:00 p.m.: Professor Davis's class.

3:00 p.m.: Symposium, "Art and Morals," which includes critics Lionel Trilling, Jacques Barzun, philosopher George Boas, artist Ben Shahn, and the poets W. H. Auden and Archibald MacLeish.

"Marty's [Marcia Brown] Champagne."

8:00 p.m.: "Symposium."

Sends telegram of birthday greetings to Mother, announces one-hundred-dollar payment from *Harper's* for three poems. *Mademoiselle* has sent ten dollars for "runner-up in third assignment."

Letter to "Dear Mother": Writing her application for O'Connor's story course at Harvard, expects to spend part of the summer learning shorthand from her mother in case she needs a secretarial job, worries about the competition for a month guest editorship at *Mademoiselle*, looks forward to gala weekend in New York with Ray Wunderlich, trying to get up the nerve to show Auden her poems, considers taking courses in psychology or sociology.

Letter to editor Russell Lynes, *Harper's Magazine*: Elated at acceptance of three poems, provides personal information he requests, says she is a junior honoring in English, working odd jobs, on scholarship. She has been a governess and farm laborer, works a "two hour daily stint in the News Office sending out releases for the town paper," mentions publications in *Seventeen*, the *Christian Science Monitor*, and *Mademoiselle* and her obsessive "ambitions for the future," including world travel.

Letter to Warren: Sends birthday card to "dearest brother," tells him to be "nice to Kathy [Preston] even though she may not be Marilyn Monroe." Brings him up to date on her activities, including boyfriends, the symposium on the arts, which she reports on ("Literary Speakers Mark Symposium at Smith College," *Daily Hampshire Gazette*, April 24), wants news from her brother: "how about it bebe?"

April 25, 9:00 a.m.: Audits science class.

10:00 a.m.–12:30 p.m.: Press board meeting.

"Type letters & contest poems."

11:00 p.m.–midnight: "Late bells."

Letter to "dearest mum": Celebrating her *Harper's* publication, her "first real professional acceptance!" Quotes the "lovely note" from editor Russell Lynes, accepting three poems since they don't "seem to be able to make up our minds which one we like best . . . which isn't just weak-mindedness on our part but real enthusiasm." Recounts various payments for her writing that she has deposited.

She has submitted to *True Story* and is "barraging" the *New Yorker*, "xxx to my birthday mummy."

April 26: Reads Auden, "mother's birthday."

April 27, 8:00–9:00 a.m.: *Smith Review* meeting.

9:00 a.m.–12:30 p.m.: News office.

"Warren's birthday."

2:00–6:00 p.m.: Shops.

7:30–9:30 p.m.: "Auden—modern poetry beer."

Writes to her mother about the "wonderful and right things" happening to her "tall stubby-nosed daughter"—elected editor of *Smith Review*, retains her "prize financial job" on the *Gazette*. Auden visits her poetry class, analyses one of his longest poems, a visit to Elizabeth Drew's "book-lined sanctuary"—"I never felt such exaltation in my life." She has been shopping for summer clothes for a New York outing, describes her purchases, including a "strapless sheath dress of blue and white pinstripe cotton cord, and an over-jacket that fits it for train travel with the parisian standup collar and long sleeves."

April 28, 9:30 a.m.: "Hair."

    10:00 a.m.–12:30 p.m.: News office.

    2:00–6:00 p.m., 7:00–10:00 p.m.: "STUDY MILTON."

April 29, 8:30 a.m.: Chapel.

    9:00–10:00 a.m.: In News Office.

    10:00 a.m.–12:30 p.m.: Studies Milton.

    2:00 p.m.: "Davis paper due."

    3:00 p.m.: "Milton Exam."

    6:00 p.m.: Press board banquet, Auden in attendance.

April 30, 8:00 a.m.: "Activities board."

    9:00 a.m.: Audits science class.

    10:00 a.m.: Bells.

    Hampshire Book Shop.

    2:00 p.m.: Class with Professor Davis.

    3:00 p.m.: Milton class.

    4:00–6:00 p.m.: Sally.

    "Phi Beta Banquet."

April 30–May 1: Letter to "Dear mother": Describes the "impressive" Phi Beta Kappa dinner. "I am getting more and more excited about harvard summer school." Expresses her increasing interest in abnormal psychology. "Love and laughter From your daft daughter! (Who gets dafter & dafter!)"

May 1, 11:00 a.m.: On the train to New York City to meet Ray Wunderlich, filet mignon and oysters at La Petitie Maison, performance of *The Crucible* (1953) by Arthur Miller with drinks and talk afterwards at Delmonico's.

May 2, 1:00 p.m.: Brunch, opera, *Carmen* (1875) by Georges Bizet, at city center, scallops at Gloucester House, performance of *Camino Real* (1953), a dance in Bard Hall, with friends, drinks, sherry, and listens to music in Ray Wunderlich's room overlooking the Hudson River.

May 3, 1:00 p.m.: Brunch at Golden Age, tour of Bard Hall, a Columbia University residence, "music," a tour of Columbia Presbyterian Hospital with Ray, in the chapel and garden, with a "nice lunch in hospital cafeteria."

    7:00 p.m.: Train home.

May 4: Sleeps until 11:00 a.m., writes Dick Norton and *Mademoiselle*.[500]

    1:30–2:30 p.m.: Press board meeting.

    2:30–5:30 p.m.: Works on Dylan Thomas paper.

    7:30–9:30 p.m.: "Modern poetry."

May 5, 8:00 a.m.: "Activities B. Poems to Auden."

9:00 a.m.: "Sr pic — $5."

Writes to Ray Wunderlich, Dick Norton,[501] and her mother, receives *Harper's* proofs.

7:00 p.m.: Meets Marcia Brown and Gordon Lameyer.

8:00 p.m.: Reports on an evening with Charles Laughton.

Letter to "Dear mother": Describes New York weekend, calls *The Crucible* a "very good play about the witch hunts in Salem," *Camino Real* "magnificently acted, shockingly surrealistic play," defends the play against critics as the "most stimulating, thought-provoking, artistic play I've ever seen in my life!" New York "enchanting," owes everything to her mother.

May 6, 8:30 a.m.: Chapel.

Works on *Smith Review*.

2:00 p.m.: Professor Davis's class.

3:00 p.m.: Milton class.

Reads proofs, fills out questionnaire for *Mademoiselle* guest editorship.

Daily Hampshire Gazette publishes "Laughton Holds Audience Spellbound with Readings."

May 7, 8:00 a.m.: Activities board meeting.

9:00 a.m.: Audits science class.

10:00 a.m.: Bells.

11:00 a.m.–12:30 p.m.: Press board meeting.

2:00 p.m.: Professor Davis's class.

3:00 p.m.: Milton class.

4:00–6:00 p.m., 7:00–10:00 p.m.: Works on Milton paper.

May 8, 8:30 a.m.: Press board meeting.

9:00 a.m.: Audits science class.

10:00 a.m.–11:00: Press board meeting.

11:00 a.m.–12:30 p.m.: Works on Milton paper.

2:00 p.m.: Professor Davis's class.

3:00–6:00 p.m.: Works on Milton paper.

7:00–10:00 p.m.: Works on Milton paper, packs for New Haven trip.

Letter to "Dearest progenitor": Works on her application for *Mademoiselle* guest editorship, includes her choices of who to interview for the magazine: J. D. Salinger, Shirley Jackson, E. B. White, Irwin Shaw. Looks forward to her first stay in a hotel (the Barbizon), thinks about the clothes she will need for a month in New York City, details of travel to New York, the *New Yorker* keeps sending rejections, but she vows to conquer it.

May 9, 9:00 a.m.: Audits science class.

9:25 a.m.: Train to New Haven to meet Myron Lotz for lunch at Silliman College, "drinking contest—park—blankets picnic—hot dogs—dance at TD.[502]—beach—party—fog horn."

May 10: Timothy Dwight dance with Myron, a lamb chop dinner, trip to Lighthouse Point[503] in New Haven, eats fudge while watching a baseball game, a talk and supper at Silliman.

May 11: Calls Antoinette ("Tony") Willard,[504] B. Mitchell, and Professor Lincoln, Milton Paper due.

May 12, 10:00 a.m.–noon: Works in News Office.

2:00 p.m.: Meets with Tony for steak dinner and a drive.

Works on "T. [Antoinette 'Tony'] Willard article,"[505] supper with Marcia Brown and Carol Pierson.

Letter to "dear mother": Describes New Haven weekend with Myron Lotz, catching up on work, including a paper on Auden and another on Milton. Taking Elizabeth Drew out to dinner with friends, then a "literary pilgrimage" to Amherst College to hear Dylan Thomas read from his work. "I am so thrilled he is coming and that I'll have the chance to hear him." Making money from *Hampshire Gazette* articles—twenty dollars so far. Through the "grapevine," she hears that Mrs. Norton now considers her selfish and not a fit match for her son Dick. "I was really appalled and very hurt." Worries about her mother working too hard, assures her that she and Warren will be able to take care of themselves financially.

May 13: Ushers at performance of *Ring Round the Moon* (1950) by Christopher Fry.

Letter to "Dearest mother": Eagerly awaits news of Warren, writing to congratulate him on his Harvard scholarship, thanks her mother for advice on food and clothing in New York City. "I'll have the chance to see what it's like living in the Big City, plus working on a magazine!" She will be as "cooperative and eager" at the magazine as she was with the Cantors. Worries about her mother's summer teaching and ulcer, expecting to write an article about her month in New York for the *Christian Science Monitor*, explains why Dick Norton could never had been her choice as a mate, notes that Myron Lotz is "emotionally insecure and uncertain of who he is."

Letter to Warren: Congratulations to "Dearest Harvard Man," wants to make sure he will have enough money from the scholarship to pay for expenses that won't be a drain on their mother. "You know, as I do, and it is a frightening thing, that mother would actually Kill herself for us if we calmly accepted all she wanted to do for us." Regrets not being at home in June to help her mother but hopes they can chip in and give her a holiday, feels "like a collegiate Cinderella" whose Fairy Godmother suddenly hops out of the mailbox and asks what her first wish is, to which Sylvia answers, "New York." With a wink and a wave of a pikestaff the wish is granted. She is proud of her brother and hopes he can learn from her mistakes, cautions him about success—"I find it expedient to keep quiet about the majority of my publications, for instance, because friends can rejoice with you for just so long without wishing they were in your place, and envying you in spite of themselves. It's sad, but that's the way it goes."

May 14, 9:00 a.m.: Audits science class.

10:00 a.m.: Bells.

11:00 a.m.–noon: Press board meeting.

Writing up profiles of seniors for *Daily Hampshire Gazette*.

Letter to "dear mother": "Life goes on fast and furiously." Busy with her journalism—"I've gotten in the habit of writing pithy, concise paragraphs, and the style is becoming pleasantly natural." She has made over $170 writing for newspapers.

May 15, 9:00 a.m.: Audits science class.

10:00 a.m.: Press board meeting.

"Davis Talk."

5:00 p.m.: Tea with Professor Lincoln, reading Milton by the fire.

Letter to "Dearest mother": Her letters are a "constant joy." Wants her mother to get rested this summer. "I forbid you to work this summer!" Expects her earnings from writing to sustain her, encourages her mother to write about her work.

May 16: Audits science class.

2:00 p.m.: With Myron Lotz, climbs Mount Holyoke in western Massachusetts, supper in Pynchon Park in Springfield, watches Myron pitch at batting practice, on to a float night on the banks of Paradise Pond, a steak dinner at the college diner.

Daily Hampshire Gazette publishes "Austrian-Born Junior [Tony Willard] in English in Women's Marine Corp."

May 17, 1:00–4:00 p.m.: Dinner with Professor Davis and his wife.

4:00 p.m.: Meets Enid at Grécourt Gates,[506] the entrance to Smith, "walk to Dippy in rain."

May 18: Works on first assignment for *Mademoiselle* about "five young teacher-poets."[507]

8:00 p.m.: Auden's speech, "Balaam and His Ass," in Sage Hall.

Letter to "Dear mother": mentions interviewing Professor Davis's wife who has written for many of the magazines that Sylvia wishes to publish in, looks forward to coffee with Mary Ellen Chase, dinner with Elizabeth Drew.

May 19, 11:00 a.m.: Meets with Chase for coffee.

Lunch with "Drew unit."

3:00 p.m.: English seminar.

6:00 p.m.: Dinner at Wiggins Tavern.

8:00 p.m.: *Smith Review* meeting.

May 20, 8:30 a.m.: Chapel.

11:00 a.m.–noon: Meets Carol Pierson at Toto's restaurant.

Daily Hampshire Gazette publishes "Many Area Students Are among the 464 Who Will Get Smith Degrees."

4:30 p.m.: To Amherst, Massachusetts, to hear Dylan Thomas read. Dinner with Marcia Brown.

May 21, 9:00 a.m.: Audits science class.

10:00 a.m.: Bells.

Packs for trip home.

Noon: Meets her mother, a drive home to see Mrs. Freeman and Mrs. Lane.

Letter to Warren: works on a "whopping" *Mademoiselle* assignment, which includes interviewing novelist Elizabeth Bowen in Cambridge, Massachusetts, prepares for Milton exam, exhausted, looking forward to a good rest.

May 22: Finishes unpacking and begins writing article on modern poets for *Mademoiselle*.

May 23: Finishes and mails *Mademoiselle* article.

1:00–5:30 p.m.: Train to Andover, Massachusetts, to watch Warren's Exeter track meet, they drive home, Sylvia begins reading Elizabeth Bowen.

May 24: Reads Bowen's early stories.

May 25: Reads Bowen's *The Death of the Heart* (1938), drives to Cambridge to interview Bowen.

May 26: "Interview for MLLE!" At May Sarton's house in Cambridge to interview Bowen.

3:38 p.m.: "Bus back to Smith?"

"To do: Miss Drew apt. Alum Q ed."

May 27: "Write Mayberry letter," returns Bowen's books to the library, calls Elizabeth Drew and Pat Epworth, works in News Office.

May 28, 10:00: "BELLS MILTON————————Pat Epworth."

May 29: BW, studies for Milton exam.

Noon: At Elizabeth Drew's house.

May 30, 8:00 a.m.: Milton exam, washes hair and packs.

1:00 p.m.: Bus home.

Plath anticipated her month-long guest editorship as an exciting turning point in her life, requiring significant adjustments, but she was not prepared for the fraught and frenetic pace of the city and of her employment at Mademoiselle.

May 31, 5:00 p.m.: "To New York!" by train.

June 1, 9:00 a.m.: In the *Mademoiselle* office for introduction, meets with editor in chief Betsy Talbot Blackwell and managing editor Cyrilly Abels.

2:00–5:45 p.m.: Works on poets article.

Supper at the Barbizon Hotel.

June 2, 9:00 a.m.: Department assignments.

10:15 a.m.: College clinic meeting at Hotel Roosevelt for fashion show.

2:00 p.m.: Appointment at Richard Hudnut for hairdressing and makeup before returning to *Mademoiselle* offices.

June 3, 9:00 a.m.: "Last word pix [photographs for "Last Word on College" feature]—LOAFERS."

10:00 a.m.–noon: Photographs for "Last Word on College" feature.

Lunch at the Oyster Bar in Grand Central Station, at the Central Park Mall for photographs of guest editors, Cyrilly Abels comments on Sylvia's manuscript.

Letter to "Dear mother": Describes three exhausting and exhilarating days, the "exquisite Barbizon"—"green lobby, light cafe-au-lait woodwork, plants, etc." The elevator whooshes her up to room 1511. The room layout—"Green wall-to-wall rug, pale beige walls, dark green bed-spread with rose-patterned ruffle, matching curtains, a desk, bureau, closet, and white enameled bowl growing like a convenient mushroom from the wall. Bath, shower, toilet, a few doors down the hall. Radio in wall, telephone by bed—and the view!" From her window, she see gardens, alleys, the Third Avenue elevated train, the United Nations, and a "snatch of the east River." From her desk at night, she looks down on a "network of lights, and the sound of car horns wafts up to me like the sweetest music. I love it." She likes her fellow guest editors. Cyrilly pronounces Sylvia's "poet-feature ready to go to the proof-room." She is surprised not to be named fiction editor but insists that she loves her "all-inclusive" work as managing editor. As usual she keeps careful track of her expenses.

June 4, 9:00 a.m.–1:30 p.m.: Works on "Last Word" feature.

Lunch with Cyrilly Abels in the Ivy Room.

2:30–6:00 p.m.: Works on "Last Word" feature.

June 5, 9:00 a.m.–noon: Works on "Last Word" feature.

Lunch with Ruth Abramson at La Champlain.

2:00–6:00 p.m.: Works on "Last Word" feature.

An evening walk with Laurie Totten up the East River, stopping for an ice cream.

June 6, 11:00 a.m.: A Barbizon breakfast, shopping at Bloomingdale's, a steak dinner.

3:00–6:00 p.m.: Visits the Museum of Modern Art, walks through the sculpture garden, encounters a "daffy Lady" on bus to Greenwich Village for an art exhibit, with Steve to a sidewalk café.

June 7: Washes hair, clothes, writes "Alum article," writes to Marcia Brown and Myron Lotz,[508] walks to Central Park Zoo and carousel with Laurie Totten.

June 8, 1:00: Appointment with Miss Ediff.

Letter to "Dearest mother": Mentions "big dinner and formal dance" at the St. Regis Hotel. Work is "continuous" as she reads manuscripts, writing rejections "signed with my own name!" She is writing friends. "Have a horrible feeling I probably won't get into O'Connor's course." Loves hearing from her mother—"Letters mean much." Learning "a lot about the world" that she wants to tell her.

June 9, 9:00 p.m.: *The Herb Shriner Show* (television show).

June 10: Paul Engle, who has started a master's degree program for writers at the University of Iowa, visits, reads some of Plath's poems, describes the graduate program.

7:30 p.m.: In Terrace Room at the St. Regis for a formal dance.

June 11: Lunch with Cyrilly Abels and writer Vance Bourjailly.

8:15 p.m.: Ballet at New York City Center.

With Melvin Woody, tours Third Avenue beer joints, lot of talk.

June 13, 10:00 a.m.: Jones Beach in Wantagh, New York.

Letter to "Dear mother": Tiring pace results in a twelve-hour sleep, the formal dance did not produce any dates, describes dinner at the St. Regis, her hopes that the O'Connor course will make an advance in her development as a writer, mentions meeting the disk jockey Art Ford, who invited Sylvia and her friends for cocktails. Meets Gregory Kamirloff, a UN translator and friend of Mrs. Norton's. Wonders about writing about television after visiting Herb Shriner's television show.

Letter to Myron Lotz: Happy to get his postcard and to imagine him striking out batters, describes living in the Barbizon Hotel "for circumspect young women," excited by meeting so many writers, publishers, and poets, listening in to Cyrilly Abels converse on the telephone with "important people," and "learning innumerable things about magazine work and human beings." The parties, the shows, the ballet, the museums, a Yankees baseball game are a thrill, but she also notices, "Lives drip away like water here, not even making a dent in the acres of concrete."

June 16, 9:00 a.m.: A tour of "Batten, Barton, Durstine, and Osborne," an ad agency, a luncheon with gifts.

7:00 p.m.: With Gregory Kamirloff, at a sidewalk café for an Italian dinner, to his penthouse, listens to music.

June 17: Guest editors get Ptomaine poisoning.

3:00 p.m.: Tour of *Vanity Fair* offices and tea.

8:00 p.m.: Movie preview of *Let's Do It Again* (1953).

June 18: UN tour with Gregory Kamirloff.

1:30 p.m.: Gregory for coffee.

4:00 p.m.: Tour of John Frederics hats.

7:00 p.m.: Dinner, listens to Mark von Slosmann, a friend of Bob Cochran's, reads his bad poetry.

The execution of the Rosenbergs, like Plath's reaction to the Suez crisis, reflects her powerful connection to public events experienced as a constituent of her own history.

June 19: Washes hair, horrified at the "blaring headline" about the execution of the Rosenbergs: "it is too bad that it could not be televised . . . so much more realistic and beneficial than the run-of-the mill crime program. Two real people being executed. No matter. The largest emotional reaction over the United States will be a rather large, democratic, infinitely bored and casual and complacent yawn." {PJ}

June 20: Watches the Yankees play the Detroit Tigers, dance in Forest Hill in Queens, New York, Meets Antonio La Vias from Lima, Peru.

New York split open Plath's mind, and later she would explore the fissures in her psyche by reading deeply in books about abnormal psychology, attempting to understand why she had come apart.

June 21, 8:45 a.m.: Picnic at Bear Mountain State Park in Bear Mountain, New York, Ray Wunderlich calls.

Letter to "Dear Warren": Proud of his "superlative honorific graduation," in the New York heat, she misses the "unsooted greenness of our backyard." The change from the hectic schedule at Smith to the frenzy of New York City has been too much. "I have been ecstatic, horribly depressed, shocked, elated, enlightened and enervated." To think of it all at once would split open her mind.

June 22, 7:30 p.m.: Meets Louis Bansci in Central Park, concert, cocktails at a sidewalk café, a talk at the Hotel St. Moritz about scenes from *Camino Real*.

June 23, noon: Lunch with Dorothy Williams.

8:30 p.m.: Performance of *Misalliance* (1910) by George Bernard Shaw.

June 24, 8:45 a.m.: Tour and breakfast at Macy's.

5:00–7:00 p.m.: Betsy Talbot Blackwell's party.

June 25, 2:30 p.m.: Visits French fashion house Trigère.

5:00 p.m.: Party at fashion house of Horwitz and Duberman.

8:30 p.m.: Meets Ilo Pill.

June 26: With Ray Wunderlich on Staten Island Ferry.

June 27: "Out by 3." Mother and Grammy meet her returning from New York City at the train station—"shocked to find her exhausted, hollow-eyed, and wearing borrowed clothes." {RC}

July 2: Picnic with Marcia Brown near the Charles River.

July 3: Meets Gordon Lameyer, a talk with Warren at lunch, evening at the Lameyers.

Letter to the director of graduate schools, Columbia University: mentions forthcoming graduation from Smith in June 1954, inquires about the graduate program in education and journalism and any bulletins and scholarship information he can send her.

July 4: "Decision." Plays tennis, cleans the car, meets Gordon Lameyer.

July 5: "New Hampshire with the Eatons and Lameyers."

July 6: ~~Harvard summer school.~~

Undated: Now that she has not been admitted to O'Connor's class, she weighs possibilities and the practicality of learning shorthand for secretarial work. Staying at home will make it harder to schedule her days. "If I can't dream up plots in my own room and backyard, I won't be able to dream them up anywhere." But she is "afraid to try writing on my own, because of the huge possibilities of failure. But I am going to. . . . The worst enemy to creativity is self-doubt. And you are so obsessed by your coming necessity to be independent, to face the great huge man-eating world, that you are paralyzed."

July 7: "Cape—Gordon [Lameyer]."

8:00–10:00 a.m.: Studies shorthand with her mother, sunbathes, cleans bathroom, studies shorthand.

July 8: Shorthand, typing.

7:30 p.m.: With Gordon Lameyer on the Charles River Esplanade.[509]

July 10: Myron Lotz's twenty-first birthday.

July 11: "Gordon [Lameyer]."

July 13: "Marcia [Brown] supper?"

July 15, 9:00 (morning or evening not specified): "Fran."

July 16, 9:30 a.m.–1:30 p.m.: "Hospital," Marcia Brown Monday? "Lunch there," "Patsy?"

"~~Mother.~~"

"~~Winthrop.~~"

July 17, 9:30 a.m.–1:30 p.m.: "Hospital."

July 18, noon: "Aldrich," "marcia [Brown] party??"

July 22: "Hampton," "Call Marty [Marcia Brown]."

July 23: "Call hospital."

Letter to Gordon Lameyer: Imagines him in the navy with a "marilyn monroeish Wave to rouse you from slumber in the morning by crooning— 'Oh, what a Beautiful Day.'" Mentions her part-time job in the Newton-Wellesley Hospital as a nurse's aide, a "new and intriguing" environment but also "sobering." Describes those suffering, crying, the "whispered consultations in the halls." Reading through all the commentaries on Joyce, she wonders whether a thesis on him is "really plausible."

July 24, 9:30 a.m.–1:00 p.m.: Hospital.

July 25: "Marblehead?"

July 26: "Not here."

July 27: Dinner at Mrs. Prouty's.

July 28: Marcia Brown's birthday.

Plath's deteriorating mental condition resulted in a series of brutally administered electric shocks, performed without any sort of sedative. To her, the treatments were torture, the equivalent of electrocution—another reason she reacted with such horror to the execution of the Rosenbergs.

July 29: "Shockt" (Shock treatments).

Letter to Gordon Lameyer: admires his mother and describes dinner with Mrs. Prouty, wants news about his "seamanship," notes that her attitudes toward the military have changed since learning about "what sort of things can be done with it."

August: *Mademoiselle* publishes "Poets on Campus."

August 4, 5:30 p.m.: "Cambridge."

August 8: "Marty [Marcia Brown]?"

August 9: "Dave tennis louise [Giesey]—party."

August 12: Letter from Gordon Lameyer. At Tillotsons'.[510]

   6:00 p.m.: Cocktails with Marcia Brown.

August 13: At the beach with Patsy O'Neil, dinner with the Cantors.

August 17: Calls Marcia Brown.

August 18: Letter to Myron Lotz: sends congratulations for continued minor league success as he advances up the hierarchy of the team, notes that "life here has been very placid," mentions giving up the idea of summer school—"the doctor ordered me to take time off and rest, and so I have been helping with the house, visiting Cambridge occasionally, and taking a few trips to the beach."

August 24, 2:00 p.m.: Leaves note for her mother that she is going on a long hike and will return the next day.

   6:00 p.m.: Plath's mother calls the police, and the search is on to discover Sylvia's whereabouts.

August 25: Aurelia discovers a bottle of fifty sleeping pills missing from the medicine cabinet, which is mentioned in newspapers reporting on the search for Sylvia.

August 26: Warren discovers sister unconscious in house's crawl space, newspapers report her rescue.

August 26–January 29: Treatment in Newton Wellesley Hospital, Massachusetts General Hospital, and McLean Hospital.

August 31: Letter to Gordon Lameyer: Acknowledges his letter and "wonderful flowers," grateful for his "constancy and friendship," mentions facial bruising treatment. "I don't know why I chose the hard way to learn who the real people are and who they aren't." Refers to making a "comeback" from her "difficult and complex situation." His letter has "meant more to me than any I've ever received . . . Or probably ever will."⁵¹¹

September 7: Letter to Gordon Lameyer: Recalls how much outings with Gordon and his mother meant to her. "I want you to know Gordy, that bearing up under the 'slings and arrows of outrageous fortune,' even if they are a result of one's own mismanagement . . . is incalculably easier when one has two such marvelous people as you and your mother to be so thoughtful."

September 14: Admitted to McLean Hospital—"Provisional Diagnosis: Psychoneurotic disorder, depressive reaction. Determined diagnosis: Sane." {HR}

*Plath comes under the care of Dr. Ruth Beuscher (aka Ruth Tiffany Barnhouse), whose treatment of Plath has been criticized in several biographies.*⁵¹²

September 15: Dictated notes—"Anamnesis,"⁵¹³ "Informant: AP. Impression of Mrs. P.: 'A quiet reserved woman who shows the strain of the past summer's experience with her daughter she is above average in intelligence, extremely interested in her children & apparently enjoys an excellent relationship with them. The reliability of her information is beyond question." A detailed account of family history, patient's personal history, early development, neurotic traits, home atmosphere and influence, sibling, play life, school, occupational history, menstrual history, habits, sex interest & practice, onset of present illness. {RB}

September 18: "A course of ambulatory insulin three times daily." {RB}

September 22: "Pleasant friendly, and cooperative. Attitude superficial. Probably still suicidal." {RB}

September 29: Mood improves, bathing and dressing properly, pleasant to other patients, reading books in the library, outdoors for long walks, averse to group activities, but avoids "talking about deeper problems. When it is suggested that she will ultimately recover, she no longer denies it vehemently, but accepts it without comment." {RB}

October 6: Insulin treatment continues, still "confused, depressed, suspicious and slightly retarded," but "more active than on admission." {RB}

October 16: Pleasant but difficult to engage, other than to talk about her "shortcomings . . . One senses she has a great a deal of hostility which she is unable to express." {RB}

October 17: Hostile feelings begin to emerge, referring to a visitor as "that old bat": "Possibly still suicidal." Feels nothing is inside her, concentrates on food preparation, wants to return home to cook for her mother and brother, responds to occupational therapy (pottery and weaving), watches movies, plays bridge, seems happy until she is questioned. Throws her mother's flowers in the basket. Dr. Beuscher works on getting Plath to admit her hostility but to prevent her from "directing it inward."{RB}

November 10: Suicide watch—"Ground privileges cancelled." Wants to get well but feels it is impossible—"There is nothing in my head." Nonetheless, "some progress is being made." {RB}

November 24: Transferred to "Women's Belknap I," where it "would be easier to relate to three patients." Drowsy after administration of chlorpromazine, "makes her feel hopeless." {RB}

At an impasse in Plath's therapy, Dr. Beuscher, earning the trust of her patient, recommends electric shock treatments.

December 8: Decision to administer "electric shock treatments since she appears to continue to be so depressed that suicide appears to be a real risk." {RB}

December 10: First electric shock treatment—a "dramatic recovery." {RB}

December 10–January 8: "From that time onward she felt certain she would be well, was cheerful, thoughtful. Cooperative, was no longer suicidal or depressed." After sixth treatment, refuses any more but persuaded to do one more, even though fearful of identity loss and longing to return to her family. {RB}

December 17: Postcard to Mother: Tells her mother about doing "occasional work in the library." She will have a sixth shock treatment tomorrow, hopes she won't have "many more," expecting to return home for two days at Christmas.

December 25: Letter to Gordon Lameyer: Pleased to be home for Christmas, spent part of the day rereading his letters,[514] which have made her want to find her way back to the world, explains her silence: "I'd been undergoing months of therapy which left me feeling rather unconversational temporarily." Feeling "100% better." Plans to finish her degree at Smith—"they've been really princely about everything." She has occupied herself in the book and record libraries.

December 28: Letter to Eddie Cohen from McLean Hospital: explains reasons for suicide attempt, the national attention it received,[515] recovery with the financial help of Mrs. Prouty and her psychiatrist, expects a "fat letter" from Eddie about his news.

1954

January 9: Sees Alec Guinness in *The Captain's Paradise* (1953) at the Astor Theatre in Boston.

January 10: Letter to Gordon Lameyer: Home for the weekend. Describes her long correspondence with Eddie Cohen without naming him and why it was important to her, but also why his sudden appearance in the flesh disturbed her.

January 13: Continued recovery, "anxious to return to college." Staff conference agrees to her beginning February semester at Smith, contingent on twice-weekly sessions with Smith psychiatrist Dr. Marion Booth. "Her attitude is good. Insight good." {RB}

January 16: Letter to Marion Freeman: The plan—return to Smith for second semester, take three instead of five courses to ease the pressure, graduate the following year. "Your messages have helped so much, dear Aunt Marion," she has enjoyed the "entertaining clippings."

January 18: Letter to Enid Mark: congratulates Enid on her marriage plans, announces her return to Smith to renew friendships, mentions friendship at McLean with Jane Anderson, who dated Dick Norton.

January 21: Letter to Sally Rogers: describes opportunities available to a Smith student, how she thrived as a scholarship student—"I think that all you have to do is figure out generally what kind of a girl you really are inside (that's pretty hard when you're still growing up, the way we are) and what sort of experience you want out of college."

January 22: Performance of *The Confidential Clerk* (1953) by T. S. Eliot at Colonial Theatre in Boston.

January 24: Visits Mr. Crockett.

January 25: Letter to Gordon Lameyer: speaks of sailing "salubriously" through his letters, reading of Kafka and T. S. Eliot, the continuing inspiration of Mr. Crockett, mourning Dylan Thomas's death, wanting to hear about Lameyer's impressions of Europe.

January 28: Officially discharged from McLean Hospital. {RB}

January 30: Returns to Smith.

February 4: Letter to Phil McCurdy: His letter made her happy. Mentions her arrival at Smith with Warren that ends almost fatally in a long downhill skid in a blizzard, enjoys courses in early American literature, modern American literature, nineteenth-century intellectual and literary history. He is one of her favorite people. She wants to see him. Regards their relationship as "platonic," and thinks it's wiser not to pursue a romance. She is quite willing to talk about it.

February 6, 9:00 a.m.: Letter to Gordon Lameyer: Feels comfortable a week after returning to Smith. Reads Nathaniel Hawthorne, Theodore Dreiser, and Fyodor Dostoevsky. Visits an Amherst friend working in a laboratory, entertaining evening listening to the "inimitable Tom Lehrer's songs," plans spring vacation in New York City.

2:30 p.m.: Listens to Professor Davis lecture on the novel.

Plays bridge, looks forward to tea with Professor Drew, lists highlights of her life—observing the birth of a baby, a spontaneous and wild ride in a small private plane, the dissection of a cadaver, appearing as the only white girl at an African American party, braving a storm in a small sailboat, picking strawberries in the blazing sun, racing a golden retriever on Nauset Beach: "little things, large things, that all are somehow very important in the formative scheme of living." Little writing since last spring, except for a "brief sarcastic bit," titled "Dirge in Three Parts," accepts Auden's criticism that she is "too glib." She believes that Gordon Lameyer, her "peregrinating Ulysses," is "kindred" and will understand her pleasure in listening to recordings of Edith Sitwell and Dylan Thomas.

February 7: Letter to Ellen Bond in the Personal and Otherwise Department of *Harper's Magazine*: provides brief biography to accompany publication of her poems.

February 8: Letter to "Dearest mother": Mentions Professor Drew, "such a dear," who hugs and kisses her, saying how happy she is to have Sylvia back. Many letters to write to Mrs. Prouty and others, describes blind date with one of those "weak" Amherst boys. Still, she managed to enjoy herself. Feels at home with her reading and the underclassmen in Lawrence House.

February 10: Letter to Gordon Lameyer: a rundown of activities—lecture, dance concert, reception at the college president's house.

February 15: Letter to "Dear Mrs. Cantor": Appreciates her loving letter, explains that, on her return to Smith, she has been met with "such love and warmth." Quotes Mary Baker Eddy: "We are sometimes led to believe that darkness is as real as light; but Science affirms darkness to be only a mortal sense of the absence of light, at the coming of which darkness loses the appearance of reality." Sylvia's darkness has dispersed "like a mist or fog, showing the clear, wonderful outline of the true world, and the true self."

February 16: Letter to Phil McCurdy: alludes to "shocking feelings" about her mother, which she will probably discuss with him "some day."

February 21: Letter to Gordon Lameyer: Responds to his letter of Joycean punning by replying in a parody of Joyce's style, reads *Winesburg, Ohio* (1919) by Sherwood Anderson, writes in the third person of "pagan heat, and the vine leaves twining in her hair, and the rough gallop of centaurs." She thinks of Ilo Pill, the Estonian artist who worked with her on the farm the summer before she entered Smith, but the "hours and hours I could spend talking, reading aloud, listening, walking and communing with you are many and multitudinous."

February 25: Letter to Jane Anderson: A dream about Anderson, then a letter from her, describes the harrowing return to Smith—"I remember the interminable seconds as we slid, utterly out of control, and I wondered if I really was living in a deterministic universe and had displeased the malicious gods by trying to assert my will," but she has acclimated, the past fading fast. She is immersed in reading Dostoevsky—"Amusingly enough, I felt conspicuous at first during the discussions of suicide in these books, and felt sure that my scar was glowing symbolically, obvious to all (the way Hester's scarlet letter burned and shone with a physical heat to proclaim her default to all)." Thinks of writing a paper on the "theme of suicide, feeling that I have somewhat of a personalized understanding of the sensations and physical and mental states one experiences previous to the act." Refers to her "new easy-going feelings," hiking, biking with Marcia Brown, good bull sessions, dating seven boys in four weeks, going to the movies, her "escapade" "had in no way made a lasting scar on my future associations" but is an advantage in understanding herself and others. Regards psychiatric help at this point as "really superfluous." She consults Dr. Booth, Smith's psychiatrist, once a week, but there is no deep exploration of her feelings. Calls herself "consistently 'happy' rather than spasmodically ecstatic." Encourages Anderson to give this letter to Dr. Beuscher—"I would like her to know how I am getting on."

March 1: Letter to Phil McCurdy: biking, picnicking, shopping with Marcia Brown, prepared for Brown's wedding, proposes various possibilities for his visit to Smith.

March 3: I. A. Richards's lecture, "The Dimensions of Reading Poetry," in Sage Hall.

A ditty addressed to Phil McCurdy begins "I try very hard / To be avant garde," wishes him a happy birthday, disgusted with a letter from a member of the Buckley family, saying no one should support Smith because it harbors Communists, including Professor Newton Arvin, whom Plath calls a "sensitive innocent guy," who is in the infirmary suffering from shock. Calls her Smith psychiatrist a "great friend."[516]

March 5: Letter to "Dear mother": "no psychological problems, actually," finds solace in her new interest—George Gebauer, with whom she can share "my humor, my ideas, and my delight in the surrounding world."

March 16: Letter to "Dear mummy": twenty-page Russian paper to write, gets As on her exams.

Letter to "Dearest Ulysses [Gordon Lameyer]": Mentions attending a "remarkably lucid" lecture by Professor Selden Bacon from Yale—"Alcoholism: Illness, Evil or Social Pathology." At Joe's pizzeria, she has a good time with next year's roommate, Nancy Hunter, talking about "every field from sex to salvation." Expresses delight in his "journeyings." Warren pays a visit. They catch up on his "academic, social and ideological life" at Harvard, where he is doing well. She may stay with Ilo Pill, her Estonian artist-friend in New York City. She has lined up a waitressing job in Orleans on the Cape.

Letter to Ramona Maher: thanks her for an article discussing a Plath poem, "Carnival Nocturne"—the first time anyone has discussed her work, provides a biography, cites Dostoevsky as her favorite novelist, Dylan Thomas as her favorite modern poet, and devotion to Joyce, Virginia Woolf, and D. H. Lawrence, and includes several of her poems.

March 24: Letter to Melvin Woody: plans for her New York City visit, lists dates when they can meet.

April 6: Letter to Gordon Lameyer: Describes visiting home, visiting Warren at Harvard, meeting Clement Moore for the first time, meeting with Dr. Beuscher—"now one of my best friends . . . only 9 years older than I, looking like Myrna Loy, tall, Bohemian, coruscatingly brilliant, and most marvelous . . . we had an excellent comradely time, and she approved heartily of my plans for spending a week in NYC this vacation and of taking an accelerated course in beginner's German at Harvard this summer." Walks a hundred blocks from Harlem in Manhattan, New York (where she is staying with Ilo Pill and his family), to Columbia University, down Broadway to the upper fifties, meeting Cyrilly Abels for a "long lunch of lobster salad and avocado pears at the Ivy Room of the Drake Hotel." Visits the Metropolitan Museum, attends performances of *The Confidential Clerk*, *Picnic* (1953), a night in Greenwich Village in Manhattan, a ride on the Staten Island Ferry, chanting "Edna St. Vincent Millay," lectures by Paul Tillich and Reinhold Niebuhr, sees *The Maltese Falcon* (1941), *Shadow of a Doubt* (1943), dinner with Cyrilly Abels, a copacetic talk at the Connecticut home of Clement Moore's mother, a successful writer, home for a dinner with the Crocketts, lunch with Mrs. Prouty, "who has literally sunk untold thousands into my scholarships and hospital bills." Disagrees with Gordon that teaching is incompatible with writing, doubts she is fit for a daily job—"last June . . . discovered that my daily work took all my creativity out of me and replaced it with weariness and a desire to relax over a drink, a dance, a show, or just plain go to bed . . . when I tried to write, I kept thinking: If I want to Get Ahead, I'll have to turn to my job reports." Mentions her experience at *Mademoiselle* is a suitable subject for a novel, considers graduate school and time to develop.

April 8: Postcard to "Dear mother": briefly describes travels and socializing.

April 10: Listens to Andres Segovia in Sage Hall.

April 11: Postcard to "Dear mother": reading a thousand pages of Herman Melville, expects a mixture of As and Bs, socializing and concert going with friends.

April 14: Postcard to "Dear mum": Enjoyed her Melville exam, requests a tin of Toll House cookies to nibble while studying, looks forward to seeing Leslie Howard in the film *Pygmalion* (1938).

Letter to Phil McCurdy: Relaxes after Melville exam, an "absolutely explosive" talk about Henrik Ibsen by Hans Kohn, a dozen purchases of novels, poetry, plays with "clots of philosophy, sociology & psych," staying put at Smith to read several thousand-page novels.

April 16: Letter to "dear mummy": Reading *War and Peace* (1867) by Leo Tolstoy, excited over writing her first poem since last May, "Doom of Exiles." Dostoevsky is her senior thesis subject.

The meeting with Richard Sassoon marked a new phase in Plath's life. Sassoon's exotic sophistication made the all-American boys, like Gordon Lameyer and Myron Lotz, seem bland and immature.

April 19: Letter to "Dearest mother": A "superlative" weekend with George Gebauer, watching a performance of *Pygmalion*, sun worshipping on Sunday with Marcia Brown, socializing, meets Richard Sassoon, whose father is a cousin of poet Siegfried Sassoon. Describes Richard as "a thin, slender Parisian fellow who is a British subject, and a delight to talk to . . . I find he's another of those men who are exactly as tall as I, but they don't seem to mind it, and I certainly don't." Calls him a "very intuitive weird sinuous little guy whose eyes are black and shadowed so he looks as if he were an absinthe addict . . . all of which helps me to be carefree and gay."

April 20: Letter to Richard Sassoon: writes a prose poem inspired by Tennessee Williams's character Kilroy in *Camino Real*.[517]

April 23: Sends birthday greeting card to Mother with lines from *Macbeth* and her own: "I'm stirring up a witches brew / That will, I hope, bring luck to you." Describes activities at Smith, including a Phi Beta Kappa dinner.

April 25, 1:00 a.m.: Letter to "Dear mother": prefers "French boy [Richard] Dick Sassoon" to "lugubrious Myron [Lotz]."

April 26: Letter to Phil McCurdy: Mentions his portrait, poster, and cartoon he sent her had made her room a "salon de Phil!" Mentions picnics, reading Henry James, Leo Tolstoy, on the sunroof, refers to her delight in a "satanic relative of siegfried sassoon."

April 28: Letter to Phil McCurdy: In infirmary with a strange "*malheureusement*," observes a "funny thing about pain: it annihilates one's pride completely." Thrilled to see her poem in the May issue of *Harper's* and the brief biography of her—"ah, *vanitas vanitatum*."

April 30: Telegram to Mother: "Smith just voted me scholarship of $1250."

May 3, 7:30 p.m.: Letter to Gordon Lameyer: Welcomes his letters, "splashes of continental color into my collegiate life." Looks forward to working on senior thesis on Dostoevsky and the "recurrence of the split personality," describes her "magnificent experience" studying with Newton Arvin and her adventures with Richard Sassoon.

May 4: Postcard to "Dear mummy": describes a farmhouse family who takes her in when Richard Sassoon's Volkswagen gets stuck in the mud— "They called me Cinderella and treated me like a queen till Sassoon came back with the reclaimed Volkswagen."

May 5: Letter to Melvin Woody: quarrels with his philosophy of life and his hedonistic view of fertility—"I am hardly ready or willing to produce the children which nature would endow me with as the understood reward of my actions."

May 7: Postcard to "Dear mother": Going to Yale to see Richard Sassoon and Melvin Woody, both of whom claim to be "intensely in love" with her—"it's a bit disconcerting to get passionate metaphysical love letters from the same mailbox & two antagonistic roommates."

Letter to Woody: she will be visiting Yale and returning some of his books just in case he does not want to be there when she arrives.

11:00 a.m.: Letter to Phil McCurdy: calls his last letter "exquisite," hopes he might be available for a date with beautiful and talented Nancy Hunter when she visits Wellesley.

May 11, 2:00 p.m.: Postcard to "Dear mother": mentions that during her visit to Yale, Melvin Woody hugs her, gives her a note, and then disappears. Richard Sassoon will be sailing for Europe soon.

May 13: Letter to Phil McCurdy: A marathon of reading—"I am so cerebralized it is annoyingly difficult to go to sleep." Thinks of her farmwork days when "struck with an uncomplicated physical exhaustion which swallowed me in a dark and dreamless sea of sleep until I woke refreshed and rejuvenated at dawn." Describes New York visit with Richard Sassoon to see Montgomery Clift in a preview of *The Seagull* (1896) by Anton Chekhov, looking forward to summer reading, Harvard summer school, classes in the fall, senior thesis.

May 18: Letter to "Dearest mother": Details arrangements for Mother's visits on May 27 and in June with friends visiting the Plath home, worries about money for the next school year and the prospect of getting a summer job.

May 19: Letter to "Dear mother": wins a poetry prize for "Doom of Exiles," elected president of Alpha Phi Kappa Psi, an honorary society of the arts, refers to the "reign of terror"—her exams.

May 20: Letter to Melvin Woody: A Shakespeare parody beginning "life's but a canceled postcard," a parody of A. E. Housman and Alexander

Pope—"oh malt does more than Melvin can / to justify my ways to man."
She wonders at their misinterpretations of each other—"I hadn't thought
I was being silent; I had thought you were. I'm just enough of a feminine
creature to give men the prerogative for inviting me to commune: you've
given it, so I commune."

May 22: Letter to Gordon Lameyer: Getting through her exams, feeling
she has learned a lot, especially from Newton Arvin, writing a paper on
Erich Fromm's *Escape From Freedom* (1941), enjoys visit to Professor George
Gibian, playing with his children, which brings out maternal instincts,
imagines mothering a "multitude of sons" "as free companions: none of
this insidious 'momism' or apron string business for me."[518]

June 11, 3:00 p.m.: Letter to Gordon Lameyer: "writing now is so different, somehow . . . there is a real, vital stimulating gordon who cuts oh,
such an endearing space out of the thin air . . . so multidimensional in
this suddenly more-than-we-think-it pluriverse, that I can scarcely become
accustomed to saying casually to myself: ah, yes."

June 12, 10:00 p.m.: Letter to Lameyer: mentions afternoon hour session with Dr. Beuscher, the first of bimonthly visits, enjoys "analyzing and
philosophizing with her."

June 22, 12:15 a.m.: Letter to Lameyer: Draws a female in a robe on a
pillow holding a pen and says this is the hour when she is prone to talking or
to a writing jag, describes a return to Winthrop with her mother, memories
of childhood when visiting the Freemans (the father has just died), draws
streets and houses and the ocean—"lawns that were continents, rocks that
were fortresses, alleys that were secret passages to magic worlds," an Eden
of dreams that never quite were reality. Remembers David Freeman, the
"Superman of my lois lane days," visits her old house, the golden rain trees
her father planted, "now flourishing giants," discusses with David their
attitudes toward death.

June 23: Letter to Lameyer: another delightful session with Dr. Beuscher.

June 29: Letter to Lameyer: describes meeting "rigid" Dick Norton for
the first time in six months—"I had lived so hard and so much and deep
that never again could I go back to the same small country of his personality which once, years ago, I had seen as vast and glittering with promise."

July 1: Drives to Dick Norton's place at the Cape, a walk with Marcia
Brown and her husband, Mike, to Nauset beach, a lobster dinner with
Warren, a movie—*Knock on Wood*,[519] starring Danny Kaye.

July 2: Returns by bus and train to Wellesley, washes hair, sunbathes,
and eats dinner and shops with Mrs. Helen Ames Lameyer.

10:00 p.m.: Letter to "Dearest mother": Reports on her activities to
her hospitalized mother—"I've never enjoyed anything so much as being

home alone . . . it seems so big and palatial and airy, with so many rooms . . . I feel I could hold a ball in the kitchen! . . . Don't worry about a thing . . . all is very fine here, and I want you to get rid of those nasty ulcer pains."

July 3: Drives to Newport with Mrs. Lameyer, tours the Cornelius Vanderbilt mansion.

Letter to Gordon Lameyer: A mishmash parody of *Dragnet* and the adventures of "Absinthe Lutely Plathered,"[520] tells him about her travels with his mother to Newport, Rhode Island. Reads *The Great Gatsby* (1925) by F. Scott Fitzgerald and *Babbitt* (1922) by Sinclair Lewis. "I want to be like a chameleon on a paisley shawl. . . . paradoxically always and yet never the same . . . the more always and vividly I love you the more newly and variously I want to tell you how this you-i linking affects me."[521]

Diary memoranda section—"write to Ruth Moynihan, Mrs Cochran, Bob Cochran, Mel [Melvin] Woody, Alison [Prentice] Smith."

July 4: Washes two loads of laundry, dinner at the Aldriches, writes letters,[522] Dave (Freeman?) for supper, "guitar and songs."

July 5: Packs for Cambridge.

3:00 p.m.: Drives with Dave (Freeman?), settles in Cambridge apartment.

Letter to Melvin Woody: Annotates *Babbitt*, reads Delmore Schwartz, Kenneth Patchen, rereads children's books, *The Little Prince* and *Alice in Wonderland* (1865), prefers Hemingway's short stories to his novels—"a personal bibliography might be as effective in describing our personality development and orientation as anything else!" Excited about Harvard summer school made possible by a scholarship, refers to her suicide attempt as the "cataclysmic downward gyre I plummeted to symbolic death in last summer, when the center did not hold because there was none, or rather (as you wrote), too many, has given me an understanding of the black and sustained hells a mind can go through." She believes they have an "amusingly ectoplasmic umbilical cord between us." Doing loads of laundry at home listening to Paul Hindemith and Francis Poulenc.

July 6: Walks in Cambridge all morning, exploring and shopping, registers for summer school, sees *Counsellor at Law*,[523] and has a drink at Wursthaus.

July 7: German and English classes, a beer at the Oxford Grille with Nancy Hunter and Edwin Akutowicz, a dance at Memorial Hall, meets with Mike Schmid and Tom Collins at Cronin's Bar.

July 8: German and English classes, coffee with Ralph Linton at the Hayes-Bickford Cafeteria.

4:00–6:00 p.m.: Naps before cocktails and supper, a trip to Lamont Library, a beer at Cronin's with Melvyn H. Dawson, a law student.

July 9: German and English classes, coffee with Jerry Alcott, a good talk with Bob Sullivan and Ruth Sullivan, home to unwind, Pat calls.

July 10: Sleeps late, sunbathes, shops, meets Gordon Lameyer and his mother for dinner, an evening on a golf course, talking in the moon and the mist.

Diary memoranda section—wash clothes, iron, "Ger ass't [German assignment]—reading."

July 11: A day at Nahant Beach in Nahant with Gordon Lameyer, swimming, sunbathing, cheeseburger dinner, supper at her apartment, studies German.

July 12, 8:00 a.m.: German class.

11:00 a.m.: German class.

Noon: English class.

2:00–4:00 p.m.: Shops for supper (meat balls, macaroni, cucumber salad, strawberries), visits with Phil McCurdy.

8:30–10:00 p.m.: At the library.

July 13, 8:00–11:00 a.m.: German classes.

Noon: English class.

2:00–5:00 p.m.: Studies.

8:00 p.m.: Meets with Dr. Beuscher.

Buys veal, salad, and rolls for supper with Lou Healy, a medical student, sees Edwin Akutowicz.

July 14, 8:00–11:00 a.m.: German classes.

Noon: English class.

2:00–5:00 p.m.: Studies for test.

Washes hair, tuna dinner.

8:00–10:00 p.m.: Great conversation with Edwin Akutowicz.

July 15, 8:00 a.m., 11:00 a.m.: "HOUR EXAM!!!"

Coffee with Don White.

Noon: English class.

Lunch with Nancy Hunter and Jim McNealy.

3:00–5:00 p.m.: Naps, supper.

8:00–10:00 p.m.: Studies at library.

July 16, 8:00 a.m., 11:00 a.m.: German class.

Noon: English class.

4:30 p.m.: Dental appointment.

Meets Mr. Lameyer at the restaurant Joseph's, meets with Mr. Spring and Howard in Brookline, Massachusetts.

Diary memoranda section—"blanket from home?" Cashes check for ten dollars, potato chips, "Ask Lissy [Snyder] out," notes to call Del Schmidt in Chatham.

July 17, 1:00–7:00 p.m.: Out with Gordon Lameyer and his mother, climbs up Mount Monadnock in New Hampshire, picnics, drives home, ice cream, popcorn, a "wonderful time together as ever."

July 18, 5:00 a.m.: A drive to Newport for an excellent sausage, pancake, and coffee breakfast at the Hotel Viking with Gordon Lameyer and a friend. They read poetry on the beach, have dinner at Hilltop Inn, then drive to Cambridge.

July 19, 8:00 a.m.: German class.

    11:00 a.m.–noon: English class.

    2:00 p.m.: Lunch, nap.

    3:30–4:30 p.m.: Shopping.

    8:30–10:00 p.m.: Studies at Widener Library.

    10:30 p.m.–1:30 a.m.: Studies at Edwin Akutowicz's apartment.

Letter to Gordon Lameyer: "I will curl up like a foetal rose petal and in the darkness of daysleep, dream of your warm nearness and rise reborn from rivering waters of love and rest." Describes meeting his mother and introducing her to roommates.

July 20, 8:00 a.m., 11:00 a.m.: German class.

    Noon: English class.

    1:30 p.m.: Lunch, washes hair, naps, cleans kitchen.

    4:00–5:00 p.m.: Writes to Bob Cochran.[524]

    Supper of salmon, peas, and pie.

    7:15–10:00 p.m.: Studies German.

July 21, 8:00 a.m., 11:00 a.m.: German class.

    Noon: English class.

    1:15–2:15 p.m.: Lunch with Jim McNealy.

    2:30 p.m.: Naps.

    5:30 p.m.: Chicken livers in sherry and cream for dinner.

    7:00 p.m.: Sees Dave.

    8:00–10:00 p.m.: Studies at Widener Library.

July 22, 8:00 a.m., 11:00 a.m.: German class, "German songs German table."

    Noon: Cuts English class.

    12:30 p.m.: Eats lunch at "Union" (Harvard Graduate Student Union?).

    1:30 p.m.: Studies at Edwin Akutowicz's, reads all afternoon, steak and wine dinner, "long evening of talk."

July 23, 8:00 a.m., 11:00 a.m.: German class.

    Noon: English class.

    Washes hair.

    1:30 p.m.: Packs for trip home.

Evening with Gordon Lameyer, meets poet Richard Wilbur "at last!" Cake at the Lameyers'.

July 24, 9:30 a.m.: A drive to the Cape, sees Warren in Chatham, to "outer bar" with Gordon Lameyer for swimming, sunbathing, walking on the beach, picnic, a "shower a deux," evening at Eastward Ho! (a private club in Chatham) of dancing, to bed at the Cochrans'.

July 25, 8:30 a.m.: A light pancake breakfast in Chatham with Warren and Gordon, a drive to Brewster to Eddie Wheeler's mansion overlooking the bay, studies, talks with Gordon in the summer house, dinner at Howard Johnson's with Gordon and his mother.

Plath's relationship with Edwin Akutowicz is complex and susceptible to many different interpretations. She continued to see him after this assault in the entry below and seems to have recovered from her trauma.[525]

July 26, 8:00 a.m., 11:00 a.m.: German class.

Noon: English class.

Cleans out kitchen, prepares for lunch.

1:00–2:00 p.m.: Lunch with Lissy Snyder.

3:00 p.m.: Meets with Dr. Beuscher.

8:15 p.m.: At library.

Assaulted at Edwin Akutowicz's apartment. {HC}

July 27, 8:00 a.m., 11:00 a.m.: German class.

Noon: English class.

Appointment with Dr. George E. Heels about excessive bleeding after Akutowicz's assault.

7:00–11:00 p.m.: Studies German.

July 28, 8:00 a.m., 11:00 a.m.: German class.

Noon: English class.

3:00 p.m.: Studies for midterm in Lamont Library, recuperates, cleans apartment.

July 29, 8:00 a.m.: German class.

9:00 a.m.: Calls Dr. Beuscher.

11:00 a.m.: German class.

Noon: Cuts English, eats lunch.

1:00–3:00 p.m.: Studies.

3:00 p.m.: Meets Dr. Beuscher.

7:00–10:00 p.m.: Studies.

July 30, 9:00–11:00 a.m.: German exam.

Noon: English class.

1:00 p.m.: Lunch at Cronin's Bar.

3:00 p.m.: Dr. Beuscher.

Walks in Cambridge, reads *Crime and Punishment* (1866) by Fyodor Dostoevsky, movie at Brattle Theatre.

July 31: Sleeps late, drives to Cambridge to pick up books from storage, dinner at the Lameyers with martinis and salad, shopping, a "long talk."

Diary memoranda section—notes to ask Debby Hoar to lunch, Del Schmidt for next week, to call Patsy, to write Bob Cochran and Mrs. Cochran, and cash ten-dollar check.

August 1: Sleeps late, wears white dress to roast beef dinner at the Lameyers, afternoon at home translating German, listening to records, after-supper drive.

August 2, 8:00 a.m., 11:00 a.m.: German class.

Noon: English class.

2:00–3:00 p.m.: Shopping.

Washes hair, prepares supper.

4:00–6:00 p.m.: Naps.

8:00–10:30 p.m.: Studies German.

August 3, 9:00–11:00 a.m.: Translates German.

11:00 a.m.: German class.

Noon: English class.

A hot toddy at lunch with a grilled peanut butter sandwich, sherry-soaked fruit salad, writes to Gordon Lameyer.[526]

4:30–6:00 p.m.: Student-faculty tea.

8:30–11:00 p.m.: Studies in Widener Library.

August 4, 8:00 a.m., 11:00 a.m.: German classes.

Noon: English class.

1:00–2:00 p.m.: Lunch.

Writes to Gordon Lameyer.

3:30–5:30 p.m.: Naps.

Salad, soup, and deviled egg supper.

8:30 p.m.: Graduate party on Trowbridge Street, cocktails, Charles Trenet.

Letter to Gordon: Describes herself as a beast of burden learning German vocabulary, "getting tense over tenses," revolving the "universe of possibilities and probabilities involving you and I and the dream of we."

August 5: Calls Dr. Heels.

8:00 a.m., 11:00 a.m.: German class.

Noon: English class.

Supper of ham and macaroni casserole with Hunter and June Brine.

7:00–9:00 p.m.: Studies in Widener Library.

Letter to Gordon Lameyer: Dreams of making love to him— "somehow, with all the difficult and dark things that have happened to me, I seem to be able to maintain a healthy, productive optimism, which eventually manages to work out crises and problems, transmuting them into positive events, such as the art of instructive philosophical development."

Mentions reveling in the "burlesque coarseness of existence" by way of explaining her desire to "give myself and (I think) unnecessary, yet indicative, tests, and cut away all the accessory males that have, for the last five years, crowded my life," reveals she lost her naïveté with a "traumatic shock last week."[527]

August 6, 8:00 a.m.: German class

    9:30–11:00 a.m.: Coffee and studies at Widener Library.

    Noon: English class.

    1:15 p.m.: Dr. Heels checkup.

    Rides home with Jeanne Woods and Betty McCurdy.

    5:15 p.m.: To bed early to sleep.

August 7, 8:00 a.m.: Up after fifteen hours of sleep.

Writes long letters to Gordon Lameyer and Claiborne Phillips and a note to Mrs. Cochran,[528] then washes her hair, eats a steak dinner, bikes to Patsy O'Neil's for a long, good talk until midnight.

Diary memoranda section—note to cash a twenty-dollar check, to call Patsy O'Neil, Del Schmidt, and Debby Hoar, and to write Bob Cochran and Mrs. Cochran.

Letter to Gordon: Pronounced intact by her doctor, she needs to repair her serenity before seeing him next weekend, spending time in the backyard in halter and shorts with her typewriter, turning herself into a "mrs. dalloway-plath," getting along "more constructively" with her mother, compares her independence to the rebellious American colonies, writes about her habits in expectation of their marriage so that he knows what to expect.

August 8: Sunbathes in backyard, studies German, plays piano, subway and bus to Cambridge for German study and conversation.

August 9, 8:00 a.m.: German class.

    9:00 a.m.: Shops with Phil McCurdy.

    11:00 a.m.: German class.

    Noon: English class.

    1:00 p.m.: Lunch with Debby Hoar at "Burr."

    3:00 p.m.: Appointment with Dr. Beuscher.

    5:00 p.m.: Prepares supper of shrimp, cheese, and onion casserole and rice.

    8:00–10:00 p.m.: Studies German.

August 10, 8:00 a.m.: German class.

    9:00–11:00 a.m.: Shopping, purchases a jumper for eleven dollars.

    11:00 a.m.: German class.

    Noon: English class.

    1:00 p.m.: Lunch with Jeanne Woods.

    5:00 p.m.: Prepares dinner of hotdogs and potatoes.

7:00 p.m.: Watches *Bicycle Thieves* (1948).[529]

August 11, 8:00 a.m.: German class.

Coffee at Hayes-Bickford Cafeteria.

11:00 a.m.: German class.

Noon: English class.

Studies at Widener Library.

2:00–5:00 p.m.: Writes to Gordon Lameyer, Marcia Brown, Mrs. Lameyer, and Sidney Schneck.[530]

7:00–9:30 p.m.: Scrubs kitchen.

"Dave & E called," studies until 12:30 a.m.

Letter to Gordon: "I have missed you increasingly like hell."

Diary memoranda section—reminder to cut hair, write to Warren, Bob, and Woody, "buy black patent bag, cash $15 check, buy party groceries ($6)."

August 15: "Delicious breakfast" with Mrs. Lameyer.

2:10 p.m.: Bus to Cambridge, meets Louise and Carl in rainy Cambridge, snacks and supper, unpacked.

9:00–11:00 p.m.: Studies.

August 16, 8:00 a.m.: Hour exam in German.

9:00–11:00 a.m.: Studies German.

11:00 a.m.: German class.

Noon: English class.

2:00–4:00 p.m.: Exam in Lamont Library.

Sunbathes on roof, "lazy supper," to bed early after a "bull session" with Joan Smith, a classmate.

August 17, 8:00 a.m.: German class.

9:00 a.m.: Shopping.

11:00 a.m.: German class.

Noon: English class.

2:00–5:00 p.m.: Studies German.

5:00–7:00 p.m.: Sidney Schneck visits.

Steak, potatoes, and peach salad supper, beer at Healy's apartment, "wonderful rapport."

August 18, 8:00 a.m.: German class.

9:00–11:00 a.m.: Studies German in the sun.

11:00 a.m.: German class.

Noon: English class.

2:30 p.m.: A gin and tonic at a "Purcell's luncheon" with Dr. Ira Scott.

8:00–10:00 p.m.: A good talk with Dr. Beuscher.

11:00 p.m.: Studies German.

August 19: Reminds herself to call the Cantors.

8:00 a.m.: German class.

9:00–10:00 a.m.: Studies German.

11:00 a.m.: German class.

Noon: English class.

1:00–4:00 p.m.: Studies German.

Jane Anderson visits.

8:00 p.m.: Ira Scott at Leveritt House, bourbon and water, listening to Louis Armstrong, talking about John Dos Passos during candlelit dinner of steak.

August 20: Coffee at College Inn with Father "Dallaire" (Delair).

8:00 a.m.: German class.

9:00–10:00 a.m.: Studies German.

11:00 a.m.: German class.

Noon: English class.

2:00–3:00 p.m.: German exam.

Washes hair, sunbathes on roof.

8:00 p.m.: Supper with Gordon Lameyer at Cronin's Bar: "Long tense bull session—problems."

August 21: Notes to call Ira Scott.

9:15 a.m.: Harvard tour.

Breakfast with Gordon Lameyer.

"Glass flowers[531]—Lou Healy—cocktails—party on."

8:00 p.m.: To Beacon Hill with medical students.

"1/2 hour hell—music & retake until early light—Satanic Sadism—6."

Diary memoranda section—note to write to Warren, Woody, Cochran, and Ruth M.[532] "Dinner with Father Delair?" Meet Schneck—"check for gas and light bill," cash fifteen-dollar check.

August 22, 9:00–11:00 a.m.: Two-hour bull session with Joan Smith.

Sunbathes, studies on roof.

3:00 p.m.: Steak dinner, three sedatives (Nembutal), "crisis of suspended animation."

Note to call the Cantors.

9:00–10:00 p.m.: Gordon Lameyer visits, "mending talk."

August 23: Notes Mother's trip to Cape.

9:15 a.m.: German final exam.

12:15 p.m.: Beach with Ira Scott.

1:30 p.m.: Dinner in Duxbury, Massachusetts, of steak, planter's punch, and bourbon, swims, sunbathes.

"Benedictine and bull session."

August 24: Meeting with Dr. Grabowski, at the beach with Ira Scott, purchases an "exquisite pink Brooks Brother shirt" in Boston, drives to

Marblehead, sails out in the bay in warm choppy water with a red-haired crew, salt spray, sandwiches, "roaring back" on Route 128 in a convertible.

August 25, 6:30 a.m.: Ira Scott calls.

Sleeps until 9:30 a.m., "leisurely breakfast," laundry, sunbathing, picnic at Crane Beach in Ipswich, Massachusetts.

5:00 p.m.: Dinner with Ira at the Crane estate near Crane Beach, a sunken garden, daiquiris, lobster Newburg, "unexpected Gordon [Lameyer] & Reese Thornton & mother."

Ira calls.

August 26: Shops for bread and milk, deposits check, picks up prescription.

Noon: Meets Ira Scott for coffee, lunch at the restaurant Meadows with daiquiris and steak while it rains.

Calls Aunt Dot, reads *Smith Review*, *Harper's*, listens to music, late supper.

August 27: In the sun, types a letter to her mother, visits Do Cruikshank, reads J. D. Salinger, veal dinner with Gordon Lameyer.

8:30 p.m.: "Long good talk"—"consider domination, paternalism, sadism."

August 28: Late breakfast with Gordon Lameyer, visit from Patsy O'Neil, reads Carson McCullers's short stories, listens to records, late chicken dinner, makes pudding and cakes, goes to bed.

Diary memoranda section—reminder to write to Bob Cochran and Ruth M., call Dr. Beuscher about next appointment, call the Cantors, Aunt Dot, and Pat.

August 29: Sunbathes all day, breakfasts, reads in backyard with Gordon Lameyer, listens to records, steak dinner with peas, macaroni and cheese, eats a sandwich after a "mutual shower," mentions "conflict at Mrs's [Gordon's mother's home]," drives home.

August 30: Deposits check, visits neighbor Betty Aldrich, shops for milk, lettuce, cakes, reads *Love Is a Bridge*,[533] window shops, sees the O'Neils, corn on the cob for supper, washes hair, "story inspiration."

Letter to "dearest mother": Mentions cooking meals for Gordon Lameyer, listening to records, Dr. Beuscher in a session that "lasted longer than usual . . ."[534] I do love her, she is such a delightful woman, and I feel that I am learning so much from her." Concentrates on discovering her "real capabilities" as a writer.

August 31: Deposits check, buys an issue of *Harper's*.

9:30 a.m.: Dental appointment.

Hurricane, calls the Cantors, reads *Writer's Digest*, writes "Insolent storm strike at the skull" by candlelight on a stormy day.

September 1: Lunch and a bull session at the Cruikshanks[535] with Bill and Do, cleanup after hurricane wreckage, packs, drives to Cambridge for cocktails at the Band Box with Candy (Bolster?) and Lou Healy—"grrr."

Letter to "dearest mother": safe after the hurricane, busy shopping, cleaning, entertaining Gordon Lameyer.

September 2: Cleans apartment, mails poems to "YR, LHJ, NY & SEP."[536] Shops, meets John Stamper and Gordon Lameyer for daiquiris at the Merry-Go-Round Bar in the Sheraton Hotel, a tuna and cheese casserole for dinner with Joan Smith, John, and Gordon, concluding a "delightful evening of talk & wine."

September 3: Sleeps until noon, brunch, packs.

3:30 p.m.: Subway to Charlestown Navy Yard in Boston where Gordon Lameyer is stationed, goes with him to the Cantors, riding with Lou Ranzini, Sherm Poppin, and Neal Farrel. They stop for supper and a beer and spend the evening with Warren at the Cantors.

September 4: "Ecstatic day"—long leisurely breakfast at the Cantors, two motorboat trips to Outer Bar at the Cape, "bracing swim in iced champagne surf," "enormous picnic" with hotdogs, hamburgers, cake, grapes, and lemonade. Naps, dance at Chatham Bars Inn—"warm rapport & delightful whirl with gordon."

Diary memoranda section—"call Cantor, Pat, deposit check."

September 5: Long, lazy breakfast at the Cantors, Christian Science service, to Andrew Hardings Beach, long walk with Gordon Lameyer—"afternoon of leisure" with turkey sandwiches, a hot bath, babysits two Cantor children, Billy and Susan, with Gordon.

September 6, 6:00 a.m.: Rides with Mother, Grammy, and Gordon to Hyannis, Massachusetts, rides back to Cambridge with Gordon and Joe Ranzini, a delightful lunch on the USS *Perry*, long talk with John Duggers about Russia, sunbathes on the roof, writes a sonnet: "Suspend This Day."

September 7: Up at 10:00 a.m., note to call Dr. Beuscher.

In the rain, taking care of laundry, shopping downtown.

12:30 p.m.: Gordon Lameyer calls, begins a sonnet: "To the Boy as Inscrutable as God."

5:45 p.m.: Meets Gordon at a park information booth for daiquiris and a lamb chop dinner at the restaurant Joseph's.

Rain reflected in the lights as she meets Mr. Lameyer.

September 8: Note to call Dr. Beuscher, cashes ten-dollar check, writes "Demon of Doom," browses in the Mandrake Bookstore, several beers with James Robert Bell and Gordon.

8:00 p.m.: Spends evening in her apartment with Gordon, a long walk, "good talk in park about life."

1:00 a.m.: In bed.

September 9: Wakes at 11:00 a.m., cashes fifteen-dollar check, shops for food, cooks Toll House cookies, Dave Neldte visits.

6:00 p.m.: Dinner at her apartment with Gordon and his father, serves them sherry, consommé, salad, shrimp casserole, parfait, and coffee.

8:00 p.m.: Sees *Gone with the Wind*.

Beer at the "Wursthaus" (Wurst Haus in Northhampton) with Gordon.

September 10: Washes hair, cashes fifteen-dollar check, manicure, pays "gas light bill, Cantor letter & gift."

Noon: Gordon calls.

Shops on a rainy afternoon, lunch, bourbons, conversation with James Robert Bell, supper with Joan Smith and Peter Davison, evening at Jim's with bourbon and music.

September 11, 11:30 a.m.: Awake, calls her mother.

"Epiphany at breakfast"—orange juice, Danish, hot coffee, listens to music on radio during "hurricane rain."

5:00 p.m.: Marcia Brown and her husband Mike call, subway to USS *Perry*, on Gordon's ship, watches movie in his cabin, reads.

Mentions "Joe Ranzini & accordion! Fred Carleton & henchmen," bourbons, moonlit walk.

6:00 p.m.: In bed.

September 12, noon: Wakes up, "lackadaisical" lunch, finishes sonnet, "Ennui," on subway to visit Jane Anderson.

2:00–5:00 p.m.: Extended session with Dr. Beuscher.

8:00 p.m.: Drives to the Navy Yard with Marcia and Mike Brown, talks over coffee with Gordon Lameyer, Reese Thornton.

September 13: In Widener Library, looking for books on psychology and Dostoevsky, shops on a beautiful sunny day with clear blue skies and "crisping leaves" with vivid colors, Phil McCurdy visits, dinner with Gordon Lameyer, Reese Thornton, and Joe Ranzini—spaghetti, anchovies, salad, garlic bread, wine, bourbon, "convivial vivacity & warmth."

September 14, 8:30 a.m.: Awakes, sends poems to the *New Yorker* on a cold, wet, gray morning.

Breakfast with Joan Smith, Phil McCurdy calls, "piano escapade in Lou Healy's apartment," walks "in sunlight" along Memorial Drive in Cambridge, reads "Promethean Will."[537]

September 15: "Over analysis on the small living experience basis."

7:15 a.m.: Packs, prepares to leave Cambridge apartment.

Appointment with Dr. Beuscher.

2:00 p.m.: "Packed and talked with Gordon [Lameyer] & Sid."

Dinner at home with Gordon, calls Patsy, unpacks.

September 16: Late breakfast, lunch with Warren, packs books for return to Smith, calls Phil McCurdy, cleans her room, buys a gray jumper, goes to the bank.

8:30 a.m.: "Dr's Apt.—Fran—nose hacked at pouring rainy night."

September 17: Finishes reading *Psychology and the Promethean Will* (1936) by William Sheldon, writes to *Seventeen*, graduate schools, Ruth M.,[538] packs clothes and books.

7:30 p.m.: A "long evening of good talk" with Patsy, Gordon Lameyer, and Mr. Crockett.

September 18, 9:30 a.m.: Appointment with Dr. Beuscher—"grand talk—'trust not merely men but be.'"

Subway to Boston, "accident—blood."

Noon: Anthony (hairdresser?), "Circle 7–8454, 93 Mass Ave."

5:00 p.m.: "Hair dyed brown."

5:30 p.m.: Calls Fran.

Dinner with Mrs. Lameyer and Gordon.

Diary memoranda Section—"Read Alpha notes," "hair dye?" "Rearrange Courses."

Sends poems to the *New Yorker*—"Circus in Three Rings," "Ennui," "Boy Inscrutable as God," and "Suspend the Day"—and notes "Bill: Dr. B to ins. co."

September 19: Meets Shirley and Perry Norton.

11:00 a.m.: With Mother, listens to sermon in church—"Exceeding Expectations."

1:00 p.m.: Dinner at Mrs. Prouty's with good talk about poetry and writing, coffee after dinner, a look at the *Stella Dallas* scrapbook.

September 20: Talks with Warren.

2:00 p.m.: Drives to Smith through the autumn countryside turning scarlet, pizza dinner at Little Italy with Warren and Joan Smith, unpacks.

Letter to Gordon Lameyer: pastes pictures of herself taken as guest editor at *Mademoiselle* and the comments on them, including one by a man who says to her "you always look as if you were going to cry even when you are laughing."

Greeting card to Gordon with several lines meant to amuse—about people "somewhat fey," who are "bundles of nerves" with "strange complexes" and the "wrong reflexes," etc.

Solicits faculty recommendations for Fulbright application, alludes to dying her hair blonde again with comments like "It makes your eyes look browner!"

September 21, 8:00 a.m.: Breakfast.

9:00 a.m.: Attendance at chapel, meeting of seniors in Sage Hall.

Noon: Honors meeting, appointment with Professor Gladys Amelia Anslow to get Fulbright application.

8:00 p.m.: Calls William Graham Cole, chaplain and assistant professor of religion.

10:15 p.m.: Waitress meeting.

Note to call professors Anslow, Drew, and Arvin.

Letter to "Dear mother": reports on settling into a charming room, concerned about getting her German underway and her Dostoevsky thesis, breakfast shift for waitressing.

September 22, 7:00–8:00 a.m.: BW.

9:30 a.m.: At the library.

Sees Dr. Booth, registers.

12:00–1:00 p.m.: Bells.

2:00–4:00 p.m.: Meets with Professor Arvin and Professor Page at Tyler House.

2:30–3:30 p.m.: Shops.

Writes Macy Gerson Feingold, a Jewish friend of the Plaths.[539]

7:00–9:15 p.m.: In the library.

September 23, 7:00–8:00 a.m.: BW.

8:00–11:00 a.m.: German.

Works in library on senior thesis, including researching article on *The Double* (1846) by Fyodor Dostoevsky.

Noon: Shakespeare class.

2:00–6:00 p.m.: Buys books for German and Shakespeare classes.

Finishes work on *The Double*.

7:00–10:00 p.m.: Washes hair and studies German.

September 24, 7:00–8:00 a.m.: BW.

8:00–11:00 a.m.: German.

Noon: Shakespeare class.

2:00 p.m.: Conference with Professor Gibian, her thesis advisor, about graduate school plans.

3:00 p.m.: Conference with Professor Drew about her thesis and Oxford.

7:00–10:00 p.m.: Translates German.

9:00 p.m.: Letter to "dearest mother": worried about her mother teaching in the evening since she will have no time to rest, notes that Dr. Booth and Dr. Beuscher won't mention her "lapse" at McLean on her Fulbright application, Sylvia considers that Mrs. Cantor might speak to her "stability," finds German difficult.

Letter to Gordon Lameyer: A "phenomenal number of conference appointments, meetings, and shoppings." Likes Professor Dunn's treatment of Shakespeare in esthetic, political, social, and historical terms, snapshots of Gordon circle her mirror. She has her first cold of the season. Believes her professors writing on her behalf for a Fulbright may "compensate for my mental hospital record." Letter from Dr. Beuscher will leave "no doubt as to the completeness of my cure." Dyes her hair back to brown to "look demure and discreet."

September 25, 7:00–8:00 a.m.: BW.

8:00–11:00 a.m.: German.

Noon: Shakespeare.

Makes note to see Paul Gerald Graham, her German professor.

6:00 p.m.: Dinner at Masters with Al Goldstein, Clement Moore, and Bill Lynn.

9:30 p.m.: A talk with Bill Lynn.

10:00 p.m.: Reads Dostoevsky.

Memoranda—"resign Press Board," scholarship applications for graduate study.

September 26: Talks with Nancy Hunter, reads *The Tales of Hoffmann*.

2:30 p.m.: Looks up F. R. Leavis in library.

Finishes draft of statement of purpose for Fulbright application.

September 27, 7:00–8:00 a.m.: BW.

Doctor's appointment, deposits twenty-two-dollar check in bank.

10:00 a.m.: German.

11:00 a.m.: Purchases German books.

Note to call Mary Ellen Chase.

2:00–5:00 p.m.: Naps.

7:00–10:00 p.m.: Works on statement of purpose for letters of recommendation.

September 28, 7:00–8:00 a.m.: BW.

8:00 a.m.: *Smith Review* meeting.

Sinus cold, infirmary visit.

10:00 a.m.–noon: "Carrells" assigned.

11:00 a.m.–1:00 p.m.: Sends poems to *Atlantic Monthly*.

2:00 p.m.: Reads Dostoevsky's *The Gambler* (1866) and *The Eternal Husband* (1870).

3:30–5:30 p.m.: Meets with Mary Ellen Chase.

7:00–10:00 p.m.: Note to call Jeannie Berkowicz, "called mother."

September 29, 7:00–8:00: BW.

8:30 a.m.: Chapel.

10:00 a.m.: German.

11:00 a.m.–noon: Gordon Lameyer visits her in the infirmary.

12:00–1:00 p.m.: Bells.

4:00–6:00 p.m.: "Mass meeting" in John M. Greene Hall.

Supper with Jeannie Berkowicz.

September 30, 7:00–8:00 a.m.: BW.

 8:00–11:00 a.m.: In the infirmary.

 11:00 a.m.: German.

 Noon: Shakespeare.

 1:30 p.m.: *Smith Review* meeting in Green Room.

 10:00 p.m.: House meeting.

October 1, 7:00–8:00 a.m.: BW.

 8:00–11:00 a.m.: "Finish German themes."

 11:00 a.m.: German.

 Noon: Shakespeare.

Meets with Miss Mensel and Professor Anslow.

 2:30 p.m.: Meets with thesis advisor, Professor Gibian.

 5:00 p.m.: Postcard to "dearest mother": Not ideal weather for "sinus victims." Groggy with shots of penicillin and cocaine sprays, cheered by Gordon's visit to her in the infirmary, auditing a course on Johann Wolfgang von Goethe, hopes her mother's medical tests "show you to be a paragon of potential longevity."

 7:00 p.m.: Walks to a waterfall with Gordon Lameyer, studies at library, beer and sandwich at Rahar's pizzeria.

October 2, 7:00–8:00 a.m.: BW.

 8:00–11:00 a.m.: Studies for German quiz.

 11:00 a.m.: German class.

 Noon: Shakespeare class with Gordon in attendance.

Lunch at Lawrence House, a walk on a hot and humid day to a hilltop to look at the colorful foliage and "smoke purple mountains," a walk after seeing *An American in Paris*.[540]

Diary memoranda Section—*Smith Review* subscriptions, note to write to Cantors, Ira Scott, Mrs. Prouty, and "Alpha letters to Tucker."

"Clear, cold, exquisite black night with <u>frozen moon</u>."

October 3: Sleeps until 10:30 a.m., coffee at Toto's with Nancy Hunter.

 Noon: Gordon arrives for a talk.

 1:00 p.m.: Dinner, coffee with Gordon.

 2:30 p.m.: In library with Gordon.

 6:00 p.m.: Supper at Little Italy.

 7:00 p.m.: Studies German.

October 4, 7:00–8:00 a.m.: BW.

 8:00–10:00 a.m.: Works on German paper.

 10:00–11:00 a.m.: German class.

 11:00 a.m.: Meets with Professor Anslow "& Do [Cruikshank]," *Smith Review* subscriptions.

Laundry, writes letter to Cambridge University,[541] a note to call Warren.

7:00–10:00 p.m.: Pajama party.

Postcard to "Dear Mother": catching up on sleep and homework, wishes her mother could have a holiday and recuperate from her hospital stay with friends and relatives.

October 5, 7:00–8:00 a.m.: BW.

8:00–10:00 a.m.: "MOUNTAIN DAY," out for crew practice.

10:00–11:00 a.m.: German class.

11:00 a.m.–1:00 p.m.: Lunch, trip to drugstore for medicine.

2:00–6:00 p.m.: Works on German paper and translations.

Tea with Sue Weller, supper with Dorrie Licht.

Letter to "Dearest mother": vows to "learn German or perish," regrets that she never spoke the language at home.

Letter to Gordon Lameyer: Tells him how charming everyone thinks he is. She is anemic and is taking iron. Enjoys the pull of crewing—"really potent!" Wishes she had more time to write poetry.

October 6, 7:00–8:00 a.m.: BW.

8:30 a.m.: Chapel.

9:00–10:00 a.m.: Works on German translations.

10:00–11:00 a.m.: German class.

11:00 a.m.–noon: Meets with Professor Page.

12:00–1:00 p.m.: Bells.

October 7, 7:00–8:00 a.m.: BW.

8:00–11:00 a.m.: Studies Shakespeare, cleans her room.

11:00 a.m.: German class.

Noon: Shakespeare class.

2:00–6:00 p.m.: Reads Poe's "William Wilson" and *Strange Case of Dr. Jekyll and Mr. Hyde* for senior thesis.

10:00 p.m.: House meeting.

October 8, 7:00–8:00 a.m.: BW.

8:00 a.m.: Crew practice.

9:00–11:00 a.m.: German homework.

11:00 a.m.: German class.

Noon: Shakespeare class.

1:30 p.m.: "Race."

2:30 p.m.: Meets with Professor Gibian about thesis.

3:00–4:00 p.m.: Meets with Professor Drew.

5:00–6:00 p.m.: German tea.

7:00–10:00 p.m.: Finishes Fulbright and Oxford applications.

Letter to Gordon Lameyer: Writes "every night I vow to go to bed early it seems that some imp of the perverse manages to fix it otherwise." Finds crewing invigorating, works on first chapter of thesis while wearing his sailor hat—"I am very happy in spite of the fact that I have so much work to do."

October 9, 7:00–8:00 a.m.: BW.

9:00 a.m.: Crew practice.

10:00–11:00 a.m.: Prepares for German class.

11:00 a.m.: German class.

Noon: Shakespeare class.

1:45–3:00 p.m.: Bells.

3:00–6:00 p.m.: Warren and Kathy Preston, Al and Pat visit.

7:00–10:00 p.m.: Reads a psychology article on Dostoevsky, takes notes on *The Double*.

Diary memoranda section—note to write to Cantors, Mrs. Prouty, consult with Professor Drew about statement of purpose, "U. specimen," and work on *Smith Review* subscriptions.

October 10, 8:30–9:30 a.m.: Reads Russian literature.

Coffee with Warren.

10:00–10:30 a.m.: Crew practice.

11:00 a.m.–1:00 p.m.: Rereads *The Double*.

1:00 p.m.: Dinner with Warren and Al.

3:00–5:30 p.m.: Works on thesis.

6:30–10:00 p.m.: Reads *The Tales of Hoffmann*.

Letter to Gordon Lameyer: "I am so inclined to introversion, and therefore must overbalance toward actual living in order to come out anywhere near even!" Expects to write an "adolescent story about doubles" after she completes her thesis—"every incident in my life begins to smack of the mirror image."

October 11, 7:00–8:00 a.m.: BW.

8:00–8:30 a.m.: Crew practice.

10:00 a.m.: Studies German.

11:00 a.m.–1:00 p.m.: Writes to Warren and Gordon.[542]

1:30 p.m.: Crew practice.

2:00–5:00 p.m.: Reads *Through the Looking-Glass* (1872) by Lewis Carroll.

5:00 p.m.: Crew practice.

7:00–10:00 p.m.: Reads *The Picture of Dorian Gray* (1890) by Oscar Wilde, takes notes on *Monsieur du Miroir* (1837) by Nathaniel Hawthorne.

In her last year at Smith, Plath began to think of studying in England for the same reason she had left home and attended Smith: to challenge herself and to grow beyond her origins.

October 12, 7:00–8:00 a.m.: BW.

8:00 a.m.: Crew race.

8:50 a.m.: Senior pictures in Davis Hall.

9:00–10:00 a.m.: Studies German.

10:00–11:00 a.m.: German class.

11:00 a.m.–1:00 p.m.: Letter to "Dearest mother": Pleased to get newsy and cheerful letter, worries about Warren, who seems "vague and negative too much of the time," stresses importance of her "healthy bohemianism" period that disrupted a "clock-regular, responsible" manner. Warren needs a social life, change of scene, companions to prod him out of his "introverted habits." As for herself, "if only england would by some miracle come through, I would be forced shivering into a new, unfamiliar world, where I had to forge anew friends and a home for myself, and although such experiences are painful and awkward at first, I know, intellectually, that they are the best things to make one grow."

1:30–3:30 p.m.: Takes notes on Yakov Petrovich Golyadkin, the protagonist in *The Double*.

3:30–4:30 p.m.: Meets with Mary Ellen Chase.

7:00–10:00 p.m.: Notes on Golyadkin, house meeting.

October 13, 7:00–8:00 a.m.: BW.

8:30 a.m.: Chapel.

10:00–11:00 a.m.: German.

11:00 a.m.–noon: Talks to Mary Ellen Chase about letter of recommendation.

12:00–1:00 p.m.: Bells.

2:00–4:00 p.m.: Meets with Alfred Kazin.

4:00 p.m.: *Smith Review* meeting in Sage Hall.

6:00 p.m.: Supper with Jeannie Berkowicz and Martha Wilson.

7:30–10:00 p.m.: Professor Sonnenfeld.

October 14, 7:00–8:00 a.m.: BW.

Cleans her room.

8:00–11:00 a.m.: Studies German.

11:00 a.m.–noon: German class.

12:00–1:00 p.m.: Shakespeare class.

2:00–4:00 p.m.: Meeting in dean's office, studies for German exam.

4:00–5:00 p.m.: Meets with Professor Daniel Aaron about the notion of doubles and her thesis.

7:00–10:00 p.m.: Studies for German exam.

10:00 p.m.: House meeting.

Letter to "dearest mother": Discouraged that she is getting no better than a B in German. A late period has made her feel "very blue," plus a cold has "thrown" her off, but she is more cheerful now. Explains her interest in Dostoevsky and doubles.

October 15, 7:00–8:00 a.m.: BW.

    8:00–11:00 a.m.: Studies for German exam.

    11:00 a.m.: One hour German exam.

    12:00–1:00 p.m.: Shakespeare class.

    2:00 p.m.: Earns two dollars and thirty cents proofreading. Writes up Kazin interview.

    4:00–6:00 p.m.: In dean's office, tea.

    7:30 p.m.: Meets Gordon Lameyer.

    8:00–10:00 p.m.: In library, a talk with Gordon.

October 16, 7:00–8:00 a.m.: BW.

    8:00 a.m.–noon: Reads Shakespeare.

    12:00–1:00 p.m.: Shakespeare class.

    2:00–6:00 p.m.: Studies Russian literature, Freud, meets Gordon in Amherst for dinner, they hitchhike to visit Ruth Freeman for an evening at Phi Psi.

Diary memoranda section—reminder to type statement of purpose for Oxford, note to see Professor Aaron, work on Kazin article.

October 17: Coffee with Gordon Lameyer, sweeps front stairs, walks with Gordon to Paradise Pond, dinner, coffee, plays piano at home.

    3:00 p.m.: "Apple cider & Dixie-Imperial Jazz band concert." Works in library.

    6:00–8:00 p.m.: Supper at coffee shop.

    9:30–11:30 p.m.: Reads Freud.

October 18, 7:00–8:00 a.m.: BW.

    8:00–10:00 a.m.: Reads Russian literature, Freud.

    10:00–11:00 a.m.: Studies German.

    3:45–5:45 p.m.: Reads Hellenic history to blind Smith professor, William Dodge Gray.

    7:00–10:00 p.m.: Babysits, reads Dostoevsky.

Postcard to "Dear mother": describes outings with Gordon Lameyer.

October 19, 7:00–8:00 a.m.: BW.

    8:00–10:00 a.m.: Purchases German books. Laundry, studies German.

    11:00 a.m.–1:00 p.m.: "Write [Professor] Drew."

    2:00–6:00 p.m.: Sees Mary Ellen Chase, Kazin interview, babysits.

    8:00–10:00 p.m.: Reads Russian literature, works on Kazin article.

October 20, 7:00–8:00 a.m.: BW.

    8:30 a.m.: Chapel.

    10:00 a.m.–noon: Studies German and Golyadkin.

    12:00–1:00: p.m. Bells, studies German.

    1:30–3:30 p.m.: Studies German.

7:30–10:30 p.m.: "German: Sonnenfeld."

October 21, 7:00–8:00 a.m.: BW.

8:00–11:00 a.m.: Cleans room.

12:00–1:00 p.m.: Cuts Shakespeare class, calls Professor Gibian.

3:30 p.m.: Washes hair.

7:30 p.m.–midnight: Types paper on Golyadkin.

October 22, 7:00–8:00 a.m.: BW.

8:00–11:00 a.m.: Works on German translations.

11:00 a.m.–noon: German class.

12:00–1:00 p.m.: Shakespeare class.

1:30 p.m.: Coffee with Elinor Friedman.

2:00–4:00 p.m.: "Kazin."

2:30 p.m.: First chapter of thesis on *The Double* due to Professor Gibian.

4:00 p.m.: At the Freemans'.

5:30 p.m.: Bus to Amherst.

10:00 p.m.–4:00 a.m.: Works on Golyadkin paper.

October 23, 8:00 a.m.–2:00 p.m.: Cuts classes, types Golyadkin paper.

2:30 p.m.: Conference with Professor Gibian on thesis.

Climbs Mount Tom with Gordon Lameyer, steak dinner with Dee (Nadine Newburg Doughty) and John Duggers.

Diary memoranda section:—note to call Kazin, work on Golyadkin chapter, letters for Professor Chase and Professor Drew.

October 24: Breakfast and bull session with Nancy Hunter, reads *Smith Review* material.

1:00 p.m.: Dinner with Gordon Lameyer, reads manuscripts by Paradise Pond.

Talk with Dee.

7:00–10:00 p.m.: Irons shirts.

Letter to "Dearest mother": Excited about interview with Alfred Kazin, very brusque and direct but becomes charming when she tells him about her writing and publications—"he'd thought I was just another pampered smith baby like the rest." He invites her to audit his class, saying "we need you!" Finds it amusing that she is writing about the double while her adviser has twins.

October 25, 7:00–8:00 a.m.: BW.

8:00–11:00 a.m.: German.

11:00 a.m.–1:00 p.m.: "Stories to Kazin."

1:30–3:30 p.m.: German.

3:45 p.m.: Reads to Professor Gray.

Quiz bowl.

October 26, 7:00–8:00 a.m.: BW.

8:00–11:00 a.m.: German.

11:00 a.m.–12:30 p.m.: Writes letters,[543] revisions for Kazin paper, sees Mary Ellen Chase, calls Holyoke College about an application to study at Oxford University.

2:00–6:00 p.m.: "Ger [German] 26 & 12," "German House."[544]

7:00–10:00 p.m.: Copies Shakespeare notes, types paper for Kazin's class.

October 27: "22nd Birthday!"

8:30 a.m.: Chapel.

10:00–11:00 a.m.: German.

12:00–1:00 p.m.: Bells.

1:30–3:00 p.m.: Washes hair, sews, finishes German translations and grammar.

3:00–6:00 p.m.: "Ed board."

7:30 p.m.: German with Professor Sonnenfeld.

10:30 p.m.: "Ger [German] 2- finish."

"Get late permission."[545]

Letter to Gordon Lameyer: "I am tempted to borrow trouble in the way of metaphors and liken myself to an aged eagle who has just been run over by time's winged chariot."

October 28, 7:00–8:00 a.m.: BW.

8:00–11:00 a.m.: Cleans room.

11:00 a.m.–noon: German class.

12:00–1:00 p.m.: Shakespeare class.

1:30–5:30 p.m.: Shakespeare.

Train and bus to Holyoke.

7:06 p.m.: Interview with Professor Joyce Horner about application to Oxford.

October 29, 7:00–8:00 a.m.: BW.

8:00–11:00 a.m.: Works on Shakespeare in library, checking secondary sources.

11:00 a.m.–noon: German class.

12:00–1:00 p.m.: Shakespeare class.

2:00–4:00 p.m.: Works on paper for Kazin class.

4:00–6:00 p.m.: Reads Shakespeare in the library.

October 30, 7:00–8:00 a.m.: BW.

8:00–11:00 a.m.: Reads Shakespeare in the library.

11:00 a.m.–noon: German class.

12:00–1:00 p.m.: Shakespeare class.

1:45–3:00 p.m.: Bells.

3:00–6:00 p.m.: Studies Shakespeare, German, works on thesis. Washes hair.

7:00 p.m.: Writes story, "Broken Glass," for Kazin.

Diary memoranda section—Kazin paper, Shakespeare question, reminders to write to Mrs. Prouty, Alison Claiborne Phillips, Marcia Brown, Ira Scott, and Mrs. Lameyer.

October 31: Works on thesis, reads literary criticism, coffee at Toto's with Warren, dinner with Kathy Preston and Warren, meets Edwin Akutowicz at Rahar's for a beer and "afternoon of dubious macchiavelian merit."

9:00–11:00 p.m.: Sherman reading.

November 1, 7:00–8:00 a.m.: BW.

8:00–10:00 a.m.: Reads German.

10:00–11:00 a.m.: German class.

11:00 a.m.–1:00 p.m.: Reads Shakespeare, Dostoevsky.

3:30 p.m.: Reads to Professor Gray.

7:00–11:30 p.m.: Shakespeare, writes Prix de Paris article.

November 2, 7:00–8:00 a.m.: BW.

8:00–10:00 a.m.: Shakespeare.

1:30 p.m.: *Smith Review* meeting.

2:00–6:00 p.m.: "Shakespeare—[Raphael] Holinshed."

5:30 p.m.: Letter to "Dear mother": Appreciates "delicious cookies" that she nibbles on while studying, mentions Professor Gray—"I do feel that this dear old Dickensian man looks most forward to my Monday afternoons with him: we get along very well." Describes Edwin Akutowicz as "very peculiar, archaic, but amusing."

7:00–10:00 p.m.: "Plays—Eliz—life."

November 3, 7:00–8:00 a.m.: BW.

8:00 a.m.–noon: Shakespeare.

12:00–1:00 p.m.: Bells.

1:30–3:30 p.m.: "KAZIN," *Richard II* (ca. 1595), and Holinshed. Supper with Professor Gibian.

7:30–10:30 p.m.: "Sonnenfeld—German—late permission" (extra tutoring).

November 4, 7:00–8:00 a.m.: BW.

8:30 a.m.: Attends chapel.

9:00–11:00 a.m.: Cleans room, types German paper.

11:00 a.m.–noon: German class.

12:00–1:00 p.m.: Shakespeare class.

4:00–6:00 p.m., 7:00–10:00 p.m.: Studies Shakespeare. House meeting.

Letter to Gordon Lameyer: Her favorite class—"the great god alfred's," says Gordon's letters are "magnificent," she is happy he visited her brother, she is "beat but beatific" as Kazin admonishes her that it is her "holy duty to write every day, spill out all, learn to give it form, and is going to let me go off on my own every week, only asking that I turn in lots and lots and not to bother with the regular class assignment. He is extremely critical and encouraging, and the fortuitous accident of interviewing him is something I'll praise fortune for all my life long. I adore him!"

November 5, 7:00–8:00 a.m.: BW.

8:00–11:00 a.m.: Studies Shakespeare.

11:00 a.m.–noon: German class.

12:00–1:00 p.m.: One hour Shakespeare exam.

3:00–5:00 p.m.: Studies German, Shakespeare.

8:00 p.m.: Party for Professor Chase.

"Bull session: Lou."

November 6, 7:00–8:00 a.m.: BW.

8:00–11:00 a.m.: Studies German.

11:00 a.m.–noon: German class.

12:00–1:00 p.m.: Shakespeare class

2:00–3:30 p.m.: Bikes with Sue Weller to Connecticut River, rides with Fred in an airplane at La Fleur Airport over "magnificent countryside."

7:00–10:00 p.m.: Begins "Superman" story.

Sandwich with Lynn.

Memoranda—reminder to write Claiborne Phillips, Prentice Smith, Ruth A.

Letter to Gordon Lameyer: Describes airplane adventure with "all the little planes lined up looking like gaudy painted toy gliders, and that Icarian lust came upon me again." She takes flight, "the shadow is parting from the earth, me screaming about how this is the fourth dimension and god isn't it a fantastic day. . . . All very naughty and dashing." Enchanting evening at the Hampshire Bookshop with Chase and the illustrator of her book, *The White Gate* (1955), who writes the "warmest inscription in my book."

November 7, 9:00 a.m.–1:00 p.m.: Types first draft of Superman story, reads *Harper's* and the *New Yorker*.

1:00 p.m.: Dinner.

3:00–5:30 p.m.: Works on Superman story.

7:00–9:00 p.m.: Coffee and talk with Jon K. Rosenthal at Little Italy.

November 8, 7:00–8:00 a.m.: BW.

8:00–10:00 a.m.: Studies German.

10:00–11:00 a.m.: German class.

11:00 a.m.–1:00 p.m.: Meets Ray Wunderlich at coffee shop.

1:30–3:15 p.m.: Reads *Brothers Karamazov* (1879–1880).

3:30 p.m.: Reads to Professor Gray.

5:30 p.m.: Supper at German house.

7:00–10:00 p.m.: Washes hair and reads Dostoevsky.

November 9, 7:00–8:00 a.m.: BW.

9:30 a.m.: Note to call Professor Gibian to discuss Ivan Karamazov—a character from *Brothers Karamazov*—and the critics of Dostoevsky and to call Mary Ellen Chase about Cambridge exam.

Lunch with Professor Gray.

2:00–6:00 p.m.: Studies German, works on thesis.

Supper with Professor Gibian.

8:00 p.m.: Attends lecture by journalist Marguerite Higgins.

November 10, 7:00–8:00 a.m.: BW.

8:30–9:00 a.m.: Attends chapel.

12:00–1:00 p.m.: Bells.

3:00 p.m.: Meets with Kazin.

4:00–6:00 p.m.: Studies German.

Dinner with Jon Rosenthal.

November 11, 7:00–8:00 a.m.: BW.

8:00–11:00 a.m.: Cleans room, studies German.

11:00 a.m.–noon: German class.

12:00–1:00 p.m.: Shakespeare class.

2:00–4:00 p.m.: Meets with Kazin.

Coffee at Toto's with Friedman.

5:00–6:00 p.m., 7:00–10:00 p.m.: Washes hair, studies for German exam.

Postcard to "Dear mother": mentions all the work she had to do, appointments with Dr. Beuscher, calls the questions on her exam for Cambridge "so general that it would have taken a year to answer anywhere near properly," asks her mother to write to the warden at Smith so that she can "go up in planes."

November 12, 7:00–8:00 a.m.: BW.

8:00–11:00 a.m.: Studies German.

11:00 a.m.–noon: One hour German exam.

12:00–1:00 p.m.: Shakespeare class.

2:00–4:00 p.m.: Meets with Alfred Kazin.

7:00–10:00 p.m.: Reads Dostoevsky, bull session with Pat.

November 13, 7:00–8:00: BW.

8:00–10:00 a.m.: Meets with Professor Sonnenfeld.

10:00 a.m.–noon: At German House.

12:00–1:00 p.m.: Shakespeare class.

2:00–4:00 p.m.: Reads Dostoevsky.

7:00–10:00 p.m.: Meets Gordon Lameyer.

Letter to "Dearest mother": a "wonderful year" working "under a healthy tension."

November 14: Begins writing a poem on "analysis and 'cold moons.'"[546]

1:00 p.m.: Sunday dinner with Gordon Lameyer, "long talk" with him "all afternoon about domination," supper afterwards at Toto's coffee shop.

November 15, 7:00–8:00 a.m.: BW.

8:15 a.m.: Senior meeting in Sage Hall.

9:00–10:00 a.m.: "Delivery job."

10:00–11:00 a.m.: German.

11:00 a.m.–1:00 p.m.: Studies Dostoevsky.

Note to call Nadia and Dr. Booth.

2:00 p.m.: "Transcript Miss [Professor]Page Dean's O."

3:00–3:30 p.m.: "Collect 1.20 scholarship."

3:30 p.m.: Reads to Professor Gray.

7:00–10:00 p.m.: "Poem."

November 16, 7:00–8:00 a.m.: BW.

8:00 a.m.: "Nadia."

10:00 a.m.: German.

10:00–11:00 a.m.: "Xray—Gym."

11:00 a.m.–1:00 p.m.: Writes poem, "Ice Age."

2:00–6:00 p.m., 7:00–10:00 p.m.: "Sassoon dostoevsky."

November 17, 9:00 a.m.–noon: German, Dostoevsky.

12:00–1:00 p.m.: Bells.

2:30 p.m.: Meets with Kazin.

7:00–11:00 p.m.: "Miss Sonnenfeld German—Late permission."

November 18, 7:00–8:00 a.m.: BW.

8:00–11:00 a.m.: Cleans room, repairs bike, studies Dostoevsky and German, meets Professor Page, Dr. Booth, finishes "Karamazov Outline."

11:00 a.m.–noon: German class.

12:00–1:00 p.m.: Shakespeare class.

2:00–3:00 p.m.: Kazin's class.

3:00–6:00 p.m., 7:00–10:00 p.m.: At coffee shop reading Dostoevsky, washes hair.

10:00 p.m.: House meeting.

November 19, 7:00–8:00 a.m.: BW.

8:00–11:00 a.m.: Studies German, Dostoevsky.

11:00 a.m.–noon: German class.

12:00–1:00 p.m.: Shakespeare class.

2:00–6:00 p.m.: Reads critics on Ivan Karamazov.

8:00 p.m.: Performance of *Twelfth Night* (ca. 1601–1602).

November 20, 7:00–8:00 a.m.: BW.

8:00–11:00 a.m.: Studies German.

11:00 a.m.–noon: German Class.

12:00–1:00 p.m.: Shakespeare class.

2:00–6:00 p.m., 7:00–10:00 p.m.: Naps, reads critics on Dostoevsky.

Diary memoranda section—reminders to write to Prentice Smith, Ruth A., Ann D., and the Sullivans.

November 21: Writes Ivan Karamazov chapter.

November 22: Kazin, paper, Shakespeare's *Henry IV* (ca. 1597–1599).

7:00–8:00 a.m.: BW.

8:00–10:00 a.m.: Types Ivan Karamazov chapter.

10:00–11:00 a.m.: Studies German.

11:00 a.m.–1:00 p.m.: Meets with Professor Gibian about Ivan Karamazov chapter.

3:30 p.m.: Reads to Professor Gray.

Writes Sullivans, Prentice Smith, and Ruth A.[547]

8:00 p.m.: Letter to "dearest Gordon [Lameyer]": Nearly sleepless after typing forty pages of her thesis, wants to be friends whether or not he decides to marry someone else. Most of Thanksgiving will be taken up with reading and writing, lining up another appointment with Dr. Beuscher.

November 23, 7:00–8:00 a.m.: BW.

9:45 a.m.: In the infirmary.

10:00–11:00 a.m.: Studies German.

11:00 a.m.–1:00 p.m.: Session with Professor Sonnenfeld.

2:00–6:00 p.m.: To Holyoke for interview about scholarship to Oxford.

7:00–10:00 p.m.: Works on "the double" in Dostoevsky for her senior thesis.

"Charmers Double in D—1933 to Gibian."

Letter to Ann Davidow: Looking forward to one of their "real talks." Reading Freud, *The Golden Bough*, E. T. A. Hoffmann's weird fairy tales for her thesis. Looking forward to end of January, finishing her thesis and exams, and a few days in New York City. "I know exactly what you mean when you say you love your work, but not necessarily what you produce." Over fifty rejections, but "I'm pigheaded and keep on sending out stuff!"

November 24, 7:00–8:00 a.m.: BW.

"Gibian: double: 1929 article."

9:00 a.m.: "Kazin."

10:00–11:00 a.m.: Studies German.

11:00 a.m.: Meets with Dr. Booth.

12:30 p.m.: "Thanksgiving—Bob Prynne vacation—drive home in rain."

"Call Beuscher," "Gordon [Lameyer]—roses & candy! Dinner & talk."

November 25, 10:00 a.m.: Awakes to turkey liver and bacon breakfast, a talk with Mother, Gordon Lameyer, Warren, and Steve Clark at dinner.

Does dishes with Gordon, reads, drowses, talks, supper with Warren and Steve, reads *Notes from the Underground* (1864).

November 26: Shops in Wellesley, at Filene's in Boston for "lingerie, etc."

1:00 p.m.: Hair appointment at Anthony's.

1:30–4:00 p.m.: At Adams House, Harvard, dinner with Warren and Phil McCurdy at Luigi's, meets Ira Scott at Widener Library, they drive to Old Colonial Inn in Concord to drink "champagne!"

November 27: "Need for being & experiencing—who knows what's 'good' in the long run anyhow? Trial & error."

10:30 a.m.: Has a "wonderful talk" with Dr. Beuscher about "maturity—necessity of paradox—need for wait for 'ebb-tide'—look up 'Psychology & Promethean Will' for sustenance."

Memoranda—notes to see Dr. Beuscher, call Pat Tschiżewskij,[548] Mr. Crockett, and the Cantors. List of items to purchase: slippers, brush and combs, girdle, "bra?," stockings, slip, blouse. Reminder to "rewrite Golyadkin chapter" and note on "Kazin story."

November 28, 11:30 a.m.–2:25 p.m.: A drive to Framingham with Gordon Lameyer.

2:35 p.m.: Meets Richard Sassoon for cognac on Mount Tom.

3:00 p.m.: Long drive to Greenfield, Massachusetts, for a steak and shrimp dinner at "Elite Cafe—all very lovely."

November 29, 7:00–8:00 a.m.: BW.

8:00–10:00 a.m.: Works on Golyadkin chapter.

10:00–11:00 a.m.: German.

11:00 a.m.–1:00 p.m.: Writes introduction to thesis.

3:30–6:00 p.m.: Reads to Professor Gray.

November 30, 7:00–8:00 a.m.: BW.

10:00–11:00 a.m.: German with Professor Sonnenfeld.

1:30 p.m.: "Alpha meeting in Davis Ballroom."

2:00–6:00 p.m., 7:00–10:30 p.m.: Rewrites first chapter of thesis.

December 1, 7:00–8:00 a.m.: BW.

8:30 a.m.: Chapel.

9:00 a.m.–noon: Studies German, attends German classes.

12:00–1:00 p.m.: Bells.

"Nina paper[549] & translation 'The Opera house of Parma: Stendahl.'"

8:00 p.m.: "Kazin lecture."

Letter to "Dearest mother": wants her mother to ask Mrs. Cantor to recommend her for a Woodrow Wilson Fellowship.

December 2, 7:00–8:00 a.m.: BW.

8:00–11:00 a.m.: Cleans room.

11:00 a.m.–noon: German class.

12:00–1:00 p.m.: Shakespeare class.

2:00–6:00 p.m., 7:00–10:00 p.m.: Writes Kazin paper, washes hair.

Letter to Jon Rosenthal: describes her holiday, praises his poetic letter, considering a holiday in Vermont skiing or the culture of New York City—perhaps they could arrange a meeting?

December 3, 7:00–8:00 a.m.: BW.

8:00–9:30 a.m.: Studies German.

9:30–11:00 a.m.: Finishes writing Kazin paper.

11:00 a.m.–noon: German class.

12:00–1:00 p.m.: Shakespeare class.

2:00–4:00 p.m.: Types Kazin paper.

4:00 p.m.: Coffee and cakes with Kazin.

7:00–9:15 p.m.: "50 Paradise Ger [German] 12 Mrs. K. [Kazin?]."

9:15–10:30 p.m.: Bells.

December 4, 7:00–8:00 a.m.: BW.

8:00 a.m.–noon: Studies German and attends class.

10:30 a.m.: Turns in revised Golyadkin chapter to Professor Gibian, who returns chapter on Ivan Karamazov.

12:00–1:00 p.m.: Shakespeare class.

3:00–6:00 p.m.: "Clai Simmons."

"Superman to NY."

7:00–10:00 p.m.: "Bull session" with Claiborne Phillips.

Diary memoranda section—notes to rewrite Golyadkin chapter, work on Kazin and German papers, read *Charterhouse of Parma* (1839), *The Possessed* (1871), *Henry IV*, work on letters for Woodrow Wilson Fellowship.

December 5, 8:00–8:30 a.m.: "Scully" breakfast trays.

10:00 a.m.–1:00 p.m.: Writes to Richard Sassoon,[550] coffee with Clai.

2:00–6:00 p.m.: Begins Kazin story.

7:00–10:00 p.m.: "[Richard] Sassoon & Farmhouse."

December 6, 7:00–8:00 a.m.: BW.

"Grampy's birthday cash $10 check."

8:00 a.m.–1:00 p.m.: Finishes Kazin story.

2:15 p.m.: Meets with Professor Gibian.

2:00–3:30 p.m.: Writes to Richard Sassoon, Warren,[551] and Mother.

3:30 p.m.: Reads to Professor Gray.

5:00 p.m.: Vocational meeting in alumni house.

7:00–10:00 p.m.: "Ger poem."

Letter to "dearest mother": Suffering her periodic cold and sore throat with "doses of codeine," close to finishing thesis with professor's approval, looks forward to writing poetry, short stories, visiting friends, reads "Superman and Paula Brown's Snowsuit" at Kazin's home over "coffee and lovely pastry," pleased to hear about her mother's visits to Mrs. Prouty and Mrs.

Cantor. She is in suspense over submissions to *Atlantic Monthly*: "I love building up my hopes, even though nothing may come of it." If she is admitted to Cambridge University, her "whole life would explode in a rainbow."

December 7, 7:00–8:00 a.m.: BW.

8:00 a.m.–1:00 p.m.: Works on thesis.

10:00 a.m.: Meets with Professor Sonnenfeld.

2:00–6:00 p.m.: Rewrites chapter on Ivan Karamazov, washes hair, cashes check.

7:00–10:00 p.m.: A performance of *For the Time Being* (1944) by W. H. Auden at St. John's.

December 8, 7:00–8:00 a.m.: BW.

Chapel.

9:00 a.m.–noon: Works on German translations.

12:00–1:00 p.m.: Bells.

1:30 p.m.: *Smith Review* meeting.

2:30 p.m.: Meets with Alfred Kazin about letter of recommendation for Woodrow Wilson Fellowship.

5:00 p.m.: *Smith Review* meeting in Sage Hall.

7:15–9:30 p.m.: "Sonnenfeld—German: poem."

Letter to "Dear mother": Looks forward to New York City visit, seeing friends over the holidays, studying and translating Rainer Maria Rilke, Kazin is "an inspiration which comes seldom in a lifetime. And it is so wonderful to know he admires me in return! Oh, yes, I do worship him."

December 9, 7:00–8:00 a.m.: BW.

8:00–11:00 a.m.: Cleans room, reads Shakespeare.

11:00 a.m.–noon: German class.

12:00–1:00 p.m.: Shakespeare class.

3:00–4:00 p.m.: Meets with Kazin.

4:00–5:00 p.m.: In Hatfield Hall.

7:00–10:00 p.m.: Works on thesis conclusion.

Letter to Gordon Lameyer: calls Kazin her "guardian angel," excited about the appearance of "Circus in Three Rings" in *Smith Review*.

December 10, 7:00–8:00 a.m.: BW.

8:00–11:00 a.m.: Studies German, German class.

12:00–1:00 p.m.: Shakespeare class.

2:00–6:00 p.m.: Washes hair, train to New Haven with Sue Weller.

7:00–10:00 p.m.: Drives to New York City.

December 11, 7:00–8:00 a.m.: BW.

8:00–11:00 a.m.: Cuts classes.

12:00–1:00 p.m.: Dinner with Richard Sassoon at Le Veau d'or: "magnificent! Escargot! Chicken—vine rosé!—wonderful rapport—adjoining table of charming absurd people."

Sees *The Bad Seed*[552] by Maxwell Anderson.

Diary memoranda section—note on "poems—[Professor Alfred] Fisher" and to write to Mrs. Cantor and Ira Scott.[553]

December 12: Has a "magnificent" brunch at Steuben's with oysters, stirred eggs, calf's liver, in police station after suitcases are stolen, a "lovely coffee session" with Claiborne Phillips and her husband, strawberries and sour cream, drives back to New Haven.

December 13, 8:00 a.m.–1:00 p.m.: Finishes working on thesis conclusions.

    9:30 a.m.: Meets with Professor Fisher about her poetry.

    2:00–3:30 p.m.: Writes Christmas cards and letters.[554]

    3:30 p.m.: Reads to Professor Gray, coffee with Dorrie Licht.

    7:00–10:00 p.m.: Works on thesis.

Letter to "dearest mother": "It is monday morning again and the world settles back from the miraculous to the mundane." Describes her happy trip to see Claiborne Phillips, wonderful time window shopping, browsing in Brentano's bookstore, looking forward to a second semester with Professor Fisher in a "private course" about poetics and Alfred Kazin's class on modern American literature.

Letter to Jon Rosenthal: looks forward to him picking her up in Wellesley on the twentieth, suggests they might go skiing—"I have a very attractive, but nervous mother, whom I see as little as possible . . . seriously though, I do love her, and am not contemplating matricide."

December 14, 8:00 a.m.–1:00 p.m.: Works on thesis and application for Woodrow Wilson Fellowship.

    Lunch with Alfred Kazin at Little Italy.

    2:25 p.m.: Thesis meeting with Professor Gibian.

    5:45 p.m.: Cleans room, works on story for Kazin.

    7:00–10:00 p.m.: "Xmas dinner."

December 15, 9:00 a.m.–noon: Purchases bus ticket, shops for brush, comb, toothbrush, toothpaste, and soap cakes.

    12:00–1:00 p.m.: Bells, writes letters.[555]

    2:00–6:00 p.m.: Cleans room, laundry, works on Kazin story.

    7:30–10:00 p.m.: German with Professor Sonnenfeld.

December 16: "Kazin plots."

    9:30 a.m.: Meets with Miss Mensel.

    11:00 a.m.–noon: German class.

    12:00–1:00 p.m.: In Shakespeare class, studying *Henry IV* and *Henry V* (ca. 1599).

    2:00–4:00 p.m.: Naps.

    4:00 p.m.: Sherry with Ann Birstein (Mrs. Kazin), who reads from her new novel.

7:00–10:00 p.m.: Finishes packing, washes hair.

December 17: "FIRST DRAFT OF THESIS DUE!"

8:00–11:00 a.m.: German study and class.

12:00–1:00 p.m.: Shakespeare class.

12:40 p.m.: Christmas vacation begins.

1:00 p.m.: Rides to Worcester, Massachusetts, with Lou Ackerman.

4:00 p.m.: Meets Warren in Worcester, to Adams House at Harvard, a beer at Cronin's Bar with Warren, Clement Moore, and Moore's date.

Letter to Melvin Woody: apologizes for the long letter she owes him, even though he has been in her thoughts, happy with thesis, certain that "dostoevsky has been the greatest philosophical influence on my life . . . along with [Friedrich] nietzsche, huxley, fromm and a few others," describes Kazin as the "light that incandesces my year," notes that "[Richard] sassoon . . . is explosive as ever."

December 18: At home, late breakfast of coffee and apple cake, plays piano, shops with Warren, purchases black velvet dress, ski jacket, gloves, wool scarf, gold slippers, powder, lipstick, rhinestone, tie clip, and stockings, dinner and dance at Robin Hood's Ten Acres with Gordon Lameyer and Warren.

Diary memoranda section—notes on presents for Gordon and Warren, to see Patsy, Ruth Giesel, the Crocketts, the Cantors, Mrs. Prouty, and to "replenish wardrobe!"

December 19: Church with Warren, Gordon, and Gordon's mother.

Dinner at home with Gordon.

3:00–4:30 p.m.: Meets Bob Cochran for a talk.

Cocktails at the Cantors, supper at Gordon's, visit with the Freemans, washes hair, packs.

December 20: Ski trip to Stowe, Vermont, with Jon Rosenthal, supper with Ann Ralston and Paul Green, visits ski shop, cold room with warm quilts, "more snow—wonderful sleep."

December 21: Huge breakfast with Jon Rosenthal, drive in snow to Mount Mansfield, an hour on the slope, lunch at Toll House, "magnificent 2 hour ski class."

December 22: Sleeps late, after breakfast "enormous feud" with Jon Rosenthal, silent ride back through "Grandma Moses Landscape" for a steak supper with Jon at home. Prentice Smith arrives.

December 23: Sleeps until noon, wraps Warren's present after late breakfast, window shops at Hathaway House and other stores, "magnificent" buffet dinner at the Cantors with Gordon Lameyer, Reese Thornton, Prentice Smith, and Betsy Bragg, cocktails at Gordon's house.

December 24: Prentice Smith departs after breakfast, Sylvia plays piano, wraps presents, and reads stories, Marcia Brown calls.

December 25: Late breakfast, opens presents—gift of white gloves from Mrs. Lameyer, Tabu perfume from Gordon plus "colored snapshots," William Empson's *Seven Types of Ambiguity* (1930), Phillis McGinley's book of poetry from Warren, twenty dollars, and Jacob Grimm and Wilhelm Grimm's fairy tales from Mother, traveling iron from Aunt Dot, earrings and stockings from the Cantors.

Diary memoranda section—reminders for "Prix de Paris: 4 articles," the Kazin story, poems to write, German stories to read and translate, and to work on story, "The Smoky Blue Piano," for *Ladies Home Journal.*

December 26, 9:00 a.m.: Coffee and long talk with Dr. Beuscher— "impossibility of argument or logic—retirement in dignified silence—moral honesty—each situation judged in itself," note to write *Vogue* articles and thank-you letters.

December 27: Finishes "Mary Ventura and the Ninth Kingdom," writes business letters and thank-you notes,[556] rewrites "The Smoky Blue Piano."

6:30 p.m.: Scott for a dinner of steak, salad, and daiquiris at Meadows, long bull session.

December 28: Late breakfast, sends "The Smoky Blue Piano" to the *Ladies Home Journal*, calls Mrs. White.

3:00–4:00 p.m.: Visits Mrs. Prouty in Brookline.

6:00 p.m.: In Cambridge, shops for ski books.

Supper at Wursthaus with Marcia and Mike Brown and Gordon Lameyer—"beef & pastrami & good talk," performance of *Bread, Love, and Dreams*[557] at Exeter Theatre.

December 29, 9:00 a.m.: Dental appointment, note to call Ruth Freeman and Patsy O'Neil, writes a thank-you to Mr. and Mrs. Lameyer,[558] writes two feature articles for *Vogue.*

7:00 p.m.: Punch party at Laurie Totten's.

9:00 p.m.–midnight: Long talk with Gordon Lameyer.

December 30: Outlines a story for Kazin's class, Calls O'Neil, Ruth Geisel, Claiborne Phillips, begins studying German, bathes, shaves.

7:30 a.m.: "Gordon: ask Mrs. L. [Lameyer] Re. Vogue."

8:00–noon: At the home of Mrs. White, 30 Summit Road.

December 31: Works on German paper and grammar, outlines "The Day Mr. Prescott Died."

4:00–5:00 p.m.: Trip to junk yard with Warren.

Reads *Mademoiselle.*

1955

January 1: Works on German paper and grammar, types rough draft of story for Alfred Kazin's class, eggnog at Aldriches, calls Patsy O'Neil and Ruth Geisel, sends "Christmas Encounter" to *Good Housekeeping*, bull session with Warren, writes rough draft of "The Day Mr. Prescott Died."

January 2: Packs for return to Smith.

Types Kazin paper.

2:45 p.m.: Packs car.

Drives to Navy Yard in Charlestown in Boston to see Gordon Lameyer, drives to Smith, calls Professor Gibian about thesis.

January 3: Works on German paper.

9:15: a.m. Appointment with Professor Gibian.

9:30 a.m.: Appointment with Professor Fisher.

Works on German translations.

Purchases red cashmere sweater, gray and brown wool dress, black sweater, striped shirt, tan jumper, silk blouse, gold earrings, necklace, and a pink nightgown, types footnotes and bibliography for thesis.

Letter to "dearest mother": describes bargains she bought, meetings with professors, busy three weeks ahead of her, including an article on Smith's social life for the *Smith Review*—"everybody is so wonderful up here—know that I'm well & happy even if I don't write till after exams—Hope you are the same."

January 4, 7:00–8:00 a.m.: BW.

Morning in library, begins "Gargoyle article research," purchases typing paper.

4:00–5:00 p.m.: Hair appointment.

7:00–10:00 p.m.: Begins German paper.

January 5, 7:00–8:00 a.m.: BW.

8:00 a.m.–noon: Finishes German paper.

12:00–1:00 p.m.: Bells.

3:00 p.m.: *Smith Review* meeting.

7:00–10:00 p.m.: German with Profession Sonnenfeld.

January 6, 7:00–8:00 a.m.: BW.

8:00–11:00 a.m.: Cleans room.

11:00 a.m.–noon: German class.

12:00–1:00 p.m.: Shakespeare class.

3:00 p.m.: Meets with Professor Fisher.

4:00 p.m.: In infirmary, works on story for Kazin's class.

Letter to "Dear mother": feeling "miserable," cough and cold treated with nose drops and gargles, requests a book she wants to read again—*Psychology and the Promethean Will.*

January 7, 7:00–8:00 a.m.: BW.

8:00–10:00 a.m.: Sees warden, Professor Russell.

11:00 a.m.–noon: German class.

12:00–1:00 p.m.: Shakespeare class.

2:00 p.m.: Honors meeting.

4:00 p.m.: Meets with Mrs. Pauline C. Walker, typist in the president's office, about her thesis.

January 8, 7:00–8:00 a.m.: BW.

8:00–11:00 a.m.: "Gargoyle article."

11:00 a.m.–noon: German class.

12:00–1:00 p.m.: Shakespeare class.

2:00–6:00 p.m., 7:00–10:00 p.m.: Works on several poems— "Ballade Banale," "Item: Stolen, One Suitcase," "Morning in the Hospital Solarium," and "New England Winter without Snow."

January 9: Rewrites "Ballade Banale" and "Harlequin Love Song!"

"Out of Infirmary!" Types poems, letters to Mr. Rice, Claiborne Phillips, Richard Sassoon,[559] Gordon Lameyer, and Mother, sends seven poems to the *New Yorker*, works on Smith "scholarship blanks."

Letter to Gordon: Won't be able to write for two weeks because of a "dantean inferno of exams and articles," describes her delight in replenishing her wardrobe—"I dreamt I went to Guantanamo Bay in my Maidenform nightie!"[560] Thesis is being typed. Describes Albert Fisher, her poetry professor: "the handsomest elderly man I've ever seen, very British, with keen blue eyes, white hair and mustache, and most tweedy clothes. I do hope he propositions me by the end of the year, (but perhaps, after his 3rd wife, he's wearied of that)." She is working with Fisher on the Elizabethan poet John Ford. Writes poems in spite of her "codeine stupor," mentions Peter Davison, a young editor at Harcourt Brace introduced to her by Alfred Kazin. Davison wants to see her first novel.

January 10, 7:00–8:00 a.m.: BW.

8:00 a.m.–1:00 p.m.: Reading period.

10:00 a.m.: Meets with thesis typist.

1:30–3:30 p.m.: Calls Professor Gray.

3:30 p.m.: Reads to Professor Gray.

5:30 p.m.: Turns in fellowship applications.

7:00–10:00 p.m.: Writes Gargoyle article.

January 11, 8:00 a.m.–1:00 p.m.: Works on Gargoyle article.

Gordon Lameyer sails to Cuba.

2:00–6:00 p.m.: Works on German paper, shops, works on "scholarship blanks."

January 12, 7:00–8:00 a.m.: BW.

9:00 a.m.–noon: Works on German grammar and paper.

12:00–1:00 p.m.: Bells, types German paper.

2:00–6:00 p.m.: German grammar.

4:00–6:00 p.m.: Naps.

7:00–10:00 p.m.: "German: paper due! Discuss stories—Marlene Dietrich."

January 13, 7:00–8:00 a.m.: BW.

Gargoyle article due.

8:00–11:00 a.m.: Works on German grammar.

11:00 a.m.–noon: German class.

2:00 p.m.: Posture picture in Scott Gym.

3:00 p.m.: Meets with Professor Fisher.

4:00–6:00 p.m., 7:00–10:00 p.m.: Reads and revises poems.

January 14, 7:00–8:00 a.m.: BW.

8:00–11:00 a.m.: Proofreads thesis.

11:00 a.m.–noon: German class.

Finishes Shakespeare's Henry plays.

2:00–6:00 p.m., 7:00–10:00 p.m.: Tea, coffee, revisions of poems.

January 15, 8:00–11:00 a.m.: Proofreads, "THESIS IN!"

11:00 a.m.–noon: German class.

12:00–1:00 p.m.: "Smoky Blue Piano" rejected and returned.

2:00–6:00 p.m.: Rewrites story, mails it at the post office.

Letter to "Dear mother": Pleased with her thesis and the way it has been professionally typed, elated at the *Ladies Home Journal* rejection that asks her to rewrite "Smoky Blue Piano," "keeping the nice sparkle it now has." Plans to rewrite "Tongues of Stone," which *Mademoiselle* rejected.

January 16: "Finish Shakespeare."

9:00–11:00 a.m.: Studies German grammar.

11:00 a.m.–noon: Bells.

2:00–6:00 p.m., 7:00–10:00 p.m.: Reads criticism of Shakespeare's Henrys and *The Rogues and Vagabonds of Shakespeare's Youth* (1907) by Edward Viles and Frederick James Furnivall.

January 17: 8:00 a.m.–1:00 p.m.: Notes to "finish Henrys."

Withdraws fifty dollars from the bank, renews books about John Ford, calls Professor Gray.

2:00–3:30 p.m.: Reads to Professor Gray.

5:30 p.m.: "Books & review stories & play."

January 18, 9:25 a.m.: Train to New York City, brings along German stories and a poem "Ceremony."[561]

1:00–2:00 p.m.: Meets Claiborne Phillips in the lobby of Prince George Hotel for lunch, window shops.

3:15 p.m.: "Cavanaugh."

5:05 p.m.: Train back to Northampton, supper at Toto's.

9:00 p.m.: Studies German grammar.

January 19, 8:00 a.m.–noon: Studies German grammar.

12:00–1:00 p.m.: Bells, reviews stories and vocabulary.

2:00–6:00 p.m.: Organizes and studies notes for *Rogues and Vagabonds*.

7:00–10:00 p.m.: "Study Folio & printing & learn quotes."

January 20, 7:00–8:00 a.m.: BW.

8:00–10:00 a.m.: "Brush up on your Shakespeare."

10:30 a.m.–12:50 p.m.: Shakespeare exam.

Lunch at Toto's.

2:30–4:50 p.m.: German exam, packs.

5:45 p.m.: Taxi to train station.

6:06 p.m.: "Train!"

Calls the airport, Richard Sassoon, and Dr. Beuscher.

7:15–8:45 p.m.: "Springfield."

Supper and bath.

January 21: Writes and mails application to Harvard.

3:30 p.m.: Hair appointment at Anthony's.

7:30 p.m.: Appointment with Dr. Beuscher, "a long bull session" about "religion & honesty & selfishness."

January 22: Shaves, shops, packs for trip to New York City.

4:00 p.m.: Laurie Totten's wedding.

5:15 p.m.: Grueling Woodrow Wilson Fellowship interviews at Harvard, four men with a barrage of questions.

8:00 p.m.: Flight to New York City.

Diary memoranda section—note on "RL Stevenson & EA Poe on Poetics."

January 23: Clams, steak, and coffee for lunch at Toffantetti's, sees *Gate of Hell*[62]—"exquisite Japanese symphony of color," Russian caviar sandwich and French pastry before performance of *The Dybbuk* (1913–1916) by S. Ansky, "absorbing fantasy."

January 24: Breakfast of grapefruit juice, eggs, bacon, coffee, toast, and jam—"most revitalizing," visits Museum of Modern Art, watches "Temptation of St. Joan"—"excruciatingly beautiful silent symbolic," a horse cab around Central Park, dinner at Le Gourmet.

January 25: "Magnificent dinner at Chez St Denis": onion soup, lamb chops, Vermouth cassis, and eclair and pear tart for dessert with good talk about art and life, then a drive through a "gray cold Connecticut landscape to New Haven and the train back to Northampton, unpacking, a hot dog at Toto's, and "back to routine."

January 26, 7:00–8:00 a.m.: BW.

8:00 a.m.–noon: Writes seven letters to Mother, Melvin Woody, Enid Mark, Gordon Lameyer, Ruth, and Mrs. Prouty.[563]

12:00–1:00 p.m.: Laundry.

2:00–6:00 p.m.: Naps

7:00–10:00 p.m.: Types poems, sends them to *Harper's* and *Kenyon Review*.

Letter to "Dear mother": Describes her "vacation"—"I rested and played and whirled until I really wanted to come back to Smith." Describes the plane to NYC—"I kept my nose pressed to the window watching the constellations of lights below as if I could read the riddle of the universe in the braille patterns of radiance." Describes her overpowering reaction to watching "Temptation of St. Joan," in which she has to ride through Central Park to calm down—"Human beings cannot bear very much reality, as Eliot says."

Letter to Enid Mark: "I am becoming a fatalist and think that somehow this postponed senior year was necessary for me to grow more slowly in time." She would like to see Enid's stories—"I'm so deep in rejections that I am hardly equipped to criticize!" She has put off the idea of marrying Gordon Lameyer. Mentions her New York frolic with Richard Sassoon.

Letter to Gordon: Gives him a rundown of her last two months at Smith, a visit home, and in New York City. During a trip home she purchases music—"These Foolish Things," "September Song," "I'm in the Mood for Love," sits at the piano "for hours soupily crooning to myself in bad french, and getting a hell of a kick out of it." A "bull session" with Dr. Beuscher about "religion, philosophy, honesty, selfishness, and a lot of other potent, and perhaps more intimate, topics." Details all the "merciless questions" four professors asked during her interview for a Woodrow Wilson Fellowship.

Letter to Melvin Woody: Notes "the future is drastically up in the air, and will be for months." Proud of her senior thesis, writing about five poems a week, inspired by her sessions with Professor Fisher. "New York soothed, assuaged, gorged, glutted, indulged."

January 27, 7:00–8:00 a.m.: BW.

8:00 a.m.–1:00 p.m.: Cleans room, begins application to Columbia University, "letter from WW [Woodrow Wilson Fellowship]—refusal shock!"

2:00–6:00 p.m.: Writes a housewife story, washes hair, shaves.

4:00 p.m.: "Bells: Tanya."

7:00–10:00 p.m.: Types "Home Is Where Heart Is."

Letter to "Dear mother": Distressed over Woodrow Wilson Fellowship rejection, worried that it dooms her other applications. "You were only too right when you challenged me about my ability to be an English teacher on the college level. . . . You seem to be more of a realist than I about my future prospects."

January 28, 7:00–8:00 a.m.: BW.

8:00 a.m.–1:00 p.m.: Writes eight pages of "teenage story" outline, "Tomorrow Begins Today."

2:00–6:00 p.m., 7:00 p.m.–midnight: For Christopher Awards, polishes "Mr. Prescott," rewrites "Tongues of Stone" with new ending for *Mademoiselle* contest, accompanied with a letter to Cyrilly Abels.

January 29, 7:00–8:00 a.m.: BW.

8:00 a.m.–1:00 p.m.: Sleeps, works on application to Columbia University.

2:00–6:00 p.m.: Reads *Tonio Kroger* (1903) by Thomas Mann, Heinrich von Kleist, and Busse.

To the post office to mail two contest envelopes.

4:30–6:00 p.m.: Bells.

7:00 p.m.–midnight: Babysitting for Professor Gibian's children, earns one dollar and seventy-five cents.

Letter to "Dear Mother": Responding to her mother's illness—"our little family is altogether too prone to lie awake at nights hating ourselves for stupidities—technical or verbal, or whatever—and to let careless cruel remarks fester until they blossom in something like ulcer attack or vomiting . . . I know that during these last days I've been fighting an enormous battle with myself." Describes the stories she is working on and her hope that she will succeed as a writer if not as an academic. "Chin up, mother, and get well for me!"

January 30, 8:00 a.m.–12:30 p.m.: Sleeps late, writes "down among strict roots & rocks," "Danse Macabre" poem.

January 31, 7:00–8:00 a.m.: BW.

8:00 a.m.–1:00 p.m.: Works on Columbia University application.

2:00–3:30 p.m.: Meets with Professor Page.

3:30–5:30 p.m.: Reads to Professor Gray.

7:30 p.m.: "Mr. Arvin."

February 1, 7:00–8:00 a.m.: BW.

8:00 a.m.–1:00 p.m.: Buys *Vogue*, renews library books, studies German, John Ford, visits vocational office to inquire about summer jobs.

2:00–6:00 p.m.: Writes "Temper of Time" and "Winter Words."

7:00–10:00 p.m.: Notes "3 poems to N[ew] Y[orker]."

February 2, 7:00–8:00 a.m.: BW.

8:30 a.m.: Chapel.

9:00 a.m.–noon: Writes "Apparel for April."

12:00–1:00 p.m.: Bells.

Meets with Professor Gibian, washes hair.

2:00–6:00 p.m.: "Tanya's dishes."

7:00–10:00 p.m.: "German unit: Sonnenfeld."

Letter to "Dearest mother": Mentions that *Ladies Home Journal* has rejected "Smoky Blue Piano," but she feels comforted by friends. "I have felt great advances in my poetry, the main one being a growing victory over word's nuances and a superfluity of adjective."

February 3, 7:00–8:00 a.m.: BW.

8:00–10:00 a.m.: Reads John Ford.

10:00–11:00 a.m.: Kazin's class.

11:00 a.m.–noon: German class.

12:00–1:00 p.m.: Shakespeare class.

1:30 p.m.: Cleans room, shaves, mails letters to Columbia University. Note to "buy [Father James] Keller Bk."

2:00–6:00 p.m.: Work on poems for Professor Fisher, coffee with him for a "grand talk."

7:00–10:00 p.m.: House meeting.

Postcard to "Dearest mother": delighted with her mother's "fat letter," mentions Professor Fisher's interest in her work and that she is considering a teaching job at an American school in Morocco if she can go with Sue Weller.

February 4, 7:00–8:00 a.m.: BW.

8:00–10:00 a.m.: Works on German translations.

10:00–11:00 a.m.: Kazin's class.

11:00 a.m.–noon: German class.

12:00–1:00 p.m.: Shakespeare class.

2:00–6:00 p.m.: Dinner with Sue Weller and her date at Little Italy.

7:00–10:00 p.m.: Daiquiris at Rahar's.

February 5, 7:00–8:00 a.m.: BW.

8:00–10:00 a.m.: Writes "Dirge"—"the sting of bees took away my father."

10:00–11:00 a.m.: Kazin's class.

11:00 a.m.–noon: German class.

12:00–1:00 p.m.: Shakespeare class.

2:00–6:00 p.m.: Meets Richard Sassoon for martinis at Rahar's.

7:00–10:00 p.m.: Pizza at Little Italy.

Letter to "Dear mother": Responds to letter about her father's colleague whose "'personality' was criticized by his students—as with daddy, disease twisted an otherwise good nature." Relieved to hear that her Woodrow Wilson rejection will not affect her other applications. "Poems come better and better." Feels better about her "prospects."

February 6: "Breakfast trays," long talk with Nancy Hunter.

    10:00 a.m.–1:00 p.m.: Writes "Elegy."

    4:00 p.m.: Meets with Mary Ellen Chase.

    7:00–10:00 p.m.: Writes poems, including "Notes on Zarathustra."

February 7, 8:00 a.m.–1:00 p.m.: Writes "The Dream."

    1:00 p.m.: Lunch with Elinor Friedman.

    2:00–3:30 p.m.: Cashes ten-dollar check, goes to scholarship office.

    3:30–5:30 p.m.: Reads to Professor Gray.

    7:30–10:40 p.m.: "Anglo-Saxon [poetry]."

February 8, 9:25 a.m.: Train to New York City with Richard Sassoon.

    2:00–6:00 p.m.: At the Whitney Museum, art exhibit, martinis.

    8:00 p.m.: "Kronenberg [Louis Kronenberger?] on Chekhov."

    9:07 p.m.: Train to Northampton.

February 9, 8:30 a.m.: Writes "Prologue to Spring."

    9:00 a.m.–noon: Finishes reading *Sister Carrie* by Theodore Dreiser (1900).

    12:00–1:00 p.m.: Bells.

    2:00–6:00 p.m.: At vocational office.

    7:30–10:00 p.m.: Notes "dishes—Randi German."

February 10, 8:00–10:00 a.m.: Works on German translations, cleans room.

    10:00–11:00 a.m.: Kazin's class.

    11:00 a.m.–noon: German class.

    12:00–1:00 p.m.: Shakespeare class.

    1:00 p.m.: Interview about a teaching job with Robert Shea, an American consulate representative in Morocco.

    2:00–3:00 p.m.: "Coffee."

    3:00–4:00 p.m.: Meets with Professor Fisher.

    4:00–6:00 p.m.: "Great talk."

    7:00–10:00 p.m.: "Sheas Talk! with Sue [Weller]."

Letter to "Dear mother": Enjoys her mother's "delicious" cookies, proud of her brother, who is doing so well, and laments her own B average in German and Shakespeare classes, discusses the state of her finances—"I depend on my dates for food, plays, and wine." Dismisses her mother's objections to taking a job in Morocco. She is not going to learn shorthand because she won't take the kind of job that interferes with her writing and is excited about the "vitality of this small international community" in Morocco, where she would be among those trying to set a good example and spread good will, as explained to her by Mr. Shea. She does not understand why her mother does not see the advantage of experience abroad instead of taking college courses. A year in England or Morocco would equip her better than just book learning. She is attracted to Morocco's "cool, dark climate with a hot sun." The teacher in charge, Mr. Shea, is "like the intelligent, loving, liberal father I have always longed for, and I can think of no man except Mr. Crockett who so much made me think that there are saints on earth, with a radiance and love of service and helping others to grow which is almost superhuman." She wants to "counteract [Joseph] McCarthy and much adverse options about the US." She believes that "new races are going to influence the world in turn, much as America did in her day, and however small my part, I want a share in giving to them." She and Sue Weller will know in late April or early May whether their applications are successful. She has the full approval of Professor Fisher, who has recommended her for the job, which is also endorsed by the Smith vocational office. She has gone to the trouble of explaining so much because to her mother her "goals in life" may seem "strange to you."

Letter to Gordon Lameyer: Believes the four men on the Woodrow Wilson Fellowship committee found her wanting because she was a woman. In spite of several magazine rejections, she is "happier in this wave of refusal than I ever was two years ago on my flashy crest of success." Professor Fisher has buoyed her belief in herself. She has been writing at least five poems a week. Claims she would follow Shea, head of the school in Morocco, to the "ends of the earth." She calls herself and Sue Weller "desiring ulysses!"

February 11, 8:00–10:00 a.m.: Reads German.

10:00–11:00 a.m.: Kazin's class.

11:00 a.m.–noon: German class.

12:00–1:00 p.m.: Shakespeare class.

Writes "Epitaph in Three Parts."

2:00–6:00 p.m.: Dorothy Wrinch and Elizabeth Sewell poetry reading.

7:00–10:00 p.m.: "Magnificent 'Supreme rearranging.'"

February 12, 8:00–10:00 a.m.: Reads Shakespeare, *Sister Carrie*.

10:00–11:00 a.m.: Kazin's class.

11:00 a.m.–noon: Shakespeare class.

Writes to Mr. Crockett.[564]

2:00–6:00 p.m.: Babysits at Professor Gibian's home.

7:30–10:00 p.m.: Talks with the Gibians.

Letter to *Atlantic Monthly*: inquires about seven poems sent five months ago, encloses six more poems, mentions her publications in *Mademoiselle*, *Seventeen*, and *Harper's*.

February 13, 8:00 a.m.–1:00 p.m.: Finishes *Sister Carrie*.

2:00 p.m.: Bells.

2:00–4:30 p.m.: "[Professor] Fisher & Hill readings," in the library Browsing Room, reads Dylan Thomas and Guy de Maupassant.

6:30 p.m.: Reads "The Secret Life of Walter Mitty" (1939) and Dickens, copies notes for Shakespeare class.

February 14, 8:00 a.m.–1:00 p.m.: Calls Mary Ellen Chase, reads Shakespeare's *Antony and Cleopatra* (ca. 1607).

2:00–3:30 p.m.: Writes "Spring Sacrament."

3:30–5:00 p.m.: "[Professor] Gray (?)."

4:30 p.m.: Meets with Chase.

7:30–10:30 p.m.: "Middle Ages—40b: Williams."

Letter to Ruth Cohen, principal of Newnham College, Cambridge: Accepts admission as an "affiliated student at Newnham College to read for the English Tripos." She plans to arrive at the university in October 1955 even if her Fulbright application is not successful.

ACKNOWLEDGMENTS

Peter K. Steinberg's assistance has been invaluable. I'm deeply indebted to his many, many responses to my queries. His extensive work on Plath is available at https://te992faff27c68c1d.starter1ua.preservica.com/portal/en-US.

I am eternally grateful to my copy editor, Laura J. Vollmer. The amount of detail in this book is overwhelming and the opportunities for error are immense. Laura identified countless mistakes and oversights, but in the end, what I failed to correct is my fault alone.

NOTES

INTRODUCTION

1. Steinberg and Kukil, *The Letters of Sylvia Plath*, 1:897. The English Tripos is the final honors examination for a BA degree at Cambridge University.

TIMELINE

1. Plath will later write a series of poems about her beekeeping at her home, Court Green, in Devon, UK.

2. Plath writes about the hurricane in "The Disquieting Muses" and in "Ocean 1212w," included in Sylvia Plath, *Johnny Panic and the Bible of Dreams: Short Stories, Prose, and Diary Excerpts* (New York: HarperPerennial, 1977).

3. Plath's time spent with her grandparents on Shirley Street is memorialized in "Point Shirley."

4. It is not clear why Aurelia is not home, but she may already have been suffering from an ulcer that resulted in a March hospitalization.

5. Hayworth (1918–1987) and Lamarr (1914–2000) were two glamorous movie stars of the time.

6. One of the two poems she wrote at this time was probably "Camping," published in the *Weetamoe Megaphone*, July 18, 1943, 2.

7. Marjorie Kinnan Rawlings's novel *The Yearling*, first published in 1938, became a huge best seller and an instant classic. It is a coming-of-age story about Jody Baxter, a boy with a love of animals who lives in the Florida backwoods of the 1870s.

8. Jack Benny (1894–1974) was a popular comedian on radio, in film, and later on television. On radio, he had a cast of characters who often poked fun at his preening and conceit, displaying an astringent humor that suffuses Plath's writing as well. For the episode Plath listened to that day, see *Jack Benny Program*, "New Year's (War Baseball)," January 2, 1944, available at This Day in Jack Benny, "New Year's (War Baseball)," n.d., audio, 32:39, https://thisdaybenny.com/2018/05/27/new-years-war-baseball/.

9. *The Great Gildersleve* was a popular radio situation comedy and one of Sylvia's favorites. The show centered on Throckmorton P. Gildersleeve's love interests and family. For the episode Plath listened to, see *The Great Gildersleve*, "New Year, New Man," January 2, 1944, available at Old Time Radio Downloads, "GG (107) New Year, New Man (Re Creation)," n.d., audio, 31:51, https://www.oldtimeradiodownloads.com/comedy/the-great-gildersleeve/gg-44-01-02-107-new-year-new-manre-creation.

10. Plath was very competitive and often recorded her grades and those of other high-ranking students, but in most cases, I have not included those entries.

11. See *Jack Benny Program*, "Jack Has a Pet Camel," January 9, 1944, mentioned at This Day in Jack Benny, "The Jack Benny Program 1944," n.d., https://thisdaybenny.com/2018/04/29/the-jack-benny-program-1944/.

12. See *The Great Gildersleeve*, "Gildy in Hospital," January 9, 1944, available at Old Time Radio Downloads, "Gildy in Hospital," n.d., audio, 29:13, https://www.oldtimeradiodownloads.com/comedy/the-great-gildersleeve/gildy-in-hospital-1944-01-09.

13. Minstrel shows were performed in school. See Grace Brigham, "Minstrel Shows at School?" Music 345: Race, Identity, and Representation in American Music, October 2, 2019, https://pages.stolaf.edu/americanmusic/2019/10/02/minstrel-shows-at-school/.

14. For examples of Arden's wardrobe, see Monte Barrett and Russell E. Ross, "Jane Arden Paper Doll," clipping, created August 20, 1939, University of North Texas Libraries Special Collections, Portal to Texas History, added July 28, 2020, https://texashistory.unt.edu/ark:/67531/metadc1705371/.

15. See *Jack Benny Program*, "From Camp Muroc California," January 23, 1944, mentioned at This Day in Jack Benny, "The Jack Benny Program 1944," n.d., https://thisdaybenny.com/2018/04/29/the-jack-benny-program-1944/.

Smith costarred with Errol Flynn in *Gentleman Jim* (1942) as the upper-class beauty that Flynn wins as his love, and in *The Constant Nymph* (1943), she plays the beautiful and sophisticated Florence Creighton.

16. See *The Great Gildersleeve*, "Eve and Gildy Get Together," January 23, 1944, available at Old Time Radio Downloads, "Eve and Gildy Get Together," n.d., audio, 28:57, https://www.oldtimeradiodownloads.com/comedy/the-great-gildersleeve/eve-and-gildy-get-together-1944-01-23.

17. According to a Girl Scouts handbook: "As a Patrol, you can choose the things you would like to do in Patrol and troop meetings. As a Patrol, you help make the plans to do those things." See Girl Scouts: Greater Los Angeles, "A Leader's Guide to the Patrol System," n.d., http://girlscoutsla.dreamhosters.com/documents/Patrol_Handbook_v2.pdf.

18. The product details for the Girl Scouts Scribe badge are as follows:

Explore what you can do with words and find out how you can encourage, entertain, and excite people with your writing.

1. Start with a poem
2. Create a short story
3. Use words to share who you are
4. Write an article
5. Tell the world what you think

When you've earned this badge, you'll know how to write different kinds of stories—both true tales and ideas from your imagination.

See Girl Scouts, "Junior Scribe Badge," n.d., https://www.girlscoutshop.com/JUNIOR-SCRIBE-BADGE.

19. See *The Great Gildersleeve*, "Marjorie the Actress," January 30, 1944, available at Old Time Radio Downloads, "Marjorie the Actress," n.d., audio, 29:50, https://www.oldtimeradiodownloads.com/comedy/the-great-gildersleeve/marjorie-the-actress-1944-01-30.

20. See *The Great Gildersleeve*, "Sleigh Ride," February 6, 1944, available at Old Time Radio Downloads, "Sleigh Ride," n.d., audio, 28:52, https://www.oldtimeradiodownloads.com/comedy/the-great-gildersleeve/sleigh-ride-1944-02-06.

21. Selected issues of *Calling All Girls* are available online. See Harvard Library, "Calling All Girls: Chicago, Ill, Parents' Magazine Press, 1941–," n.d., http://listview.lib.harvard.edu/

lists/drs-422585194. The January 1944 issue features articles such as "Who's Who Among Junior Scientists," "Kathy, a Story about a Girl and a Lonely Soldier," "Date with the Opera," "Girls in the News," "In the Movies," "Only Brother to Dance With" (which states: "Sure, brothers are fine in their place. But no fun being 'stuck' with your kid brother at a dance. That's next to being a wallflower!"), a comic strip entitled "A Girl from Norway," a comic strip about a female flyer, "Judy Wing," a contribution about craft projects with paper, "Fun Foods for Holiday Parties," and "Learn to Jitterbug at Home in 15 Minutes." Some of the advertisements include "The Soda Shop Gang Drools for This Jumper" and "The Blazer of Your Dreams."

22. *Maida's Little House*, by Inez Haynes Irwin, was published in 1921. It is the second book in the Maida Westabrook series about the orphaned daughter of Jerome Buffalo Westabrook, a Wall Street tycoon.

23. Plath earned her Child Care badge by babysitting.

24. See *Superman*, "Mystery of the Transport Plane Crashes," February 16, 1944. I have not been able to find a link to this particular broadcast. In the radio version of *Superman*, much is made of his work as a journalist and his involvement in current events. See Wikipedia, "*The Adventures of Superman* (Radio Series)," last modified July 16, 2022, https://en.wikipedia.org/wiki/The_Adventures_of_Superman_(radio_series). See also *The Superman Radio Scripts, Volume 1: The Original Scripts in the 1940s Radio Series* The Adventures of Superman, compiled and edited by DC Comics (New York: Watson-Guptill Publications, 2001).

25. *Terry and the Pirates*, a radio-series adaptation of the comic strip, features Terry Lee and his encounters with various evildoers. For the audio of various episodes, see Old Time Radio Catalog, "Terry and the Pirates," n.d., https://www.otrcat.com/p/terry-and-the-pirates.

26. See *The Lone Ranger*, "Too Many Shares," Blue Network, New York: NBC, February 16, 1944. The Lone Ranger, a masked hero, is another version of a Superman hero out to do good, vanquish evil, and fight for justice. For a list of episodes, see Fandom, "List of Lone Ranger Episodes," Lone Ranger Wiki, n.d., https://loneranger.fandom.com/wiki/List_of_Lone_Ranger_Radio_Episodes. For downloads of some episodes, see Old Time Radio Westerns, "The Lone Ranger," n.d., https://www.otrwesterns.com/westerns/the-lone-ranger/.

27. The Hathaway Bookshop was built in ca. 1830. See Wellesley History, "The History of Central Street," May 31, 2014, https://wellesleyhistory.wordpress.com/2014/05/.

28. *The White Isle* (1940), by Caroline Dale Snedeker, is about an enchanted land in Roman Britain.

29. By "turock," Plath possibly meant "tarock," a card game with Bavarian and Austrian origins.

30. Set in Depression-era Yorkshire, *Lassie Come Home* (1943) was perhaps Plath's first look at the country her future husband, Ted Hughes, would come from. The story is about Lassie's perilous adventures as she makes her way home to the boy Joe Carraclough, her first and most beloved master.

31. Bobbsey Twins is a series of children's novels, beginning in 1904, about a family with two sets of fraternal twins and their adventures.

32. *A Girl of Limberlost* (1909) is about Elnora Comstock who lives with her widowed mother in Limberlost, a fictional town in northeast Indiana. The mother scorns her daughter's desire for an education. Eventually Elnora wins her mother's love.

33. *Silver Theater* features movie stars in radio dramas.

34. See *Jack Benny Program*, "Hollywood Canteen," February 27, 1944, mentioned at This Day in Jack Benny, "The Jack Benny Program 1944," n.d., https://thisdaybenny.com/2018/04/29/the-jack-benny-program-1944/.

35. *Quiz Kids* is a game show often featuring radio stars, like Benny and Fred Allen. For some episodes, see Old Time Radio Downloads, "Quiz Kids The," n.d., https://www.oldtimeradiodown loads.com/quiz/quiz-kids-the.

36. The eponymous Charlie McCarthy is Edgar Bergen's ventriloquist's dummy, by turns whimsical, mischievous, and obnoxious. See Old Time Radio Catalog, "Edgar Bergen and Charlie McCarthy," n.d., https://www.otrcat.com/p/bergen-and-mccarthy-edgar-bergen-and-charlie-mccarthy.

37. *Scarlet Pimpernel* is a British film first released in 1934, starring Leslie Howard whose character is leading a double life, pretending to be an effete aristocrat while actually working to free a French nobleman from the Reign of Terror during the French Revolution.

38. *Love Crazy* is a 1941 screwball comedy starring William Powell and Myrna Loy, a couple on the verge of a breakup over the husband's former girlfriend and the wife's disapproving mother.

39. "Old Ironsides," by Oliver Wendell Holmes Sr., is a tribute to the USS Constitution, a ship engaged in many conflicts, including the War of 1812. Although the poem proclaims that the ship should be consigned to a burial at sea, an aroused public clamored for its preservation. It remains the oldest commissioned ship still afloat.

40. *The Trumpeter of Krakow* (1928) is a young adult historical novel, with many plot twists, set in medieval Krakow and involving precious jewels, evil alchemists, and other nefarious characters as well as plundering Tartars.

41. *The Secret of the Barred Window* is a part of a thirty-eight-volume series featuring Judy Bolton, a feminist-behaving character who grows up during the series, which deals with serious issues.

42. *Riding High* is a 1943 anthology film starring Dorothy Lamour as a burlesque queen.

43. Betsy Powley's home was in the northeastern part of the Berkshires. For more information, see Town of Colrain, home page, n.d., https://colrain-ma.gov.

44. See note 25.

45. Sky Ryders is a board game that was released in 1940. "The object of the game is for players to move around the solar system collecting the rare element, Coronium, and then return it to Earth without it being stolen by other players. Bags of Coronium are represented by yellow or green discs." See Board Game Geek, "Sky Riders (1940)," n.d., https://boardgamegeek.com/ boardgame/283693/sky-riders.

46. *The Great Gildersleeve*, "Gildy Wants to Run for Mayor," March 19, 1944, available at Old Time Radio Downloads, "Gildy Wants to Run for Mayor," n.d., audio, 29:00, https://www.old timeradiodownloads.com/comedy/the-great-gildersleeve/gildy-wants-to-run-for-mayor-1944-03-19.

47. *Jack Benny Program*, "Barbara Stanwyck (Mairzy Doats)," March 19, 1944, available at This Day in Jack Benny, "Barbara Stanwyck (Mairzy Doats)," n.d., audio, 34:00, https://thisdaybenny. com/2021/03/28/barbara-stanwyck-mairzy-doats/.

48. *Madame Curie* (1943) stars Greer Garson and Walter Pidgeon as Marie and Pierre Curie.

49. *Riding High* (1943) is a musical Western starring Dorothy Lamour, Dick Powell, and Cass Daley.

50. *What a Woman!* (1943) stars Rosalind Russell as a female literary agent who tries to make her star client behave as adventurously as his most famous character.

51. The Court of Awards is a Scout's ceremony during which badges are awarded and other achievements from the year are recognized.

52. For the rules of kickball, see World Kickball Association, "Official WAKA Kickball Rules," n.d., https://kickball.com/rules/.

53. For rules and tips for jump rope, see JumpRoapSpring, "Rules and Tips," n.d., http://jumprope sprint.com/rules-and-tips/.

54. For the rules of dodgeball, see Rules of Sport, "Dodgeball Rules," n.d., https://www.rulesof sport.com/sports/dodgeball.html.

55. *When a Cobbler Ruled the King* was published in 1911 and is the story of the "lost Dauphin" set during the French Revolution.

56. *Johnny Tremain* was published in 1943. This young adult novel is set in Boston in 1773 and follows the adventures of a fourteen-year-old boy caught up in revolutionary events.

57. A Sugar Daddy is a caramel lollipop.

58. *The Lucky Sixpence*, by Emile Benson Knipe and Alden Arthur Knipe, was published in 1912: "Twelve year old Beatrice outwits the English officers in her effort to deliver an important message to the colonial rebels during onset of the Revolutionary War." See the product description at Google Books, "Lucky Sixpence," n.d., https://books.google.com/books/about/The_Lucky_Sixpence .html?id=_EoDAAAAYAAJ.

59. *Treasure of Carcassonne*, published in 1928, is Albert Robida's story about a treasure hunt in a fabled French city.

60. *Happy House*, Jane D. Abbott's book published in 1919, is about how an old family quarrel and how an old homestead becomes a happy home.

61. *The Great Gildersleeve*, "Engaged," April 30, 1944, available at Old Time Radio Downloads, "Engaged," n.d., audio, 29:50, https://www.oldtimeradiodownloads.com/comedy/ the-great-gildersleeve/engaged-1944-04-30.

62. *Eight Cousins* is a Louisa May Alcott novel published in 1875 about a sickly girl who gets well in the care of her unorthodox Uncle Alec and holds her own in her large family.

63. *A Boy of the Lost Crusades*, a novel by Agnes Danforth Hewes published in 1923, is about a little French boy, Roland Arnot, who sets off in search of his father who has gone off to fight the Saracens.

64. *Kilmeny of the Orchard*, a novel by Lucy Maud Montgomery, published in 1910, is about a mute girl, Kilmeny Gordon, and a teacher, Eric Marshall, who falls in love with her. She rejects him because of her disability, but he persists in finding a way to get her to speak and return his love.

65. *The Great Gildersleeve*, "Campaign Gets Hot," May 7, 1944, available at Old Time Radio Downloads, "Campaign Gets Hot," n.d., audio, 29:50, https://www.oldtimeradiodownloads.com/ comedy/the-great-gildersleeve/campaign-gets-hot-1944-05-07.

66. *The Wind in the Willows* is Kenneth Grahame's classic 1908 book about a mole, rat, toad, and badger and their lives in pastoral England.

67. "In Flanders Fields" is a famous memorial poem about the fallen in World War I who speak of their lives, who "felt dawn, saw sunset glow, / Loved and were loved, and now we lie / In Flanders fields." McCrae, "In Flanders Fields," Poetry Foundation, n.d., https://www.poetryfoundation .org/poems/47380/in-flanders-fields.

68. *Freckles* is Gene Stratton-Porter's 1904 novel, set in the Limberlost swamp in Indiana, about an orphaned young man with a freckled complexion and a hand missing at the wrist who works for a lumber company, overcoming his fears of nature and learning about his family background while devoting himself to his new home.

69. *Nadita* is a 1927 novel by Grace Moon about Nadita (English: "Little Nothing") who is cast out from her home after adopting a little dog and has to make her own way in the world.

70. See note 13.

71. *Meet Corliss Archer* is a radio serial about a young girl and her bumbling boyfriend, Dexter Franklin. RUSC, "Dexter Franklin," n.d., https://www.rusc.com/old-time-radio/Dexter-Franklin .aspx?t=4828.

72. Russia is a board game about the Russian theater of war.

73. *The Great Gildersleeve*, "Gildy Engaged to Eve But Kissing Leila," May 14, 1944, available at Old Time Radio Downloads, "Gildy Engaged to Eve But Kissing Leila," n.d., audio, 29:15, https://www.oldtimeradiodownloads.com/comedy/the-great-gildersleeve/gildy-engaged-to-eve-but -kissing-leila-1944-05-14.

74. *One Man's Family* holds the record for the longest-running soap opera on radio (1932–1959). Set in the Sea Cliff area of San Francisco, the show is about a stockbroker, his wife, and five children.

75. See note 13.

76. *The Story Girl* is a 1911 novel by Lucy Maud Montgomery following the adventures of young people on Prince Edward Island, Canada.

77. *Heidi* is an 1881, world-famous novel by Johanna Spyri about an orphaned Swiss girl.

78. *The Little Colonel's Holidays* is a 1901 novel by Annie Fellows Johnston about a little girl in Victorian Louisville, Kentucky.

79. *The Diary of Selma Lagerlof* by Selma Lagerloff (1858–1940), published in 1937, is the story of growing up in a busy, happy family. The protagonist never lets her lameness interfere with her interest in life and in writing stories.

80. *An Old Fashioned Girl* is a novel by Louisa May Alcott about old-fashioned Polly Milton who is shocked by her visit to a well-to-do and fashionable family who do not care for one another.

81. *Henry Aldrich* follows the adventures of high school hero Henry Aldrich. Old Radio World, "The Aldrich Family: 11 MP3 Downloads Available," n.d., https://www.oldradioworld.com/shows/ Aldrich_Family.php.

82. *Susie Sugarbeet* is Margaret Asmum's novel, published in 1930, about Susie Siegefried and her happy family on a sugar beet farm.

83. *The Blue Aunt*, by Elizabeth Orne White and published in 1918, is the story of an aunt called "blue" but is in fact a godsend to the children of a family that expected the worst. Internet Archive, "The Blue Aunt," June 23, 2018, https://archive.org/details/blue_aunt_1806_librivox.

84. Fairy Rock is on the Boulder Brook Reservation Trail. The Swellesley Report, "Wellesley, Mass. Rocks," n.d., https://theswellesleyreport.com/wellesley-rocks/.

85. *Uncharted Ways* is a novel by Caroline Dale Snedeker, a fictional story about Mary Dyer, better known as the "Quaker Martyr," who was hanged for her devotion to her faith.

86. *The Great Gildersleeve*, "Eve's Mother Arrives," June 4, 1944, available at Old Time Radio Downloads, "Eves Mother Arrives," n.d., audio, 29:42, https://www.oldtimeradiodownloads.com/ comedy/the-great-gildersleeve/eves-mother-arrives-1944-06-04.

87. *The Army Hour* is a radio news program with reports about the war and entertainment. Wikipedia, "The Army Hour," last modified December 26, 2021, https://en.wikipedia.org/wiki/ The_Army_Hour.

88. *Otto of the Silver Hand*, first published in 1888, is a tale of thirteenth-century Germany with unusually realistic detail.

89. *Edward MacDowell and His Cabin in the Pines* by Opal Wheeler, published in 1940, is a biography of the famous composer who lived in Peterborough, New Hampshire.

90. *Mozart the Wonder Boy* is by Opal Wheeler, published in 1943.

91. Morses Pond is a one-hundred-acre site. Wellesley Town Hall, "About Morses Pond," n.d., https://www.wellesleyma.gov/788/About-Morses-Pond.

92. *The Great Gildersleeve*, "Dinner for Eve's Mother," June 11, 1944, available at Old Time Radio Downloads, "Dinner for Eves Mother," n.d., audio, 29:50, https://www.oldtimeradiodownloads.com/comedy/the-great-gildersleeve/dinner-for-eves-mother-1944-06-11.

93. *Up in Arms* is a 1944 musical, starring Danny Kaye, about a draftee's adventures in the army. For more on the film, see Carl Rollyson, *Hollywood Enigma: Dana Andrews* (Jackson: University Press of Mississippi, 2012), 166–67.

94. *Passport to Destiny* is a 1944 RKO war film, starring Elsa Lanchester as an English char-woman who believes her magic-eye amulet will protect her on a mission to assassinate Adolf Hitler.

95. Still popular today, the chair-o-plane is a carnival ride with fast-moving, swinging chairs hanging by chains and spinning around up in the air. Community Stories, "Chair-O-Plane, Circa 1930s," n.d., https://www.communitystories.ca/v2/bingo-hauser_fur-for-iron-la-fourrure-contre-le-fer/gallery/chair-o-plane-ride/.

96. Sandy Bottom refers to Little Bottom Sandy Pond in Pembroke, Massachusetts. It has a small beach. Google Maps, "Little Sandy Bottom Pond," n.d., https://www.google.com/maps/place/Little+Sandy+Bottom+Pond/@42.0399088,-70.8360713,17z/data=!4m5!3m4!1s0x89e49866b9d59b7d:0xf79070882adec5aa!8m2!3d42.040626!4d-70.8313198?hl=en-us.

97. "Aunt Helen" possibly refers to Patsy O'Neil's mother, a family friend.

98. In *Lost Angel* (1943), "six year old foundling Alpha, who has ostensibly lived her entire life at and under the strict control of the Pickering Institute in New York City, has been their scientific ex-periment since her arrival." IMDb, "Lost Angel (1943): Plot," n.d., https://www.imdb.com/title/tt0036120/plotsummary?ref_=tt_ov_pl.

99. In *Rationing* (1944), "a village butcher bickers with the postmistress in charge of World War II ration stamps." IMDb, "Rationing," n.d., https://www.imdb.com/title/tt0037211/.

100. Pencil games include tic-tac-toe, for example.

101. Hangman is a pencil-and-paper, guessing game.

102. The first extant letter to Aurelia Plath is a postcard dated July 14. Earlier letters are lost, missing, or possibly in private hands, suggests Peter K. Steinberg, coeditor of Plath's letters.

103. Steal the bacon is a game of tag.

104. *The House at Pooh Corner* is the second volume of stories about Winnie-the-Pooh.

105. Sink the ship is probably some version of a game with bowling pins on each corner of mats that act as the ships. Balls are thrown at the pins to sink the ship. Mrs. Carly Glanzman, "Sink the Ship: Best P.E. Game," February 27, 2015, 2:40, https://youtu.be/4wFE8kR9qCQ.

106. *Mystery at the Moss-Covered Mansion* is a Nancy Drew mystery published in 1941.

107. Some of these letters are lost or in private hands.

108. "Nosebag supper" is a Girl Scout term for a meal "tied in a bandanna (enough room for a sandwich, a few chips and a cookie or piece of fruit . . .)." PippinTBK, "Definition of 'Nosebag Lunch,'" Leader/Guider Cyber Council, Delphi Forums, March 20, 2003, http://forums.delphiforums.com/gsleaders/messages/7099/7.

109. *Fog Magic* (1943) is Julia L. Sauer's fantasy novel set in Nova Scotia in which a young girl travels in the fog back to the past of an abandoned village. Wikipedia, "*Fog Magic*," last modified October 21, 2021, https://en.wikipedia.org/wiki/Fog_Magic; Penguin Random House, "Fog Magic," n.d., https://www.penguinrandomhouse.com/books/296740/fog-magic-by-julia-l-sauer/.

110. Liverpool is a card game—a version of rummy.

111. *An Ear for Uncle Emil* is Eva Roe Gaggin's 1939 novel set in Switzerland and has been compared to *Heidi* (1880). See *Kirkus Reviews*, review of *An Ear for Uncle Emil*, by Eva Roe Gaggin, June 15, 1939, https://www.kirkusreviews.com/book-reviews/a/eva-r-gaggin/an-ear-for-uncle-emil/.

112. *Cornelli* is a novel by Johanna Spyri, published in 1920, about a heroine under suspicion by her elders.

113. *A Date with Judy* is a comedy series aimed at a teenage audience. Wikipedia, "*A Date with Judy*," last modified March 26, 2022, https://en.wikipedia.org/wiki/A_Date_with_Judy.

114. *Mystery Theatre* is an NBC series. The episode from that day was "Fifty Candles," in which "a ruthless businessman has been stabbed, leaving five obvious suspects." See the description at Old Time Radio Downloads, "Fifty Candles," n.d., https://www.oldtimeradiodownloads.com/thriller/molle-mystery-theater/fifty-candles-1944-07-25.

115. *Mr. and Mrs. North* is about a married couple of amateur detectives solving cases in New York City. Internet Archive, "Mr and Mrs North: Single Episodes," September 28, 2013, https://archive.org/details/OTRR_Mr_and_Mrs_North_Singles.

116. Frank was in the army.

117. Little Maid is a historical series set in different locales. See, e.g., ThirftBooks, "The Little Maid's Historical Series," n.d., https://www.thriftbooks.com/series/little-maid/50584/.

118. *Cavalcade of America* is an anthology drama series. Internet Archive, "Cavalcade of America: Single Episodes," March 30, 2010, https://archive.org/details/OTRR_Cavalcade_of_America_Singles.

119. *Destination Tokyo* (1943) is about a submarine on a secret mission. IMDb, "Destination Tokyo," n.d., https://www.imdb.com/title/tt0035799/.

120. *Schoolgirl Allies* is a 1917 novel, by Rebecca Middleton Samson, about a boy and girl in a Belgian boarding school. The full text is available at Library of Congress, "Schoolgirl Allies," n.d., https://www.loc.gov/item/17023653/.

121. *I Love a Mystery* is a radio series about a group of crime solvers. See Old Time Radio Catalog, "I Love a Mystery (ILAM)," n.d., https://www.otrcat.com/p/i-love-a-mystery.

122. *Pollyanna* is a classic of children's literature, with eleven sequels about a young girl who overcomes her travails with an optimistic outlook. "Pollyanna" has become a word for someone who is excessively optimistic.

123. Ginny Simms was a big-band vocalist and actress with her own radio show. IMDb, "Ginny Simms (1913–1994)," n.d., https://www.imdb.com/name/nm0799963/.

124. *A Little Maid of New York* is a historical novel set in 1783 during the British occupation of New York.

125. *The Open Gate* is a 1943 novel by Kate Seredy, set during World War II, and about a family on a run-down farm.

126. *The Middle Moffat* is a 1942 novel by Eleanor Estes about Jane Moffat, neither the youngest nor oldest member of the family, so she decides to be mysterious.

127. "Peace and Plenty" is possibly a jigsaw puzzle.

128. Crater Lake is in Oregon. National Park Service, "Crater Lake," last modified September 29, 2022, https://www.nps.gov/crla/index.htm.

129. A flutter board is sometimes called a "kick board."

130. The game 156 pickup is possibly a variant of fifty-two-card pickup using three decks of cards.

131. For a description of the game hoist the green sail, see Diane Bradshaw, *The Girl from 21 Wakullah Street* (Bloomington, IN: AuthorHouse, 2013), 27–28.

132. Mary Poppins is a series of eight books by P. L. Travers, first published in 1934, about an English nanny who pops in and out of the lives of children.

133. *Home in Indiana* (1944) is a horse-racing film, starring Walter Brennan.

134. *The Scarlet Claw* (1944) is a Sherlock Holmes film, starring Basil Rathbone.

135. "Relivo" perhaps refers to ring-a-levio, a "game in which players on one team are given time to hide and are then sought out by members of the other team who try to capture them, keep them in a place of confinement, and keep them from being released by their teammates." Merriam-Webster Dictionary, s.v. "ring-a-levio," n.d., https://www.merriam-webster.com/dictionary/ring-a-levio.

136. *Come Soon, Tomorrow*, published in 1943, is by Gladys Swarthout. WorldCat, "Come Soon, Tomorrow: The Story of a Young Singer," n.d., https://www.worldcat.org/title/come-soon-tomorrow -the-story-of-a-young-singer/oclc/25271170.

137. *Cousins' Luck in the Louisiana Bayou Country*, published in 1940, is by Rose Bell Knox and set in the Louisiana bayou. WorldCat, "Cousins' Luck in the Louisiana Bayou Country," n.d., https://www.worldcat.org/title/2970476.

138. *Blondie* is a situation comedy based on the comic strip by the same name. It is about Blondie and her husband, Dagwood. Some episodes are available at Old Radio World, "Blondie: 5 MP3 Downloads Available," n.d., https://www.oldradioworld.com/shows/Blondie.php; and at Old Time Radio Downloads, "Blondie," n.d., https://www.oldtimeradiodownloads.com/comedy/blondie/2.

139. By "Kenny Aldrich," perhaps Plath was referring to Henry Aldrich, the protagonist of the family situation comedy *The Aldrich Family*. See Old Time Radio Catalog, "The Aldrich Family (Henry Aldrich)," n.d., https://www.otrcat.com/p/aldrich-family-henry-aldrich?gclid=CjwKCAiAr6-A BhAfEiwADO4sfatVwrOYvVfzmKGxSrF9DRQ9ssmL4HrZ5HI9GfmvJhVhAJJ9Abaklho CzAAQAvD_BwE.

140. *The Heavenly Body* (1944) is about the beautiful wife of an astronomer. IMDb, "The Heavenly Body," n.d., https://www.imdb.com/title/tt0035980/.

141. *Tampico* (1944) is a war drama. IMDb, "Tampico," n.d., https://www.imdb.com/title/ tt0037346/?ref_=fn_al_tt_1.

142. *The Golden Skylark, and Other Stories* (1941) is Elizabeth Goudge's stories about childhood and the English countryside. For more information, see the Elizabeth Goudge Society, last modified 2022, https://www.elizabethgoudge.org.

143. See *The Great Gildersleeve*, "Water Commissioner Is a Fired Rainmaker," September 10, 1944, https://www.oldtimeradiodownloads.com/comedy/the-great-gildersleeve/water-commissioner-is -fired-rainmaker-1944-09-10.""

144. On the rules of rummy, see Bicycle, "Rummy (Rum)," n.d., https://bicyclecards.com/ how-to-play/rummy-rum/.

145. On the rules of Go Fish, see Bicycle, "Go Fish," n.d., https://bicyclecards.com/how-to-play/ go-fish.

146. *The Rise of Our Free Nation*, published in 1942, is by Edna McGuire and Thomas B. Portwood.

147. *Pollyanna's Door to Happiness*, published in 1936, is by Elizabeth Borton. It is volume 9 in the Pollyanna series. On the origin of the series, see Encyclopedia.com, "Pollyanna: The Glad Book," n.d., https://www.encyclopedia.com/children/academic-and-educational-journals/ pollyanna-glad-book.

148. See note 54.

149. *The Riddle of River Acres* is part of a series by Augusta Seaman about girl sleuths. For more information, see Series Books for Girls, "River Acres Riddle and Charlemonte Crest by Augusta Seaman," August 3, 2018, https://series-books.blogspot.com/2018/08/river-acres-riddle-and -charlemonte.html.

150. For the rules of beat ball, see Pedago, "Beat Ball," n.d., https://www.pedagonet.com/PhysEd/game19.htm.

151. *Jack Benny Program*, "From Gardner Field Taft California," October 15, 1944, mentioned at This Day in Jack Benny, "The Jack Benny Program 1944," n.d., https://thisdaybenny.com/2018/04/29/the-jack-benny-program-1944/.

152. "The object of the game [red rover] is to call over one player from the other team to try and break through your team's wall." See Fun Games Kids Play, "Red Rover Game," n.d., https://fungameskidsplay.com/redrovergame.htm.

153. *Swiss Family Robinson*, published in 1812 and by Johann David Wyss, is about a resource-ful shipwrecked family. Britannica, "Swiss Family Robinson," n.d., www.britannica.com/topic/The-Swiss-Family-Robinson.

154. There are many different versions of the game who am I. Icebreakers, "Who Am I," n.d., https://www.icebreakers.ws/medium-group/who-am-i.html.

155. These letters are lost or in private hands.

156. *Rebecca of Sunnybrook Farm* (1903), an American classic by Kate Douglas Wiggin, is a tale of Rebecca and her two very different aunts and reactions to her trials and tribulations. Wikipedia, "*Rebecca of Sunnybrook Farm*," last modified October 2, 2022, https://en.wikipedia.org/wiki/Rebecca_of_Sunnybrook_Farm.

157. By "Paderewski," Plath is referring to celebrated Polish pianist Ignacy Jan Paderewski (1860–1941). For more information, see YourDictionary, "Ignace Jan Paderewski," n.d., https://biography.yourdictionary.com/Ignace-jan-paderewski.

158. *Greenwich Village* (1944) is a Twentieth Century-Fox musical about a composer. IMDb, "Greenwich Village," n.d., https://www.imdb.com/title/tt0036881/.

159. Bibi is a series of novels by Karin Michaelis about a little Danish girl. See the product description at Google Books, "Bib: A Little Danish Girl," n.d., https://books.google.com/books/about/Bibi.html?id=mgmZXwAACAAJ.

160. *Road to Down Under*, published in 1944 and by Maribelle Cormack, is about a young girl's adventures on the way to Australia. See the product description at Bookworm Blessings, "Road to Down Under: By Maribelle Cormack," n.d., https://bookwormblessings-676131.square .site/product/road-to-down-under-by-maribelle-cormack/160/.

161. In July 1939, a twelve-year-old boy was lost on Maine's Mount Katahdin and, after a manhunt involving hundreds of volunteers, was found nine days later dehydrated, mosquito-bitten, and sixteen pounds lighter. He attributed this survival to his training as a Boy Scout. William Grimes, "Donn Fendler, Who Was Lost in Wilds of Maine as a Boy, Dies at 90," *New York Times*, October 11, 2016. https://www.nytimes.com/2016/10/12/us/donn-fendler-who-was-lost-in-wilds -of-maine-as-a-boy-dies-at-90.html.

162. In the game of pickup sticks, sticks are dropped as a loose bunch onto a surface, and the challenge is to remove one at a time without disturbing the pile. The winner picks up the most sticks. See How Do You Play It, "Pick Up Sticks Rules," n.d., https://howdoyouplayit.com/pick-up -sticks-rules/.

163. *All Aboard the Whale!* first published in 1944 and by Richard Hatch, is about Susanne, Peter, and Jonathan and their wild summer of adventure. See the product description at AbeBooks, "All Aboard the Whale!" n.d., https://www.abebooks.co.uk/Aboard-Whale-Hatch-Richard-W-Jonathan/18786308380/bd.

164. Braddock's Campaign was part of a massive British campaign against the British in the summer of 1755. Encyclopedia.com, "Braddock's Expedition," n.d., https://www.encyclopedia.com/history/dictionaries-thesauruses-pictures-and-press-releases/braddocks-expedition.

165. The Albany Plan of Union was proposed in 1754 as a way of uniting the colonies in a common defense against the French. Office of the Historian, "Albany Plan of Union, 1754," Department of State, n.d., https://history.state.gov/milestones/1750-1775/albany-plan.

166. *The Magical Walking-Stick* (1932) by John Buchan, is about a thirteen-year-old boy and the magical stick that can take him anywhere he wishes. FadedPage, "The Magic Walking-Stick," n.d., https://www.fadedpage.com/showbook.php?pid=20140867.

167. *Jack Benny Progam,* "From San Bernardino California," December 10, 1944, mentioned at This Day in Jack Benny, "The Jack Benny Program 1944," n.d., https://thisdaybenny.com/2018/04/29/the-jack-benny-program-1944/.

168. *Holiday Inn* is a 1942 musical with Bing Crosby and Fred Astaire. IMDb, "Holiday Inn," n.d., https://www.imdb.com/title/tt0034862/.

169. In *A Night of Adventure* (1944): "A wealthy lawyer begins to suspect that his inattention to his wife is making her cheat on him. When he discovers the truth, he's charged with murder." IMDb, "A Night of Adventure," n.d., https://www.imdb.com/title/tt0037130/.

170. *Bright Morning*, published in 1942 and by Margery Williams Bianco, is about her childhood in London. Enyclopedia.com, "Bianco, Margery Williams (1881–1944)," n.d., https://www.encyclopedia.com/women/encyclopedias-almanacs-transcripts-and-maps/bianco-margery-williams-1881-1944.

171. Published in 1944, *The Silver Pencil*, by Alice Dalgliesh, is a novel based on her childhood in Trinidad and England. WorldCat, "The Silver Pencil," n.d., https://www.worldcat.org/title/silver-pencil/oclc/1281081.

172. Published in 1944, *New Worlds for Josie*, by Kathryn Worth, is "a boarding school story about American Josie's and her sister's year in Switzerland." GoodReads, "New World for Josie," n.d., https://www.goodreads.com/en/book/show/1785614.New_Worlds_for_Josie.

173. Published in 1933, *Peddler's Pack* is by Mary Owen Lewis. *New York Times*, "Peddler's Pack: By Mary Owens Lewis. 64 pp. Philadelphia: David McKay Company. $1.50," January 14, 1934, https://www.nytimes.com/1934/01/14/archives/peddlers-pack-by-mary-owens-lewis-64-pp-philadelphia-david-mckay.html.

174. Published in 1944, *A Separate Star*, by Loula Grace Erdman, is "a career book aimed at young women interested in pursuing a career in teaching." West Texas A&M University, "Biographical Information," n.d., https://www.wtamu.edu/library/speccoll/erdman/bio.shtml.

175. *Jack Benny Program*, "From St Albans Naval Hospital in New York," February 4, 1945, mentioned at This Day in Jack Benny, "The Jack Benny Program 1945," n.d., https://thisdaybenny.com/2018/04/29/the-jack-benny-program-1945/.

176. Juliette Gordon Low (1860–1927) founded the Girl Scouts. Girl Scouts, "Juliette Gordon Low," n.d., https://www.girlscouts.org/en/about-girl-scouts/our-history/juliette-gordon-low.html.

177. In *The Forgotten Daughter*, Caroline Snedeker's 1933 novel, "Chloe, the young daughter of a noble Roman man, has been lost to her father, and has spent her life unknown to him, as a slave on one of his own villas. Cruelly treated, and with no hope of freedom, her only escape is

into the stories of her Grecian mother's home town [*sic*] of Eresos, as told to her by Melissa, a fellow-slave and her mother's dearest friend." GoodReads, "The Forgotten Daughter," n.d., https:// www.goodreads.com/book/show/1649088.The_Forgotten_Daughter.

178. Published in 1909, *The Adventure of Princess Sylvia* is by A. M. Williamson. See A. M. Williamson, *The Adventure of Princess Sylvia* (1909; Project Gutenberg, 2013), https://www .gutenberg.org/files/42357/42357-h/42357-h.htm.

179. For more information on a central balance design, see Rick Mess, "Balance in Composition: How to Balance Design," May 24, 2020, https://www.outcrowd.io/blog/balance-in -composition-how-to-balance-design.

180. For more information on intermediate colors, see Yundle, "Intermediate Colors Definition," n.d., https://www.yundle.com/terms-definitions/i/intermediate-colors.

181. *Thirty Seconds over Tokyo* is a 1944 film. IMDb, "Thirty Seconds over Tokyo," n.d., https:// www.imdb.com/title/tt0037366/.

182. Published in 1941, *The Middle Button*, by Kathryn Worth, is about heroine Maggie in 1880s North Carolina who is determined to become a doctor but must first obtain family support and learn to control her temper. Google Books, "The Middle Button," n.d., https://books.google .com/books/about/The_Middle_Button.html?id=5is_OAAACAAJ.

183. This is an inexact quotation from William Wordsworth's "I Wandered Lonely as a Cloud."

184. See note 109.

185. The Babson Institute is a private business school in Wellesley. Babson College, "Who We Are," n.d., https://www.babson.edu/academics/centers-and-institutes/.

186. "The Centerville Ghost" actually refers to *The Canterville Ghost*, released in 1944. This film is an adaptation of Oscar Wilde's story about a ghost in an English castle and his American relative. IMDb, "The Canterville Ghost," n.d., https://www.imdb.com/title/tt0036696/.

187. *Show Business* (1944) is about a couple (dancers) and their transition from burlesque to vaudeville. IMDB, "Show Business," n.d., https://www.imdb.com/title/tt0037274/.

188. *The Fighting Lady* (1944) is a documentary about the aircraft carrier USS Yorktown. IMDb, "Fighting Lady," n.d., https://www.imdb.com/title/tt0036823/.

189. Albert Schweitzer was a theologian and humanitarian, and he won the 1952 Nobel Peace Prize. Plath studied him in a religion class and owned a copy of *Out of My Life and Thought: The Autobiography of Albert Schweizer* (1931). See SPL.

190. These letters are either lost or in private hands.

191. In *The Open Gate*, published in 1943, "a laid-off advertising man places a starting bid at a country auction and finds out that he bought a run-down farm—a humorous and somewhat idyllic picture of a family adapting to country living (although for Gran, it is a return to the farm life she loved) as World War II steadily worsens in Europe." GoodReads, "The Open Gate," n.d., https://www.goodreads.com/book/show/299465.The_Open_Gate.

192. *The Little Colonel's Holidays*, by Annie Fellows Johnston, was published in 1901. "Several chapters of this 1900–1901 tale are set in 'Old Louisville.' The Little Colonel and the Two Little Knights of Kentucky have grown a bit, and are joined by the Waltons, modeled after the family of General H. W. Lawton, a fallen hero of the Spanish American War. The story revolves around the search for a little girl who has been 'kidnapped' by her drunken father." GoodReads, "The Little Colonel's Holidays," n.d., https://www.goodreads.com/book/show/1845874.The_Little_Colonel _s_Holidays.

193. "The Man without a Country" is Edward Everett Hale's classic story, first published in 1863, about a treasonous American Army lieutenant, Philip Nolan, sentenced to spend the rest of his days at sea separated from all news about his native land.

194. IMDb, "Brazil," n.d., https://www.imdb.com/title/tt0036670/.

195. "Riverside Park" refers to either Riverside Park in Weston, Massachusetts, or the one in Newton, Massachusetts.

196. "The Courtship of Miles Standish" is Longfellow's famous narrative poem, published in 1858, about early colonial settlement.

197. See Plath's later poem, "Cut."

198. "Scrub" is perhaps baseball or another game that is informal, not arranged by teams, and sometimes refers to practice for a game.

199. "Johnny-jump-ups" refers to violets. Anne Baley, "Johnny Jump Up Flowers: Growing A Johnny Jump Up Violet," last modified June 29, 2021, https://www.gardeningknowhow.com/ornamental/bulbs/violet/johnny-jump-up-flowers.htm.

200. *She*, published in 1887, is set in the African interior region ruled by a white queen, Ayesha, the "She-who-must-be-obeyed."

201. The "four freedoms" refers to those outlined in Franklin D. Roosevelt's January 6, 1941, address about freedom of speech and worship and freedom from want and fear.

202. "The Mummy's Foot" is Théophile Gautier's 1840 story about what happens with the four-thousand-year-old foot of Princess Hermonthis purchased in a Parisian curiosity shop.

203. "The Necklace" was published in 1884 and is by Guy de Maupassant, known for his irony and ending his stories with a twist.

204. "Lulu's Triumph" was published in 1891 and is by Matilde Serao, "a great champion of the emancipation of women and their higher education." Matilde Serao, "Lulu's Triumph," trans. by Leader Scott, *The Parents' Review* 2 (1891–1892): 740–54, https://www.amblesideonline.org/PR/PR02p740LulusTriumph.shtml.

205. "Kivvers" refers to pond perch.

206. On the game of flinch, see GameRules.com, "Flinch," n.d., https://gamerules.com/rules/flinch/.

207. As Plath scholar Emily Van Duyne comments, Sylvia was never one to take the easy road.

208. Britannica, "Blindman's Buff," n.d., https://www.britannica.com/topic/blindmans-buff.

209. John Taylor, "Go Fish Game Rules," PlayingCardDecks.com, August 4, 2019, https://playingcarddecks.com/blogs/how-to-play/go-fish-game-rules.

210. How Plath played this game is not certain. For an example, see Google Play, "Solitaire Social: Classic Game," last updated February 22, 2019, https://play.google.com/store/apps/details?id=air.com.kosmos.km&hl=en_US&gl=US.

211. *Singing Tree*, published in 1940, is set in Budapest after World War I.

212. *Sung under the Silver Umbrella*, published in 1935, contains poems for children. GoodReads, "Sung under the Silver Umbrella," n.d., https://www.goodreads.com/book/show/2816256-sung-under-the-silver-umbrella.

213. "Jenny Cracked Corn" is usually called "Jimmy Crack Corn," a popular minstrel song. Liquisearch, "Jimmy Crack Corn: History and Interpretation," n.d., https://www.liquisearch.com/jimmy_crack_corn/history_and_interpretation.

214. These letters are either lost or in private hands.

215. In the game of loose caboose, "the loose cabooses try to attach themselves to an end of a train, then the person at the front of that train becomes a loose caboose." Mr. N's Physical Education Resource, "Loose Caboose," n.d., https://physed.tripod.com/loosecaboose.htm.

216. This sketch is included in Kathleen Connors and Sally Bailey, eds., *Eye Rhymes: Sylvia Plath's Art of the Visual* (Oxford: Oxford University Press, 2007).

217. Published in 1937, *White Stag*, by Kate Seredy, is a story of the Huns and Magyars roaming across Asia and into Europe, including the life of Attila the Hun.

218. Published in 1943, *Stand Fast and Reply*, by Lavinia R. Davis, is about a young girl growing up in Ohio.

219. These letters are lost or in private hands.

220. The Loungways are Aurelia's friends.

221. The point of the game keep away is apparently to intercept the ball as it is passed between players.

222. In one version of the game drop the handkerchief, "one player runs behind the other players as they stand in a circle and drops a handkerchief behind one of them who then must pick up the handkerchief and run around the circle after the first player and try to tag, catch, or kiss the first player before he or she gets to the vacant place in the circle left by the second player." Merriam-Webster Dictionary, s.v. "drop the handkerchief," n.d., https://www.merriam-webster .com/dictionary/drop%20the%20handkerchief.

223. The Flying Dutchman is a game that involves forming a circle by joining hands while two players outside the circle, representing the lost ship the *Flying Dutchman*, break into the circle, making the two players with unjoined hands the new Flying Dutchman. Ultimate Camp Resource, "Flying Dutchman," n.d., https://www.ultimatecampresource.com/camp-games/circle-games/ flying-dutchman/.

224. A spatter print "is a simple type of stenciling in which the paint or ink is sprayed over a shape or natural object which keeps the ink from touching the material." Chest of Books, "Projects: Spatter Printing," n.d., https://chestofbooks.com/crafts/camping/Creative/Projects-Spatter -Printing.html.

225. Kick the can is a complicated version of hide-and-seek. Hella Entertainment, "How to Play Kick the Can," n.d., https://www.considerable.com/entertainment/games/kick-the-can/.

226. *Quiz of Two Cities* features competitions between two cities. Fandom, "The Quiz of Two Cities," US Game Shows Wiki, n.d., https://gameshows.fandom.com/wiki/The_Quiz_of _Two_Cities.

227. This letter is lost or in private hands.

228. See entries for July 5, 6, 8, and 14, 1945. This letter is lost or in private hands.

229. This refers to a frappe, often called a "frap" in Boston.

230. See note 174.

231. Lake Waban is on the Wellesley campus. Trip Advisor, "Things to Do in Wellesley," n.d., https://www.tripadvisor.com/Attraction_Review-g41891-d7140134-Reviews-Lake_Waban-Wellesley _Massachusetts.html.

232. In *Son of Lassie* (1945), the protagonist is trapped in Norway in 1942. IMDb, "Son of Lassie," n.d., https://www.imdb.com/title/tt0038097/.

233. In *Gentle Annie* (1944), set in 1901, "an undercover US Marshal is sent to Oklahoma Territory to investigate a string of train robberies and arrest the culprits." IMDb, "Gentle Annie," n.d., https://www.imdb.com/title/tt0036859/.

234. *Bulldog Drummond* is a crime drama. Some episodes are available at Classic Radio Shows, "Bulldog Drummond," n.d., https://www.myclassicradio.net/bulldog-drummond.html.

235. Published in 1934, *Invincible Louisa* is by Cornelia Meigs. GoodReads, "Invincible Louisa: The Story of the Author of Little Women," n.d., https://www.goodreads.com/book/show/680154 .Invincible_Louisa.

236. Spit is played with two decks of cards with the aim of getting rid of all the cards as fast as possible. Bicycle, "Spit," n.d., https://bicyclecards.com/how-to-play/spit/.

237. I doubt it is a version of the game spit. Bicycle, "I Doubt It," n.d., https://bicyclecards.com/how-to-play/i-doubt-it/.

238. Published in 1916, *Gulliver the Great: And Other Dog Stories* is by Walter A Dyer. Forgotten Books, "Gulliver the Great," n.d., https://www.forgottenbooks.com/en/books/Gulliver theGreat_10530475.

239. *A Sea Between* is a "four-square stand against anti-Semitism. The heroine encounters the dragon of anti-Semitic prejudice early in the story during a visit to her fiancé's family in a locality resembling Cape Cod." Dorothy Adelson, "Elsie Dinsmore's New Problem," review of *A Sea Between*, by Lavinia R. Davis, *Commentary*, December 1945, https://www.commentarymagazine.com/articles/dorothy-adelson/a-sea-between-by-lavinia-r-davis/.

240. This letter is lost or in private hands.

241. *Daddy-Long-Legs* is a 1912 epistolary novel, by the American writer Jean Webster, about an orphan sent to college by an unknown benefactor. GoodReads, "Daddy-Long-Legs," n.d., https://www.goodreads.com/book/show/1499952.Daddy_Long_Legs.

242. This letter is lost or in private hands.

243. Lowell (1855–1916) was an astronomer famous for claiming there were canals on Mars.

244. *Tello-Test* was a radio show in which random people were called to answer a question to win a prize. Dave Lehner, "July 24: Minot Memories—Old Minot Radio," July 24, 2017, https://kcjb910.iheart.com/content/2017-07-19-july-24-minot-memories-old-minot-radio/.

245. Plath does not name the book, but it may be the classic work *Madame Curie: A Biography* (1937), by Curie's daughter Eve, which has had a lasting impact on young women, including Susan Sontag. See entry for October 24, 1945.

246. *The Perilous Seat*, published in 1929, is by Caroline Dale Snedeker and set in ancient Greece. Google Books, "The Perilous Seat," n.d., https://books.google.com/books/about/The_Perilous_Seat .html?id=ZgIqAQAAMAAJ.

247. *Story Girl* is a 1911 novel by L. M. Montgomery, featuring fourteen-year-old Sara Stanley, her stories, and adventures on Prince Edward Island. See L. M. Montgomery, *The Story Girl* (1911; Project Gutenberg, 2004), https://www.gutenberg.org/files/5342/5342-h/5342-h.htm.

248. *The Golden Road* is a 1913 novel by L. M. Montgomery and the sequel to *The Story Girl*. See L. M. Montgomery, *The Golden Road* (1913; Project Gutenberg, 2008), https://www.gutenberg .org/files/316/316-h/316-h.htm.

249. Cape Juby is off the coast of southern Morocco.

250. The convention attended was the Norfolk County Teachers' Convention along with a concert at Tremont Temple, 88 Tremont Street, Boston, Massachusetts.

251. See Wikipedia, "GI Joe Trading Card Game," n.d., https://en.m.wikipedia.org/wiki/G.I._Joe _Trading_Card_Game.

252. See note 66.

253. The photograph is missing.

254. Wheat Sparkies is a puffed wheat cereal introduced in 1940. MrBreakfast.com, "Puffed Wheat Sparkies," n.d., https://www.mrbreakfast.com/cereal_detail.asp?id=745.

255. See note 177.

256. In the film *Our Vines Have Tender Grapes* (1945), "a Norwegian farmer lovingly raises his daughter in rural World War II–era Benson Junction, Wisconsin." IMDb, "Our Vines Have Tender Grapes," n.d., https://www.imdb.com/title/tt0037963/.

257. The thank-you notes are lost or in private hands.

258. Junket is a dish of sweetened and flavored curds of milk, often served with fruit.

259. Russian bank is "a competitive patience game for two players." For details, see Pagat, "Russian Bank," last modified April 19, 2022, https://www.pagat.com/patience/crapette.html.

260. Edward MacDowell was an American composer. Library of Congress, "Edward Alexander MacDowell (1860–1908)," n.d., https://www.loc.gov/item/ihas.200035715/.

261. On spool knitting, see Needlepointers.com, "Spool Knitting: How to Spool Knit," n.d., https://www.needlepointers.com/main/youtubecontent.aspx?youtubepageid=82.

262. *Her Highness and the Bellboy* is a 1945 film. IMDb, "Her Highness and the Bellboy," n.d., https://www.imdb.com/title/tt0037769/.

263. *Dangerous Partners* is a 1945 film. IMDb, "Dangerous Partners," n.d., https://www.imdb.com/title/tt0037634/.

264. "Horatius at the Bridge" is a poem by Thomas Babington Macaulay about a noble Roman who beats back the Etruscan invaders. N. S. Gill, "'Horatius at the Bridge' by Thomas Babington Macaulay," last modified January 13, 2019, https://www.thoughtco.com/horatius-at-the-bridge-4070724.

265. *The Dragon's Secret*, published in 1921, involves a young girl, the seashore, and a mysterious treasure chest. Amazon, "The Dragon's Secret," n.d., https://www.amazon.com/Dragons-Secret-Augusta-Huiell-Seaman-ebook/dp/B004TRNKE8.

266. *The Life of Riley* is a situation comedy that originated the phrase "life of Riley," meaning an easy, carefree life. Episodes available at Old Time Radio Downloads, "The Life of Riley," n.d., https://www.oldtimeradiodownloads.com/comedy/the-life-of-riley/3.

267. In *Granite Harbor*, published in 1946, a teenage girl reluctantly moves to Granite Harbor, Michigan, from Texas with her parents and ultimately adapts to her new home. It is set in the Marquette area on Lake Superior. GoodReads," Granite Harbor," n.d., https://www.goodreads.com/en/book/show/5187212.

268. In *A Year to Grow*, published in 1943 and by Helene Conway, "Anne was not sure that she was going to like Maple Grove, the convent school outside of Boston which her mother had attended when she was a girl." GoodReads, "A Year to Grow," n.d., https://www.goodreads.com/book/show/55856611-a-year-to-grow.

269. Raymond Ditmars was "an American herpetologist, writer, public speaker and pioneering natural history filmmaker." *Scarsdale Inquirer*, "Raymond L. Ditmars, Expert on Reptiles, Dies in Hospital," May 15, 1942, Historical Newspapers, https://news.hrvh.org/veridian/?a=d&d=scarsdaleinquire19420515.2.69&e=-------en-20--1--txt-txIN-------.

270. *The Strange Romance of Evelyn Winters* is a soap opera. See Internet Archive, "The Strange Romance of Evelyn Winters," December 2021, https://archive.org/details/OTRR_Curated_Strange_Romance_of_Evelyn_Winters.

271. See note 234.

272. A box coat is a loose coat fitted at the shoulders.

273. See note 138.

274. In *Barberry Gate*, published in 1925 and by Jane D. Abbott, "a boy flyer opened the Barberry Gate, closed since the day great-grandfather Colfax locked it, and Winsome learned the romantic story behind it all." GoodReads, "Barberry Gate," n.d., https://www.goodreads.com/book/show/42360195-barberry-gate.

275. *Island Adventure*, published in 1935, is a story about an American family's trip to Bali. *New York Times*, review of *Island Adventure*, by Adele de Leeuw, March 3, 1935, https://www.nytimes.com/1935/03/03/archives/island-adventure-a-novel-for-girls-by-adele-de-leeuw-pictures-by.html.

276. *Career for Jennifer*, published in 1941, is a "juvenile novel about a teenage girl who rescues a cat, which turns out to belong to a world-famous woman photographer—who, to show her appreciation, offers to teach Jennifer all about photography, and in so doing helps her launch a career." Antiquarian Booksellers' Association of America, "Career for Jennifer," n.d., https://www.abaa.org/book/304489140.

277. *Kitty Foyle* is a radio show based on the movie starring Ginger Rogers who appears in the April 6, 1946, episode available at Old Time Radio Downloads, "Kitty Foyle," n.d., audio, 29:56, https://www.oldtimeradiodownloads.com/drama/academy-award-theater/kitty-foyle-1946-04-06.

278. *Jack Benny Program*, "Weekend at the Acme Plaza," April 7, 1946, mentioned at This Day in Jack Benny, "The Jack Benny Program 1946," n.d., https://thisdaybenny.com/2018/04/30/the-jack-benny-program-1946/.

279. *Beloved Enemy* is a 1936 film. IMDb, "Beloved Enemy," n.d., https://www.imdb.com/title/tt0027345/.

280. For more on this the film *Come and Get It* (1936), see Carl Rollyson, *A Real American Character: The Life of Walter Brennan* (Jackson: University Press of Mississippi, 2015), 57–59.

281. *Jenny's Secret Island*, published in 1943 and by Phillis Garrard, is a coming-of-age story set in pre–World War II Bermuda.

New York Times, review of *Jenny's Secret Island*, by Phillis Garrard, June 27, 1943, https://timesmachine.nytimes.com/timesmachine/1943/06/27/85108300.html?pageNumber=57.

282. *The Piper* was first produced in 1909 and is based on the tale of the Pied Piper of Hamelin. My Poetic Side, "Josephine Preston Peabody," n.d., https://mypoeticside.com/poets/Josephine-preston-peabody-poems.

283. *The Bandit of Sherwood Forest* is a 1946 film. IMDb, "The Bandit of Sherwood Forest," n.d., https://www.imdb.com/title/tt0038326/.

284. *Masquerade in Mexico* is a 1945 film. IMDb, "Masquerade in Mexico," n.d., https://www.imdb.com/title/tt0037903/.

285. "Evangeline" is Longfellow's poem, published in 1847, about an Acadian girl in search of her lost love. It is a surprisingly modern story of displacement.

286. For more information, see International Order of the Rainbow for Girls, home page, n.d., https://www.gorainbow.org.

287. *The Spanish Main* is a 1945 adventure film full of treachery, pirates, and political corruption. IMDb, "The Spanish Main," n.d., https://www.imdb.com/title/tt0038108/.

288. *The Enchanted Forest* is a 1945 film about a hermit who talks to animals. IMDb, "The Enchanted Forest," n.d., https://www.imdb.com/title/tt0037672/.

289. *At the Back of the North Wind* was published in book form in 1871. It is a fantasy novel about a boy named Diamond and his adventures.

290. In *Doctor Ellen*, first published in 1944, "Lovely Ellen Paige met a host of violent reactions every time she affirmed her intention of being a doctor. 'It's—well, it's so unfeminine.' 'It's hard for a man; it's even harder for a woman.' 'I want a doctor—one with pants on!' 'No woman should be a doctor—and you, least of all.'" See the product description at Amazon, "Doctor Ellen," n.d., https://www.amazon.com/Doctor-Ellen-Vintage-Romance-F-163/dp/044106163X.

291. *Mystery in Blue* was published in 1945.

292. In *With a High Heart*, first published in 1945, "to her dismay, library science student Anne McLane is assigned a summer-long practicum at an underfunded country library, where she ends up as a bookmobile driver." GoodReads, "With a High Heart," n.d., https://www.goodreads.com/book/show/15097971-with-a-high-heart.

293. This letter is lost or in private hands.

294. This letter is lost or in private hands.

295. For a description of a peplum skirt, see Merriam-Webster, s.v. "peplum," n.d., https://www.merriam-webster.com/dictionary/peplum.

296. A shadowgraph is a "picture produced by throwing a shadow, as of the hands, on a lighted screen, wall, or the like." Dictionary.com, s.v. "shadowgraph," n.d., https://www.dictionary.com/browse/shadowgraph. See also Wolfgang Merzkirch, "Shadowgraph Technique," Thermopedia, last modified February 8, 2011, https://thermopedia.com/content/1117/.

297. Rickrack is a braided trim in the form of a zigzag. Merriam-Webster, s.v. "rickrack," n.d., https://www.merriam-webster.com/dictionary/rickrack.

298. For information on the game of hearts, see Bicycle, "Hearts," n.d., https://bicyclecards.com/how-to-play/hearts/.

299. The letters she wrote were to stamp companies and do not seem to be extant.

300. This letter is lost or in private hands.

301. In *Meet Corliss Archer*, "Corliss' life revolves around the men in her life, which are her father and Dexter Franklin, the boy next door." See Old Time Radio Catalog, "Meet Corliss Archer," n.d., https://www.otrcat.com/p/meet-corliss-archer, where some episodes are also available.

302. For information on the game tripoli, see Pagat, "Tripoli," last modified November 3, 2016, https://www.pagat.com/stops/3in1.html.

303. See note 172.

304. Published in 1937, *Bright Island* is by Mabel L. Robinson. Katie Fitzgerald, review of *Bright Island*, by Mabel L. Robinson, Read-at-Home Mom, October 28, 2012, http://www.readathomemom.com/2012/10/bright-island.html.

305. In *Going on Sixteen*, published in 1946 and by Betty Cavanna, "Fourteen-year-old Julie tries to escape her own sense of inadequacy and her friends' talk of boys and parties by devoting herself to raising an orphaned collie pup." GoodReads, "Going on Sixteen," n.d., https://www.goodreads.com/book/show/1621660.Going_on_Sixteen.

306. This letter from her Belgian pen pal is lost or in private hands.

307. In *Girl without a Country*, published in 1944 and by Martha Lee Poston, "when the Japanese invade China, a young American girl remains in China with her doctor father to help in the hospital, but after Pearl Harbor she makes a dangerous journey across China to the airport to escape the war." GoodReads, "Girl without a Country," n.d., https://www.goodreads.com/book/show/40236975-the-girl-without-a-country.

308. *The Falcon's Alibi* is a 1946 film. IMDb, "The Falcon's Alibi," n.d., https://www.imdb.com/title/tt0038519/.

309. *Centennial Summer* is a 1946 film. IMDb, "Centennial Summer," n.d., https://www.imdb
.com/title/tt0038406/. See also a discussion of the film in Carl Rollyson, *A Real American Character: The Life of Walter Brennan* (Jackson: University Press of Mississippi, 2015), 119–21.

310. "Forfeits are stunts or actions that a person who has made a mistake or lost a game are required to carry out as punishment (and for the amusement of their fellow players). . . . If a group of teenagers uses the kissing forfeits, the odds are good that someone will *want* to earn a forfeit so they'll have an excuse to kiss their boyfriend or girlfriend." Victorian Games, "Forfeits," n.d., https://historicalgames.neocities.org/Victorian/forfeits.html. Emphasis original.

311. Correctly spelled "Mortimer Snerd." See Fandom, "Mortimer Snerd," Muppet Wiki, n.d., https://muppet.fandom.com/wiki/Mortimer_Snerd

312. Published in 1940, *Growing Pains* is a portrait of the artist as a young girl.

313. *People are Funny* is a TV series in which contestants are asked to "carry out stunts in order to prove that 'People Are Funny.'" IMDb, "People are Funny," n.d., https://www.imdb.com/title/tt0046635/.

314. O. Henry is the pen name of William Sydney Porter (1862–1910).

315. *California*, a 1947 film, is an "epic account of how California became a state, featuring a wagon train, the Gold Rush, a wicked saloon queen, and an evil profiteer." IMDb, "California," n.d., https://www.imdb.com/title/tt0038392/.

316. *Susie Steps Out* (1946) is about what happens when fifteen-year-old Susie lies about her age and gets a job in a nightclub. IMDb, "Susie Steps Out," n.d., https://www.imdb.com/title/tt0038999/.

317. Published in 1941, *Forty Faces*, by Mary Urmston, is about a young girl studying to be a teacher.

318. In *The Cuckoo Clock*, published in 1877 and by Mary Louisa Molesworth, "a small child and a cuckoo from a cuckoo clock become unlikely friends. At night the clock transports her to magical places." Wikipedia, "*The Cuckoo Clock*," last modified April 15, 2022, https://en.wikipedia.org/wiki/The_Cuckoo_Clock.

319. *The Fat Man* is a take off of Dashiell Hammett's detective stories. Great Detectives of Old Time Radio, "The Fat Man," n.d., https://www.greatdetectives.net/detectives/fat-man/.

320. *The Adventures of the Thin Man* is based on Dashiell Hammett's novel *The Thin Man*. Old Time Radio Downloads, "The Thin Man," n.d., https://www.oldtimeradiodownloads.com/crime/the-thin-man.

321. Published in 1939, *Wind, Sand, and Stars*, by Antoine de Saint-Exupéry, is about his hazardous career flying to deliver the mail.

322. *The Inner Sanctum* was a popular mystery show, emphasizing horror. Old Time Radio Downloads, "Inner Sanctum Mysteries," n.d., https://www.oldtimeradiodownloads.com/thriller/inner-sanctum-mysteries.

323. This letter is lost or in private hands.

324. These letters are lost or are in private hands.

325. Jibing is shifting the sail from one side of the ship to the other.

326. This letter is lost or in private hands.

327. *Mrs. Mike: The Story of Katherine Mary Flannigan* (1947), by Benedict Freedman, "is the love story of Katherine Mary O'Fallon, a young Irish girl from Boston, and Sergeant Mike Flannigan of the Canadian Mounted Police, who is priest, doctor and magistrate to all in the great Canadian wilderness area under his supervision." LibraryThing, "Mrs. Mike: The Story of Katherine Mary Flannigan," n.d., https://www.librarything.com/work/10011.

328. For more on Cowl, see IMDb, "Jane Cowl," n.d., https://www.imdb.com/name/nm 0184785/.

329. For information on Mohonk Mountain House, see Mohonk Mountain House, "Welcome to Mohonk Mountain House," n.d., https://www.mohonk.com.

330. *Vacation Days* is a 1947 film. IMDb, "Vacation Days," n.d., https://www.imdb.com/title/ tt0039948/.

331. *Calcutta* is a 1946 film. IMDb, "Calcutta," n.d., https://www.imdb.com/title/tt0039235/.

332. William Dana Orcutt was a writer about books and book design. SNAC, "Orcutt, William Dana, 1870-1953," n.d., https://snaccooperative.org/ark:/99166/w6kw5kqd.

333. Published in 1938, *In Hazard* is "based on detailed research into an actual event, Richard Hughes's tale of high suspense on the high seas is an extraordinary story of men under pressure and the unexpected ways they prove their mettle—or crack." *New York Review of Books*, "In Hazard," n.d., https://www.nyrb.com/products/in-hazard?variant=1094929861.

334. *Thunderbolt* is William Wyler's 1947 documentary about the Twelfth Air Force in northern Italy. Wikipedia, "*Thunderbolt* (1947 film)," last modified September 11, 2022, https://en.wikipedia .org/wiki/Thunderbolt_(1947_film).

335. For how to play honeymoon bridge with two players, see Pagat, "Honeymoon Bridge," last modified November 15, 2013, https://www.pagat.com/auctionwhist/honeymoon.html.

336. "City Streets" is included in Steinberg and Kukil, *The Letters of Sylvia Plath*, 1:157.

337. See entry for July 12, 1947. "Cynthia Clubs" were part of a marketing campaign, as reported in *Motion Picture Herald*, October 18, 1947 (courtesy of Kathleen Spaltro).

338. *Jack London* is a 1943 film. IMDb, "Jack London," n.d., https://www.imdb.com/title/ tt0036051/.

339. *Nob Hill* is a 1945 Technicolor film about a Barbary Coast saloon keeper, starring George Raft and Joan Bennett. IMDb, "Nob Hill," n.d., https://www.imdb.com/title/tt0037946/.

340. What Pollard did is not clear, but see the entry for December 13, 1947.

341. The Maugus Club is a social and sports club established in 1893. See Maugus Club, "Welcome to Our Club!" n.d., http://maugus.clubhosting.org.

342. "P. N." refers to Perry Norton.

343. In *Killer McCoy* (1947), "following a mishap in the ring, hard-nosed lightweight Tommy 'Killer' McCoy gets mixed-up with a big-time gambler and falls for his educated daughter, Sheila, against her father's better wishes." IMDb, "Killer McCoy," n.d., https://www.imdb.com/title/ tt0039531/. Rooney was cast against the type of all-American boy he usually played.

344. In *Her Husband's Affairs* (1947), "a scientist invents a formula that removes old, thinning hair and replaces it with thick, new hair. Complications ensue." IMDb, "Her Husband's Affairs," n.d., https://www.imdb.com/title/tt0039456/.

345. See Irwin Edman, "A Reasonable Life in a Mad World," *The Atlantic*, March 1949, https:// www.theatlantic.com/magazine/archive/1949/03/a-reasonable-life-in-a-mad-world/643562/.

346. Tall, athletic, and handsome, he is mentioned in Plath's letters and in HC.

347. The great German novelist, a Nobel Prize winner, was exiled in the United States during the Third Reich (1933-1945). Plath read several of his novels including *Buddenbrooks* (1921) and *The Magic Mountain* (1924). See SPL.

348. Ten Acres is apparently a private school in Wellesley.

349. Ilo Pill's letters are lost or in private hands.

350. It is puzzling that she wants to learn bridge since earlier diary entries report that Plath knew how to play the game already.

351. The relief method of printing is a "process consisting of cutting or etching a printing surface in such a way that all that remains of the original surface is the design to be printed. Examples of relief-printing processes include woodcut, anastatic printing (also called relief etching), linocut, and metal cut. Britannica, "Relief Printing," n.d., https://www.britannica.com/art/relief-printing.

352. This is a quotation from *The Mayor of Casterbridge* (1886), by Thomas Hardy.

353. See the section Abbreviations.

354. As part of her scholarship terms, Plath waited on tables in Haven House and later used the abbreviation "BW" to refer to this activity, which is used in this book.

355. Francestown is a farmhouse in New Hampshire that belonged to Brown's aunt.

356. One of the people she is referring to is Cohen.

357. Pearl Primus was a dancer and choreographer. For more information, see John Perpener, "Dance of the African Diaspora: Pearl Primus," Jacob's Pillow Dance Interactive, May 2017, https://danceinteractive.jacobspillow.org/themes-essays/african-diaspora/pearl-primus/.

358. For more on Morrow House, see Smith College, "Morrow House," n.d., https://www.smith.edu/student-life/residence-life/houses/morrow-house.

359. Rally Day is a Smith tradition since 1876, commemorating the birthday of George Washington. Rally Day is "highlighted by a festive all-college gathering at which distinguished alums are awarded Smith College Medals by the president." Smith College, "Rally Day," n.d., https://www.smith.edu/about-smith/college-events/rally-day.

360. Niebuhr was an American theologian and commentator on politics, history, and society. One of his important books is *The Irony of American History* (1952), in which he explores the evil that sometimes results from idealism and good intentions.

361. *Darkness at Noon* is a famous novel about the Stalinist purge of the 1930s.

362. See entry for May 4, 1951.

363. The film she is referring to is *Un Chien Andalou* (1929).

364. See entry for May 9, 1951.

365. Ford was a scholarship donor to Smith College.

366. The senior step sing is a "major event . . . where the senior class gathers at the front of Neilson Library as members of Sophomore Push sing to them." Smithipedia, "Ivy Day and Commencement Weekend," n.d., https://sophia.smith.edu/blog/smithipedia/traditions/ivy-day-and-commencement-weekend/.

367. Mensel was the director of scholarships.

368. Edith Sitwell is an important British poet and member of the famous Sitwell family, many of them prominent literary figures. Plath owned seven volumes of Sitwell's poetry, including her most famous collection, *The Canticle of the Rose* (1949), as well as books about Sitwell's work. See SPL.

369. Sachem's Head is a private yacht club in Guildford, Connecticut.

370. See Smith College, "Float Night," n.d., https://socialnetwork.smith.edu/event/505044.

371. By "M," Plath is possibly referring to Marcia Brown.

372. Wheaton was a high school principal in Concord, New Hampshire, who had a son, David, and a wife, Lucy.

373. The poem is a parody of Alfred Tennyson's poem, "The Eagle."

374. See SPL for the titles of books Plath read and which ones she owned.

375. Plath is referring to *Modern Christian Revolutionaries: Kierkegaard, Gill, Chesterton, Andrews and Berdyaev* (1947), edited by Donald Attwater. See SPL.

376. Savin Rock is a popular park in West Haven, Connecticut, with a boardwalk, beach, and restaurants.

377. "Mr. C" probably refers to her teacher, Mr. Crockett.

378. The *Mistral* was a sixty-six-foot yacht.

379. Plath describes Stanway, a Canadian, as a "ruddy, snubnosed chap" in a letter to Aurelia Plath, July 26, 1951.

380. "Eastern" refers to the Eastern Yacht Club in Marblehead.

381. Esther Blodgett was the sister of Plath's employer, Mrs. Mayo. Marcia Brown worked for the Blodgetts.

382. Michael was a junior at Dartmouth.

383. She is possibly referring to Ventura, a high school classmate.

384. Giesey and O'Neil were Smith classmates.

385. Arrowsmith was a Wesleyan student that Plath called the "most handsome thing I ever laid eyes on" in a letter to her mother, October 1, 1951.

386. See note 189.

387. Hirsch was a Smith classmate.

388. See entry for September 23, 1951.

389. For more on the dance, see entry for October 8, 1951.

390. Mountain Day is a tradition at Smith during which the president cancels classes.

391. "Press board" refers to the Smith College News Office.

392. Powell was a Smith classmate, "very sweet . . . very friendly—red haired."

393. Plath's notes on Buckley's talk are at the Lilly Library, Indiana University, as are her reports on many other events at Smith.

394. Sophia's circus is a Smith event. Plath kept a ticket stub from the 1950 circus in her scrapbook. See Peter K. Steinberg, "Sylvia Plath's High School Scrapbook," Sylvia Plath Info Blog, May 1, 2017, https://sylviaplathinfo.blogspot.com/2017/05/sylvia-plaths-high-school-scrapbook.html.

395. Plath owned several editions of Eliot's poems and plays. See SPL.

396. Plath owned a copy of Eugene O'Neill's play. See SPL.

397. She is referring to Marion Freeman, mother of Ruth Freeman, Sylvia's childhood friend. Sylvia sometimes addresses her as "Aunt Marion."

398. By "Review Sec-Gov," Plath means reviewing a section of government.

399. By "Fran," Plath is possibly referring to Frances Yvonne White MacKenzie, a Smith student.

400. For information on the Davis Center's recreational and other events, see Smithipedia, "Davis Center," n.d., https://sophia.smith.edu/blog/smithipedia/places/david-center/.

401. College Hall is the oldest building on the Smith College campus. Smithipedia, "College Hall," n.d., https://sophia.smith.edu/blog/smithipedia/places/college-hall/.

402. Tenney House is a Smith College cooperative. Smith College, "Tenney House," n.d., https://www.smith.edu/student-life/residence-life/houses/tenney-house.

403. The Jimmy Fund Building is part of the Dana Farmer Cancer Institute, established in 1948. The Jimmy Fund, "About the Jimmy Fund," n.d., https://www.jimmyfund.org/about-us/about-the-jimmy-fund/.

404. *Lady's Not for Burning* is a Christopher Fry play. Wikipedia, "*Lady's Not for Burning*," last modified May 12, 2022, https://en.wikipedia.org/wiki/The_Lady%27s_Not_for_Burning.

405. "Mrs. B—call" perhaps refers to a call to Brown's mother about Marcia's measles.

406. The People's Institute teaches an introductory art course to children in Northampton.

407. The "Harlow case" probably had to do with Plath's service on the Honor Board, which adjudicated student misconduct.

408. The case briefs were perhaps for the Honor Board.

409. She is referring to the Pines Hotel and resort in Cotuit, Massachusetts. Plath considered working there.

410. "Hamp-library" refers to the Northampton Public Library.

411. "David" perhaps refers to her childhood friend David Freeman.

412. Plath perhaps meant William Graham Cole, Smith College chaplain, who debated William F. Buckley Jr. on the Smith College campus.

413. Plath's mention of "newspapers" seems to be part of an assignment for her government class.

414. This marks the beginning of her work on her prize-winning story later published in *Mademoiselle*, "Sunday at the Mintons."

415. By "Cong. On trial," Plath means *Congress on Trial* (1950) by James McGregor Burns.

416. Plath owned copies of Drew's books about T. S. Eliot and modern poetry. See SPL.

417. "White House" perhaps refers to Sessions House, a part of which once housed the White House Inn.

418. By "Old Mill," Plath perhaps meant Old Mill Inn in Springfield, Massachusetts.

419. "Enid" probably refers to Enid Epstein.

420. "Carol" probably refers to Carol Pierson, a housemate.

421. Plath owned a collection of this important twentieth-century poet's work. See SPL.

422. "Club women" were interested in education and culture but were often scorned as earnest but tiresome dilettantes not fully integrated into society—similar to "career women," another negative term in Plath's lexicon.

423. By "Carol," Plath probably meant Carol Pierson.

424. *Campus Cat* is a humor magazine.

425. "Mrs. Sherk" probably refers to the wife of Kenneth Sherk, a professor of chemistry at Smith.

426. "Maria" refers to Maria Canellakis Michaelides.

427. Senior personals are profiles of graduating seniors. See entry for May 27, 1952.

428. See note 427.

429. "Savoy Coral" refers to Cohen's coral convertible.

430. *Three Lives* (1909) is by Gertrude Stein.

431. "Bill" probably refers to William Norton, father of Dick and Perry.

432. Brewster is where the Nortons rented a summer cottage.

433. The apron skirt was probably used for waitressing.

434. The Herring River is an estuary in Wellfleet, Massachusetts.

435. The head waiter offered Plath extra hours so she could earn more money, but she decided the increased work would exhaust her.

436. Plath worked briefly for Mrs. Williams.

437. This letter is lost or in private hands.

438. Otha is the name of an African American cook who worked with Dick Norton at his summer job.

439. This refers to Art Kramer's employers.

440. Kathy was the oldest Cantor child, a seventeen-year-old living in Holland.

441. This letter is lost or in private hands.

442. These letters are lost or in private hands.

443. These letters are lost or in private hands.

444. Valerie Gendron was a magazine writer Sylvia visited to talk about writing.

445. This letter is lost or in private hands.

446. For more on the handwriting analysis, see entry for August 4, 1952.

447. These letters are lost or in private hands.

448. These letters are lost or in private hands.

449. These letters are lost or in private hands.

450. The science she studied may have been Christian science.

451. These letters are lost or in private hands.

452. On Camp Tonset, see Tim Weller, "When the Cape Was Summer Camp HQ," Chatham Historical Society, n.d., https://chathamhistoricalsociety.org/wp-content/uploads/When-The -Cape-Was-Summer-Camp-HQ.pdf.

453. On Crystal Lake, see Orleans Pond Coalition, "Crystal Lake," n.d., https://www.orleans pondcoalition.org/healthy-waters/freshwater/crystal-lake/.

454. "Merrythought" most likely refers to a toy shop.

455. These letters are lost or in private hands.

456. This letter is lost or in private hands.

457. Dudley was a Northeastern University freshman.

458. "Richard" perhaps refers to Richard Newell.

459. Smythe was a Yale student.

460. "Aunt M." probably refers to Mildred Norton.

461. See next entry, September 4, 1952.

462. Besides the letter to Mrs. Cantor, these letters are lost or in private hands.

463. This letter is lost or in private hands.

464. *Carrie* (1952) is based on Theodore Dreiser's novel *Sister Carrie* (1900).

465. *Don't Bother to Knock* (1952) features Marilyn Monroe as a mentally disturbed babysitter.

466. Heavenly Hash is a fruit dessert. Steve Gordon, "Heavenly Hash Recipe," Taste of Southern, March 24, 2019, https://www.tasteofsouthern.com/heavenly-hash-recipe/.

467. These letters are lost or in private hands.

468. On the Quabbin Reservoir, see Wikipedia "Quabbin Reservoir," last modified September 8, 2022.

469. "CW" possibly refers to creative writing class.

470. See entry for October 6, 1952.

471. The Green Room is an exhibition space in Smith College Museum of Art.

472. "Enid" perhaps refers to Enid Epstein.

473. Neuberg was a classmate and resident of Lawrence House.

474. This refers to Smith College Warden Alison Loomis Cook. The warden is the dean of students. Plath was probably calling her about Honor Board work. See Smith College, "History of the Warden, Dean of Students at Smith College, January 17, 1978," n.d., https://findingaids .smith.edu/repositories/4/archival_objects/24829.

475. Walsh probably refers to the then president of the Hampshire Book Shop. She had given a talk at Smith about publishing.

476. Decker was her Princeton date.

477. This dinner took place at the home of Professor Davis.

478. Little was a *Mademoiselle* College Board editor.

479. These letters are lost or in private hands.

480. This letter is lost or in private hands.

481. These letters are lost or in private hands.

482. This letter is lost or in private hands.

483. Plath was visiting Dick Norton, who had tuberculosis. For more information on the sanitarium, see Wikipedia, "Adirondack Cottage Sanitarium," last modified July 26, 2022, https:// en.m.wikipedia.org/wiki/Adirondack_Cottage_Sanitarium.

484. Lynn was a doctor and friend of Dick Norton's.

485. The doctor was Lynn. See entry for December 26, 1952.

486. For more on Scudder, see Smith College, "Scudder, Vida," n.d., https://findingaids.smith .edu/agents/people/39466.

487. Plath's letters to Cohen were destroyed.

488. There are several books about the holy grail that Plath studied, and it is not certain which work this refers to. See SPL.

489. A book about Chaucer written by Professor Patch. He wrote several. Plath owned two of his books. See SPL.

490. This story was rejected by *Mademoiselle*, later published by Harper in the US and Faber and Faber in England in 2019.

491. This letter is lost or in private hands.

492. Plath is quoting Henley's famous poem "Invictus" (1888).

493. See SPL.

494. In her calendar, Plath always refers to "Davis," never the subject matter of the class. For a description of the course, see Peter K. Steinberg, "The Education of Sylvia Plath, Smith College, 1952–1953," Sylvia Plath Info Blog, September 11, 2017, https://sylviaplathinfo.blogspot .com/2017/09/the-education-of-sylvia-plath-smith.html.

495. West Rock Ridge overlooks New Haven.

496. Shirley Baldwin, Perry Norton's girlfriend and future wife, was a Middlebury student.

497. *True Confessions* is a magazine aimed at young women readers. Wikipedia, "*True Confessions*," last modified April 21, 2022, https://en.m.wikipedia.org/wiki/True_Confessions_(magazine).

498. This letter is lost or in private hands.

499. "Ransom analysis" is possibly a reference to poet and critic John Crowe Ransom. Poetry Foundation, "John Crowe Ransom," n.d., https://www.poetryfoundation.org/poets/john-crowe -ransom.

500. These letters are lost or in private hands.

501. The letters to Wunderlich and Norton are lost or in private hands.

502. See next entry, May 10, 1953.

503. On Lighthouse Point, see City of New Haven, "Our Parks," n.d., https://www.newhavenct .gov/Home/Components/FacilityDirectory/FacilityDirectory/16/664.

504. Plath was writing about a student who had enlisted in the Women's Marine Corps.

505. For more on the Willard article, see entry for May 16, 1953.

506. On Grécourt Gates, see Smith College, "Grécourt Gates, West Street and Elm Street Project to Begin," May 6, 2015, https://www.smith.edu/news/grecourt-gates-west-elm-project.

507. See the undated entry for August 1953.

508. These letters are lost or in private hands.

509. On the Charles River Esplanade, see Esplanade Association, home page, n.d., https://esplanade.org.

510. Kenneth J. Tillotson was Plath's psychiatrist.

511. The ellipses are Plath's.

512. For more positive treatments of Beuscher/Barnhouse, see Carl Rollyson, *The Last Days of Sylvia Plath* (Jackson: University Press of Mississippi, 2020); and Lee Kravetz, *The Last Confessions of Sylvia P.* (New York: Harper, 2022). Kravetz is a trained therapist and novelist. See also Carl Rollyson, *The Making of Sylvia Plath* (forthcoming).

513. "Anamnesis" usually refers to a patient's account of a medical history.

514. Plath received fourteen letters from Gordon Lameyer between August 30, 1953, and December 2, 1953.

515. The impact of this "national attention" is explored in Carl Rollyson, *The Making of Sylvia Plath* (forthcoming).

516. Plath's relationship with Arvin is explored in Carl Rollyson, *The Making of Sylvia Plath* (forthcoming).

517. This letter is lost or in private hands.

518. The reference to "momism" is an allusion to Philip Wylie's book, *Generation of Vipers* (1943), an attack on the adoration of mothers and their undue control over their progeny.

519. *Knock on Wood* (1954) is about the love problems of a ventriloquist and his dummy.

520. Plath is making up a name for herself, mimicking the Joycean language Gordon Lameyer likes.

521. The ellipses are Plath's.

522. These letters are lost or in private hands.

523. *Counsellor at Law* (1933) is about the rise of a Jewish ghetto boy, who becomes a successful attorney. The film stars one of Plath's favorites: Myrna Loy.

524. This letter is lost or in private hands.

525. For an interpretation of the Plath-Akutowicz relationship, see Carl Rollyson, *The Making of Sylvia Plath* (forthcoming).

526. This letter is lost or in private hands.

527. The "traumatic shock" is a reference to her sexual encounter with Edwin Akutowicz. In spite of the trauma, she professed to regard the incident as necessary in her understanding of the sexual current between women and men.

528. These letters are lost or in private hands.

529. *Bicycle Thieves* (1948) is about postwar Italy. IMDb, "Bicycle Thief," n.d., https://www.imdb.com/title/tt0040522/.

530. Some of these letters are lost or in private hands.

531. On glass flowers, see Harvard Museum of Natural History, "Glass Flowers: The Ware Collection of Blaschka Models of Plants," n.d., https://hmnh.harvard.edu/glass-flowers.

532. These letters are lost or in private hands.

533. *Love Is a Bridge* is Charles Bracelen Flood's novel about Harvard life published in 1952.

534. The ellipses are Plath's.

535. The Cruikshanks were her next-door neighbors.

536. "YR, LHJ, NY & SEP" presumably refers to the *Yale Review*, *Ladies Home Journal*, the *New Yorker*, and the *Saturday Evening Post*, respectively.

537. She is referring to William H. Sheldon's *Psychology and the Promethean Will* (1936).

538. These letters are lost or in private hands.

539. This letter is lost or in private hands.

540. In *An American in Paris* (1951), "three friends struggle to find work in Paris." IMDb, "An American in Paris," n.d., https://www.imdb.com/title/tt0043278/.

541. This letter is lost or in private hands.

542. These letters are lost or in private hands.

543. These letters are lost or in private hands.

544. For more on the German House, see *New York Times*, "Students at Smith Fill German House: Twenty-Three Live There in Atmosphere of the Country and Its Language," November 28, 1937, https://www.nytimes.com/1937/11/28/archives/students-at-smith-fill-german-house-twentythree-live-there-in.html.

545. "Get late permission" refers to a request to add or drop a course after the enrollment period has ended.

546. This poem is included in *Collected Poems* (London: Faber and Faber, 1981) as "Metamorphoses of the Moon."

547. These letters are lost or in private hands.

548. Tschiżewskij was the daughter of a Harvard professor that Plath knew.

549. "Nina paper" perhaps refers to a paper on Nina Leeds from Eugene O'Neill's *Strange Interlude*, although such a paper is not in any archive. The play is in Plath's library, on which see SPL.

550. This letter is lost or in private hands.

551. These letters are lost or in private hands.

552. *The Bad Seed* (1956) is about Rhoda Penmark, who knows how to get what she wants.

553. These letters are lost or in private hands.

554. Some of these letters are lost or in private hands.

555. These letters are lost or in private hands.

556. These notes and letters are lost or in private hands.

557. *Bread, Love, and Dreams* (1953) is an Italian romantic comedy.

558. This note is lost or in private hands.

559. These letters are lost or in private hands.

560. Plath is referencing Maidenform advertisements. See Sally Edelstein, "Maidenform Dream Ads: Iconic and Ironic," Envisioning the American Dream, March 6, 2018, https://envisioningtheamericandream.com/2018/03/06/maidenform-dream-ads-iconic-and-ironic/.

561. Though Plath refers to simply "Ceremony," the full title is "Ceremony after a Fire Raid."

562. On *Gate of Hell* (1953), see Stephen Prince, "*Gate of Hell*: A Colorful History," Criterion Collection, April 10, 2013, https://www.criterion.com/current/posts/2727-gate-of-hell-a-colorful-history.

563. The letters to Ruth and Mrs. Prouty are lost or in private hands.

564. This letter is lost or in private hands.

INDEX

ABOUT THE AUTHOR

Self-portrait courtesy of the author

Carl Rollyson, professor emeritus of journalism at Baruch College, CUNY, has published fifteen biographies—*A Real American Character: The Life of Walter Brennan* (2015), *A Private Life of Michael Foot* (2015), *To Be a Woman: The Life of Jill Craigie* (2005), *Amy Lowell Anew: A Biography* (2013), *American Isis: The Life and Art of Sylvia Plath* (2013), *Hollywood Enigma: Dana Andrews* (2012), *Marilyn Monroe: A Life of the Actress* (revised and updated 2014), *Lillian Hellman: Her Life and Legend* (2017), *Beautiful Exile: The Life of Martha Gellhorn* (2000), *Norman Mailer: The Last Romantic* (2008), *Rebecca West: A Modern Sibyl* (2017), and *Susan Sontag: The Making of an Icon* (revised and updated 2016), *The Life of William Faulkner* (2020), *The Last Days of Sylvia Plath* (2020), *William Faulkner Day by Day* (2022)—and three studies of biography, *A Higher Form of Cannibalism? Adventures in the Art and Politics of Biography* (2005), *Biography: A User's Guide* (2007), and *Confessions of a Serial Biographer* (2016). His reviews of biography have been collected in *Reading Biography, American Biography, Lives of the Novelists, Essays in Biography*, the *Wall Street Journal*, the *Weekly Standard*, the *New Criterion*, and other newspapers and periodicals. He has also published four biographies for young adults on Pablo Picasso, Marie Curie, Emily Dickinson, and Thurgood Marshall.